1st Corinthians
Preaching Verse-by-Verse

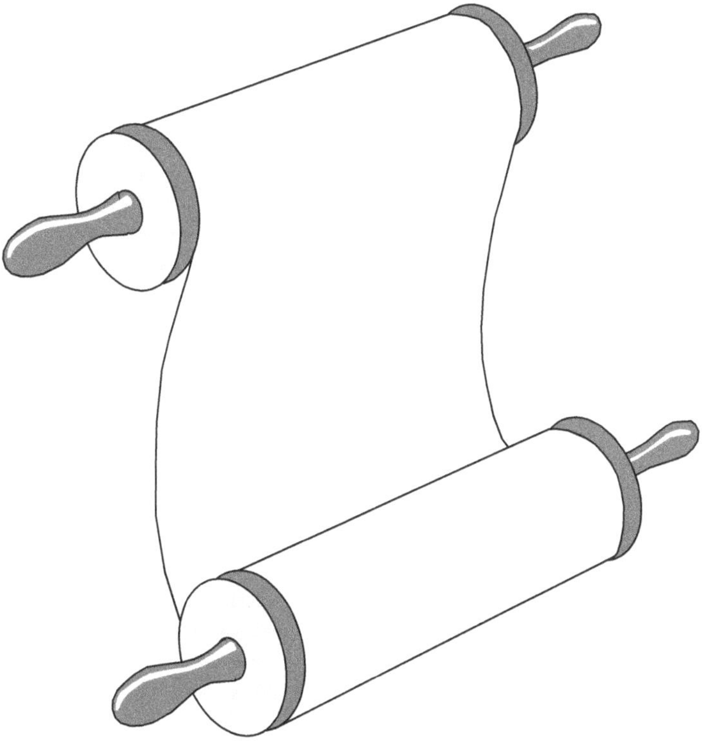

Pastor D. A. Waite, Th.D., Ph.D.

Published by
THE BIBLE FOR TODAY PRESS
900 Park Avenue
Collingswood, New Jersey 08108 U.S.A.
Pastor D. A. Waite, Th.D., Ph.D.
𝔅ible 𝔉or 𝔗oday 𝔅aptist 𝔆hurch
Church Phone: 856-854-4747
BFT Phone: 856-854-4452
Orders: 1-800-John 10:9
e-mail: BFT@BibleForToday.org
Website: www.BibleForToday.org

FAX: 856-854-2464
We Use and Defend
the King James Bible

Publishing assisted by

The Old Paths Publications, Inc.
www.theoldpathspublications.com

Copyright, 2019
All Rights Reserved
November, 2018
BFT #4174
ISBN #978-1-56848-117-3

Acknowledgments

I wish to thank and to acknowledge the assistance of the following people:

- **The Congregation of the Bible For Today Baptist Church**–for whom these messages were prepared, to whom they were delivered, and by whom they were published. They listened attentively and encouraged their Pastor.
- **Yvonne Sanborn Waite**–my wife, who encouraged the publication of these sermons, read the manuscript, developed the various boxes, and gave other helpful suggestions and comments. The boxes help the reader to see some of the more important topics that are covered in the various chapters.
- **Pastor Daniel Waite**–our church's Assistant Pastor for helping to keep our computers up-to-date and working properly day by day so that this book could be written and published.
- **Patricia Canter**–a friend of mine and Mrs. Waite who volunteered to take the cassette tapes of the verse-by-verse exposition of the book of 1 Corinthians and put these words into the computer in digital format to be used for this book. She also volunteered to help with the final step of proofreading the entire book once the first draft was completed. Without her assistance, this book, and many other books she has worked on, could not be completed for publication.
- **Bonlyn Walls**–one of our email friends who volunteered to proofread this book. She spent many hours in this important task. We're very grateful for her assistance and skill in this important work of proofreading.
- **Dr. Kirk DiVietro**–a friend for many years, one of our Dean Burgon Society faithful Vice Presidents, who is an expert on the use of computers. He has helped in many ways to make the computer work easier and in the proper manner when performing the tasks needed to complete this book.

Foreword

- **The Beginning.** This book is the **sixteenth** in a series of verse-by-verse preaching from various New Testament books of the Bible. It is an attempt to bring to the minds of the readers two things: (1) the **meaning** of the words in the verses, and (2) some practical **applications** of those words to the lives of both genuine Christians and non-Christians.
- **Preached Sermons.** These were messages that I preached to our **Bible For Today Baptist Church** in Collingswood, New Jersey. They were broadcast over the Internet by computer-streaming around the world. I preached verse-by-verse on half a chapter of the book each Sunday as the messages were preached. All verses quoted are from the King James Bible.
- **Other Verses.** In connection with both the **meaning** and **application** of the verses in this book, there are many verses from other places in the Bible that have been quoted for further elaboration on the teachings in this book. All the verses of Scripture that were used to illustrate further truth are written out in full for easy reference.
- **A Transcription.** This entire book was typed into computer format by Patricia Canter from the tape recordings of the messages as they were preached. In addition to the words used as I preached these sermons, I have added other words for clarification as needed.
- **The Audience.** The intended audience for this book is the same as the audience that listened to the messages in the first place. These studies are not meant to be overly scholarly, though there are many references to various Greek or Hebrew Words used. My aim and burden was to try to help genuine Christians to understand and follow the Words of God. It is also my hope that my children, grandchildren, great grandchildren, and others might profit from this study. There is an **11-page INDEX** of words and phrases to help the reader easily find the various topics they are looking for.

Yours For God's Words,
D. A. Waite
Pastor D. A. Waite, Th.D., Ph.D.
Bible For Today Baptist Church

Table of Contents

Publisher's Data i
Acknowledgments ii
Foreword iii
Table of Contents iv
1 Corinthians Chapter One 1
1 Corinthians Chapter Two 41
1 Corinthians Chapter Three 69
1 Corinthians Chapter Four 97
1 Corinthians Chapter Five 125
1 Corinthians Chapter Six 153
1 Corinthians Chapter Seven 175
1 Corinthians Chapter Eight 199
1 Corinthians Chapter Nine 225
1 Corinthians Chapter Ten 247
1 Corinthians Chapter Eleven 275
1 Corinthians Chapter Twelve 303
1 Corinthians Chapter Thirteen 323
1 Corinthians Chapter Fourteen 351
1 Corinthians Chapter Fifteen 375
1 Corinthians Chapter Sixteen 405
Index of Words and Phrases 431
About the Author 443
Order Blank Pages 445
Defined King James Bible Orders 453

1 Corinthians
Chapter One

Background Of The Book Of 1 Corinthians

The Approximate Date Of 1 Corinthians. This book was written in about 59 A.D. after Paul had been at Ephesus for three years preaching the Words of God. The city of Corinth is in Greece; it's about 40 miles west of Athens. It was a popular city. Paul went there on his second missionary journey. It was a large city with many commercial businesses and schools.

The Sinful And Pagan Practices At Corinth. However, the city of Corinth was a city where gross sin was practiced with approval. As such, it resembled some of the large cities in our own nation today such as Los Angeles, San Francisco, Philadelphia, New York, and many others. The entire city of Corinth was steeped in immorality of various kinds. It was known for drunkenness, gluttony, and religiously-licensed prostitution. The Greek goddess Aphrodite was worshipped there. Moral corruption was so great in the city of Corinth that people living in other cities at the time, who were living in sinful practices, were often referred to acting like those who lived in Corinth.

The Three Most Wicked Ancient Cities. In the ancient world, there were three cities that were considered the most wicked, evil, and sinful of them all. They all began, in the Greek language
with the letter "KAPPA" or a "K." This is similar to our English letter "C." They were:
1. Cappadocia
2. Crete
3. Corinth

The apostle Paul knew that he had invaded Satan's playground, and that he was not fighting only against flesh and blood, but against the very Devil himself and the emissaries of Hell.

Why Paul Wrote This Letter. When Paul arrived at the city of Corinth, he was disquieted by some reports from the household of Chloe, that many evil things had sprung up in that local church which he had founded some years before. This is what prompted Paul to write this letter.

Some Background Verses From Acts 18. Paul departed from Athens and came from Athens over to Corinth, just forty miles to the West. He found there Aquila and his wife Priscilla. With Paul, they were all tentmakers.

- **Acts 18:6**

"And <u>when they opposed themselves</u>, and blasphemed, he shook *his* raiment, and said unto them, Your blood *be* upon your own heads; I *am* clean: from <u>henceforth I will go unto the Gentiles</u>."

So Paul left the Jewish synagogues and went to the Gentiles. He departed there and went into the house of Justus.

- **Acts 18:8**

"And Crispus, the chief ruler of the synagogue, believed on the Lord with all his house; and <u>many of the Corinthians hearing believed, and were baptized</u>."

- **Acts 18:9**

"<u>Then spake the Lord to Paul in the night by a vision</u>, Be not afraid, but <u>speak, and hold not thy peace</u>:"

- **Acts 18:10**

"For I am with thee, and no man shall set on thee to hurt thee: for I have much people in this city."

- **Acts 18:11**

"And <u>he continued *there* a year and six months</u>, teaching the word of God among them."

So Paul remained in the city of Corinth for a year and a half, teaching and preaching to them.

1 Corinthians 1:1

"Paul, called to be an apostle of Jesus Christ through the will of God, and Sosthenes *our* brother,"

Paul was the writer of this book. Sosthenes, apparently, was with him as Paul was writing and delivering this letter. Notice, Paul was called by the Lord Jesus Christ to be an apostle. The Lord called him first for salvation, and then for service. Paul's calling to be an apostle was not by man's will, but by the will of God. An "*apostle*" is a messenger sent forth with orders.

Paul was converted to genuine faith in the Lord Jesus Christ when he was on the road toward Damascus. He had orders from the chief priests to round up genuine Christians and put them in prison where they would be killed at a later time.

In Acts, Chapter 9, Paul's conversion to Christ is recorded. The Lord Jesus met Paul with a light from heaven that shined brighter than the sun. He was blinded by that light. The Lord Jesus Christ spoke to Paul, and Paul trusted Him as His Saviour. *"And Saul, yet breathing out threatenings and slaughter against the disciples of the Lord, went unto the high priest, And desired of him letters to Damascus to the synagogues, that if he found any of this way, whether they were men or women, he might bring them bound unto Jerusalem. And as he journeyed, he came near Damascus: and suddenly there shined round about him a light from heaven: And he fell to the earth, and heard a voice saying unto him, Saul, Saul, why persecutest thou me? And he said, Who art thou, Lord? And the Lord said, I am Jesus whom thou persecutest: it is hard for thee to kick against the pricks. And he trembling and astonished said, Lord, what wilt thou have me to do? And the Lord said unto him, Arise, and go into the city, and it shall be told thee what thou must do. And the men which journeyed with him stood speechless, hearing a voice, but seeing no man. And Saul arose from the earth; and when his eyes were opened, he saw no man: but they led him by the hand, and brought him into Damascus. And he was three days without sight, and neither did eat nor drink."* (Acts 9:1-9)

Paul became a genuine Christian. The Lord Jesus Christ commissioned him as an apostle to take the place of Judas Iscariot the traitor. It was not Matthias who was to take the place of Judas, as some people teach, but it was Paul. Matthias was chosen by Peter and the other disciples. Paul was chosen, like all of the original twelve apostles, by the Lord Jesus Christ.

So true Christians have been called, by the will of God, not only to salvation and redemption by genuine faith in the Lord Jesus Christ, but also for some kind of service for Him. That service might be just to live for Him consistently and grow in His grace by faithfully reading God's Words from Genesis through Revelation each year. Or the service might be missionary service, pastoral service, evangelistic service, or some other kind of Christian ministry, if God calls them to it.

1 Corinthians 1:2

"Unto the church of God which is at Corinth, to them that are sanctified in Christ Jesus, called to be saints, with all that in every place call upon the name of Jesus Christ our Lord, both theirs and ours:"

Paul writes unto the church of Corinth, this evil city. He doesn't hit them over the head in this verse of the book, but he'll do this very clearly later in this letter. Though the book of Corinthians is loaded with the mention of sins of this church, Paul doesn't bring them up to begin with, but later in the letter.

In this verse, Paul writes *"to them that are sanctified in Christ Jesus, called to be saints with all that in every place call upon the name of Jesus Christ our Lord, both theirs and ours:"* These were genuine Christians who were both sanctified and called to be saints. They belong to the Lord Jesus Christ.

THE MEANING OF THE GREEK WORD, HAGIAZO

The Greek Word for *"sanctified"* is HAGIAZO. Some the meanings of that Greek Word are:

"1) to render or acknowledge, or to be venerable or hallow; 2) to separate from profane things and dedicate to God;)"

God wanted the genuine Corinthian Christians to be separated from the wickedness of the world and separated unto Himself. He wants the same thing for true Christians who are living in our days as well.

Verses On Sanctification

- **John 17:19**

"And for their sakes I sanctify myself, that they also might be sanctified through the truth."

The Greek Word for *"saint"* is HAGIOS. It refers to sanctified ones who have been set apart from the world through genuine faith in the Lord Jesus Christ.

- **Acts 20:32**

"And now, brethren, I commend you to God, and to the word of his grace, which is able to build you up, and to give you an inheritance among all them which are sanctified."

The Words of God can build true Christians up if they read it and follow it day by day. This applies to all who are genuine Christians whom God calls, those who are sanctified or set apart to Him.

- **Acts 26:18**
"To open their eyes, *and* to turn *them* from darkness to light, and *from* the power of Satan unto God, that they may receive forgiveness of sins, and <u>inheritance among them which are sanctified by faith that is in me</u>."

People can only be sanctified by genuine faith in the Lord Jesus Christ. This sets them apart for the Lord. They can never be sanctified by the church of Rome or by any other church. Only the Lord Jesus Christ can perform this.

- **Romans 15:16**
"That I should be the minister of Jesus Christ to the Gentiles, ministering the gospel of God, that the offering up of the Gentiles might be acceptable, <u>being sanctified by the Holy Ghost</u>."

Present and continuous sanctification of true Christians is done by the power of God the Holy Spirit Who indwells them.

- **1 Corinthians 6:11**
"And such were some of you: but ye are washed, but <u>ye are sanctified</u>, but ye are justified in the name of the Lord Jesus, and by the Spirit of our God."

These Corinthian genuine Christians were formerly very evil, but now they have been positionally sanctified by the Lord.

- **2 Timothy 2:21**
"If a man therefore purge himself from these, he shall be a vessel unto honour, <u>sanctified, and meet for the master's use</u>, *and* prepared unto every good work."

Biblical separation demands separation from sin and evil. God wants true Christians sanctified and holy in their living.

- **Hebrews 10:10**
"<u>By the which will we are sanctified</u> through the offering of the body of Jesus Christ once *for all*."

Genuine Christians have been positionally sanctified by the offering of the Lord Jesus Christ at the cross.

1 Corinthians 1:3

"Grace *be* unto you, and peace, from God our Father, and from the Lord Jesus Christ."

"*Grace*" is the common greeting among the Greeks and "*peace*" is the common greeting among the Jews. Both grace and peace are given to true Christians by God the Father and God the Son after they are truly saved. There is a unity between God the Father and God the Son. Both of these terms are full of important meanings.

THE MEANING OF THE GREEK WORD, CHARIS

The Greek Word for *"grace"* is CHARIS. Some of the meanings of that Greek Word are:

"1) grace; 1a) that which affords joy, pleasure, delight, sweetness, charm, loveliness: grace of speech; 2) good will, loving-kindness, favour; 2a) of the merciful kindness by which God, exerting his holy influence upon souls, turns them to Christ, keeps, strengthens, increases them in Christian faith, knowledge, affection, and kindles them to the exercise of the Christian virtues; 3) what is due to grace; 3a) the spiritual condition of one governed by the power of divine grace; 3b) the token or proof of grace, benefit; 3b1) a gift of grace; 3b2) benefit, bounty; 4) thanks, (for benefits, services, favours), recompense, reward."

THE MEANING OF THE GREEK WORD, EIRENE

The Greek Word for "*peace*" is EIRENE. Some meanings of that Greek Word are:

"1) a state of national tranquillity; 1a) exemption from the rage and havoc of war; 2) peace between individuals, i.e. harmony, concord; 3) security, safety, prosperity, felicity, (because peace and harmony make and keep things safe and prosperous); 4) of the Messiah's peace; 4a) the way that leads to peace (salvation) 5) of Christianity, the tranquil state of a soul assured of its salvation through Christ, and so fearing nothing from God and content with its earthly lot, of whatsoever sort that is; 6) the blessed state of devout and upright men after death."

1 Corinthians 1:4

"I thank my God always on your behalf, for the grace of God which is given you by Jesus Christ;"

Paul was thankful always for every genuine Christian who was given grace by God the Father because they genuinely received the Lord Jesus Christ as their Saviour. That grace was not given by works, but it was given because of their true faith in the Saviour.

- **Ephesians 2:8-9**
 "For <u>by grace are ye saved through faith</u>; and that not of yourselves: *it is* the gift of God: Not of works, lest any man should boast."

God's great saving grace has its source in God Himself through a person's genuine faith in the Lord Jesus Christ as their Saviour. Though some teach this falsehood, it can never be earned by the works and deeds of people.

1 Corinthians 1:5

"That in every thing ye are enriched by him, in all utterance, and in all knowledge; "

These true Christians in Corinth were enriched by the Lord Jesus Christ in two areas that are listed here.

    1. Enriched In Utterance. Once a people are born-again by the Spirit of God through genuine faith in the Lord Jesus Christ, they are given the ability and guidance to speak on behalf of their Saviour effectively so they can tell others about Him. Their testimony must be guided by God the Holy Spirit Who lives within them. If they are thus guided, the enrichment in all utterance will become evident in their lives.

    2. Enriched In Knowledge. The Lord Jesus Christ has given those whom He has saved the knowledge that they need to know in order to serve Him acceptably. He gave them the Bible in which they are able to find all the important knowledge they need to live to please Him. (He did this through giving God the Holy Spirit His Words to give to the writers of the Bible.) It is up to all true Christians to make use of these Words daily, not only in knowledge of them, but also in obedience to them.

1 Corinthians 1:6
"Even as the testimony of Christ was confirmed in you:"
The testimony of the Lord Jesus Christ was confirmed and accepted by the genuine Christians at Corinth by Paul for a year and a half by his preaching and teaching ministry. He had much Jewish opposition during that time, but he continued serving the Saviour faithfully in spite of such persecution.

1 Corinthians 1:7
"So that ye come behind in no gift; waiting for the coming of our Lord Jesus Christ: "
The genuine Christians in the church at Corinth did not come behind in any of the temporary spiritual gifts that were then in the church prior to about A.D. 90-100 A.D. when the New Testament was completed.

Regardless of what temporary gifts they may have had, one thing is certain. They were waiting for the coming of the Lord Jesus Christ.

The Two Phases Of Christ's Second Coming
1. **The first phase of His coming.** This first phase is called the Rapture, when the Lord Jesus Christ will come in the clouds to take to Heaven all genuine Christians, both the living and the dead. I believe this is what Paul was referring to and what the Christians at Corinth and in other churches believed in that day. They were *"waiting for the coming of our Lord Jesus Christ"* even though He did not come back then, nor has He come back yet as I am writing this book. But true Christians should still *"wait"* and look forward to His return, whenever this event happens.

2. **The second phase of His coming.** This second phase takes place after the tribulation period when the Lord Jesus Christ comes to earth to judge the Antichrist and his followers and to set up His 1,000-year millennial reign.

Six Positions On Christ's Rapture Of True Christians
I believe this verse refers to the Rapture of the true Christians when He meets all of them in the air. That event may occur at any time. There are many false views of the timing of the Rapture. Let me list briefly some of these false views.

1. **The True Pre-Tribulation Rapture Position.** This is the true view of the Rapture which is backed up by many verses from the Bible when they are rightly interpreted. This coming is imminent, that is, it might occur at any time without any event that needs to precede it, including any part of the seven-year Tribulation period. At that time, the Lord Jesus Christ will return in the clouds to catch away every genuine Christian, living or dead, after they have been bodily raised from the dead and given glorified bodies like unto the body of the Lord Jesus Christ.

2. **The False Mid-Tribulation Rapture Position.** This is a false view of the Rapture which holds that the Lord Jesus Christ's Rapture will not occur until all the true Christians then living will go through the first three-and-one-half years of the seven-year Tribulation period.

3. **The False Pre-Wrath Rapture Position.** This is a false view of the Rapture which holds that the Lord Jesus Christ's Rapture will not occur until some part of the seven-year Tribulation period when there is a great wrath of God that takes place.

4. **The False Post-Tribulation Rapture Position.** This is a false view of the Rapture which holds that the Lord Jesus Christ's Rapture will not occur until all the true Christians then living will go through the entire seven-year Tribulation period.

5. **The False Partial-Rapture Position.** This s a false view of the Rapture which holds that not all the genuine Christians will be Raptured to Heaven, but only those who are walking with the Lord at the time. Those who are carnal or fleshly Christians will be left on earth to pass through the Tribulation period.

6. **The False Anti-Rapture Position.** This is a false view of the Rapture that denies that there is any such thing as the coming back of the Lord Jesus Christ at any time. Those who hold this false view do not believe there is anything in the Bible that teaches this.

Verses On The Second Coming Of Christ
- **Matthew 24:3**
"And as he sat upon the mount of Olives, the disciples came unto him privately, saying, Tell us, when shall these things be? and what *shall be* the sign of thy coming, and of the end of the world?"

This would refer to the 2nd phase of Christ's return to set up His thousand-year reign. After the Millennium, *"the end of the world,"* as we know it, will take place.

- **Matthew 24:27**

"For as the lightning cometh out of the east, and shineth even unto the west; <u>so shall also the coming of the Son of man be</u>."

This is a picture of the 2nd phase of the Lord Jesus Christ's glorious coming to the earth to rule and reign during the Millennium. Lightning is a picture of His glorious return to earth once again.

- **Matthew 24:30**

"And then shall appear the sign of the Son of man in heaven: and then shall all the tribes of the earth mourn, and <u>they shall see the Son of man coming in the clouds of heaven with power and great glory</u>."

This refers to the 2nd phase of the Lord's return. The Rapture is the first stage.

- **Matthew 24:37**

"But as the days of Noe *were*, <u>so shall also the coming of the Son of man be</u>."

This is also a reference to the 2nd phase of Christ's coming.

- **Matthew 24:39**

"And knew not until the flood came, and took them all away; <u>so shall also the coming of the Son of man be</u>."

And so there will be a surprise. This refers to the 1st phase of the coming of the Lord Jesus Christ in the Rapture.

- **Mark 13:26**

"And then shall they see <u>the Son of man coming in the clouds with great power and glory</u>."

This is another reference to the 2nd phase of Christ's coming with great power and glory.

- **1 Corinthians 15:23**

"But every man in his own order: Christ the firstfruits; afterward <u>they that are Christ's at his coming</u>."

They were waiting for his coming. This refers to the 1st phase of the Lord Jesus Christ's coming in the Rapture for the genuine Christians out of this life.

- **1 Thessalonians 2:19**

"For what *is* our hope, or joy, or crown of rejoicing? <u>*Are* not even ye in the presence of our Lord Jesus Christ at his coming</u>?"

This refers to the Rapture again. Genuine Christians will be in His presence when He returns in the clouds of the heavens.

- **1 Thessalonians 4:15**

"For this we say unto you by the word of the Lord, that <u>we which are alive *and* remain unto the coming of the Lord shall not prevent them which are asleep</u>."

When the Lord Jesus Christ comes back in the clouds in the Rapture, the dead in Christ will rise first, then those who are alive at His return.
- **1 Thessalonians 5:23**
"And the very God of peace sanctify you wholly; and *I pray God your whole spirit and soul and body be preserved blameless unto the coming of our Lord Jesus Christ*."

This was Paul's wish for those true Christians who will be alive when Christ returns in the Rapture.
- **2 Thessalonians 2:1**
"Now we beseech you, brethren, by the coming of our Lord Jesus Christ, and *by* our gathering together unto him,"

This is a very clear reference to the Rapture of all genuine Christians.
- **2 Thessalonians 2:8**
"And then shall that Wicked be revealed, whom the Lord shall consume with the spirit of his mouth, and shall destroy with the brightness of his coming:"

This refers to the coming of the Lord Jesus Christ to earth at the end of the Tribulation period to destroy the Antichrist with the brightness of His coming.
- **James 5:7**
"Be patient therefore, brethren, unto the coming of the Lord. Behold, the husbandman waiteth for the precious fruit of the earth, and hath long patience for it, until he receive the early and latter rain."

This might refer either to the first phase or the second phase of the coming of the Lord Jesus Christ.
- **2 Peter 3:4**
"And saying, Where is the promise of his coming? for since the fathers fell asleep, all things continue as *they were* from the beginning of the creation."

Since it implies there is no change in the world, it probably refers to Christ's coming to earth to set up the Millennium where many changes will take place.
- **1 John 2:28**
"And now, little children, abide in him; that, when he shall appear, we may have confidence, and not be ashamed before him at his coming."

This is a reference to the Rapture of the Lord Jesus Christ. John hopes that no true Christian will be ashamed before Him when He comes in the Rapture to take them to Heaven

I hope that will be the case of every genuine Christian who reads this book, that their lives will be honoring to the Lord Jesus

Christ so they will not be ashamed before Him at His coming in the Rapture which might occur at any moment.

1 Corinthians 1:8

"Who shall also confirm you unto the end, *that ye may be* blameless in the day of our Lord Jesus Christ."

Paul is telling the true Christians at Corinth that the Lord Jesus Christ will confirm and strengthen them until either the end of their lives, or until He comes for them at the time of the Rapture. He especially wants them to live blameless lives right up to the time of His imminent coming for them in the Rapture.

THE MEANING OF THE GREEK WORD, ANEGKLETOS

The Greek Word for *"blameless"* is ANEGKLETOS. Some meanings of that Greek Word are:

> *"1) that cannot be called into account, unreproveable, unaccused, blameless."*

When the Lord Jesus Christ comes back at the Rapture, every genuine Christian, (either dead or alive), will be changed and transformed unto His likeness. If they are living, their mortal bodies, which are subject to death, will become immortal and not subject to death. If these true Christians have already died, their corruptible bodies will become incorruptible (1 Corinthians 15:51-54).

Then, and only then, will genuine Christians be perfectly blameless and spotless. Paul has a problem on his hands because he's writing to these Corinthian Christians that are not perfectly blameless. Would to God that all true Christians living today would have as their goal to be blameless in their lives as they wait for the return of the Lord Jesus Christ in the Rapture.

Verses On Blameless

- **Philippians 2:15**

> "That ye may be blameless and harmless, the sons of God, without rebuke, in the midst of a crooked and perverse nation, among whom ye shine as lights in the world;"

Right now, in this life, God wants genuine Christians to be *"blameless,"* as defined above, as lights in the world.

- **1 Thessalonians 5:23**

> "And the very God of peace sanctify you wholly; and *I pray God* your whole spirit and soul and body be preserved blameless unto the coming of our Lord Jesus Christ."

The entire three parts of Christians' bodies–spirits, souls, and bodies–should be preserved blameless until the coming of the Lord Jesus Christ in the Rapture.
- **1 Timothy 3:2**
"<u>A bishop then must be blameless</u>, the husband of one wife, vigilant, sober, of good behaviour, given to hospitality, apt to teach;"

Among other requirements for pastors-bishops-elders (one office with three different responsibilities) is that they must be "*blameless.*"
- **1 Timothy 3:10**
"And let these also first be proved; then let them use the office of a deacon, being *found* blameless."

One of the qualifications for deacons is that they must be found "*blameless.*"
- **Titus 1:6-7**
"<u>If any be blameless</u>, the husband of one wife, having faithful children not accused of riot or unruly. For a bishop must be blameless, as the steward of God; not selfwilled, not soon angry, not given to wine, no striker, not given to filthy lucre;"

Blamelessness is another requirement for elders (that is, pastors-bishops-elders).
- **2 Peter 3:14**
"Wherefore, beloved, seeing that ye look for such things, be diligent that <u>ye may be found of him</u> in peace, without spot, and <u>blameless</u>."

The Apostle Peter urged true Christians to be diligent in being found to be "*blameless*" in their lives.

1 Corinthians 1:9

"God *is* faithful, by whom ye were called unto the fellowship of his Son Jesus Christ our Lord."

The true Christians in the church at Corinth were called into the fellowship of God's Son, the Lord Jesus Christ. One of the attributes of their God and ours is His faithfulness.

Verses On Faithfulness
- **1 John 1:9**
"<u>If we confess our sins, he is faithful and just to forgive us *our* sins</u>, and to cleanse us from all unrighteousness."

God is faithful in forgiveness and cleansing of true Christians if they understand what "*confess*" means and use it. It comes from the Greek Word HOMOLOGEO. HOMO is "*sa*m*e*" and LOGEO is "*to say.*" The resultant meaning is:

"to say the same thing about our sins as God says, that is to agree with God about them that they are sins."

Only if this is true will their sins be forgiven and they be cleansed.
- **1 Corinthians 4:2**
"Moreover it is required in stewards, <u>that a man be found faithful</u>."

A steward is responsible for his master's goods. It is required of that steward that he be faithful. Otherwise, he should be fired. God expects all true Christians to be faithful to Him and to His Words in the Bible.

1 Corinthians 1:10

"Now I beseech you, brethren, by the name of our Lord Jesus Christ, *that* ye all speak the same thing, and that there be no divisions among you; but *that* ye be perfectly joined together in the same mind and in the same judgment."

Paul urges these genuine Christians in Corinth in the Name of the Lord Jesus Christ to do a number of things.

    1. <u>**Speak The Same Things Without Divisions.**</u> The first thing Paul urges them to do is to *"speak the same thing"* without any *"divisions"* among them. As all of us know, this is not an easy task in churches. The question I have for true Christians today in our Bible-believing and faithful churches is, "How can they speak the same things, one with another, if you have different Bibles"? You can't. It's impossible!

There are multiple Bible versions used in many churches that are not founded on the same Hebrew, Aramaic, and Greek Words. As such, there are numerous additions, subtractions, and other changes in each of these various versions.

That's why, at Bible for Today Baptist Church, we use and stand for one Bible version. We use the King James Bible in the English language for all of our ministries. We believe strongly that it is based on the only true and proper foundation of the Hebrew, Aramaic, and Greek Words that underlie it. Because of this, we can *"speak the same thing"* about the doctrines and teachings found in our Bibles. We are not divided in any of these doctrines.

Some of these English Bible versions teach things that contradict our King James Bible. If some use one version and others use other versions, there are divisions in doctrines scattered throughout the Bible, compared to the King James Bible.

This is true for the Revised Version of 1881 (RV), the American Standard Version (ASV), the New International Version (NIV), the English Standard Version (ESV), as well as many other versions in English and in other languages all around the world. The errors of these versions that are founded on the erroneous Gnostic Critical New Testament Greek text have been found by Dr. Jack Moorman to be at least 356 doctrinal passages that exist in Bible versions based upon that false text. See his book, *Early Manuscripts, Church Fathers, and the Authorised Version* (**BFT #3230 @ $20.00 + $8.00 S&H**).

Even with those who use the King James Bible, there are doctrinal differences based upon various interpretations of some verses. But at least with the same English words, there is a far greater possibility to speak the same thing and not to be divided than if these falsely-based versions are used.

2. Be Perfectly Joined Together In The Same Mind And Judgment. The second thing Paul urged the genuine Christians at Corinth was to have a unity in mind and judgment. He was going to start right out in the next few verses to list all of the various divisions that were present among them. He's approaching it cautiously. He hopes they don't have divisions, and that they are perfectly joined together in mind and judgment. That would be great, if it were true.

That's why we should have clearly written doctrinal statements in our local churches that people must agree to and adhere to before becoming members. Here are 28 beliefs and doctrines that are included in our own doctrinal statement that might also be included in other churches as basis of unity in mind and judgment:

3. 28 Doctrines That Could Join Together Genuine Christians

Below is a list, among many other doctrines and beliefs, of 28 different Christian and Biblical doctrines that, if firmly believed by true Christians, could unite them in the same mind and judgment.

1. The Deity of Christ
2. The Perfect and sinless Humanity of Christ
3. The miraculous virgin birth of Christ
4. The miracles of Christ
5. The substitutionary death of Christ bearing the sins of the entire world in His body on the cross

6. The promise of eternal life for those who have genuine faith in and receive Christ as their Saviour who bore their sins in His own body on the cross
7. The bodily resurrection of Christ
8. The bodily ascension of Christ
9. The presence of Christ in Heaven at the right hand of God.
10. The belief that all people are considered by God to be sinners
11. Belief in a real Heave.
12. Belief in a real, literal, and eternal Hell
13. Belief in the Trinity
14. Belief in a real and powerful Devil
15. Belief in the return of Christ in two phases, the Rapture of all genuine Christians before the Tribulation
16. Belief in eternal life for those who truly trust the Lord Jesus Christ as their Saviour
17. Salvation by grace and faith, not by good works
18. The 1,000-year millennial reign of Christ for 1,000 years
19. The seven-year Tribulation before Christ's millennial reign
20. Belief that the miracle of speaking in foreign language tongues ceased when the Bible was completed in 90 to 100 A.D.
21. Belief in the inspiration of the Hebrew, Aramaic, and Greek Words of the Bible
22. Belief in God's preservation of those inspired and inerrant Words to this date
23. Belief that these preserved Words should be the basis of every Bible in all the languages of the world
24. Belief that the King James Bible is a skilled and accurate translation into English of the preserved Masoretic Hebrew and Aramaic Old Testament Words, as well as the Traditional Received Greek New Testament Words
25. Belief in a dispensational understanding of the Bible
26. Belief in the various ministries of God the Holy Spirit in the genuine Christians
27. Belief in the permanence of genuine salvation and the eternal security of every true Christian
28. And many, many other additional doctrines and Biblical beliefs

1 Corinthians 1:11

"For it hath been declared unto me of you, my brethren, by them *which are of the house of Chloe, that there are contentions among you.*"

Paul founded this church at Corinth some years before he wrote this. Some people told him that there were some contentions among them. When the church began, there were no contentions, but now, after some years, there were some arguments and fighting going on in the church.

THE MEANING OF THE GREEK WORD, ERIS

The Greek Word for "*contention*" is ERIS. Some meanings of that Greek Word are:

"1) contention, strife, and wrangling"

In the previous verse, Paul hoped this was not so, but he is writing the church about it to find out the truth.

Verses On Contention
- **Proverbs 13:10**

"Only by pride cometh contention: but with the well advised *is* wisdom."

What is really wrong with letting other people win their point of view? I realize that, when they are Biblically correct, it takes humility to do this, but isn't humility better than contention and fighting?

- **Proverbs 22:10**

"Cast out the scorner, and contention shall go out; yea, strife and reproach shall cease."

In churches, sometimes there are some that disagree with some of the doctrines of the church or with the pastor, or with others who attend. After many weeks, months, or years, such scorners and contenders must be asked to leave so that the strife and disturbing contention will cease in the church family. Sometimes this is difficult to do, but it must be done to maintain peace and tranquility in the fellowship.

- **Philippians 1:16**

"The one preach Christ of contention, not sincerely, supposing to add affliction to my bonds:"

Even some preachers preach Christ in a fleshly way, rather than in the strong power of God the Holy Spirit.

- **1 Thessalonians 2:2**
  "But even after that we had suffered before, and were shamefully entreated, as ye know, at Philippi, we were bold in our God to speak unto you the gospel of God with much contention."

If there is contention and contending for the Gospel and God's truth, this is a proper contending if done in the proper spirit. Wrong contention is the kind motivated by fleshly actions and attitudes. Jude 1:3 mentions this proper contention:

"Beloved, when I gave all diligence to write unto you of the common salvation, it was needful for me to write unto you, and exhort you that ye should earnestly contend for the faith which was once delivered unto the saints."

This proper contending for the faith I have sought to do in all of my ministries, past and present.

1 Corinthians 1:12

"Now this I say, that every one of you saith, I am of Paul; and I of Apollos; and I of Cephas; and I of Christ."

Paul mentions four different names that people in the church at Corinth were following: (1) Paul, (2) Apollos, (3) Cephas, and (4) Christ. We know who Paul was because of his many apostolic journeys and writings. We also know about the Lord Jesus Christ. Let's look at some verses about Apollos and Cephas. Perhaps those groups each sat in different areas of the church. Perhaps front left, front right, back left, and back right. Perhaps they argued with one another about the merits of their leaders.

Verses on Apollos

- **Acts 18:24**
  "And a certain Jew named Apollos, born at Alexandria, an eloquent man, *and* mighty in the scriptures, came to Ephesus."

He was born in Alexandria, Egypt, eloquent, and mighty in the Scriptures.

- **Acts 19:1**
  "And it came to pass, that, while Apollos was at Corinth, Paul having passed through the upper coasts came to Ephesus: and finding certain disciples,"

Apollos spent some time in Corinth and Ephesus as well.

- **1 Corinthians 3:6**

"I have planted, <u>Apollos watered</u>; but God gave the increase." Apollos was a fellow preacher and fellow missionary with Paul. Paul planted the gospel and Apollos watered it by further Bible ministry and teaching.

- **1 Corinthians 16:12**

"<u>As touching *our* brother Apollos</u>, I greatly desired him to come unto you with the brethren: but <u>his will was not at all to come at this time</u>; but <u>he will come when he shall have convenient time</u>."

Paul wanted Apollos to come to Corinth, but he would come to visit this church when he had a convenient time.

Verses On Cephas

- **John 1:42**

"And he brought him to Jesus. And when Jesus beheld him, he said, Thou art Simon the son of Jona: <u>thou shalt be called Cephas, which is by interpretation, A stone.</u>"

Cephas means stone. He's later called Peter, which also means stone.

- **1 Corinthians 9:5**

"Have we not power to lead about a sister, a wife, as well as other apostles, and <u>as the brethren of the Lord, and Cephas</u>?" Paul said he and the other apostles were able to marry as Cephas did.

- **1 Corinthians 15:5**

"And that <u>he was seen of Cephas, then of the twelve</u>:" After the bodily resurrection of the Lord Jesus Christ, He was seen of Cephas before the other apostles.

- **Galatians 2:9**

"And <u>when James, Cephas, and John, who seemed to be pillars</u>, perceived the grace that was given unto me, they gave to me and Barnabas the right hands of fellowship; that we *should go* unto the heathen, and they unto the circumcision."

James, Cephas and John were pillars in the early church. They took the leadership of the Twelve on many occasions in the New Testament.

1 Corinthians 1:13

"Is Christ divided? was Paul crucified for you? or were ye baptized in the name of Paul?"

Paul asks three questions in this verse. The answer to all three of them is "No." Christ is not divided. Paul was not crucified for the genuine Christians at Corinth. These Christians were not baptized in the name of Paul.

In this way, Paul chided the true Christians at Corinth for their various leaders, whether Paul, Apollos, or Cephas. Though many, if not all, denominations and local churches are very divided on many and various issues, the Lord Jesus Christ is not divided.

- **1 John 2:19**
"<u>They went out from us, but they were not of us</u>; for if they had been of us, they would *no doubt* have continued with us: but *they went out*, that they might be made manifest that they were not all of us."

One of the greatest and important divisions is the theological antitheses between the liberal, modernist, apostate beliefs and positions on the Bible and all of its doctrines on one side, and the conservative, Fundamentalist, Bible-believing, beliefs and positions. Based upon the clear teachings of 2 Corinthians 6:14-18, Bible-believing Christians should separate from Biblical apostasy:

> *"Be ye not unequally yoked together with unbelievers: for what fellowship hath righteousness with unrighteousness? and what communion hath light with darkness? And what concord hath Christ with Belial? or what part hath he that believeth with an infidel? And what agreement hath the temple of God with idols? for ye are the temple of the living God; as God hath said, I will dwell in them, and walk in them; and I will be their God, and they shall be my people. Wherefore come out from among them, and be ye separate, saith the Lord, and touch not the unclean thing; and I will receive you, And will be a Father unto you, and ye shall be my sons and daughters, saith the Lord Almighty."* (2 Corinthians 6:14-18)

1 Corinthians 1:14

"I thank God that I baptized none of you, but Crispus and Gaius;"

In this verse, the Bible records that these two men were the only people that Paul baptized. The baptism of Crispus is recorded in Acts 18:8. When Paul was in Corinth, Crispus was the chief ruler of the synagogue. He truly believed in the Lord Jesus Christ with all his house and because of that, Paul baptized him. The baptism of Gaius is mentioned only in this verse. Paul was called to preach and teach about the Lord Jesus Christ as his primary duty rather than to baptize the converts to Christianity.

1 Corinthians 1:15

"Lest any should say that I had baptized in mine own name."

Paul believed in water baptism, but he didn't want anyone to believe that he baptized in his own name, rather than in the Name of God the Father, God the Son, and God the Holy Spirit, as these verses direct.

"Go ye therefore, and teach all nations, baptizing them in the name of the Father, and of the Son, and of the Holy Ghost: Teaching them to observe all things whatsoever I have commanded you: and, lo, I am with you alway, even unto the end of the world. Amen." (Matthew 28:19-20)

Water baptism does not save a person, as some churches wrongly believe. It is done in obedience to the Bible's commands after people become genuine Christians by truly receiving the Lord Jesus Christ as their Saviour. The Greek Word for baptism means to dip under or to immerse. This is why our church practices water baptism by immersion.

1 Corinthians 1:16

"And I baptized also the household of Stephanas: besides, I know not whether I baptized any other."

In this verse, Paul mentioned that, in addition to Crispus and Gaius, he baptized the household of Stephanas. He didn't remember any others that he baptized. That does not mean that Paul was against water baptism. He left it to be performed primarily by the pastors of the local churches.

1 Corinthians 1:17

"For Christ sent me not to baptize, but to preach the gospel: not with wisdom of words, lest the cross of Christ should be made of none effect."

When the Lord Jesus Christ saved Paul, He gave him a commission which included a number of things. He did not get sent to baptize. He was sent forth, to the Gentiles primarily, to preach the Gospel of the Lord Jesus Christ in simple terms, not with words that would show off his own wisdom, lest the cross of Christ should be made of none effect.

When the Lord Jesus Christ called Paul as an apostle, He sent him forth to the Gentiles, all over the then-known world. In obedience to his call, Paul made three missionary journeys to many parts of the world in order to preach the New Testament's good news Gospel as clearly as he was able.

Verses On The Cross of Christ

- **Galatians 5:11**

   "And I, brethren, if I yet preach circumcision, why do I yet suffer persecution? then is the offence of the cross ceased."

Salvation by genuine faith in the Lord Jesus Christ, Who bore the sins of the world in the cross, is an offence to some, but it means salvation and redemption to those who believe it.

- **Galatians 6:12**

   "As many as desire to make a fair shew in the flesh, they constrain you to be circumcised; only lest they should suffer persecution for the cross of Christ."

Those who preach the cross of the Lord Jesus Christ and the meaning of that sacrifice where He died for the sins of the world, often causes persecution. That sacrifice, that He made is the only basis for any person's salvation before a righteous God, persecution or not.

- **Galatians 6:14**

   "But God forbid that I should glory, save in the cross of our Lord Jesus Christ, by whom the world is crucified unto me, and I unto the world."

Paul gloried in the cross and what was accomplished by the Saviour's death thereon.

- **Ephesians 2:16**

   "And that he might reconcile both unto God in one body by the cross, having slain the enmity thereby:"

Both Jews and Gentiles can be reconciled by truly trusting in the Lord Jesus Christ Who died upon the cross to save their souls.

- **Philippians 2:8**

   "And being found in fashion as a man, he humbled himself, and became obedient unto death, even the death of the cross."

Crucifixion is a terrible, ignominious, shameful death. Yet the Lord Jesus Christ willingly humbled Himself and bore our sins on the cross.

- **Philippians 3:18**

   "(For many walk, of whom I have told you often, and now tell you even weeping, *that they are* the enemies of the cross of Christ:"

Those that deny that salvation is only by genuine faith in the Lord Jesus Christ, who shed His blood for the forgiveness of their sins, are considered by God as the enemies of the cross of Christ.
- **Colossians 1:20**
"And, having made peace through the blood of his cross, by him to reconcile all things unto himself; by him, *I say*, whether *they be* things in earth, or things in heaven."

Peace was made possible by acceptance of the blood of the cross of the Lord Jesus Christ by personal faith in Him.
- **Hebrews 12:2**
"Looking unto Jesus the author and finisher of *our* faith; who for the joy that was set before him endured the cross, despising the shame, and is set down at the right hand of the throne of God."

Every genuine Christian should look unto the Lord Jesus Christ Who is the Author and Finisher of their faith. They need His help and assistance day by day and even moment by moment. He endured the cross of shame for the joy set before Him--that because of His voluntary death on that cross of shame, multitudes would be ushered into His presence at their deaths to be with Him for all eternity to come.

When the Lord Jesus Christ had, in obedience to His Father's will, endured that cross, He arose bodily from the grave, ascended bodily, and then sat down at the place of honor at His Father's right hand.

Verses On Wisdom
- **1 Corinthians 1:19**
"For it is written, I will destroy the wisdom of the wise, and will bring to nothing the understanding of the prudent."

The worldly wisdom of the wise of this world will be destroyed by God. Only His wisdom is eternal.
- **1 Corinthians 1:24**
"But unto them which are called, both Jews and Greeks, Christ the power of God, and the wisdom of God."

The Lord Jesus Christ is the manifestation of the wisdom of God. This should be understood and accepted by everyone.
- **1 Corinthians 2:1**
"And I, brethren, when I came to you, came not with excellency of speech or of wisdom, declaring unto you the testimony of God."

Paul had much wisdom of this world, about the law of Moses, and of many other things. But when he came to the Corinthian church, he didn't come with that human wisdom when he declared to them the testimony of God, he came with the wisdom and leading of the Holy Spirit.

- **1 Corinthians 2:4-5**
"And my speech and <u>my preaching was not with enticing words of man's wisdom,</u> but in demonstration of the Spirit and of power: <u>That your faith should not stand in the wisdom of men,</u> but in the power of God."

Paul used the wisdom that God had given him to impart to the church at Corinth the things they should know. He did not use the wisdom of men that he had learned through the many years. He didn't write to the church to impress anybody. He could have done this because he was brought up at the feet of Gamaliel. Though he was a very wise preacher, he forsook the wisdom that he had learned; he used the wisdom that God gave Him from the Scriptures and from the Lord Jesus Christ Himself.

1 Corinthians 1:18

"For the preaching of the cross is to them that perish foolishness; but unto us which are saved it is the power of God."

Yes, indeed, the preaching of the cross of the Lord Jesus Christ to them who will perish in Hell is foolishness. They do not accept it, but think that those who proclaim it as truth are really the fools. They do not understand it, nor do they wish to understand it.

Let me tell you about what happened to me many years ago, when I was a Navy Chaplain on active duty for five years. Near the end of those five years as an active duty Navy Chaplain, I was stationed at the Naval Air Station in Corpus Christi, Texas.

The Senior Chaplain was an apostate Presbyterian named Chaplain Carter. One Sunday, it was my turn to preach at the Navy chapel morning service. When I entered the Naval Chaplain Corps, our motto was *"CO-OPERATION WITHOUT COMPROMISE."* I was sponsored by a Bible-believing Baptist organization. Because of that, I preached in these services according to my strongly held Bible-believing doctrines.

The title of my sermon on that occasion was *"Taming The Untamed."* It was about the maniac of Gadara. <u>I told how the man was soundly converted to the Lord Jesus Christ by genuine faith in Him</u>. I also told the sailors about faith in the Lord Jesus Christ, and how people today can be saved. I assured those who were present that they could become genuine Christians in the same way. At the end of the service, this apostate Presbyterian senior chaplain told me:

"Chaplain Waite, that sermon was spiritually sterile and intellectually barren."
He also banned me from preaching in the morning services for a month or two and told me I would be called to Washington. I wrote the Chaplains department in Washington and told them what Chaplain Carter had done. Instead of calling me to Washington, they called him there and told him to restore my preaching immediately! Paul was correct when he said that preaching the Gospel is *"to them that perish foolishness;"* To Chaplain Carter, an apostate Navy Chaplain, it was foolishness, but to the true Christians, it's the *"power of God."*

Verses On Power
- **Matthew 6:13**

"And lead us not into temptation, but deliver us from evil: For <u>thine is the kingdom, and the power</u>, and the glory, for ever. Amen."

The Lord has great and unlimited power. He is omnipotent!
- **Matthew 22:29**

"Jesus answered and said unto them, <u>Ye do err, not knowing</u> the scriptures, nor <u>the power of God</u>."

The Scriptures and the Lord of Heaven and earth give power to those who believe in them and use them rightly.
- **Matthew 28:18**

"And Jesus came and spake unto them, saying, <u>All power is given unto me in heaven and in earth</u>."

There is no limit to the power of God the Son, the Lord Jesus Christ.
- **Luke 9:43**

"And they were all amazed at the mighty power of God. But while they wondered every one at all things which Jesus did, he said unto his disciples,"
- **John 1:12**

"But <u>as many as received him, to them gave he power to become the sons of God</u>, *even* to them that believe on his name:"

The Lord Jesus Christ gave those who genuinely believe on His Name, the power to become the children of God by true faith.
- **Acts 1:8**

"But <u>ye shall receive power, after that the Holy Ghost is come upon you</u>: and ye shall be witnesses unto me both in Jerusalem, and in all Judaea, and in Samaria, and unto the uttermost part of the earth."

With the coming of God the Holy Spirit into the world and especially into the bodies of every genuine Christian, they have the power to witness for the Lord Jesus Christ *"unto the uttermost part of the earth."* This can be through our faithful verse-by-verse preaching, through our missionaries at home and abroad, through radio, through the Internet, through our books and tapes, and in many other ways, including, through individual Christian lives as God provides opportunities.

1 Corinthians 1:19

"For it is written, I will destroy the wisdom of the wise, and will bring to nothing the understanding of the prudent."

Paul was alluding to Isaiah 29:14, which says:
- **Isaiah 29:14**

"Therefore, behold, I will proceed to do a marvellous work among this people, *even* a marvellous work and a wonder: for the wisdom of their wise *men* shall perish, and the understanding of their prudent *men* shall be hid."

The Words, *"it is written,"* are in the Greek Perfect tense. This tense implies something that happened in the past, that is preserved in the present, and will continue to be preserved in the future. This signifies the preservation of the Hebrew and Aramaic Words of the Old Testament, and the Greek Words of the New Testament.

The King James Bible is an accurate translation of the proper and preserved Hebrew, Aramaic, and Greek Words. This Bible translation departs from over 99% of the other so-called modern Bible translations which are based on improper Hebrew, Aramaic, and Greek Words and which use improper translation techniques in their so-called translations.

This verse teaches that the Lord will not agree with the wisdom and understanding of those who might be "wise" in this world, without His wisdom that comes from the proper understanding of His Words in the Bible. Worldly wisdom includes a myriad of human views and practices which are out of strict conformity with God's eternal and preserved Words in our Bible.

1 Corinthians 1:20

"Where is the wise? where is the scribe? where is the disputer of this world? hath not God made foolish the wisdom of this world?"

Anything that is contrary to the Word of God in the accurately-translated Bible, is merely the *"wisdom of this world"* which God has made *"foolish."* This worldly wisdom might come from a Ph.D. level, or whatever intellectual level that can be named. This foolish wisdom includes scribes, or writers of articles, magazines or books. It includes all the debaters and disputers of the world who conjure up many intellectual arguments against God's Words in the Scripture. It includes many of the hundreds of schools and seminaries around the world that differ from God's wisdom and Words.

1 Corinthians 1:21

"For after that in the wisdom of God the world by wisdom knew not God, it pleased God by the foolishness of preaching to save them that believe."

Through philosophy and vain worldly false "wisdom," people did not know God in any way. They forsook Him in all of their thoughts and ways. Yet God, in His love for their souls, was pleased to save them who truly believed in His Son as their Saviour. This was done by what the fools of this world would refer to as the *"foolishness of preaching"* of the Gospel of God's grace.

It is important that this "preaching" should be done in a proper and truthful manner. For all the years of our Bible For Today Baptist Church, I have used the method of verse-by-verse preaching from the books of the Bible. I have taken that method as I have preached from Romans through Revelation. I take a half of a chapter each Sunday morning for this.

I have also used this verse-by-verse method in my Bible study discussion services on Sunday afternoons and Thursday evenings. In these classes, I ask questions on parts of each of the verses and ask those present to make comments on the teachings of these verses.

Verses On Preaching

- **Jonah 3:2**

"Arise, go unto Nineveh, that great city, and <u>preach unto it the preaching that I bid thee</u>."

God told Jonah to go to Nineveh and preach to them that judgment was coming if they did not repent of their sins. He was a faithful preacher of God's Words. They repented and judgment did not come to them at that time.

- **Matthew 12:41**

"The men of Nineveh shall rise in judgment with this generation, and shall condemn it: because <u>they repented at the preaching of Jonas</u>; and, behold, a greater than Jonas *is* here."

Jonah's preaching was used by God to save thousands of lives of all ages and positions.
- **Acts 8:4**
"Therefore <u>they</u> that were scattered abroad <u>went every where preaching the word</u>."

The early Christians were faithful in preaching God's Words to all areas of the then-known world.
- **Acts 8:12**
"But when <u>they believed Philip preaching the things concerning</u> the kingdom of God, and <u>the name of Jesus Christ</u>, they were baptized, both men and women."

These people believed Philip as he preached concerning the Name of the Lord Jesus Christ. After their salvation, they were baptized.
- **Acts 10:36**
"The word which *God* sent unto the children of Israel, <u>preaching peace by Jesus Christ</u>: (he is Lord of all:)"

The apostles preached peace by trusting the Lord Jesus Christ as their Saviour. He is the only source of peace with God the Father.
- **Acts 15:35**
"<u>Paul also and Barnabas continued</u> in Antioch, teaching and <u>preaching the word of the Lord</u>, with many others also."

Neither of these two disciples ceased teaching and preaching the Word of the Lord. They continued in this important activity.
- **Romans 16:25**
"Now <u>to him that is of power to stablish you according to</u> my gospel, and <u>the preaching of Jesus Christ</u>, according to the revelation of the mystery, which was kept secret since the world began,"

We need Biblical preachers today who will preach the Lord Jesus Christ by means of God's power.
- **1 Corinthians 15:14**
"And <u>if Christ be not risen, then *is* our preaching vain</u>, and your faith *is* also vain."

The bodily resurrection of the Lord Jesus Christ was an essential truth so that Paul's preaching would not be in vain.
- **2 Timothy 4:2**
"<u>Preach the word</u>; be instant in season, out of season; <u>reprove, rebuke, exhort with all longsuffering and doctrine</u>."

The preaching must be about God's Words. If faithfully preached, it will include reproof, rebuke, and exhortation with both longsuffering and doctrine.
- **Titus 1:3**
"But <u>hath in due times manifested his word through preaching</u>, which is committed unto me according to the

commandment of God our Saviour;"
God's Words are manifested when Biblical and faithful preaching is followed carefully and faithfully.

> **THE MEANING OF THE GREEK WORD, KERUGMA**
>
> The Word for "preaching" is KERUGMA. Some of the meanings of this Greek Word are:
>
> *"1) that which is proclaimed by a herald or public crier, a proclamation by herald; 2) in the NT the message or proclamation of the heralds of God or Christ."*

1 Corinthians 1:22

"For the Jews require a sign, and the Greeks seek after wisdom:"

In Paul's day, and probably in our day as well, the Jews were looking for various spiritual signs of one kind or another. The Greeks were more interested in some sort of human wisdom.

Verses On Signs

- **Exodus 4:8**

"And it shall come to pass, if they will not believe thee, neither hearken to the voice of the first sign, that they will believe the voice of the latter sign."

Moses was told by the Lord that if the people wouldn't believe the first sign, they would not believe the next sign either.

- **Deuteronomy 13:1-2**

"If there arise among you a prophet, or a dreamer of dreams, and giveth thee a sign or a wonder, And the sign or the wonder come to pass, whereof he spake unto thee, saying, Let us go after other gods, which thou hast not known, and let us serve them;"

This was common among the Jews to have prophets who gave the people certain signs or wonders.

- **1 Samuel 2:34**

"And this *shall be* a sign unto thee, that shall come upon thy two sons, on Hophni and Phinehas; in one day they shall die both of them."

God fulfilled that sign. Both Hophni and Phinehas died the same day.

- **Isaiah 7:14**

"Therefore the Lord himself shall give you a sign; Behold, a virgin shall conceive, and bear a son, and shall call his name Immanuel."

God gave Isaiah the sign of the virgin birth of the Lord Jesus Christ. This miracle birth came to fulfillment in the New Testament.

- **Matthew 12:38**
"Then certain of the scribes and of the Pharisees answered, saying, Master, we would see a sign from thee."

The Lord Jesus Christ was asked by the scribes and Pharisees for some kind of a sign.

- **Matthew 16:4**
"A wicked and adulterous generation seeketh after a sign; and there shall no sign be given unto it, but the sign of the prophet Jonas. And he left them, and departed."

Jonah was the only sign the Lord Jesus Christ gave to the wicked generation in His day.

- **Luke 2:12**
"And this *shall be* a sign unto you; Ye shall find the babe wrapped in swaddling clothes, lying in a manger."

The wise men were given a sign of where the Lord Jesus Christ was to be born.

- **John 6:30**
"They said therefore unto him, What sign shewest thou then, that we may see, and believe thee? what dost thou work?"

When the Lord Jesus Christ was on earth, the Jews asked Him for a sign.

1 Corinthians 1:23

"But we preach Christ crucified, unto the Jews a stumblingblock, and unto the Greeks foolishness;"

Paul was faithful in preaching the Lord Jesus Christ crucified, regardless of what the Jews or Greeks thought of it, whether a stumblingblock or foolishness. Sad to say, today, many preachers are seeking to please people, rather than Christ. Not Paul!

- **Romans 11:9**
"And David saith, Let their table be made a snare, and a trap, and a stumblingblock, and a recompence unto them:"

THE MEANING OF THE GREEK WORD, SKANDALON

The Greek Word for "***stumblingblock***" is "SKANDALON." Some of the meanings for that Greek Word are:

> "*1) the movable stick or trigger of a trap, a trap stick; 1a) a trap, snare; 1b) any impediment placed in the way and causing*

> *one to stumble or fall, (a stumbling block, occasion of stumbling) i.e. a rock which is a cause of stumbling; 1c) fig. applied to Jesus Christ, whose person and career were so contrary to the expectations of the Jews concerning the Messiah, that they rejected him and by their obstinacy made shipwreck of their salvation; 2) any person or thing by which one is (entrapped), drawn into error or sin."*

1 Corinthians 1:24

"But unto them which are called, both Jews and Greeks, Christ the power of God, and the wisdom of God."

To those who have accepted the Lord Jesus Christ's call to come unto Him in true faith, whether Jews or Greeks, He is both the Power of God and the Wisdom of God.

- **John 1:29b**
   "Behold <u>the Lamb of God</u>, which <u>taketh away the sin of the world</u>."

When you preach, make it clear that the Lord Jesus Christ was crucified and shed His Divine blood as an offering for all people, but they must genuinely receive Him as their Saviour in order to become a true Christian. If you truly trust Him, He will forgive your sins. You who are reading this book, have you responded favorably to His call for salvation? If not, accept Him Who died for your sins. Don't put it off. He is God's Power and God's Wisdom.

- **Acts 1:8**
   "But <u>ye shall receive power, after that the Holy Ghost is come upon you</u>: and ye shall be witnesses unto me both in Jerusalem, and in all Judaea, and in Samaria, and unto the uttermost part of the earth."

The power for the genuine Christian is both in the Lord Jesus Christ and in God the Holy Spirit Who indwells every true Christian.

1 Corinthians 1:25

"Because the foolishness of God is wiser than men; and the weakness of God is stronger than men."

With all the man-centered, so-called "wisdom," God equates it in this verse to what might be called God's foolishness. In God's eyes, man's wisdom is foolish when judged by the infinite standards of the God of the Bible.

Verses On Wisdom And Knowledge
- **Job 37:16**

"Dost thou know the balancings of the clouds, the wondrous works of <u>him which is perfect in knowledge</u>?"
God's knowledge is perfect. He is omniscient and knows everything there is to know.

- **Proverbs 2:6**

"For <u>the LORD giveth wisdom</u>: out of his mouth *cometh* knowledge and understanding."
The Lord is the source of all wisdom. He has revealed some of it within the pages of the Bible.

- **Romans 11:33**

"O <u>the depth of the riches both of the wisdom and knowledge of God</u>! how unsearchable *are* his judgments, and his ways past finding out!"
God's wisdom and knowledge is so vast and unsearchable that no human being can know or understand them all.

- **Colossians 2:3**

"<u>In whom are hid all the treasures of wisdom and knowledge</u>."
This refers to the Lord Jesus Christ. In Him, God has hidden all the treasures of both wisdom and knowledge. He is all-knowing.

1 Corinthians 1:26

"For ye see your calling, brethren, how that not many wise men after the flesh, not many mighty, not many noble, *are called*:"

Paul is referring to the genuine Christians in the church at Corinth. They should understand that not many wise, mighty, or noble have received the Lord Jesus Christ as their Saviour. These true Christians should realize that they are numbered among the very few out of the whole world who have received God's eternal life and answered His call upon their lives.

Verses On Calling

- **1 Corinthians 7:20**
"Let every man abide in the same calling wherein he was called."

God has called genuine Christians to salvation. He has called some of them to a special calling such as to special service for Him--missionary service, evangelistic service, pastoral service, soul-winning service–whatever that might be.

- **Ephesians 4:4**
"*There is* one body, and one Spirit, even as ye are called in one hope of your calling;"

True Christians are called in one hope–the hope of eternal life.

- **2 Thessalonians 1:11**
"Wherefore also we pray always for you, that our God would count you worthy of *this* calling, and fulfil all the good pleasure of *his* goodness, and the work of faith with power:"

May every genuine Christian who has answered God's call for salvation and service be worthy of such a calling.

- **2 Timothy 1:9**
"Who hath saved us, and called *us* with an holy calling, not according to our works, but according to his own purpose and grace, which was given us in Christ Jesus before the world began,"

All true Christians that are saved have a calling from the Lord to do His will according to His Words.

- **Hebrews 3:1**
"Wherefore, holy brethren, partakers of the heavenly calling, consider the Apostle and High Priest of our profession, Christ Jesus;"

All genuine Christians are partakers in God's heavenly calling.

- **2 Peter 1:10**
"Wherefore the rather, brethren, give diligence to make your calling and election sure: for if ye do these things, ye shall never fall:"

True Christians must have confidence that they have been saved by sincere faith in the Lord Jesus Christ.

1 Corinthians 1:27

"But God hath chosen the foolish things of the world to confound the wise; and God hath chosen the weak things of the world to confound the things which are mighty;"

In His saving the souls of genuine Christians, God has chosen those whom the world counts as foolish to confound those whom the world considers to be wise.

For example, the giant, Goliath, thought that it was the craziest thing in the world, to have this little lad, named David, to come out to do battle with him. And yet, God enabled this young man to slay the mighty giant, Goliath.

Another example of how God used a small group of men to defeat a much larger group is found in the battle between Gideon and his men with the Philistine armies. Gideon's 300 chosen men, by following God's explicit instructions, were used by Him to defeat the many thousands in the Philistine army. They were outnumbered about ten to one, but God used them to defeat the pagan Philistines, who were so confused that they began killing each other.

Another illustration of the weak to defeat the strong was in the case of Samson. When he was blinded by the Philistines, he became their servant. As he was doing work where the Philistines were assembled, he had a lad to show him where the pillars were that held up the building. He showed him the pillars. Then he prayed unto the Lord to avenge him of these enemies. The Lord answered his prayer and allowed him to pull down those main pillars, slaying more in his death than he had slain throughout his life.

A further example of the small being able to help the many was when the Lord Jesus Christ fed the five thousand men plus women and children. He asked His disciples if they had any bread. They said they did not. But there was a little lad there who had five loaves and two fishes. He gave them to the Lord Jesus Christ Who then multiplied them to feed that entire throng.

These illustrations teach us that God, the Mighty One, can use the smallest and the weakest things, if given over to His might and strength, to defeat and conquer the mighty and many who are His enemies.

1 Corinthians 1:28

"And base things of the world, and things which are despised, hath God chosen, *yea*, and things which are not, to bring to nought things that are:"

In addition to the foolish and weak things of the world to confound the worldly-wise and strong, He has also the things the world considers to be base, and even non-existent, to bring to nought the things that are. The Lord Jesus Christ is able to assist the genuine Christians who are faced with such obstacles. God does not merely stifle these various things that are against His genuine Christians, but He brings them *"to nought."*

THE MEANING OF THE GREEK WORD, KATARGEO

The Greek Word for *"bring to nought"* is KATARGEO. Some of the meanings of that Greek Word are:

> *"1) to render idle, unemployed, inactivate, inoperative; 1a) to cause a person or thing to have no further efficiency; 1b) to deprive of force, influence, power; 2) to cause to cease, put an end to, do away with, annul, abolish; 2a) to cease, to pass away, be done away; 2b) to be severed from, separated from, discharged from, loosed from any one; 2c) to terminate all intercourse with one."*

The Help Of The Lord Jesus Christ
- Acts 4:13

"Now when they saw the boldness of Peter and John, and perceived that they were unlearned and ignorant men, <u>they marvelled; and they took knowledge of them, that they had been with Jesus.</u>"

Apostles Peter and John were unlearned and ignorant men, but their enemies saw their boldness and could see that they had been with the Lord Jesus Christ Who had given them their spiritual strength. May people see this in the lives of genuine Christians today.

- **Hebrews 5:1-2**
"For every high priest taken from among men is ordained for men in things *pertaining* to God, that he may offer both gifts and sacrifices for sins: <u>Who can have compassion on the ignorant, and on them that are out of the way</u>; for that he himself also is compassed with infirmity."

The Lord Jesus Christ is the Heavenly High Priest who has greater compassion on the out of the way and the ignorant than the earthly high priests. He cares for those He has saved from the quagmire of sin. This is the case of all true Christians living today. May they be thankful unto Him, and live to please Him every day of their lives, despite those who are lost sinners, religious compromisers, and apostates who might despise them.

1 Corinthians 1:29

"That no flesh should glory in his presence."

The reason God has used people whom the world considers to be foolish, weak, and base, is so that they should not glory in His presence.

Verses On Glory
- **Ephesians 2:8-9**
"For by grace are ye saved through faith; and that not of yourselves: *it is* the gift of God: <u>Not of works, lest any man should boast</u>."

God does not want any Christians to boast or glory in their own deeds. Their glory should be in the Lord and His grace.

- **Jeremiah 9:23-24**
"Thus saith the LORD, Let not the wise *man* glory in his wisdom, neither let the mighty *man* glory in his might, let not the rich *man* glory in his riches: <u>But let him that glorieth glory in this, that he understandeth and knoweth me</u>, that I *am* the LORD which exercise lovingkindness, judgment, and righteousness, in the earth: for in these *things* I delight, saith the LORD."

Every true Christian should glory in the Lord Jesus Christ and what He has done for them rather than in their fleshly attainments.

In the hymn, "*The Sands of Time Are Sinking*," the hymn-writer declared, "*The Lamb is all the glory in Immanuel's land.*" Another hymn comes to mind on this theme as well. It is "*The Meeting in the Air.*" It speaks of the Rapture of all genuine Christians before any part of the seven-year Tribulation. The last phrase of that hymn states: "*And God's own Son will be the leading One, in that meeting in the air.*" It is the Lord Jesus Christ Who deserves and should receive all the glory.

1 Corinthians 1:30

"But of him are ye in Christ Jesus, who of God is made unto us wisdom, and righteousness, and sanctification, and redemption:"

Those who are "*in Christ,*" are genuine Christians on whom God has bestowed four tremendous positional gifts: (1) wisdom, (2) righteousness, (3) sanctification, and (4) redemption.

All four of these tremendous gifts are bestowed immediately when people become true Christians by their personal faith in the Lord Jesus Christ as their Saviour. These are part of their standing in Christ. There should also be an attempt to make these possessions a part of their state as well as their standing.

Every genuine Christian should do the following in a practical way as often as possible:

(1) They should seek to avail themselves of God's wisdom by reading and heeding His Words in the Bible day by day.
(2) They should seek to live righteously by following God's Words and be guided by God the Holy Spirit Who dwells within them.
(3) They should be sanctified and set apart unto the Lord Jesus Christ and separated from the works of their flesh, from the world, and from Satan's wiles.
(4) They should be grateful for God's redemption they have received because of their true faith in the work of the Lord Jesus Christ on the cross. In addition, they should tell others that they should avail themselves of this redemption.

1 Corinthians 1:31

"That, according as it is written, He that glorieth, let him glory in the Lord."

Paul is referring to Jeremiah 9:24. Remember that the expression, "*it is written*" is in the Greek perfect tense. As such, it refers to something that happened in the past with the results occurring down to the present and on into the future. This is one of the proofs that not only the Words in Jeremiah 9:24 have been preserved in Hebrew down to the present time, but it is true that all of God's original Hebrew, Aramaic, and Greek Words have been thus preserved as well.

For the true Christians, there should never be a time that they glory and boast in themselves. Their glory and boast should be in the things that the Lord Jesus Christ, God the Father, and God the Holy Spirit have done for them.

- **Jeremiah 9:24**

"But let him that glorieth glory in this, that he understandeth and knoweth me, that I *am* the LORD which exercise lovingkindness, judgment, and righteousness, in the earth: for in these *things* I delight, saith the LORD."

Jeremiah reminds all genuine Christians to glory in the fact that they understand and know the Lord of the Bible Who has redeemed them and given them everlasting life.

1 Corinthians Chapter Two

1 Corinthians 2:1

"**And I, brethren, when I came to you, came not with excellency of speech or of wisdom, declaring unto you the testimony of God.**"

Paul did not present himself to the church in Corinth by the use of excellency of speech or of wisdom when he declared to them God's testimony. That doesn't mean he didn't speak clearly, but he didn't use flowery speech that called attention more to his words and phases than to the message that was being spoken.

When he went to Mars Hill that is mentioned in Acts 17, he differed with those who emphasized philosophy and the worship of many gods. He told them of the unknown God whom they didn't worship, that they had never heard of. He told them of the Lord Jesus Christ and His saving power.

In Acts 18, Paul came to the city of Corinth. He had had his fill of the philosophy and debate with the Athenians on Mars Hill. When he arrived at Corinth, he left his wisdom behind. Not that he didn't have wisdom. He was brought up in the Jewish law being taught by Gamaliel, but he wanted to speak in a true and simple manner when addressing those in Corinth. He wanted people to understand him rather than to have them admire his excellence of speech.

Verses On Excellency
- **2 Corinthians 4:7**
"But we have this treasure in earthen vessels, <u>that the excellency of the power may be of God</u>, and not of us."

God did not want His excellency to be bypassed by exalting any human being. This is why God put His treasure of the Holy Spirit within earthen vessels of clay so God would get the glory, not human beings.

- **Philippians 3:8**
"Yea doubtless, and <u>I count all things *but* loss for the excellency of the knowledge of Christ</u> Jesus my Lord: for whom I have suffered the loss of all things, and do count them *but* dung, that I may win Christ."

The true excellency should be found in the knowledge of the Lord Jesus Christ, rather than any human being considered as excellent.

Verses On Speech

- **Proverbs 7:21**
"<u>With her much fair speech</u> she caused him to yield, with the flattering of her lips <u>she forced him</u>."

The speech of the prostitute urges her customers to pay her price and commit the wicked, godless sin of sexual immorality.

- **Isaiah 28:23**
"Give ye ear, and hear my voice; hearken, and <u>hear my speech</u>."

The prophet Isaiah urged his readers to hear his speech concerning their errors and sins.

- **Isaiah 32:9**
"Rise up, ye women that are at ease; hear my voice, ye careless daughters; <u>give ear unto my speech</u>."

Isaiah is pleading to the lazy, careless women to listen to his speech.

- **2 Corinthians 10:10**
"For *his* letters, say they, *are* weighty and powerful; but *his* bodily presence *is* weak, and <u>*his* speech contemptible</u>."

The church at Corinth didn't like Paul's speech, but he got his point across. Perhaps he had some kind of speech defect, but he preached God's Words faithfully.

- **2 Corinthians 11:6**
"But <u>though *I be* rude in speech</u>, yet not in knowledge; but we have been throughly made manifest among you in all things."

Paul admitted he had some defect in his speech, but he had no defect in his knowledge of God's Words and His will.

- **Colossians 4:6**
"<u>Let your speech *be* alway with grace, seasoned with salt</u>, that ye may know how ye ought to answer every man."

Genuine Christians should have gracious speech which is seasoned with salt so they know how to answer every person tactfully.

- **Acts 14:3**
"Long time therefore abode they <u>speaking boldly in the Lord</u>, which gave testimony unto the word of his grace, and granted signs and wonders to be done by their hands."

True Christians should be able to speak boldly for the Lord Jesus Christ.

- **Ephesians 5:19**
"<u>Speaking to yourselves in psalms and hymns and spiritual songs</u>, singing and making melody in your heart to the Lord;"

Speaking and singing the proper kind of psalms and hymns is needful. The present contemporary Christian music (CCM) is often similar to the rock music of the world.

1 Corinthians 2:2

"For I determined not to know any thing among you, save Jesus Christ, and him crucified."

Paul was determined not to exalt what he knew, though he knew a lot. He wanted to know more about the Lord Jesus Christ, and Him crucified. He's the One that Paul wanted to know more about and to exalt. This was a determination for him.

Verses On Crucifixion

- **John 19:6**
"When the chief priests therefore and officers saw him, they cried out, saying, <u>Crucify *him*, crucify *him*</u>. Pilate saith unto them, <u>Take ye him, and crucify *him*</u>: for I find no fault in him."

Why would Paul want to know nothing except Jesus Christ crucified? Crucifixion is a horrible, painful, and ignominious death. Paul knew that the Lord Jesus Christ's death at Calvary was essential for people to become genuine Christians. On that cross, The Lord Jesus Christ bore the sins of the world so that those who truly trusted Him might heave everlasting life.

- **Acts 2:23**
"Him, being delivered by the determinate counsel and foreknowledge of God, <u>ye have taken, and by wicked hands have crucified and slain</u>:"

God was not surprised when the crucifixion of His Son took place. It occurred by the determinate counsel and foreknowledge of God. The Lord Jesus Christ was the Lamb slain before the foundation of the world. God the Father foreordained that His Son would come to this earth, not just to live, but also to die and suffer on that cross, as an offering for the sins of the world.

- **Acts 2:36**
"Therefore let all the house of Israel know assuredly, that God hath made that same Jesus, whom ye have crucified, both Lord and Christ."

God the Father made His crucified Son both Lord and Christ, the Anointed One.

- **1 Corinthians 1:23**
"But we preach Christ crucified, unto the Jews a stumblingblock, and unto the Greeks foolishness;"

Paul preached Christ not simply living, but Christ suffering and dying, for the sins of the world.

- **Revelation 11:8**
"And their dead bodies *shall lie* in the street of the great city, which spiritually is called Sodom and Egypt, where also our Lord was crucified."

The place where these two witnesses will be buried is in Jerusalem, that wicked city, which spiritually is called Sodom and Egypt.

1 Corinthians 2:3

"And I was with you in weakness, and in fear, and in much trembling."

When Paul came to Corinth, he was not strong in body or in spirit. Instead, he had weakness and trembling.

THE MEANING OF THE GREEK WORD, TROMOS

The Greek Word for *"trembling"* is TROMOS. Some of the meanings of this Greek Word are:

"1) a trembling or quaking with fear;
2) with fear and trembling, used to describe the anxiety of one who distrusts his ability completely to meet all requirements, but religiously does his utmost to fulfil his duty."

Verses On Weakness

- **2 Corinthians 12:9**
"And he said unto me, My grace is sufficient for thee: for my strength is made perfect in weakness."

And if Paul were strong and not weak, then the power of God might not flow through him. Perhaps if he were strong, he might rely totally on himself and his own power rather than on God's power. God's strength was made perfect and evident when it contrasted with Paul's own human weakness. The difference would be obvious.

- **Hebrews 11:34**
"Quenched the violence of fire, escaped the edge of the sword, <u>out of weakness were made strong</u>, waxed valiant in fight, turned to flight the armies of the aliens."

This eleventh chapter of Hebrews lists the many heroes of the Old Testament who, though they were weak in themselves, God made them strong so they could be valiant and turn back the armies of the alien unbelievers.

1 Corinthians 2:4

"And my speech and my preaching was not with enticing words of man's wisdom, but in demonstration of the Spirit and of power:"

Paul preached with the power of God the Holy Spirit rather than with enticing words of man's wisdom. Preachers today should follow his example.

Verses On Power

- **Psalms 21:13**
"Be thou exalted, LORD, in thine own strength: *so* will <u>we sing and praise thy power</u>."

Biblical songs should praise God's power. God's power is great.

- **Psalms 147:5**
"<u>Great *is* our Lord, and of great power</u>: his understanding *is* infinite."

God is great and has great power.

- **Isaiah 40:29**
"<u>He giveth power to the faint</u>; and to *them that have* no might he increaseth strength."

God is able to help His genuine Christians who are faint. He can give them power.

- **Jeremiah 32:17**
"Ah Lord GOD! behold, <u>thou hast made the heaven and the earth by thy great power</u> and stretched out arm, *and* there is nothing too hard for thee:"

God showed His mighty power by His creation of the heaven and the earth. Nothing is too hard for Him.

- **Zechariah 4:6**
"Then he answered and spake unto me, saying, This *is* the word of the LORD unto Zerubbabel, saying, <u>Not by might, nor by power, but by my spirit</u>, saith the LORD of hosts."

God's remedy for true Christians to accomplish things is not by might or power, but by His Spirit.

- **Matthew 28:18**
  "And Jesus came and spake unto them, saying, <u>All power is given unto me in heaven and in earth</u>."

The Lord Jesus Christ told His disciples just before He ascended to Heaven, that He had all power in heaven and in earth. He is, He was, and He will ever be all-powerful.

- **Acts 1:8**
  "But <u>ye shall receive power, after that the Holy Ghost is come upon you</u>: and ye shall be witnesses unto me both in Jerusalem, and in all Judaea, and in Samaria, and unto the uttermost part of the earth."

Another thing the Lord Jesus Christ told His disciples before He ascended to Heaven was that God the Holy Spirit would come upon them and they would receive His power for their ministries. So today, our church needs His power in our missionary ministry, in our church ministry, in our Internet ministry, and all other ministries that we have.

- **Acts 4:33**
  "And <u>with great power gave the apostles witness of the resurrection</u> of the Lord Jesus: and great grace was upon them all."

The apostles of the Lord Jesus Christ were given great power as they witnessed about His bodily resurrection.

- **Romans 1:16**
  "For I am not ashamed of <u>the gospel of Christ</u>: for it <u>is the power of God unto salvation</u> to every one that believeth; to the Jew first, and also to the Greek."

When the Gospel of Christ is faithfully and Biblically proclaimed, it is God's power that leads people to genuine salvation. The Gnostic Critical New Testament Greek texts omit "*Christ*" from this verse. So do 99.9% of the modern English and other language versions because they follow slavishly and consistently these false and perverted Greek texts.

- **Ephesians 6:10**
  "Finally, my brethren, <u>be strong in the Lord, and in the power of his might</u>."

Paul urged these genuine Christians to be strong in the Lord Jesus Christ and in the power of His might. His power is mighty. It should be relied upon every moment of every day.

1 Corinthians 2:5
"That your faith should not stand in the wisdom of men, but in the power of God."

The reason that Paul wanted to speak with the power of the Lord rather than with the wisdom of man was because he didn't want the faith of his listeners to stand in the wisdom of men, but in God's power. Mormons follow the wisdom of men in their *Book Of Mormon*. Christian Science, Jehovah Witnesses, Roman Catholicism, modern Judaism, the National and World Counsels of Churches, Apostate theological seminaries, humanists, atheists, apostate ministers and missionaries–and many, many others–are all following the false wisdom of men rather than the power of God found in the written and preserved Words of God in the Hebrew, Aramaic, and Greek Texts and their accurate translations in the languages of the world. That's where God's wisdom is to be found.

1 Corinthians 2:6
"Howbeit we speak wisdom among them that are perfect: yet not the wisdom of this world, nor of the princes of this world, that come to nought:"

Though Paul did not use the wisdom of this world or the wisdom of the leaders of this world that comes to nought, he did speak the wisdom that God has given us in His written Words.

Verses On Wisdom
- **Psalms 111:10**

"The fear of the LORD *is* the beginning of wisdom: a good understanding have all they that do *his commandments*: his praise endureth for ever."

Trusting the Lord Jesus Christ as your Saviour is when you first have the "fear of the Lord." This is the beginning of Godly wisdom.

- **Proverbs 9:10**

"The fear of the LORD *is* the beginning of wisdom: and the knowledge of the holy *is* understanding."

As I said in the verse before: *"Trusting the Lord Jesus Christ as your Saviour is when you first have the 'fear of the Lord.' This is the beginning of Godly wisdom."*

- **Isaiah 47:10**

"For thou hast trusted in thy wickedness: thou hast said, None seeth me. Thy wisdom and thy knowledge, it hath perverted thee; and thou hast said in thine heart, I *am*, and none else beside me."

One of the possible sad results of the use of human wisdom by itself are perversion in many areas, including egotism, pornography, homosexuality, bestiality, rape, adultery, fornication, lying, murder, and many other sins.

- **Jeremiah 9:23-24**

"Thus saith the LORD, Let not the wise *man* glory in his wisdom, neither let the mighty *man* glory in his might, let not the rich *man* glory in his riches: But let him that glorieth glory in this, that he understandeth and knoweth me, that I *am* the LORD which exercise lovingkindness, judgment, and righteousness, in the earth: for in these *things* I delight, saith the LORD."

Those who are wise in this world must not glory in that wisdom, but glory that they understand and know the Lord.

- **Ezekiel 28:12**

"Son of man, take up a lamentation upon the king of Tyrus, and say unto him, Thus saith the Lord GOD; Thou sealest up the sum, full of wisdom, and perfect in beauty."

The king of Tyrus is a picture of Satan who is full of a perverted wisdom that fooled Adam and Eve in the Garden of Eden. He's fooled many other people into following his wicked, crafty, and devilish wisdom. He tried to order around the Lord Jesus Christ for 40 days in the wilderness, but did not succeed in his efforts, and was defeated. Satan uses lying and deceptive wisdom to lure people into following him.

- **1 Corinthians 1:30**

"But of him are ye in Christ Jesus, who of God is made unto us wisdom, and righteousness, and sanctification, and redemption:"

God the Father permits true Christians to have the Lord Jesus Christ made unto them true wisdom.

- **Colossians 1:28**

"Whom we preach, warning every man, and teaching every man in all wisdom; that we may present every man perfect in Christ Jesus:"

Paul preached the Lord Jesus Christ and taught in wisdom everyone to whom he ministered.

- **Colossians 2:3**

"In whom are hid all the treasures of wisdom and knowledge."

In the Lord Jesus Christ are hid all the treasures of true wisdom and knowledge.
- **James 1:5-6**
"If any of you lack wisdom, let him ask of God, that giveth to all *men* liberally, and upbraideth not; and it shall be given him. But let him ask in faith, nothing wavering. For he that wavereth is like a wave of the sea driven with the wind and tossed."

Genuine Christians who lack God's wisdom should ask God the Father about it, and he has promised to give Godly wisdom to them.
- **Colossians 4:5**
"Walk in wisdom toward them that are without, redeeming the time."

True Christians must not only have proper wisdom, but they must also walk in wisdom toward the unsaved multitudes that surround them in this world.
- **James 3:17**
"But the wisdom that is from above is first pure, then peaceable, gentle, *and* easy to be intreated, full of mercy and good fruits, without partiality, and without hypocrisy."

God's wisdom that is from above is pure, peaceable, gentle, entreatable, full of mercy, full of good fruits, without partiality, and without any hypocrisy.

1 Corinthians 2:7

"But we speak the wisdom of God in a mystery, even the hidden wisdom, which God ordained before the world unto our glory:"

Paul spoke to his listeners about God's hidden wisdom which He had before the world began. This wisdom was a mystery or a secret until He revealed it to mankind in the Bible. Paul used this wisdom from the Old Testament Scriptures as well as the wisdom God revealed to him by Divine inspiration as he taught and preached to people everywhere.

1 Corinthians 2:8

"Which none of the princes of this world knew: for had they known *it*, they would not have crucified the Lord of glory."

None of the princes and political rulers of this world knew God's wisdom. Had they known it, they would never have crucified the Lord Jesus Christ Who is the Lord of Glory. In our present day, most of the rulers of nations, states, counties, and cities do not know the Lord of Glory either. For this reason, they often look down on genuine Christians and Biblically-sound churches in their areas.

Verses On Glory
- **Exodus 16:10c**

"Behold, the glory of the LORD appeared in the cloud."

After Moses had set up the tabernacle as God had directed him, the very presence of the Lord appeared in a shekinah glory. It could be seen by all of the Israelites.

- **Numbers 20:6**

"And Moses and Aaron went from the presence of the assembly unto the door of the tabernacle of the congregation, and they fell upon their faces: and the glory of the LORD appeared unto them."

On this occasion, Moses and Aaron went into the door of the tabernacle, and they fell on their faces because the glory of the Lord appeared unto them.

- **Exodus 24:15**

"And Moses went up into the mount, and a cloud covered the mount."

The glory of the Lord also appeared to Moses as he went up onto Mount Sinai. The cloud of glory covered the entire mountain on this occasion.

- **Exodus 24:17**

"And the sight of the glory of the LORD *was* like devouring fire on the top of the mount in the eyes of the children of Israel."

At the top of Mount Sinai, the glory of the Lord was like bright, devouring fire.

- **2 Chronicles 7:1-3**

"Now when Solomon had made an end of praying, the fire came down from heaven, and consumed the burnt offering and the sacrifices; and the glory of the LORD filled the house. And the priests could not enter into the house of the LORD, because the glory of the LORD had filled the LORD's house. And when all the children of Israel saw how the fire came down, and the glory of the LORD upon the house, they bowed themselves with their faces to the ground upon the pavement, and worshipped, and praised the LORD, *saying*, For *he is* good; for his mercy *endureth* for ever."

When the temple was completed, King Solomon prayed to the Lord concerning His leadership and greatness. When he finished his prayer, fire came down and the glory of the Lord filled the

temple. When the Israelites saw this, they bowed themselves with their faces to the ground and worshipped and praised the Lord.
- **Matthew 17:1-2**
"And after six days Jesus taketh Peter, James, and John his brother, and bringeth them up into an high mountain apart, And <u>was transfigured before them: and his face did shine as the sun, and his raiment was white as the light.</u>"

In the New Testament, Peter, James, and John were with the Lord Jesus Christ. While there, the Lord Jesus Christ's garments were whiter than snow as He was transfigured before them. This was a New Testament example of the glory of the Lord being seen by human beings.
- **John 1:14**
"And the Word was made flesh, and dwelt among us, (and <u>we beheld his glory, the glory as of the only begotten of the Father</u>,) full of grace and truth."

The Word is the Name of the Lord Jesus Christ Who dwelt among people on earth after He was incarnated. The perfect God the Son became perfect Man. Though He usually veiled His glory, the Apostles Peter, James, and John beheld His glory on the mount where He was transfigured before them.

1 Corinthians 2:9

"But as it is written, Eye hath not seen, nor ear heard, neither have entered into the heart of man, the things which God hath prepared for them that love him."

Notice in verse nine, "*But as it is written*," That's a perfect tense in the Greek language and that perfect tense means something that happened in the past, that continues into the present, and that continues into the future. This Greek perfect tense is one of the proofs of the Bible preservation of the Hebrew, Aramaic, and Greek Words of God.

THE MEANING OF THE GREEK WORD, "GRAPHO"

The Greek Word for "*write*" is GRAPHO. Some of the meanings of this Greek Word are:

"1) to write, with reference to the form of the letters; 1a) to delineate (or form) letters on a tablet, parchment, paper, or other material; 2) to write, with reference to the contents of the writing; 2a) to express in written

> *characters; 2b) to commit to writing (things not to be forgotten), write down, record; 2c) used of those things which stand written in the sacred books (of the OT); 2d) to write to one, i.e. by writing (in a written epistle) to give information, directions; 3) to fill with writing 4) to draw up in writing, compose."*

From the above definition, to "*write*" includes the meaning of "*to delineate (or form) letters on a tablet, parchment, paper, or other material.*" In this sense, every letter in the Hebrew, Aramaic, and Greek Old and New Testament Words, written in the past, has been preserved by God. Paul is quoting from Isaiah 64:4. These Hebrew Words were preserved by God from Isaiah's day to Paul's day, to our days, and on into the future.

- **Isaiah 64:4**
"For since the beginning of the world *men* have not heard, nor perceived by the ear, neither hath the eye seen, O God, beside thee, <u>what he hath prepared for him that waiteth for him</u>."

So, this is a quotation of the Old Testament. Things which God hath prepared.

Verses On Prepared Things
- **Psalms 23:5**
"<u>Thou preparest a table before me in the presence of mine enemies</u>: thou anointest my head with oil; my cup runneth over."

God prepares a table for His own, even in the presence of their enemies.

- **Amos 4:12**
"Therefore thus will I do unto thee, O Israel: *and* because I will do this unto thee, <u>prepare to meet thy God, O Israel</u>."

Every person who ever lived must prepare to meet the God of the Bible. This preparation is done by believing and trusting in their hearts the Lord Jesus Christ as their Saviour. This is the preparation necessary for people to meet the Lord in Heaven for all eternity to come.

- **Matthew 25:34**
"Then shall the King say unto them on his right hand, Come, ye blessed of my Father, <u>inherit the kingdom prepared for you</u> from the foundation of the world:"

Genuine Christians have a prepared kingdom in Heaven.

- **Matthew 25:41**

"Then shall he say also unto them on the left hand, Depart from me, ye cursed, into <u>everlasting fire, prepared for the devil and his angels</u>:"

Just as the Heavenly kingdom is prepared for true Christians, so Hell and everlasting fire is also prepared for those who reject the Lord Jesus Christ as their Saviour.

- **John 14:2-3**

"In my Father's house are many mansions: if *it were* not *so*, I would have told you. <u>I go to prepare a place for you</u>. And if I go and prepare a place for you, I will come again, and receive you unto myself; that where I am, *there* ye may be also."

The Lord Jesus Christ is preparing a place in Heaven for genuine Christians who are redeemed by His precious Blood.

- **Revelation 21:2**

"And I John saw the holy city, new Jerusalem, coming down from God out of heaven, <u>prepared as a bride adorned for her husband</u>."

What God has prepared!

All these prepared things have not been seen by the eye, or heard by the ear, nor entered into the heart, although John got a preview.

Verses On The Heart

- **Proverbs 23:26**

"<u>My son, give me thine heart</u>, and let thine eyes observe my ways."

The very center of people's emotions and feelings is their heart. God wants the heart of all true Christians; He desires that unsaved people become Christians and give Him their hearts as well. No one knows what God has prepared for them that love Him but, as the next verse says, God has revealed this to them.

1 Corinthians 2:10

"**But God hath revealed them unto us by his Spirit: for the Spirit searcheth all things, yea, the deep things of God.**"

Though eye can't see about God's prepared things, nor can the ear hear them, nor can they enter into people's hearts, God has revealed them to genuine Christians by His Holy Spirit. God's Spirit searches all things, even the deep things about God.

God's revelation was given in the Hebrew and Aramaic Words of the Old Testament and the Greek Words of the New

Testament. At that point, His revelation has ceased, despite the various cults who teach that they have further revelation of one kind or another. This includes Christian Science, the Mormons, and the Charismatics with all their alleged special revelations, among many others.

Verses On Revealed

- **Deuteronomy 29:29**

"The secret things belong unto the LORD our God: but <u>those things which are revealed</u> *belong* unto us and to our children for ever, that *we* may do all the words of this law."

Both parts of our Bibles, Old and New Testaments, in the Hebrew, Aramaic, and Greek have been accurately translated in the languages of the world–like our King James Bible in English has been–are facts, teachings, and doctrines God has revealed to people down through the years.

- **1 Samuel 3:7**

"Now Samuel did not yet know the LORD, <u>neither was the word of the LORD yet revealed unto him</u>."

Samuel lived with Eli for a while before God called Samuel as a prophet and then revealed His will to him.

- **1 Samuel 3:21**

"And the LORD appeared again in Shiloh: for <u>the LORD revealed himself to Samuel in Shiloh</u> by the word of the LORD."

Shiloh was the first place where the Lord revealed Himself to Samuel.

- **Daniel 2:19**

"<u>Then was the secret revealed unto Daniel</u> in a night vision. Then Daniel blessed the God of heaven."

God gave Daniel the answer to the situation that was requested; The answer was by God's special revelation.

- **Daniel 2:28**

"But <u>there is a God in heaven that revealeth secrets</u>, and maketh known to the king Nebuchadnezzar what shall be in the latter days. Thy dream, and the visions of thy head upon thy bed, are these;"

God is the One Who revealed things to Daniel that were needed and necessary in his days.

- **Daniel 2:29-30**

"As for thee, O king, thy thoughts came *into thy mind* upon thy bed, what should come to pass hereafter: and <u>he that revealeth secrets maketh known to thee what shall come to pass</u>. But as for me, this secret is not revealed to me for *any* wisdom that I have more than any living, but for *their* sakes

that shall make known the interpretation to the king, and that thou mightest know the thoughts of thy heart."
It was God Who revealed the king's questions. It was not any wisdom that Daniel had.

- **Amos 3:7**
"Surely the Lord GOD will do nothing, but he revealeth his secret unto his servants the prophets."

We have in the prophets in the Old Testament and New Testaments, God's revelation about secrets that otherwise we could never have known.

- **Matthew 11:27**
"All things are delivered unto me of my Father: and no man knoweth the Son, but the Father; neither knoweth any man the Father, save the Son, and _he to whomsoever the Son will reveal him._"

If you want to know the Lord Jesus Christ as your Saviour, He can reveal God the Father to you.

- **Ephesians 3:5**
"Which in other ages was not made known unto the sons of men, as it is now revealed unto his holy apostles and prophets by the Spirit;"

Unknown things in ages past were revealed by God to his apostles and prophets by God the Holy Spirit. God the Holy Spirit is perfect God, just as God, the Son, is perfect God, and God, the Father, is perfect God. The Holy Spirit is the One who has revealed His Words and what He wants us to know.

1 Corinthians 2:11

"For what man knoweth the things of a man, save the spirit of man which is in him? even so the things of God knoweth no man, but the Spirit of God."

This verse shows what part of the three parts of human beings--spirit, soul, and body--is their "knowing" part. It is the "_spirit of man which is in him._" It is the human "spirit." So with the things of God. They are only known by the Spirit of God.

- **1 Thessalonians 5:23**
"And the very God of peace sanctify you wholly; and _I pray God_ your whole spirit and soul and body be preserved blameless unto the coming of our Lord Jesus Christ."

This verse shows us that every human being has three parts--a tripartite being with spirit, soul, and body. There are some genuine Christians who don't believe that. They think that human beings are just dual--material and immaterial. They say, the spirit and the soul are the same. No, the Bible distinguishes and differentiates these two. They are NOT the same. If God makes a distinction in His Word, then we must make such a distinction. We cannot combine the spirit and the soul and make them one.

1 Corinthians 2:12

"Now we have received, not the spirit of the world, but the spirit which is of God; that we might know the things that are freely given to us of God."

The true Christians at Corinth had received the "*Spirit which is of God*," **not** the "*spirit of the world*." This happened to all of them the minute they genuinely accepted the Lord Jesus Christ as their Saviour. Their bodies became the temple of God the Holy Spirit.

Verses On Spirit

- **Ephesians 2:2**
"Wherein in time past ye walked according to the course of this world, according to the prince of the power of the air, the spirit that now worketh in the children of disobedience:"

That's the spirit of the world. According to this verse, that's a spirit from Satan. That's an unbelieving spirit. Everyone, when they are born, receives an evil spirit from the Devil. They are not God's children, but are Satan's children. They have the spirit of the world and are "*the children of disobedience.*"

- **1 John 4:1**
"Beloved, believe not every spirit, but try the spirits whether they are of God: because many false prophets are gone out into the world."

Genuine Christians are not to believe every spirit, but are to try or test out the spirits to see if they are from God. Many false prophets were in John's day and many, many more are in our day.

- **1 John 4:6**
"We are of God: he that knoweth God heareth us; he that is not of God heareth not us. Hereby know we the spirit of truth, and the spirit of error."

John points out there are two spirits: (1) the spirit of truth Who is God the Holy Spirit, and (2) the spirit of error which abides in non-true Christians all around the world.

THE MEANING OF THE GREEK WORD, "KOSMOS"

The Greek Word for "world" is KOSMOS. Some of the many shades of meanings of this Greek Word are:

"1) an apt and harmonious arrangement or constitution, order,

> *government; 2) ornament, decoration, adornment, i.e. the arrangement of the stars, 'the heavenly hosts', as the ornament of the heavens. 1 Pet. 3:3; 3) the world, the universe; 4) the circle of the earth, the earth; 5) the inhabitants of the earth, men, the human race; 6) the ungodly multitude; the whole mass of men alienated from God, and therefore hostile to the cause of Christ; 7) world affairs, the aggregate of things earthly; 7a) the whole circle of earthly goods, endowments, riches, advantages, pleasures, etc, which although hollow and frail and fleeting, stir desire, seduce from God and are obstacles to the cause of Christ; 8) any aggregate or general collection of particulars of any sort; 8b) the Gentiles as contrasted to the Jews (Rom. 11:12 etc); 8a) of believers only, John 1:29; 3:16; 3:17; 6:33; 12:47; 1 Cor. 4:9; 2 Cor. 5:19."*

This sense of the "world" is not the created world, but the evil that is found in many of the people, groups and institutions found in this world. As such, along with the flesh and the Devil, the world is the enemy of all genuine Christians.

Our former pastor for many years, Pastor Earl Willetts, of the Berea Baptist Church in Berea, Ohio, had a very good definition of the "*world*" in the sense used in this verse. Speaking to true Christians, he said:

> "*Anything is of the "world" which lessens your love for the Lord Jesus Christ.*"

1 Corinthians 2:13

"Which things also we speak, not in the words which man's wisdom teacheth, but which the Holy Ghost teacheth; comparing spiritual things with spiritual."

The things which were freely given to us by God through the inspiration of the Holy Spirit, Paul spoke about wherever he went. He did not speak about the words that man's wisdom might teach.

On the contrary, he the things taught by God the Holy Spirit found in the Hebrew and Aramaic Old Testament and in the Greek New Testament. As such, he compared these spiritual things of God with words which were his own that were in line with God's spiritual Words.

Verses On Words

- **2 Peter 1:21**

  "For the prophecy came not in old time by the will of man: but <u>holy men of God spake</u> *as they were* moved by the Holy Ghost."

The source of the prophecy and Words of the Bible, as found in both the Old Testament and in the New Testament, did not originate by the will of the men who wrote them down, but the prophets wrote and spoke God's Words as they were moved and led by the Holy Spirit. These Words were inspired and God-breathed Words.

We believe in the verbal, plenary, inspiration of God's Words in the Bible. "Plenary" means full and complete. It refers to every Word of the original Hebrew, Aramaic, and Greek Words. "Verbal" refers to the "Words" given by God. "Inspiration" refers to the fact that these Words were THEOPNEUSTOS, or "God-breathed." We teach that the very Hebrew, Aramaic, and Greek Words have been preserved, not only the "concepts," ideas, or "thoughts." God did not give the writers only concepts, but He gave them "Words" which He has preserved.

The style and Words that were chosen by God were taken from the human writers' own vocabularies. This is why the styles of Peter, James, Paul, Jude and other writers differ slightly. Yet God chose the Words they were to use. At the Dallas Theological Seminary in Dallas, Texas, where I attended and was graduated after five years of study, they did not like to hold the "*dictation theory*" of Bible inspiration of the original Scriptures. I see nothing wrong with this term. Out of the writers' own vocabulary, God dictated the very Words of Hebrew, Aramaic, and Greek that He wanted them to write down.

- **Psalms 12:6-7**

  "<u>The words of the LORD *are* pure words</u>: *as* silver tried in a furnace of earth, purified seven times. <u>Thou shalt keep them</u>, O LORD, thou shalt preserve them from this generation for ever."

The words of God, the Hebrew, Aramaic, and Greek, are preserved by God throughout the centuries.

- **Matthew 24:35**
 "Heaven and earth shall pass away, but <u>my words shall not pass away</u>."

All the Words of the Old and New Testaments were given by the Lord Jesus Christ to God the Holy Spirit Who gave them to the human writers. The Lord Jesus Christ said those Words would be preserved and would never pass away.

Many teachers and preachers today, who call themselves "Fundamentalists," have denied the verbal, plenary, inspiration of the Bible. Dr. Tom Strouse called this denial of the proper and Biblical view of preservation "dynamic or concept preservation." This is a false view which is held in part or in whole by such men as Dr. Stewart Custer and Dr. Samuel Snyder of Bob Jones University, and other schools such as Central Baptist Seminary, Calvary Baptist Seminary, and many others. They hold only to a dynamic theory of inspiration that deals only with the thoughts, ideas, or concepts, but not the very Words of God.

- **John 6:63**
 "It is the spirit that quickeneth; the flesh profiteth nothing: <u>the words that I speak unto you, *they* are spirit, and *they* are life</u>."

The Words John wrote here are the Words that bring eternal life, if people will trust the Lord Jesus Christ as their Saviour.

- **2 Timothy 1:13**
 "<u>Hold fast the form of sound words</u>, which thou hast heard of me, in faith and love which is in Christ Jesus."

We must hold fast to the "*sound*" Words that are the preserved Hebrew, Aramaic, and Greek Words that underlie our King James Bible as well as the accurate English translation of those Words. The other versions in English and other languages based on the false Hebrew, Aramaic, and Greek Words, are not "sound words." No one should hold fast to those <u>unsound</u> words.

- **Jude 1:17**
 "But, beloved, <u>remember ye the words which were spoken before of the apostles</u> of our Lord Jesus Christ;"

It's vital to remember the Words spoken by the apostles that are written down in the Bible. But, let me ask you a question. How can you remember the Words spoken by the apostles, if those Words are no longer with us? We must believe in the verbal, plenary preservation of the original Hebrew, Aramaic, and Greek Words. Otherwise, how can you remember "Words" that are not all there? The only way people can "remember" God's Words is by reading them each year from Genesis through Revelation.

1 Corinthians 2:14

"But the natural man receiveth not the things of the Spirit of God: for they are foolishness unto him: neither can he know them, because they are spiritually discerned."

The Greek Word for "*natural*" is PSUCHIKOS. Some of the meanings of this Greek Word are:

> **THE MEANING OF THE GREEK WORD, "PSUCHIKOS"**
>
> "1) of or belonging to breath; 1a) having the nature and characteristics of the breath; 1a1) the principal of animal life, which men have in common with the brutes; 1b) governed by breath; 1b1) the sensuous nature with its subjection to appetite and passion."

When Paul speaks of the "natural man," he is talking about every man or woman who has not received the Lord Jesus Christ as their Saviour and Redeemer. The natural or soulish man, woman, boy, or girl governed by the soul only, not by their human spirit, and certainly not by the Holy Spirit of God, can not receive the things from Him, including especially the Words of the Bible.

All these Biblical Words are foolishness with these natural and lost people. They can't understand these Words because they are only discerned by those who are genuine Christians who are indwelt by God the Holy Spirit.

Unsaved and non-Christian people don't understand the Gospel of the Lord Jesus Christ. They don't understand why the Lord Jesus Christ came into the world to seek and to save that which was lost. They don't understand Calvary and what the Saviour accomplished there.

Verses On Natural

- **1 Corinthians 15:44**

"It is sown a natural body; it is raised a spiritual body. There is a natural body, and there is a spiritual body."
This verse speaks of the "natural" human body contrasted with a "spiritual" body that genuine Christians will have when they go Home to be with their Saviour.

- **1 Corinthians 15:46**

"Howbeit that *was* not first which is spiritual, but that which is natural; and afterward that which is spiritual."

The natural human body is first. The spiritual body for true Christians will come next at their death, or at the Rapture of all genuine Christians, whichever comes first.

Verses On Discerning

- **Hebrews 4:12**

"For <u>the word of God</u> is quick, and powerful, and sharper than any twoedged sword, piercing even to the dividing asunder of soul and spirit, and of the joints and marrow, and <u>is a discerner of the thoughts and intents of the heart</u>."

Notice, the Word of God is a discerner of the thoughts and intents of the hearts of all people.

- **Hebrews 5:14**

"But strong meat belongeth to them that are of full age, *even* those who <u>by reason of use have their senses exercised to discern both good and evil</u>."

True Christians who are mature in their faith who have used the strong meat of the Scripture, have their senses able to discern both good and evil. They have spiritual discernment.

Verses On Foolishness

- **Mark 7:21-22**

"For from <u>within, out of the heart of men, proceed</u> evil thoughts, adulteries, fornications, murders, Thefts, covetousness, wickedness, deceit, lasciviousness, an evil eye, blasphemy, pride, <u>foolishness</u>:"

One of the things that proceeds out of the heart of human beings is foolishness.

- **1 Corinthians 1:18**

"For <u>the preaching of the cross is to them that perish foolishness</u>; but unto us which are saved it is the power of God."

Those who are not genuine Christians consider the preaching of the cross of the Lord Jesus Christ to be foolishness.

- **1 Corinthians 1:21**

"For after that in the wisdom of God the world by wisdom knew not God, <u>it pleased God by the foolishness of preaching to save them that believe</u>."

The preaching of the Gospel of the Lord Jesus Christ is considered foolishness to those who are lost, but that Gospel message is able to save those who believe it.

- **1 Corinthians 1:23**

"But <u>we preach Christ crucified</u>, unto the Jews a stumblingblock, and <u>unto the Greeks foolishness</u>;"

Preaching Christ crucified is a disappointment to both of these groups, both the Jews and the Gentile Greeks.

- 1 Corinthians 3:19

"For <u>the wisdom of this world is foolishness with God</u>. For it is written, He taketh the wise in their own craftiness."

Using the term of "foolishness," God has His own opinion about the wisdom of this world. God considers that wisdom to be foolishness.

1 Corinthians 2:15

"But he that is spiritual judgeth all things, yet he himself is judged of no man."

The founder and president of Dallas Theological Seminary was Dr. Louis Sperry Chafer. He was one of my teachers for four years at that seminary. He was a godly man. He went Home to be with the Lord in the summer of 1952. It was right after our class had completed four years of class work for the Master of Theology (Th.M.) Degree.

Dr. Chafer wrote an excellent book whose title was taken from the words in this verse. It was entitled *He That Is Spiritual*. It means that a genuine Christian who is filled and controlled by God the Holy Spirit is one who is a "spiritual" person. Such a person is able to judge all things and yet is not rightly judged by any other person.

Verses On Spiritual

- 1 Corinthians 9:11a

"<u>If we have sown unto you spiritual things</u>,"

Spiritual things are those things that pertain to the various truths and doctrines that are found in the Bible.

- **Galatians 6:1**

"Brethren, if a man be overtaken in a fault, <u>ye which are spiritual, restore such</u> an one in the spirit of meekness; considering thyself, lest thou also be tempted."

This refers to someone, either a genuine Christian or even a non-Christian, who has fallen into some kind of serious sin. The only ones who should try to restore that person should be true Christians who are controlled by the Holy Spirit. This is to insure that the one who is attempting to restore this person will not fall into this same sin. Spiritual discernment is especially necessary in this case.

Verses On Judging

- John 5:22

"For <u>the Father judgeth no man, but hath committed all judgment unto the Son</u>:"

God the Father has committed all judgment unto His son. The Lord Jesus Christ will be the Judge: (1) at the Judgment Seat of Christ when genuine Christians will be judged, (2) at the Great White Throne judgment when all the non-Christians will be judged, (3) at the judgment of angels, and at all other judgments.

- **John 8:50**

"And I seek not mine own glory: <u>there is one that seeketh and judgeth</u>."

God the Father was the One Who was the Judge of His Son while He was here on earth as the perfect Son of Man.

- **John 12:48**

"He that rejecteth me, and receiveth not my words, hath one that judgeth him: the word that I have spoken, the same shall judge him in the last day."

At all the judgments mentioned above, the standards of judgment will be the Words of God.

1 Corinthians 2:16

"For who hath known the mind of the Lord, that he may instruct him? But we have the mind of Christ."

Nobody can know the mind of the Lord but the Lord himself. He is the One that's omniscient, all knowing. Humans have only a partial knowledge. Different people have different levels of knowledge and understanding, but the Lord knows everything. Frail human beings aren't going to instruct the Lord. He instructs us. That's why we must go to the Bible. We must never change the Bible to suit us. God says that genuine Christians have "*the mind of Christ.*" That is difficult to understand, but we must accept it because the Bible tells us that it is so.

Verses On The Mind

- **Proverbs 29:11**

"<u>A fool uttereth all his mind</u>: but a wise *man* keepeth it in till afterwards."

We must be very careful on what we say. Let our words be few rather than many. Certainly we should not act like these fools spoken of in this verse.

- **Isaiah 26:3**

"Thou wilt keep *him* in perfect peace, <u>*whose* mind *is* stayed *on thee*</u>: because he trusteth in thee."

True Christians should keep their minds fixed and trusting the Lord Jesus Christ. This will give them perfect peace.

- **Matthew 22:37**
"Jesus said unto him, Thou shalt <u>love the Lord thy God</u> with all thy heart, and with all thy soul, and <u>with all thy mind</u>."

Genuine Christians must trust in the Lord, not only with all their heart and soul, but with all their mind as well.

- **Mark 5:15**
"And they come to Jesus, and see <u>him that was possessed with the devil</u>, and had the legion, sitting, and clothed, and <u>in his right mind</u>: and they were afraid."

After this demon-possessed man was healed by the Lord Jesus Christ, he was clothed again and in his right mind. The Lord Jesus Christ has a way of getting our minds straightened out even today.

- **Acts 17:11**
"These were more noble than those in Thessalonica, in that <u>they received the word with all readiness of mind</u>, and searched the scriptures daily, whether those things were so."

True Christian nobility is found in not only reading the Scriptures, but also receiving them with a readiness of mind.

- **Acts 20:19a**
"<u>Serving the Lord with all humility of mind</u>,"

Genuine Christian service must always be with humility of mind rather than any boasting or egotism.

- **Romans 7:23**
"But I see <u>another law in my members, warring against the law of my mind</u>, and bringing me into captivity to the law of sin which is in my members."

Like the non-Christians, the true Christians still have their flesh which wars against their new nature and indwelling Holy Spirit.

- **Romans 7:25**
"I thank God through Jesus Christ our Lord. So then <u>with the mind I myself serve the law of God</u>; but with the flesh the law of sin."

This shows a tremendous struggle between the flesh and the mind. Paul had a real battle in Romans 7 between these two battling natures within him.

- **Romans 11:34**
"For <u>who hath known the mind of the Lord</u>? or who hath been his counsellor?"

No one has the wisdom and knowledge to counsel the Lord. Many are trying to do this. But it should never be done. He must counsel everyone in the world, saved and lost.

- **Romans 12:2**

    "And be not conformed to this world: but <u>be ye transformed by the renewing of your mind</u>, that ye may prove what *is* that good, and acceptable, and perfect, will of God."

Genuine Christians must renew their minds in order to understand and do God's acceptable and perfect will.

- **Romans 15:6**

    "<u>That ye may with one mind</u> *and* one mouth <u>glorify God</u>, even the Father of our Lord Jesus Christ."

There should be unity among all true Christians to glorify God with one mind and one mouth.

- **2 Corinthians 8:12**

    "For <u>if there be first a willing mind</u>, *it is* accepted according to that a man hath, *and* not according to that he hath not."

Willingness of mind to think and to do the will of God should be a part of every genuine Christian's thinking.

- **Ephesians 2:3**

    "Among whom also we all had our conversation in times past in the lusts of our flesh, <u>fulfilling the desires</u> of the flesh and <u>of the mind</u>; and were by nature the children of wrath, even as others."

Let the past be the past. Once people become strong and true Christians, they should not fulfill either the desires of the flesh or of the mind.

- **Ephesians 4:23**

    "And <u>be renewed in the spirit of your mind;</u>"

Genuine Christians should be renewed in their minds.

- **Philippians 2:5**

    "<u>Let this mind be in you, which was also in Christ Jesus</u>:"

True Christians should think with their minds, as much as possible, like the Lord Jesus Christ did in dealing with the many people while He was here on this earth. They must read their Bibles carefully to see just how the Lord Jesus Christ used His perfect and sinless mind in dealing with people and events.

1 Corinthians Chapter Three

1 Corinthians 3:1

"**And I, brethren, could not speak unto you as unto spiritual, but as unto carnal, *even* as unto babes in Christ.**"

All genuine Christians should ask themselves whether they are "carnal" or "spiritual." Evidently, like churches today, the Corinthian Church was a mixed bag of all kinds of problems. He couldn't speak to these true Christians as those who were spiritual, (guided and directed by the Holy Spirit of God), but unto carnal and as unto babes in Christ. There are various references in the scriptures to those who are spiritual, that is guarded, guided, led, and filled with the Holy Spirit of God.

Verses On The Work Of The Holy Spirit
- **Galatians 5:22-23**

"But <u>the fruit of the Spirit is love, joy, peace, longsuffering, gentleness, goodness, faith, Meekness, temperance</u>: against such there is no law."

The fruit of the Spirit is produced by Him when genuine Christians are filled and controlled by the Holy Spirit. This makes them "spiritual."

- **Galatians 6:1**

"Brethren, <u>if a man be overtaken in a fault, ye which are spiritual, restore such an one</u> in the spirit of meekness; considering thyself, lest thou also be tempted."

Those in the local church who should be the ones who seek to restore true Christians who are overtaken in some fault are the spiritual Christians who are controlled by the Holy Spirit. They must be careful lest they fall into the same sin.

Verses On Carnal Or Fleshly
- **Romans 8:7**

"Because <u>the carnal mind *is* enmity against God</u>: for it is not subject to the law of God, neither indeed can be."

The carnal or fleshly mind is against God and His laws.

- **2 Corinthians 10:4**

   "(For <u>the weapons of our warfare *are* not carnal</u>, but mighty through God to the pulling down of strong holds;)"

Genuine Christians must use mighty spiritual weapons in their warfare for the Lord. They must not be carnal or fleshly.

- **Galatians 5:19-21**

   "Now <u>the works of the flesh are manifest</u>, which are *these*; Adultery, fornication, uncleanness, lasciviousness, Idolatry, witchcraft, hatred, variance, emulations, wrath, strife, seditions, heresies, Envyings, murders, drunkenness, revellings, and such like: of the which I tell you before, as I have also told *you* in time past, that they which do such things shall not inherit the kingdom of God."

All this list of carnal works of the flesh are against God's will for all true Christians. They must be led and controlled by the Holy Spirit in order to avoid all these fleshly and sinful actions.

The Greek Word for "***carnal***" is SARKIKOS. Some of the meanings of this Greek Word are:

THE MEANING OF THE GREEK WORD, "SARKIKOS"

"1) fleshly, carnal; 1a) having the nature of flesh, i.e. under the control of the animal appetites; 1a1) governed by mere human nature not by the Spirit of God; 1a2) having its seat in the animal nature or aroused by the animal nature; 1a3) human: with the included idea of depravity; 1b) pertaining to the flesh; 1b1) to the body: related to birth, linage, etc;"

Verses On Babes

- **Romans 2:20**

   "An instructor of the foolish, <u>a teacher of babes</u>, which hast the form of knowledge and of the truth in the law."

True Christians who are newly saved are babes. They must grow in the things of the Lord. They need some instructions and teachings in order to assist them in their growth.

- **1 Peter 2:2**

   "<u>As newborn babes, desire the sincere milk of the word</u>, that ye may grow thereby:"

Newly regenerated genuine Christians are spiritual babes. They should have a sincere desire for the basic things of God's Words in order to grow in their faith. Bible reading, believing, and practicing Biblical principles enable that needed growth. The spiritual condition of this church in Corinth was that of a spiritual little child.

A baby has to grow, and we have to grow spiritually rather than remain in spiritual babyhood. To grow, true Christians must also grow in the knowledge of our Lord and Saviour Jesus Christ.

Verse On The Need For Spiritual Growth
- 2 Peter 3:18

"But grow in grace, and *in* the knowledge of our Lord and Saviour Jesus Christ. To him *be* glory both now and for ever. Amen."

Babes in Christ are to grow daily in the knowledge of and obedience to the Lord Jesus Christ. This knowledge is found only as they read, understand, and obey truths from the Bible.

1 Corinthians 3:2

"I have fed you with milk, and not with meat: for hitherto ye were not able *to bear it,* neither yet now are ye able."

Paul fed the genuine Christians at Corinth with the spiritual milk of God's Words but not with spiritual meat. They weren't able to understand it when he visited them, and still are not able to grasp it. They were still spiritual babies able only to drink milk, but not able to eat solid food.

Verses On Christian Spiritual Babies
- Hebrews 5:12-14

"For when for the time ye ought to be teachers, ye have need that one teach you again which *be* the first principles of the oracles of God; and are become such as have need of milk, and not of strong meat. For every one that useth milk *is* unskilful in the word of righteousness: for he is a babe. But strong meat belongeth to them that are of full age, *even* those who by reason of use have their senses exercised to discern both good and evil."

Paul writes of these true Christians in these verses who were also spiritual babies. They should have been Bible teachers, instead; they had to have someone teach them. They could only understand "baby talk." Is that your condition? If so, grow in God's grace and the understanding of His Words.

1 Corinthians 3:3

"**For ye are yet carnal: for whereas** *there is* **among you envying, and strife, and divisions, are ye not carnal, and walk as men?**"

Paul repeats to these genuine Christians at Corinth that they are carnal or fleshly, walking after their flesh rather than being obedient to the Holy Spirit Who indwells them. He lists, in this verse, four evidences of their carnality:
1. They have envying.
2. They have strife.
3. They have divisions.
4. They walk as men, as natural, unsaved people.

Paul asks these true Christians two different times: "*Are ye yet carnal?*" Every genuine Christian today should ask themselves this same question. It would be good if every true Christian in the world would answer "no," but, sad to say, carnality abounds in so many, many of them, just like in the church at Corinth.

Verses On Envy

- **Proverbs 23:17**

"Let not thine heart envy sinners: but *be thou* in the fear of the LORD all the day long."

Genuine Christians should not envy anyone, especially sinners.

- **Mark 15:10**

"For he knew that the chief priests had delivered him for envy."

The Jewish chief priests delivered the Lord Jesus Christ to the Roman government to be crucified because they envied Him for His powerful miracles, and His drawing multitudes to follow Him.

- **Acts 7:9**

"And the patriarchs, moved with envy, sold Joseph into Egypt: but God was with him,"

Joseph's eleven brothers envied him for good looks and his favor with their father. So they sold him as a slave to a group of slaveholders.

- **Acts 13:45**

"But when the Jews saw the multitudes, they were filled with envy, and spake against those things which were spoken by Paul, contradicting and blaspheming."

The Apostle Paul had multitudes following him and his Gospel message. The Jewish leaders were filled with envy because of this.

- **Romans 1:29**

  "Being filled with all unrighteousness, fornication, wickedness, covetousness, maliciousness; full of envy, murder, debate, deceit, malignity; whisperers,"

The heathen world spoken about in this verse had their hearts full of fleshly envy.

- **Romans 13:13**

  "Let us walk honestly, as in the day; not in rioting and drunkenness, not in chambering and wantonness, not in strife and envying."

Genuine Christians are exhorted by Paul, in this verse, to live their lives honestly, without either strife or envying. Envying is a sinful work of the flesh.

- **2 Corinthians 12:20**

  "For I fear, lest, when I come, I shall not find you such as I would, and *that* I shall be found unto you such as ye would not: lest there be debates, envyings, wraths, strifes, backbitings, whisperings, swellings, tumults:"

Paul did not want to come to Corinth and find these true Christians with envyings.

- **Galatians 5:21**

  "Envyings, murders, drunkenness, revellings, and such like: of the which I tell you before, as I have also told *you* in time past, that they which do such things shall not inherit the kingdom of God."

Of all the "*works of the flesh*" that are listed here, "*envyings*" is included as one of them.

- **Galatians 5:26**

  "Let us not be desirous of vain glory, provoking one another, envying one another."

If you are a genuine Christian, do you envy someone? If so, what are you envying about? Do you envy someone's car? Or their hat? Or their suit? Or something else that they have? That's a work of the flesh that true Christians should despise.

- **James 3:16**

  "For where envying and strife *is*, there *is* confusion and every evil work."

Strife, confusion, and every evil work come with envying. One of the marks of carnality by the true Christians at Corinth is "*divisions*" among them.

Verses On Divisions

- **Romans 16:17**

"Now I beseech you, brethren, <u>mark them which cause divisions</u> and offences <u>contrary to the doctrine</u> which ye have learned; <u>and avoid them</u>."

Modernists, liberals, and doctrinal apostates should be marked, exposed, and avoided. Genuine Christians should stand firmly for the doctrines and teachings found in the Bible, separating from all those who have departed from them.

- **1 Corinthians 1:10**

"Now <u>I beseech you, brethren</u>, by the name of our Lord Jesus Christ, that ye all speak the same thing, and *that* <u>there be no divisions among you</u>; but *that* ye be perfectly joined together in the same mind and in the same judgment."

Paul besought those genuine Christians at Corinth that they would not have any doctrinal divisions.

- **1 Corinthians 11:18**

"For first of all, when ye come together in the church, <u>I hear that there be divisions among you</u>; and I partly believe it."

Paul was told that there were many divisions among the true Christians in Corinth. He wasn't positive, but at least partly believed it.

1 Corinthians 3:4

"For while one saith, I am of Paul; and another, I *am* of Apollos; are ye not carnal?"

The carnality of the true Christians at Corinth was evidenced by their taking public positions to be followers of different leaders. Some were following Paul. Others were following Apollos. Apparently they did not do this in a quiet manner; by carnal, fleshly means and methods. They must have been seriously divided. Instead of being united on the doctrines of the Bible and unitedly following the Lord Jesus Christ, they were looking at personalities.

There is certainly nothing wrong for local churches having leaders within them. But when there is carnal war among these leaders that causes bitter carnality throughout that local church, this is fleshly sin. Such sin and divisiveness is not acceptable to the Lord Jesus Christ and should not be accepted among the members of that church. Such petty divisiveness certainly is not acceptable to the Lord Jesus Christ.

1 Corinthians 3:5

"Who then is Paul, and who is Apollos, but ministers by whom ye believed, even as the Lord gave to every man?"

When Paul asked this question, I believe he was exercising humility on his part. He was not trying to exalt himself or his office. The same is true of Apollos. Both he and Paul were only ministers or servants that the Lord used to lead many of those in the Corinthian church to a saving knowledge of the Lord Jesus Christ.

He implied that the Lord gave both Paul and Apollos the preparation, insight, and leading of the Holy Spirit so that they both could be faithful and godly ministers of the Lord Jesus Christ. Each of them had different human abilities, background, and training, and gifts from the Lord, yet they both served their Saviour to the best of their abilities.

Verses On Ministers

- **1 Corinthians 4:1**

"Let a man so account of us, as of <u>the ministers of Christ</u>, and stewards of the mysteries of God."

Paul wanted to have both Apollos and himself to be regarded as faithful ministers of the Lord Jesus Christ and good stewards of all that God led them to do and teach.

- **2 Corinthians 6:4**

"But in all *things* <u>approving ourselves as the ministers of God</u>, in much patience, in afflictions, in necessities, in distresses,"

Paul, Apollos, and all the other early "*ministers of God*" faced afflictions, necessities, distresses, and many other serious troubles with much patience. This is amazing. It should also be an example for all genuine Christians to follow today.

The phrase, "*as the Lord gave to every man,*" (verse 5) shows how Paul was different from Apollos or others. God gave different gifts to different people. So with true Christians today. None have the same gifts and abilities. Some can speak, some can sing, some can play the piano, some can think, some can succeed in business, some can build radios, and so on.

Even full-time Christian leaders have different gifts. Some are evangelists. Some are pastors. Some are teachers. This is true of all other genuine Christians. They are different and have different gifts from the Lord. None of them are the same, but they should be able to work together for the Lord Jesus Christ and appreciate each other's gifts.

1 Corinthians 3:6

"I have planted, Apollos watered; but God gave the increase."

There are three parts of raising flowers, crops, or other things.
>   1. the planting
>   2. the watering
>   3. the growth

In this verse, Paul uses this analogy referring to the process of obtaining God's salvation for others. Paul planted, Apollos watered, and God gave the increase.

Verses On Sowing And Reaping
- **Mark 4:3**

"Hearken; Behold, there went out <u>a sower to sow</u>:"
The sower was sowing seed, thus planting it.

- **Mark 4:14**

"<u>The sower soweth the word</u>."
That's what Paul planted--the Words of God. That's what our church seeks to plant--the Words of God. That's what makes us a distinctive church, by the verse-by-verse preaching and teaching of the Words of God.

Verses On Watering By Preaching God's Words
- **Proverbs 11:25**

"The liberal soul shall be made fat: and <u>he that watereth shall be watered also himself</u>."

Those who give spiritual water to others will be spiritually watered as well. It will bring a blessing to them as well as to the one who is watered.

- **Isaiah 32:20**

"<u>Blessed *are* ye that sow beside all waters</u>, that send forth *thither* the feet of the ox and the ass."

Genuine Christians should sow the Seed of the Words of God to anyone they might meet. It is for everyone to know about and believe. Especially is needful for all people to know the good news about what the Lord Jesus Christ did for them on the cross and for them to trust Him from their heart. Our church seeks to do this by streaming our services 24/7/365 all around the world on our Internet site BibleForToday.org.

- **2 Timothy 4:2**
"Preach the word; be instant in season, out of season; reprove, rebuke, exhort with all longsuffering and doctrine." The *"Word"* in this verse is God's Word. The first need in preaching the Words of God is to be certain as to where these Words are to be found. They are to be found originally in the inerrant and preserved original Words of Hebrew, Aramaic, and Greek.

Then these original and preserved Words are to be translated faithfully and accurately into all the languages of the world. In the English language, these Words have been accurately translated in the King James Bible. All of the other English Bible translations have failed in one way or another in being accurate: (1) either they have not followed the proper Hebrew, Aramaic, or Greek Words, but have tried to translate from other Words. This is true of over 99% of the current English translations today. (2) Or they have not been accurately translated from the inspired, and preserved original Words. This is true of the remaining 1% of the current Bible versions.

When I was a resident student at the Dallas Theological Seminary from 1948 through 1953 *or 1954, the seminary's motto was* **"PREACH THE WORD."** It was written in Greek in the sign in front of the seminary (**KERUXON TON LOGON**). It was taken from 2 Timothy 4:2 I don't know whether it's still their motto. I suppose it is. But even in those years we were taught in our Greek classes to use the heretical Gnostic Critical Greek text edited by Westcott and Hort. The school's acceptable English translation was not the accurate *King James Bible*, but the false *New American Standard Version*. Today, they still teach from the false Gnostic Critical Greek texts and favor many other false English versions, including the *New International Version* and the *English Standard Version*.

As a result of this, I was not taught what was either the proper Hebrew, Aramaic, and Greek "Word" to preach from or the proper English translation to follow. This was a horrible and serious failure of my seminary training. I am glad that I found out the truth about the true and proper Hebrew, Aramaic, and Greek texts to use and was able to use and defend the King James Bible in my preaching and teaching. I have been teaching and preaching knowing these truths in our Bible For Today Baptist Church since October 3, 1998–for over 19 years as this is being written. We are now in our 20th year.

In our last class at the seminary for the Master of Theology (Th.M.) degree, our church history professor, Dr. Charles Nash, (a dear, tall, silver-haired teacher), quoted the seminary's motto from:

2 Timothy 4:2:
"Preach the word; be instant in season, out of season; reprove, rebuke, exhort with all longsuffering and doctrine."

Then he added, ***"BUT NEVER COMPROMISE!!"*** I'll never forget these last words to our class from this excellent church-history teacher–and I have sought to follow them ever since that day.

The Increase Of The Planted, Watered Words Of God

- **Psalms 115:14**

"<u>The LORD shall increase you more and more</u>, you and your children."

God is the One Who causes His Seed to grow in the lives of true Christians who follow His Words.

- **2 Corinthians 9:10**

"Now he that ministereth seed to the sower both minister bread for *your* food, and <u>multiply your seed sown, and increase the fruits of your righteousness</u>;)"

It's God Who has to do the increase and growth in the lives of those genuine Christians who have been planted and watered with His Words. He's the One Who has to develop and make these people grow. Paul can plant and Apollos can water.

1 Corinthians 3:7

"So then neither is he that planteth any thing, neither he that watereth; but God that giveth the increase."

Paul did not boast of his planting the Gospel of the Lord Jesus Christ, nor did he boast about the watering of the seed by Apollos. He wanted to exalt God Who is the One that gives the increase of the seed which has been sown.

True Christians should not be like people who have proud and arrogant attitudes. There should be a humility that is in evidence on the part of these Christians. God has given them gifts He wants them to have. There should be no bragging of any kind.

God does not want genuine Christians to make themselves idols, nor does he want them to make idols of other people. Follow the Lord Jesus Christ Himself as revealed in His Words in the Bible.

John the Baptist had it right when he said, as recorded in John 3:30:
- **John 3:30**

"*He must increase, but I must decrease.*"

1 Corinthians 3:8

"Now he that planteth and he that watereth are one: and every man shall receive his own reward according to his own labour."

Paul wanted to dispel the notion that there was a division between these two preachers, himself and Apollos. They were not fighting between themselves. There was a unity between them. Paul understood that each of them had his own gift from God. At the Judgment Seat of Christ, each of them will receive their rewards from God, according to their own labour.

Verses On Rewards
- **Colossians 3:24**

"Knowing that <u>of the Lord ye shall receive the reward</u> of the inheritance: for ye serve the Lord Christ."

The Lord Jesus Christ is the One Who gives to genuine Christians the rewards according to His will.
- **Revelation 22:12**

"And, behold, <u>I come quickly; and my reward *is* with me, to give every man according as his work shall be</u>."

Rewards depend on what true Christians have done for the Lord Jesus Christ.

Verses On The Five Crowns

There are five crowns spoken of in the Bible that depict the rewards for some true Christians. The memory hint we have talked about is R-G-I-R-L.

"R" stands for the crown of righteousness.
- **2 Timothy 4:8**

"Henceforth <u>there is laid up for me a crown of righteousness</u>, which the Lord, the righteous judge, shall give me at that day: and not to me only, but <u>unto all them also that love his appearing</u>."

This crown is for genuine Christians who love the appearing of the Lord Jesus Christ at the Rapture.

"G" stands for the crown of glory.
- **1 Peter 5:4**

"And when the chief Shepherd shall appear, <u>ye shall receive a crown of glory</u> that fadeth not away."

This verse does not tell us the reason for this crown, but is one of the crowns mentioned in the New Testament.

"I" stands for the incorruptible Crown.
- **1 Corinthians 9:25**

"And every man that striveth for the mastery is temperate in all things. Now they *do it* to obtain a corruptible crown; but we an incorruptible."

This crown is given to true Christians who strive for the mastery in their Christian lives.

"R" stands for the crown of rejoicing
- **1 Thessalonians 2:19**

"For what is our hope, or joy, or crown of rejoicing? *Are* not even ye in the presence of our Lord Jesus Christ at his coming?"

This seems to be the crown given to genuine Christians who lead people to a saving knowledge of the Lord Jesus Christ.

"L" stands for the crown of life #1
- **James 1:12**

"Blessed *is* the man that endureth temptation: for when he is tried, he shall receive the crown of life, which the Lord hath promised to them that love him."

This crown is given to true Christians who endure temptation.

"L" stands for the crown of life #2

Revelation 2:10 also speaks of this crown of life as well.
- **Revelation 2:10**

"Fear none of those things which thou shalt suffer: behold, the devil shall cast *some* of you into prison, that ye may be tried; and ye shall have tribulation ten days: be thou faithful unto death, and I will give thee a crown of life."

This crown is given to genuine Christians who are faithful to their Saviour even unto their death.

All true Christians will be judged by the Lord Jesus Christ at the Judgment Seat of Christ referred to later in this chapter will receive rewards and crowns, and others will not receive any crowns; but will be judged according to their own labor they have done for the Lord Jesus Christ during their lives.

1 Corinthians 3:9

"For we are labourers together with God: ye are God's husbandry, *ye are* God's building."

Paul and Apollos were laborers together with God. They were partners in dealing with the people of Corinth. Though Paul and Apollos were the planters and builders, those genuine Christians at Corinth that they planted and watered were God's garden or cultivated field. They were also like buildings that God Himself had constructed through their ministry. They were not Paul's building or Apollos' building, but God's building.

- **Matthew 9:37**
"Then saith he unto his disciples, The harvest truly is plenteous, but the labourers are few; Pray ye therefore the Lord of the harvest, that he will send forth labourers into his harvest."

That's always the case today. The harvest of the millions of non-Christians all around the world is plenteous indeed, but those who seek to win them genuine faith in the Lord Jesus Christ are few in number. Not just sound and Biblical pastors and missionaries, but all true Christians should be ready, willing, and able to labor for the Lord Jesus Christ in whatever way possible. They should labor for their Master from the dawn to setting sun, as the Gospel song goes.

1 Corinthians 3:10

"According to the grace of God which is given unto me, as a wise masterbuilder, I have laid the foundation, and another buildeth thereon. But let every man take heed how he buildeth thereupon."

Here Paul says, "According to the grace of God which is given unto me," Paul received from God His grace. Grace has been defined as *"Getting something we don't deserve."* That's what Paul got. He was saved by his genuine faith in the Lord Jesus Christ Who shed His blood as a sacrifice for his sins and the sins of the whole world.

Paul became a genuine Christian who before led a life of wickedness, murder, and persecuting Christians. He wasn't saved by his own works. He didn't want to stop imprisoning and killing Christians.

But on the road to Damascus, the Lord Jesus Christ asked Paul why he was persecuting Him. Paul's desire for Christian conversion was found in his statement to the Saviour, *"Lord, what wilt Thou have me to do?"* Paul obeyed the Lord's wishes from then on and for the rest of his life. That's what the Saviour wants to do in the lives of all His true Christians. He wants their obedience.

God gave Paul the wisdom to be a wise masterbuilder. As such, he laid the foundation Who is the Lord Jesus Christ. But he warns the genuine Christians at Corinth and all true Christians all over the world, from his day and on into the future, to be very careful how they build upon the Lord Jesus Christ, the only true Foundation.

There are many false foundations in the past, in our present day, and there will be many in the future. Faithful Pastors and church leaders today must guide genuine Christians, their followers, to build their lives wisely on Christ, their true Foundation. They must insist on reading and following daily only translations which are accurately translated from the traditional Hebrew, Aramaic, and Greek Words. In English, this is the King James Bible.

1 Corinthians 3:11

"For other foundation can no man lay than that is laid, which is Jesus Christ."

The only Foundation that should be laid, to build a church upon, or to build a life on, is the Lord Jesus Christ. However, that's not the foundation that the false prophets, false teachers, and false Christs build upon.

Verses On False Prophets, False Teachers, And False Christs

- **Matthew 7:15**

"Beware of false prophets, which come to you in sheep's clothing, but inwardly they are ravening wolves."
They look like sheep, but inwardly, they are ravening wolves.

- **Matthew 24:11**

"And many false prophets shall rise, and shall deceive many."
We have many such false and deceiving prophets today. They lead false churches, write false books, and appear on false radio and Internet programs today.

- **Matthew 24:24**

"For there shall arise false Christs, and false prophets, and shall shew great signs and wonders; insomuch that, if it were possible, they shall deceive the very elect."
Some of these are so sharp and so smooth, that even genuine Christians are often deceived by them.

- **Mark 13:22**

"For false Christs and false prophets shall rise, and shall shew signs and wonders, to seduce, if it were possible, even the elect."
This is a prediction by the Lord Jesus Christ Himself concerning false Christs and false prophets.

- **2 Corinthians 11:13-15**

"For such are <u>false apostles, deceitful workers</u>, transforming themselves into the apostles of Christ. And no marvel; for <u>Satan</u> himself is transformed into an angel of light. Therefore it is no great thing if <u>his ministers also be transformed as the ministers of righteousness</u>; whose end shall be according to their works."

Satan is the source of all these false prophets and deceitful workers.

- **2 Peter 2:1**

"But <u>there were false prophets also among the people</u>, even as <u>there shall be false teachers among you</u>, who privily shall bring in damnable heresies, even denying the Lord that bought them, and bring upon themselves swift destruction."

False prophets in the past and false teachers in the days of the New Testament. They're still here in our days as well.

- **1 John 4:1**

"Beloved, believe not every spirit, but try the spirits whether they are of God: because <u>many false prophets are gone out into the world</u>."

All these false prophets are fakes and not built on the Lord Jesus Christ. This includes the Jehovah's Witnesses, Judaism, Roman Catholicism, Christian Science, the Muslim religion, and many groups who are not founded squarely and 100% on the Lord Jesus Christ and sound Bible doctrines.

1 Corinthians 3:12

"Now if any man build upon this foundation gold, silver, precious stones, wood, hay, stubble;"

The Foundation is the Lord Jesus Christ Himself. This verse speaks about only genuine Christians who are building on the Lord Jesus Christ. This does not have anything to do with non-Christians. Six separate building materials are mentioned in this verse. These are materials that true Christians can use in their building upon their Foundation, the Lord Jesus Christ.

Though there are six materials mentioned, they fall into two separate categories. The first three are usually small in appearance, yet they are very valuable. The second three might be able to be much larger in size, but are much less valuable than the first three. There is no specific definition of any of these six materials. They can only be understood in a figurative sense.

God is concerned that sound Christians grow in God's grace and get stronger each day and year in their genuine salvation by true faith in the Lord Jesus Christ as their Saviour. Genuine

Christians should build on the Lord Jesus Christ, their Foundation, is very important to the Lord, but, sad to say, it is not important to many Christians. Doing things in obedience to glorify the Lord Jesus Christ would be, in general, building with gold, silver, and precious stones. On the other hand, doing things selfishly in the flesh, to glorify and exalt themselves or engage in sinful habits would be, in general, building with hay, wood, and stubble.

1 Corinthians 3:13

"Every man's work shall be made manifest: for the day shall declare it, because it shall be revealed by fire; and the fire shall try every man's work of what sort it is."

All genuine Christians, whether they are men, women, or children, will have their works manifested at the Judgment Seat of Christ. This judgment is not to determine whether they are saved, but to determine, on the basis of their works after being saved, whether or not they will receive any rewards.

Verses On Things Being Manifested

- **2 Corinthians 5:10**

"For we must all appear before the judgment seat of Christ; that every one may receive the things done in his body, according to that he hath done, whether it be good or bad."

All true Christians will receive rewards according to what they have done for the Lord Jesus Christ.

- **1 Corinthians 4:5**

"Therefore judge nothing before the time, until the Lord come, who both will bring to light the hidden things of darkness, and will make manifest the counsels of the hearts: and then shall every man have praise of God."

Though human beings cannot see inside the hearts of people, our omniscient God can see these things and manifest them at the Judgment Seat of Christ.

- **1 Corinthians 14:25**

"And thus are the secrets of his heart made manifest; and so falling down on his face he will worship God, and report that God is in you of a truth."

These secret works of all genuine Christians will be manifested at this judgment of the Lord Jesus Christ.

- **2 Corinthians 4:11**
"For we which live are alway delivered unto death for Jesus' sake, that <u>the life also of Jesus might be made manifest in our mortal flesh</u>."
All true Christians should, through devotion to the Lord Jesus Christ, and have His life manifested in their bodies while on this earth.

The Meaning Of Works Tested By Fire

I believe it is clear that the "*fire*" is an illustration to show what will happen to the works of genuine Christians who build on gold, silver, and precious stones in their Christian lives, which are valuable though small, as opposed to those who build on wood, hay, and stubble, (some of which can be very large and visible, though not as valuable as gold, silver, or precious stones).

1. **What Fire Does To Gold, Silver, And Precious Stones** We know that when these precious metals are heated to high temperatures by fire, or other means, that the dross and impurities are burned off and the metals become purer than before.

2. **What Gold, Silver, And Precious Stones Mean** Though the Bible does not give us a specific answer to this question, it is most likely that when true Christians build on the Lord Jesus Christ, their Foundation, with these materials, their lives would be full of thoughts, words, and actions that do great honor to their Lord and Saviour, Jesus Christ. These Christians will receive rewards.

3. **What Fire Does To Wood, Hay, And Stubble** When fire surrounds wood, hay, or stubble, it ignites these substances, causing them to burn. When combustion is finished, there is nothing left but ashes.

4. **What Wood, Hay, And Stubble Mean** Though the Bible does not give us a specific answer to this question, it is most likely that when genuine Christians don't build on the Lord Jesus Christ, their Foundation, with precious materials, their lives wouldn't be full of thoughts, words, and actions that honor the Lord Jesus Christ. These Christians will not receive rewards.

1 Corinthians 3:14

"If any man's work abide which he hath built thereupon, he shall receive a reward."

A work abiding in and through the fire, not consumed into ashes, will bring a reward. Five types of crowns may be given as rewards. RGIRL is a reminder, each letter for a crown. A selfish motive wouldn't receive a crown.

Verses On The Five Crowns Of Rewards
- **2 Timothy 4:8**

"Henceforth there is laid up for me <u>a crown of</u> **R**<u>ighteousness</u>, which the Lord, the righteous judge, shall give me at that day: and not to me only, but <u>unto all them also that love his appearing</u>."

That's a first crown.

- **1 Peter 5:4**

"And when the chief Shepherd shall appear, <u>ye shall receive a crown of</u> **G**<u>lory</u> that fadeth not away."

That's a second crown.

- **1 Corinthians 9:25**

"And <u>every man that striveth for the mastery</u> is temperate in all things. Now they do it to obtain a corruptible <u>crown;</u> but we an **I**<u>ncorruptible</u>."

That's a third crown.

- **1 Thessalonians 2:19**

"For <u>what is our hope, or joy, or crown of</u> **R**<u>ejoicing</u>? Are not even ye in the presence of our Lord Jesus Christ at his coming?"

This a fourth crown.

- **James 1:12**

"Blessed is the man that endureth temptation: for <u>when he is tried, he shall receive the crown of</u> **L**<u>ife</u>, which the Lord hath promised to them that love him."

This a fifth crown which is a first **L**.

- **Revelation 2:10**

"Fear none of those things which thou shalt suffer: behold, the devil shall cast some of you into prison, that ye may be tried; and ye shall have tribulation ten days: <u>be thou faithful unto death, and I will give thee a crown of</u> **L**<u>ife</u>."

This a fifth crown which is a second **L**.

These five crowns are awarded to the genuine Christians who build their lives on endeavors for the Lord Jesus Christ that are considered to be gold, silver, or precious stones.

1 Corinthians 3:15

"If any man's work shall be burned, he shall suffer loss: but he himself shall be saved; yet so as by fire."

This verse refers to genuine Christians who have built upon their Foundation, the Lord Jesus Christ, with the combustible materials of wood, hay, and stubble. In the fire, all of these substances will be burned up. Nothing will be left except ashes.

They themselves will be saved, "*yet so, as by fire.*" They will be in Heaven for all eternity future without any rewards to cast at the feet of their Saviour. They just lived for themselves and their own desires rather than for the Lord Jesus Christ Who saved them. This is the picture of the Judgment Seat of Christ for all true Christians.

1 Corinthians 3:16

"Know ye not that ye are the temple of God, and *that* the Spirit of God dwelleth in you?"

All true Christians are referred to here as the "*temple of God.*" This is true because everyone of them have the Holy Spirit of God dwelling in their bodies. This is true of all genuine Christians today and will be true of all such from now on into the future. This verse is one of the verses that teaches this truth. It should never be questioned or doubted. It is not true of non-Christians.

Verses On The Holy Spirit
Indwelling Genuine Christians

- **2 Corinthians 6:16**

"And what agreement hath the temple of God with idols? for ye are the temple of the living God; as God hath said, I will dwell in them, and walk in them; and I will be their God, and they shall be my people."

God calls His genuine Christians His temple. He promises to dwell in them and walk with them.

- **1 Corinthians 6:19**

"What? know ye not that your body is the temple of the Holy Ghost which is in you, which ye have of God, and ye are not your own?"

This is another verse that makes it clear that the bodies of true Christians are the temple of the Holy Spirit Who is within them. It is true no matter what age, appearance, intelligence, strength,

gender, size, color, country, or any other feature that might be involved.
- **Romans 8:9**
"But ye are not in the flesh, but in the Spirit, <u>if so be that the Spirit of God dwell in you</u>. Now if any man have not the Spirit of Christ, he is none of his."

If these are genuine Christians, the Spirit of God indwells them.
- **Romans 8:11**
"But <u>if the Spirit of him that raised up Jesus from the dead dwell in you</u>, he that raised up Christ from the dead shall also quicken your mortal bodies by <u>his Spirit that dwelleth in you</u>."

This is another clear verse showing that true Christians have God the Holy Spirit dwelling in them. He will also make alive and quicken their mortal bodies in their bodily resurrection at the Rapture of the genuine Christians before any part of the Tribulation period.

1 Corinthians 3:17

"If any man defile the temple of God, him shall God destroy; for the temple of God is holy, which *temple* ye are."

It is clear from the preceding verses that all genuine Christians are "*the temple of God*" which is holy. The reference to "*any man*" is used for any true Christian person.

THE MEANING OF THE GREEK WORD, "PHTHEIRO"

The Greek Word for "*defile*" is PHTHEIRO. Some of the meanings of this Greek Word are:

"1) to corrupt, to destroy; 1a) in the opinion of the Jews, the temple was corrupted or "destroyed" when anyone defiled or in the slightest degree damaged anything in it, or if its guardians neglected their duties; 1b) to lead away a Christian church from that state of knowledge and holiness in which it ought to abide; 1c) to be destroyed, to perish; 1d) in an ethical sense, to corrupt, deprave."

If true Christians corrupt or defile their bodies which are the temple of God, those persons will God corrupt or defile. The Greek Word used for "*destroy*" in this verse is this same Greek Word for "*defile*" [**PHEHEIRO**]. The sense of "*destroy*" would be to understand destroy as corrupting their testimony and reputation.

In the literal sense of "*destroy,*" God does tell us about the sin unto physical death. 1 John 5:16-17 speaks about this sin:

> "*If any man see his brother sin a <u>sin which is not unto death</u>, he shall ask, and he shall give him life for them that sin not unto death. <u>There is a sin unto death</u>: I do not say that he shall pray for it. All unrighteousness is sin: and <u>there is a sin not unto death</u>.*"

This punishment was literally carried out in the sin of Ananias and Saphira in Acts 5:1-10. They both lied about the sale of their property. Because of this, God slew them both, one after the other, because they had committed the sin unto physical death.

Verses On Defilement

- **Leviticus 18:30**

"Therefore shall ye keep mine ordinance, that ye commit not any one of these abominable customs, which were committed before you, and <u>that ye defile not yourselves therein</u>: I am the LORD your God."

Just as in the case of the Jews of the Old Testament, so with genuine Christians today. By not keeping God's Words and committing sins, they defile themselves.

- **Numbers 5:2**

"Command the children of Israel, that they <u>put out of the camp</u> every leper, and every one that hath an issue, and <u>whosoever is defiled by the dead</u>:"

The Jews were not to be defiled by lepers, a person with an issue, or those who had touched dead bodies. They were to be put out of the camp.

- **Ezekiel 20:18**

"But I said unto their children in the wilderness, <u>Walk ye not in the statutes of your fathers</u>, neither observe their judgments, <u>nor defile yourselves with their idols</u>:"

The faithful Israelites were not to defile themselves either with their fathers' statutes or with their idols.

- **Ezekiel 37:23**

"<u>Neither shall they defile themselves any more with their idols, nor with their detestable things, nor with any of their transgressions</u>: but I will save them out of all their dwellingplaces, wherein they have sinned, and will cleanse them: so shall they be my people, and I will be their God."

The Old Testament Israelites were not to defile themselves with either idols, detestable things, or their transgressions.

- **Daniel 1:8**

"But <u>Daniel purposed in his heart that he would not defile himself</u> with the portion of the king's meat, nor with the wine which he drank: therefore <u>he requested of the prince of the eunuchs that he might not defile himself</u>."

Daniel was courageous in his purpose not to defile himself with any of the bad things that the king offered him.

- **Matthew 15:18-19**

"But <u>those things which proceed</u> out of the mouth come forth <u>from the heart</u>; and they <u>defile the man</u>. For <u>out of the heart</u> proceed evil thoughts, murders, adulteries, fornications, thefts, false witness, blasphemies:"

The Lord Jesus Christ said that evil things originate in the heart, come out of the mouth, and defile people. It's the heart of the old nature that defiles genuine Christians and others.

- **1 Timothy 1:10**

"For whoremongers, for <u>them that defile themselves with mankind</u>, for menstealers, for liars, for perjured persons, and if there be any other thing that is contrary to sound doctrine;"

This seems to be a reference to homosexuality. It is greatly defiling according to the Lord. Genuine Christians are not to defile themselves in any way; they should be good witnesses for the Lord Jesus Christ.

1 Corinthians 3:18

"Let no man deceive himself. If any man among you seemeth to be wise in this world, let him become a fool, that he may be wise."

This verse begins with a negative prohibition in the Greek present tense. As such, it means to stop an action already in progress. Paul is saying to the true Christians at Corinth to stop deceiving themselves. Apparently these genuine Corinthians were deceiving themselves. Paul tells them to stop it. Many times people try to make others think they are wise when they are not. If this is the case, let such people "*become a fool, that he may be wise.*" In that way, they will realize that they were wrong in thinking they **Verses On Wise And Wisdom**

- **Isaiah 5:21**

"Woe unto them that are <u>wise in their own eyes</u>, and prudent in their own sight!"

Just because people are wise "in their own eyes" doesn't make them **really** wise. They just **think** they are wise.

- **Isaiah 29:14**

"Therefore, behold, I will proceed to do a marvellous work among this people, even a marvellous work and a wonder: for <u>the wisdom of their wise men shall perish</u>, and the understanding of their prudent men shall be hid."Even the so-called wisdom of wise teachers in colleges, seminaries, and universities of our land will perish. Much of their "wisdom" is foolishness with God. Even the sound wisdom will one day come to a halt and perish.

- **Isaiah 44:25**

"That frustrateth the tokens of the liars, and maketh diviners mad; <u>that turneth wise men backward, and maketh their knowledge foolish</u>;"

God does this. God is the One Who makes the knowledge of the wise to be foolish. It's God's wisdom that they should seek—not their own!

- **Isaiah 47:10**

"For thou hast trusted in thy wickedness: thou hast said, None seeth me. <u>Thy wisdom and thy knowledge, it hath perverted thee</u>; and thou hast said in thine heart, I am, and none else beside me."

God speaks a vital and needful truth here. Knowledge, especially false knowledge, is a very powerful perversion tool. It often perverts, even those who have passed away or are genuine Christians. There is much perversion of knowledge and wisdom that has been promoted and will continue to go on in once-sound fundamental Christian schools, colleges, and seminaries. They have adopted false doctrines, false bibles, false dress codes, false music, false philosophy, and many, many other false things. They have moved or will one day move into pure and total Satanic paganism.

1 Corinthians 3:19

"For the wisdom of this world is foolishness with God. For it is written, He taketh the wise in their own craftiness."

"The wisdom of this world is foolishness with God." Since God is omniscient—He knows everything there is to know in all the languages, books, poems, radio, and Internet statements in the entire world. Compared to His marvelous wisdom, all the wisdom of this is, by comparison, complete and total foolishness.

Notice how Paul quoted Job 5:13 in this verse from God's Hebrew Old Testament. He said: "*It is written.*" Paul used the Greek Word, GEGRAPTAI. This is the Greek perfect tense form of the verb, GRAPHO ("to write"). This Greek perfect tense means something that was written in the past, is preserved to the present, and continues to be preserved into the future.

God has promised to preserve His Words which were written in Hebrew, Aramaic, and Greek in the past, preserve them into the present, and on into the future. The only way that Paul could have quoted from the Hebrew Old Testament Words is that those Words had been preserved for him in his day. Those Words have been preserved for us in our day and in all future days as well. These are inspired and preserved Words that underlie our King James Bible and which have been accurately translated into our English language.

Apostate schools and seminaries have rejected Bible inspiration and Bible preservation for centuries. Today, most of the schools and seminaries which believe many Bible truths, are sometimes weak even on **Bible inspiration**, but have totally rejected the **Bible preservation** of the Hebrew, Aramaic, and Greek Words found in the sixty-six books of the Bible. This is a very sad situation, and it's getting worse and worse, not better, as the years go on.

This unbelief in Bible **preservation**, for example, is found in such schools as Bob Jones University, Central Baptist Seminary, Detroit Baptist Seminary, Bible Baptist Seminary, Los Angeles Baptist Seminary, Dallas Theological Seminary, and most, if not all, of the professing "fundamentalist" schools, as well as ALL of the new evangelical seminaries like Dallas Theological Seminary.

1 Corinthians 3:20

"And again, The Lord knoweth the thoughts of the wise, that they are vain."

By God's miraculous omniscience, He can read the very thoughts of the so-called wise people. He knows them to be vain and empty.

Verses On Thoughts
- **Job 21:27**

"Behold, I know your thoughts, and the devices which ye wrongfully imagine against me."

God's perfect knowledge pierces even the thoughts of those who think they are wise. They wrongfully imagine things against the Lord.

- **Psalms 56:5**

"Every day they wrest my words: all their thoughts are against me for evil."

All the thoughts of the wicked unbelievers are against the Lord for evil, not for good.
- **Psalms 94:11**
"The LORD knoweth the thoughts of man, that they are vanity."

The thoughts of human being are filled with vanity. These people are just thinking of themselves rather than the Lord or other people.

1 Corinthians 3:21

"Therefore let no man glory in men. For all things are yours;"

Those genuine Christians in the Corinthian church were glorying over one leader or another. Paul asked that this be stopped. Later in the book, Paul gave some specifics about being of Paul, Apollos, Cephas, or of Christ.

Verses on Glory And Glorying

- **Psalms 4:2**
"O ye sons of men, how long will ye turn my glory into shame? how long will ye love vanity, and seek after leasing? Selah."

Many people, both men and women, turn the glory of God and His creation of all things, into the shame of idolatry and other false beliefs.

- **Jeremiah 9:23**
"Thus saith the LORD, Let not the wise man glory in his wisdom, neither let the mighty man glory in his might, let not the rich man glory in his riches:"

Those who are rich should not glory in riches that could disappear overnight in times of crisis. They should rather glory in the Lord.

- **Jeremiah 9:24**
"But let him that glorieth glory in this, that he understandeth and knoweth me, that I am the LORD which exercise lovingkindness, judgment, and righteousness, in the earth: for in these things I delight, saith the LORD."

The Lord Himself should be the One people should glory in because of His matchless lovingkindness and power.

- **Romans 8:17**
"And if children, then heirs; heirs of God, and joint-heirs with Christ; if so be that we suffer with him, that we may be also glorified together."

Genuine Christians are joint heirs with Christ. Everything the Lord Jesus Christ owns, the true Christians own as well. Joint-heirs means they are co-signers with their Saviour, the Lord Jesus

Christ. Mrs. Waite is a joint signer on our house. She and I both own it. We are joint-owners. This is true of genuine Christians being joint-heirs with their Saviour. Everything that He has is joined with His children, whether this be suffering with Him, or being glorified by Him.

1 Corinthians 3:22

"Whether Paul, or Apollos, or Cephas, or the world, or life, or death, or things present, or things to come; all are yours;"

Paul states to the genuine Christians at Corinth, all things are theirs because they are joint-heirs with the Lord Jesus Christ. This is true whether they are Paul, Apollos, Peter, the world, life, death, things present, or things to come. True Christians, whether the three leaders mentioned, or all other genuine Christians by life or by death. All things can be cared for victoriously because they are joint-heirs with the Lord Jesus Christ and share His victories both in during their lifetimes as well as when they are with Him in Heaven.

1 Corinthians 3:23

"And ye are Christ's; and Christ is God's."

This verse states clearly that genuine Christians are possessed and owned by the Lord Jesus Christ. They do not belong to themselves once they become true Christians. It is also true that the Lord Jesus Christ is part of the Trinity of God the Father, God the Son, and God the Holy Spirit.

Verses On Genuine Christians Owned By God
- **1 Corinthians 6:19**

"What? know ye not that your body is the temple of the Holy Ghost which is in you, which ye have of God, and <u>ye are not your own</u>? For <u>ye are bought with a price</u>: therefore glorify God in your body, and in your spirit, which are God's."

Once people have trusted the Lord Jesus Christ as their Saviour, they belong to Him. They are not their own to do as they please. On the contrary, they should please the Lord Jesus Christ Who bought them with His precious Blood.

- `Mark 9:41`

"For whosoever shall give you a cup of water to drink in my name, <u>because ye belong to Christ</u>, verily I say unto you, he shall not lose his reward."

True Christians belong to the Lord Jesus Christ. There's a chorus that we sing sometimes that emphases that truth:

"Now I belong to Jesus. Jesus belongs to me. Not for the years a time alone, but for eternity."

Since genuine Christians belong to the Lord Jesus Christ, they should know His will for their lives by reading and following the Biblical truths in the Bible. They should serve Him faithfully.

1 Corinthians Chapter Four

1 Corinthians 4:1

"Let a man so account of us, as of the ministers of Christ, and stewards of the mysteries of God."

When Paul said "*let a man so account of us*," he referred to himself and all those who helped him in the ministry. He says that they all are "*ministers of Christ*." They served and worked on behalf of the Lord Jesus Christ Himself Who had gone to Heaven.

Paul and his fellow-workers were also "*stewards*" of God's mysteries. A good "*steward*" is a person who should wisely and faithfully take care of another person's possessions. Paul wanted to be a good steward of God's standards and principles. This is especially true in the midst of all the sins found in the church at Corinth.

Verses On Stewards

- **Genesis 15:2**

"And Abram said, Lord GOD, what wilt thou give me, seeing I go childless, and the steward of my house is this Eliezer of Damascus?"

Eliezer was the man who took care of all of Abraham's affairs. All of the details of Abraham's house were cared for by Eliezer.

- **Matthew 20:8**

"So when even was come, the lord of the vineyard saith unto his steward, Call the labourers, and give them their hire, beginning from the last unto the first."

This steward worked for the lord of the vineyard. He took care of all the details involved in the vineyard administration, including paying for the labourers.

- **Luke 12:42**

"And the Lord said, Who then is that faithful and wise steward, whom his lord shall make ruler over his household, to give them their portion of meat in due season?"

The master was looking for a faithful and wise steward who could be promoted to be the household ruler.

- **Luke 16:1**

"And he said also unto his disciples, There was a certain rich man, which <u>had a steward</u>; and the same was <u>accused unto him that he had wasted his goods</u>."

This unjust steward was a very bad person. He was accused of wasting his rich master's goods.

- **Titus 1:7**

"For <u>a bishop must be blameless, as the steward of God</u>; not selfwilled, not soon angry, not given to wine, no striker, not given to filthy lucre;"

From Acts 20:17, 20 and 1 Peter 5:1-2, looking closely at the Greek Words mention there, I believe it is clear that the office of the leader in local churches has three names for this one office. He is the pastor-bishop-elder. He should be a blameless, good and faithful steward for the local church that has called him.

- **1 Peter 4:10**

"As every man hath received the gift, even so minister the same one to another, <u>as good stewards of the manifold grace of God</u>."

All genuine Christians, whether men or women, have been given by the Lord Jesus Christ, something special that they can and should perform and manifest the manifold grace of God.

THE MEANING OF THE GREEK WORD, "HUPERETES"

The Greek Word for "ministers" is HUPERETES. Some of the meanings of this Greek Word are:

"1) servant; 1a) an underrower, subord- inate rower; 1b) any one who serves with hands: a servant; 1b1) in the NT of the officers and attendants of magistrates as -- of the officer who executes penalties; 1b2) of the attendants of a king, servants, retinue, the soldiers of a king, of the attendant of a synagogue; 1b3) of any one ministering or rendering service; 1c) any one who aids another in any work; 1c1) an assistant; 1c2) of the preacher of the Gospel."

Among many other things, as a "*minister*," he must be the servant of the Lord Jesus Christ.

In this verse, Paul and his helpers were also to be accounted as *"stewards."*

> **THE MEANING OF THE GREEK WORD, "OIKONOMOS"**
>
> The Greek Word for *"stewards"* is OIKONOMOS. Some of the meanings of that Greek Word are:
>
> "1) the manager of household or of household affairs; 1a) esp. a steward, manager, superintendent (whether free-born or as was usually the case, a freed-man or a slave) to whom the head of the house or proprietor has entrusted the management of his affairs, the care of receipts and expenditures, and the duty of dealing out the proper portion to every servant and even to the children not yet of age; 1b) the manager of a farm or landed estate, an overseer; 1c) the superintend- ent of the city's finances, the treasurer of a city (or of treasurers or quaestors of kings); 2) metaph. the apostles and other Christian teachers and bishops and overseers."

Paul wanted himself and his fellow-workers to be good managers in their conduct in the churches and in their proper teaching of the doctrines of the Bible.

1 Corinthians 4:2

"Moreover it is required in stewards, that a man be found faithful."

If a man is a steward, he must not be unfaithful in his stewardship. It is incumbent upon him to be found faithful. The Bible recognized the extreme importance of faithfulness and has given us many verses on it.

Verses On Faithfulness

- **Numbers 12:7**

"My servant <u>Moses</u> is not so, who is <u>faithful in all mine house</u>."

God chose Moses because he was a faithful man. At first, he did not want to lead God's people out of Egypt, but finally he obeyed the Lord.

- **Deuteronomy 7:9**

"Know therefore that <u>the LORD thy God, he is God</u>, <u>the faithful God</u>, which keepeth covenant and mercy with them that love him and keep his commandments to a thousand generations;"

Every genuine Christian should be very thankful that our God is faithful in all His thoughts and ways.

- **Nehemiah 9:7-8**

"<u>Thou art the LORD the God, who didst choose Abram</u>, and broughtest him forth out of Ur of the Chaldees, and gavest him the name of Abraham; <u>And foundest his heart faithful before thee</u>, and madest a covenant with him to give the land of the Canaanites, the Hittites, the Amorites, and the Perizzites, and the Jebusites, and the Girgashites, to give it, I say, to his seed, and hast performed thy words; for thou art righteous:"

God chose Abraham to serve Him because he had a faithful heart. Would that all true Christians might have faithful hearts as well!

- **Psalms 119:138**

"<u>Thy testimonies</u> that thou hast commanded <u>are righteous and very faithful</u>."

Not only is the God of the Bible faithful, but His Words are also very faithful.

- **Proverbs 28:20**

"<u>A faithful man shall abound with blessings</u>: but he that maketh haste to be rich shall not be innocent."

Blessings abound with genuine Christians who are faithful to the Lord and His Words.

- **Daniel 6:4**

"Then <u>the presidents and princes sought to find occasion against Daniel</u> concerning the kingdom; <u>but they could find none occasion nor fault; forasmuch as he was faithful</u>, neither was there any error or fault found in him."

Daniel was faithful to the Lord and His Words in this heathen land, even if it caused his enemies to want the lions to tear him to pieces. They knew that he was faithful to the law of his God and would never cease praying to Him.

- **Matthew 25:21**

"His lord said unto him, <u>Well done, thou good and faithful servant: thou hast been faithful</u> over a few things, I will make thee ruler over many things: enter thou into the joy of thy lord."

The man with five talents turned it into ten talents. I wonder if genuine Christians will hear this from the Lord Jesus Christ at the Judgment Seat of Christ. What do you think?

- **Matthew 25:23**

"His lord said unto him, <u>Well done, good and faithful servant; thou hast been faithful</u> over a few things, I will make thee ruler over many things: enter thou into the joy of thy lord."

The man with two talents turned them into four talents and the master said *"well done"* to him as he said to the other servant in verse 21.

- **Luke 16:10**

"<u>He that is faithful in that which is least is faithful also in much</u>: and he that is unjust in the least is unjust also in much."

We've got to be faithful in the little things. Everything God has given to us as stewards requires excellent management.

- **1 Corinthians 1:9**

"<u>God is faithful</u>, by whom ye were called unto the fellowship of his Son Jesus Christ our Lord."

God is always faithful. He will never give up that marvelous character trait.

- **1 Corinthians 4:17**

"For this cause have I sent unto you <u>Timotheus, who is my beloved son, and faithful in the Lord</u>, who shall bring you into remembrance of my ways which be in Christ, as I teach every where in every church."

Timothy was Paul's beloved son whom he led to faith in his Saviour. He was to be faithful in telling the Corinthian Christians about Paul's ways in Christ.

- **1 Corinthians 10:13**

"There hath no temptation taken you but such as is common to man: but <u>God is faithful, who will not suffer you to be tempted above that ye are able</u>; but will with the temptation also make a way to escape, that ye may be able to bear it."

God is faithful to true Christians when temptations come to them. He will provide a way of escape in order for them to bear them.

- **Ephesians 6:21**

"But that ye also may know my affairs, and how I do, <u>Tychicus, a beloved brother and faithful minister in the Lord</u>, shall make known to you all things:"

May all genuine Christian pastors be as Tychicus and his faithful ministry for the Lord Jesus Christ.

- **Colossians 1:7**

"As ye also learned of <u>Epaphras</u> our dear fellowservant, who is for you <u>a faithful minister of Christ</u>;"

Though most are ot faithful to God's Words today, it would be great if all of our true Christian pastors would be faithful ministers of the Lord Jesus Christ as Epaphras was.
- **Colossians 4:9**
"With <u>Onesimus, a faithful and beloved brother</u>, who is one of you. They shall make known unto you all things which are done here."

Onesimus is the fourth of the men in the New Testament who were faithful in their ministries.
- **1 Thessalonians 5:24**
"<u>Faithful is he that calleth you</u>, who also will do it."

As in the many verses before, the Lord Jesus Christ is faithful.
- **2 Thessalonians 3:3**
"But <u>the Lord is faithful, who shall stablish you, and keep you from evil</u>."

The Lord is faithful to establish and keep from evil those genuine Christians at Thessalonica.
- **1 Timothy 1:12**
"And I thank <u>Christ Jesus our Lord</u>, who hath enabled me, for that he <u>counted me faithful, putting me into the ministry</u>;"

The reason that the Lord Jesus Christ met Paul on the road to Damascus and called him to be an Apostle because He knew that Paul would be faithful to Him.
- **1 Timothy 3:11**
"Even <u>so must their wives be</u> grave, not slanderers, sober, <u>faithful in all things</u>."

This is a requirement for the wives of church deacons. They must be, as their husbands, *"faithful in all things."*
- **2 Timothy 2:2**
"And <u>the things that thou hast heard of me</u> among many witnesses, <u>the same commit thou to faithful men</u>, who shall be able to teach others also."

Paul wanted Pastor Timothy to commit to faithful men the teachings and doctrines that he had heard from Paul. That's what I seek to do here in our Bible For Today Baptist Church. I try to preach God's Words on a verse-by-verse method to faithful people in our church and over the Internet. This is in hopes that they might teach others also. I hope that our missionaries will do the same.
- **Hebrews 2:17**
"Wherefore in all things it behoved him to be made like unto his brethren, <u>that he might be a merciful and faithful high priest</u> in things pertaining to God, to make reconciliation for the sins of the people."

The Lord Jesus Christ is a sinless and holy High Priest to whom true Christians can confess their sins and receive forgiveness and be cleansed from all unrighteousness.

- **Hebrews 10:23**

"Let us hold fast the profession of our faith without wavering; (for <u>he is faithful that promised</u>;)"

God the Father and God the Son are faithful to their promises.

- **1 Peter 5:12**

"By <u>Silvanus, a faithful brother unto you</u>, as I suppose, I have written briefly, exhorting, and testifying that this is the true grace of God wherein ye stand."

Silvanus is another faithful Christian brother who was serving the Lord Jesus Christ in Peter's day.

- **1 John 1:9**

"<u>If we confess our sins, he is faithful and just to forgive us our sins, and to cleanse us from all unrighteousness</u>."

For genuine Christians who agree with God that they have sinned, God is both faithful and just to forgive them and cleanse them.

1 Corinthians 4:3

"But with me it is a very small thing that I should be judged of you, or of man's judgment: yea, I judge not mine own self."

Now Paul is faithful, regardless of how these Corinthians thought his message was. "But with me it is a very small thing that I should be judged of you," Now, why were the Corinthians judging Paul? Because he was preaching sound and straight and many preachers are judged by people who listen because he preaches sound and straight. That's a very small thing. The Lord Jesus is the one who is going to judge. There are a few verses on that,

Verses On Judgment

- **John 5:22**

"For <u>the Father judgeth no man</u>, but hath committed <u>all judgment unto the Son</u>:"

God the Father has committed all judgment to His Son, the Lord Jesus Christ. This includes the judgment of Christians, of the non-Christians, of Israel, of angels, and any other judgment.

- **John 5:30**

"I can of mine own self do nothing: <u>as I hear, I judge: and my judgment is just</u>; because I seek not mine own will, but the will of the Father which hath sent me."

The Lord Jesus Christ's judgment on any matter is always perfectly just and righteous.

- **John 7:24**
  "Judge not according to the appearance, but <u>judge righteous judgment</u>."

Sometimes people say that genuine Christians should never judge anyone for anything. In this verse, the Lord Jesus Christ commands that they are to judge in a righteous judgement. He never said not to judge at all. They need righteousness in all their judgment and decisions.

- **John 8:16**
  "And yet <u>if I judge, my judgment is true</u>: for I am not alone, but I and the Father that sent me."

The Lord Jesus Christ is omniscient, omnipresent, and omnipotent. He knows the hearts of every person who ever lived. His judgments are always true.

- **Romans 14:10**
  "But <u>why dost thou judge thy brother</u>? or why dost thou set at nought thy brother? for we shall all stand before the judgment seat of Christ."

The Lord Jesus Christ will judge all true Christians at the Judgment Seat Of Christ. He will be the Righteous Judge.

- **2 Corinthians 5:10**
  "For <u>we must all appear before the judgment seat of Christ</u>; that every one may receive the things done in his body, according to that he hath done, whether it be good or bad."

This Judgment Seat is where all genuine Christians will be judged according to their works after becoming Christians. They will not lose their salvation, but may lose their rewards.

- **Revelation 20:11**
  "And <u>I saw a great white throne</u>, and him that sat on it, from whose face the earth and the heaven fled away; and there was found no place for them."

The Lord Jesus Christ was sitting on that Great White Throne to judge all non-Christians who have never trusted Him as their Saviour. Their sentence is the Lake of Fire in Hell.

1 Corinthians 4:4

"For I know nothing by myself; yet am I not hereby justified: but he that judgeth me is the Lord."

Paul said that he knows nothing by himself, but only what the Lord Jesus Christ has revealed to him. He is not justified by this revelation. The One Who judges him is the Lord Jesus Christ. All true Christians are declared righteous before God by having genuine faith in His Son, the Lord Jesus Christ.

This gives them a righteous standing before God. They should then live righteously in accord with God's Words in the Bible before all. When they sin, they must do what 1 John 1:9 commands:
- **1 John 1:9**
"If we confess our sins, he is faithful and just to forgive us our sins, and to cleanse us from all unrighteousness."

Genuine Christians must confess any of their sins unto God. The Greek Word *"confess"* is HOMOLOGEO. It is a compound Greek Word. HOMO means *"the same."* LOGEO means *"to say."*

"The whole word, HOMOLOGEO, means to say the same thing about our sins as God says, that is, to agree with God that the things confessed are sins in the sight of God."

True Christians must confess their sins of the heart, mind, word, and deed, immediately to God and He has promised, in this verse, (1) He will forgive them, and (2) He will cleanse them from all unrighteousness. Every time they sin, this verse must be followed.

1 Corinthians 4:5

"Therefore judge nothing before the time, until the Lord come, who both will bring to light the hidden things of darkness, and will make manifest the counsels of the hearts: and then shall every man have praise of God."

This verse uses a negative present Greek tense. This indicates a command to stop an action already in progress. The genuine Christians at Corinth were judging others about serious matters. Paul told them to stop this practice. At His coming in the air, the Lord Jesus Christ will judge all true Christians at the Judgment Seat of Christ, all non-Christians at the Great White Throne Judgment. He will be the Final Judge of all matters that concern all genuine Christians and all non-Christians.

Many times the judgment of genuine Christians is misjudgment. It's a very sad thing when a situation is misjudged. Sometimes you can never take it back and make things right. People often get angry and friendship is lost.

"A brother offended is harder to be won than a strong city: and their contentions are like the bars of a castle." (Proverbs 18:19)

1 Corinthians 4:6

"**And these things, brethren, I have in a figure transferred to myself and to Apollos for your sakes; that ye might learn in us not to think *of men* above that which is written, that no one of you be puffed up for one against another.**"

Paul was very concerned about some who might think of him and Apollos above what was written in the Bible. The Bible is clear that "*all have sinned and come short of the glory of God.*" (Romans 3:23). He didn't want anyone to be puffed up with any pride, but to refer to them as it has been written in the Bible. The Greek Word for "*written*" is HAGIAZO. It is in the Greek perfect tense which describes a Word that was written in past, preserved up to the present and even preserved on into the future. This teaches the plenary verbal preservation of the Words of God in the original Hebrew, Aramaic, and Greek Words.

THE MEANING OF THE GREEK WORD, "PHUSIOO"

The Greek Word for "*puffed up*" is PHUSIOO. Some of the meanings of this Greek Word are:

> "1) to make natural, to cause a thing to pass into nature; 2) to inflate, blow up, to cause to swell up; 2a) to puff up, make proud; 2b) to be puffed up, to bear one's self loftily, be proud."

Verses On Puffed Up

- **1 Corinthians 4:18-19**

"Now <u>some are puffed up</u>, as though I would not come to you. But I will come to you shortly, if the Lord will, and will know, <u>not the speech of them which are puffed up, but the power</u>."

As mentioned above, "*puffed up*" refers to be proud and be lofty. That is not what true Christians should ever be.

- **1 Corinthians 8:1**

"Now as touching things offered unto idols, we know that we all have knowledge. <u>Knowledge puffeth up</u>, but charity edifieth."

This is warning about the wrong use of knowledge. It is very able to puff up the people who possess much of it. This would be true in reference to secular knowledge as well as knowledge of the Bible and its many teachings. On the other hand, love does not purr up, but builds up.

- **Colossians 2:18**

"Let no man beguile you of your reward in a voluntary humility and worshipping of angels, intruding into those things which he hath not seen, vainly puffed up by his fleshly mind."

Have you ever met a know-it-all? You probably have. There are some people that think they know it all. Is it possible for any human being to know it all? It is absolutely impossible, is it not? There are too many facts in this world to have any one person to know about them all.

There is now what is called a knowledge explosion. Knowledge has multiplied greatly More things are known today than we ever knew before. In any event, whatever people might know, they should never be puffed up and arrogant because of it.

1 Corinthians 4:7

"For who maketh thee to differ *from another*? and what hast thou that thou didst not receive? now if thou didst receive *it*, why dost thou glory, as if thou hadst not received *it*?"

Genuine Christians have received many things from the Lord, including forgiveness, redemption, eternal life, salvation, and especially all of His Words found in both the Old and the New Testaments. All true Christians differ from one another in one way or another. But all of God's eternal gifts that have been bestowed upon them are from Him, not from themselves. Because this is true, they should not have self-glory for these things, because they are not the source of them.

Verses On Glory

- **2 Corinthians 10:17**

"But he that glorieth, let him glory in the Lord."

True Christians should glory in the Lord and what He has done for them rather than in themselves and their deeds and actions.

- **2 Corinthians 12:9**

"And he said unto me, My grace is sufficient for thee: for my strength is made perfect in weakness. Most gladly therefore will I rather glory in my infirmities, that the power of Christ may rest upon me."

The Lord had given Paul His power and strength, even in his own physical infirmities, Paul gloried in these infirmities that the Lord Jesus Christ's power would rest upon him.

- **Galatians 5:26**
"Let us not be desirous of vain glory, provoking one another, envying one another."

Vain and empty glory should never be desired by genuine Christians. Their glory should be in the Lord Jesus Christ and all that He has done for them in time and in eternity.

- **Galatians 6:14**
"But God forbid that I should glory, save in the cross of our Lord Jesus Christ, by whom the world is crucified unto me, and I unto the world."

The only thing that the Apostle Paul wanted to glory in was the cross of the Lord Jesus Christ and all that He accomplished by His substitutionary, expiatory death for the sins of all the people in the world.

1 Corinthians 4:8

"Now ye are full, now ye are rich, ye have reigned as kings without us: and I would to God ye did reign, that we also might reign with you."

Paul talks here about the Corinthians being full, rich, and reigning like kings "*without us*." They were on their own, without Paul and his helpers. They were different than the apostles who were impoverished, going to different places without knowing which town was going to accept them, or try to kill them.

Those genuine Christians in the church at Corinth were sitting in Corinth which was one of the three most wicked cities in the ancient world along with Crete and Cappadocia. Those in Corinth who were genuine Christians possessed the riches of God in the Lord Jesus Christ. They certainly did have spiritual riches. Paul wished they really did "*reign*" so that he and his helpers could reign with them. It doesn't seem true that they were really reigning as earthly kings.

1 Corinthians 4:9

"For I think that God hath set forth us the apostles last, as it were appointed to death: for we are made a spectacle unto the world, and to angels, and to men."

Paul reminds the genuine Christians at Corinth that he and the other apostles of the Lord Jesus Christ were set forth last as far as the world thought of them. In addition, they were, in a very real sense, were appointed to death. Every one of the twelve original apostles but John, were killed in a brutal manner.

According to tradition, they were either crucified, sawed asunder, stoned, burned at the stake, or died in some other painful way. Paul himself was decapitated by the Roman government. Only the Apostle John died a natural death. He was sent to the isle of Patmos as a prisoner.

The reason for their cruel deaths is that they were faithful preachers of the Person and work of the Lord Jesus Christ. By their cruel deaths, the apostles were made a spectacle to the world, to angels, and to the non-Christian men and women of that day.

> **THE MEANING OF THE GREEK WORD, "THEATRON"**
> The Greek Word for *"spectacle"* is THEATRON. Some of the meanings of this Greek Word are:
> *"1) a theatre, a place in which games and dramatic spectacles are exhibited, and public assemblies held (for the Greeks used the theatre also as a forum); 2) a public show; 2a) metaph., a man who is exhibited to be gazed at and made sport of."*

During Paul's two Roman imprisonments, he was led of the Lord to write five or six books of the Bible. During his first Roman imprisonment, he wrote what are called the "prison epistles." They are the Bible books of Ephesians, Philippians, Colossians, and Philemon. At a later date, Paul was imprisoned again by Rome. While in prison that time, he wrote 2 Timothy, and possibly 1 Timothy. 2 Timothy was his last book before being executed by Rome.

At the beginning of every morning service of our Bible For Today Baptist Church (which can be heard at BibleForToday.org 24/7) we sing a chorus written by my mother-in-law entitled *"Faithful To The Fight."* We then quote part of 2 Timothy 4:7: ". . . *I have fought a good fight, I have finished my course, I have kept the faith."*

- **2 Timothy 4:6-7**

"For I am now ready to be offered, and the time of my departure is at hand. **I have fought a good fight, I have finished my course, I have kept the faith.**"

Paul was ready to depart to be with the Lord Jesus Christ which was far better than living in this sin-cursed earth. He had done nothing worthy of death. Rome slew him because he preached the Lord Jesus Christ as the only Saviour and Redeemer of the world.

1 Corinthians 4:10

"We are fools for Christ's sake, but ye are wise in Christ; we *are* weak, but ye *are* strong; ye *are* honourable, but we are despised."

Apparently, the genuine Christians at Corinth lived comfortably in their homes. They seemed to be "*wise,*" "*strong,*" and "*honourable.*" But Paul and the other apostles, as far as the non-Christians were concerned, seemed to be "*fools,*" "*weak,*" and "despised."

Just look at what Paul was like in the past. He left his home in Jerusalem to be a roving missionary. He left his status as one of the key members of the Jewish Sanhedrin. He was learned in all the wisdom of the Jewish law. He sat at the feet of Gamaliel, a chief teacher of the law of Moses. He had everything going for him.

He hated the Christians so much that he took a journey on the road to Damascus to imprison and kill as many Christians as he found there. But the Lord Jesus Christ had other plans for this Jewish Pharisee. He met Paul on that road, blinded him with a light brighter than the sun.

Paul said, "*Lord, what will Thou have me to do?*" Then he submitted to the will of the Lord Jesus Christ and became a genuine Christian. He was turned "*from darkness to light.*" The Lord Jesus Christ gave Paul a commission to go to the Gentiles and tell them about the Saviour Who came to save them from sin.

As he says in this verse, Paul and the other apostles became "*fools for Christ's sake.*" The preaching of the cross to men that perish is foolishness, but to them that are saved, it's the power of God. And this is what he means by being called fools for the sake of the Lord Jesus Christ.

Comparatively speaking, Paul was not weak but people might have thought he was weak. Paul was really strong. His accusers were the weak ones. Paul was following the wisdom of 2 Timothy 2:15. He was seeking to be approved unto God.

- **2 Timothy 2:15**
"Study to shew thyself approved unto God, a workman that needeth not to be ashamed, rightly dividing the word of truth."

Paul was studying and diligently showing himself approved unto God. He was filling his mind with God's Words of truth and rightly dividing it so it could be understood by his listeners. Paul was going to give an account one day at the Judgment Seat of Christ, along with every other genuine Christian who ever lived.

At that Judgment Seat for the true Christians, it will not be a question of whether or not they were successful, whether loud or soft in their speech, whether they were tall or short, whether rich or poor, whether fat, skinny, or just right. The one and only issue that every genuine Christian will face is whether they have they been absolutely faithful to their Lord Jesus Christ in their service for Him. Nothing else matters at that Judgment Seat of Christ for every genuine Christian throughout all the ages.

1 Corinthians 4:11

"Even unto this present hour we both hunger, and thirst, and are naked, and are buffeted, and have no certain dwellingplace;"

There are five serious hardships that Paul mentioned in this verse that were true up to the time of this letter. All five hardships concerned Paul and all the other apostles and genuine Christian leaders. Every one of these five situations was tragic.

THE MEANING OF THE GREEK WORD, "GUMNETEUO"

The Greek Word for *"naked"* is GUMNETEUO. Some of the meanings of this Greek Word are:

"1) to be lightly or poorly clad; 2) to be a light armed soldier."

You can see from the meaning above that this does not mean *"nude"* as it does in English. It can mean lightly clothed. When the Apostle Peter went back to fishing after the bodily resurrection of the Lord Jesus Christ, John 21:7 uses this same word, *"naked,"* describing Peter. He just had his undergarments on apparently, and then put on his outer coat.

John 21:7

*"Therefore that disciple whom Jesus loved saith unto Peter, It is the Lord. Now <u>when Simon Peter heard that it was the Lord, he girt his fisher's coat unto him, (for **he was naked**,)</u> and did cast himself into the sea."*

Notice all the buffeting and problems that Paul wrote about to the genuine Christians at Corinth. His fellow workers had their share of hardships as well, I am sure.

2 Corinthians 11:23-28

"Are they ministers of Christ? (I speak as a fool) I am more; in labours more abundant, in stripes above measure, in prisons more frequent, in deaths oft. Of the Jews five

times received I forty stripes save one. Thrice was I beaten with rods, once was I stoned, thrice I suffered shipwreck, a night and a day I have been in the deep; In journeyings often, in perils of waters, in perils of robbers, in perils by mine own countrymen, in perils by the heathen, in perils in the city, in perils in the wilderness, in perils in the sea, in perils among false brethren; In weariness and painfulness, in watchings often, in hunger and thirst, in fastings often, in cold and nakedness. Beside those things that are without, that which cometh upon me daily, the care of all the churches."

1 Corinthians 4:12

"And labour, working with our own hands: being reviled, we bless; being persecuted, we suffer it:"

Paul was not a loafer, but a laborer. He was a faithful worker for the Lord Jesus Christ Who saved him. When people reviled him—and there were many who did this—Paul blessed them. When Paul was persecuted, as he was often, he and his fellow helpers put up with it without backing down.

THE MEANING OF THE GREEK WORD, "KOPIAO"

The Greek Word used here for *"labour"* is KOPIAO. Some of the meanings of this Greek Word are:

"1) to grow weary, tired, exhausted (with toil or burdens or grief); 2) to labour with wearisome effort, to toil; 2a) of bodily labour"

Verses On Labor
- Acts 18:2-3

"And found a certain Jew named Aquila, born in Pontus, lately come from Italy, with his wife Priscilla; (because that Claudius had commanded all Jews to depart from Rome:) and came unto them. And because <u>he was of the same craft, he abode with them, and wrought: for by their occupation they were tentmakers</u>."

Though I have never made a tent of any kind, I am sure it was not a simple feat for Paul and others to labor in tent construction. It was hard work.

- **Ephesians 4:28**
"Let him that stole steal no more: but rather <u>let him labour, working with *his* hands the thing which is good</u>, that he may have to give to him that needeth."

Paul urged the genuine Christians at Ephesus to labour and working with their hands to help themselves and others who needed help.

- **2 Thessalonians 3:10**
"For even when we were with you, this we commanded you, that <u>if any would not work, neither should he eat</u>."

The Greek Word for "*would*" means someone who is able to work but is not "*willing*" to work. If that is the case, that person should not be given food until he began to work again. This was quite a severe penalty.

1 Corinthians 4:13

"Being defamed, we intreat: we are made as the filth of the world, *and are* the offscouring of all things unto this day."

Paul continues telling the church at Corinth about his mistreatment by his enemies. He was "*defamed*" and also made as the "*filth*" of the world and the "*offscouring*" of all things. There are some unusual meanings of these Words for you to see.

MEANING OF THE GREEK WORD, "BLASPHEMEO"
The Greek Word for "defamed" is BLASPHEMEO. Some of the Meanings of this Greek Word are:
> "1) to speak reproachfully, rail at, revile, calumniate, blaspheme; 2) to be evil spoken of, reviled, railed at"

MEANING OF THE GREEK WORD, "PERIKATHAMA"
The Greek Word for "*filth*" is PERIKATHAMA. Some of the meanings of this Greek Word are:
> "*1) ... refuse; 2) metaph.; 2a) the most abject and despicable men; 2b) the price of expiation or redemption, because the Greeks used to apply the term "katharmata" to victims sacrificed to make expiation for the people, and even to criminals who were maintained at the public expense, that on the outbreak of a*

> *pestilence or other calamity they might be offered as sacrifices to make expiation for the state."*

THE MEANING OF THE GREEK WORD, "PERIPSEMA"

The Greek Word for *"offscouring"* is PERIPSEMA. Some of the meanings of this Greek Word are:

> *"1) what is wiped off; 2) dirt rubbed off; 3) off scouring, scrapings; The Athenians, in order to avert public calamities, yearly threw a criminal into the sea as an offering to Poseidon; hence the term became used for an expiatory offering, a ransom, for our child, i.e. in comparison with the saving of our son's life let it be to us a despicable and worthless thing. It is used of a man who in behalf of religion undergoes dire trials for the salvation of others."*

Perhaps you have had some of these terms used by your enemies about you, the same as they used about the Apostle Paul by some of your enemies, or whatever people might call true Christians because they disagree with the Lord Jesus Christ and the Bible. These bad names did not silence Paul, and these should not silence genuine Christians today either.

1 Corinthians 4:14

"I write not these things to shame you, but as my beloved sons I warn you."

Paul was an apostle who was faithful to those "beloved" ones he had led to the Lord Jesus Christ. He didn't want to shame them, but he felt he needed to warn them about certain things that were amiss in the church at Corinth. The ministry of faithful and Biblical warning from pastors is almost completely eliminated these days. This is something that is very needful, and yet is seriously missing.

Verses On Warning

- **Ezekiel 3:21**

"Nevertheless <u>if thou warn the righteous *man*, that the righteous sin not</u>, and he doth not sin, <u>he shall surely live, because he is warned</u>; also thou hast delivered thy soul."

Proper warning against sin on the part of righteous people which causes them to turn from sin is useful and needful.

- **Ezekiel 33:2b-3**

"When I bring the sword upon a land, if the people of the land <u>take a man of their coasts, and set him for their watchman</u>: If when he seeth the sword come upon the land, <u>he blow the trumpet, and warn the people;</u>"

The nation of Israel had watchmen on the walls of their cities in order to warn the cities of approaching enemies. Today, we need watchmen in our church pulpits to warn their attendees of dangerous enemies of Bible truths. They should be watching for false teachings and all varieties of unscriptural doctrines that are all around the churches.

Many people don't like to be warned and awakened in the presence of imminent danger. They prefer to remain asleep as to these pending dangers. They do not want the trumpets of warning to blow. They say,

"Don't wake me. Don't blow any trumpets.
I'm sleeping, and I want to keep on sleeping.
Don't wake me up. Don't warn me about
anything. Just let me be injured or die."

Ezekiel was a faithful watchmen for the Lord. He warned the people when the enemy was approaching the city.

- **Acts 20:31**

"Therefore watch, and remember, that by the space of three years <u>I ceased not to warn every one night and day with tears.</u>"

The Apostle Paul is writing to the pastors-bishops-elders of the church at Ephesus. He warned them because after he left them, he knew that there were going to be people among them who would raise up false teachings that were against the truths of the Scriptures.

- **1 Thessalonians 5:14**

"Now we exhort you, brethren, <u>warn them that are unruly</u>, comfort the feebleminded, support the weak, be patient toward all *men.*"

But warn them, the unruly ones. Many people don't like to be warned. When ice in a stream is thin and not well frozen, signs are often placed to warn people not to walk on the thin ice.

In our churches and schools today there are all kinds of things to warn genuine Christians about. These things include not only the modernism and liberalism in most Protestant churches and schools, but also in the many churches and schools of Roman Catholicism. There are also cults and world religions that need to be warned against as well.

1 Corinthians 4:15

"For though ye have ten thousand instructors in Christ, yet *have ye* not many fathers: for in Christ Jesus I have begotten you through the gospel."

The true Christians at Corinth had many instructors, but not many fathers. Paul said that on his missionary journey to Corinth, he led many of them to Christ. I was your father in the faith. *"I have begotten you through the Gospel."* Paul was their father in that sense and he led them in the new birth and so on. The question is, have we been leading people to the Lord. By the way, this word 'begotten.' Many of these new Bible versions and perversions have followed the wrong understanding of that Greek Word and have eliminated *"begotten"* altogether.

Verses On Begotten

- **John 1:14**

  "And the Word was made flesh, and dwelt among us, (and we beheld his glory, the glory as of the only begotten of the Father,) full of grace and truth."

The Lord Jesus Christ had an eternal relationship with God the Father as no one else has ever had.

- **John 1:18**

  "No man hath seen God at any time; the only begotten Son, which is in the bosom of the Father, he hath declared *him*."

The only begotten Son declared and explained God the Father.

- **John 3:16**

  "For God so loved the world, that he gave his only begotten Son, that whosoever believeth in him should not perish, but have everlasting life."

God the Father sent His Only begotten Son into the world so sinners might genuinely trust Him as their Saviour and receive everlasting life.

- **John 3:18**

  "He that believeth on him is not condemned: but he that believeth not is condemned already, because he hath not believed in the name of the only begotten Son of God."

Sinners must truly trust God's only begotten Son in order to receive eternal life.

1 Corinthians 4:16
"Wherefore I beseech you, be ye followers of me."
   Why did Paul beseech them? Because he was their father in the faith. To the extent that Paul followed the Lord Jesus Christ, he urged the genuine Christians at Corinth to follow him as he followed the Saviour.

Verses On Follow
- **1 Corinthians 11:1**
"Be ye followers of me, even as I also *am* of Christ."

His readers were to follow Paul as he was following the Lord Jesus Christ.
- **Ephesians 5:1**
"Be ye therefore followers of God, as dear children;"

Paul wrote to the true Christians at Ephesus from his Roman prison cell. He wished them to follow God, even if they landed in prison because of it, as Paul did.
- **Philippians 3:17**
"Brethren, be followers together of me, and mark them which walk so as ye have us for an ensample."

Paul was an example to those at Philippi to follow the Lord Jesus Christ, no matter what the cost. He was a good example of that.
- **1 Thessalonians 1:6**
"And ye became followers of us, and of the Lord, having received the word in much affliction, with joy of the Holy Ghost:"

The genuine Christians at Thessalonica followed Paul and the Lord. Because he was following the Lord, they became followers of Paul.
- **Hebrews 6:12**
"That ye be not slothful, but followers of them who through faith and patience inherit the promises."

Paul told these Hebrew Christians that they should be followers of those who inherit the promises of God.

1 Corinthians 4:17
"For this cause have I sent unto you Timotheus, who is my beloved son, and faithful in the Lord, who shall bring you into remembrance of my ways which be in Christ, as I teach every where in every church."
   Paul was going to send Timothy to the church at Corinth because he was faithful to the Lord Jesus Christ. He would bring to their remembrance his ways and doctrines that he taught in

every one of the churches he had founded. Timothy was the pastor of the church at Ephesus. Paul led him to trust the Lord Jesus Christ as his Saviour. After that, he was faithful to the work of the Lord. Paul could trust Timothy to try to straighten out the various problems among the true Christians in the Corinthian church. He will also bring to their remembrance Paul's ways and teachings.

Verses On Remembrance
- **1 Corinthians 11:24-25**

"And when he had given thanks, he brake it, and said, Take, eat: this is my body, which is broken for you: this do in remembrance of me. After the same manner also he took the cup, when he had supped, saying, This cup is the new testament in my blood: this do ye, as oft as ye drink it, in remembrance of me."

The Lord's Supper was to be a picture and a remembrance of what the Lord Jesus Christ suffered on the cross as a penalty for the sins of the entire human race.

- **John 14:26**

"But the Comforter, *which is* the Holy Ghost, whom the Father will send in my name, he shall teach you all things, and bring all things to your remembrance, whatsoever I have said unto you."

The Lord Jesus Christ told His disciples that God the Holy Spirit would bring to their remembrance all the things that He had taught them. This enabled them to be guided by the Holy Spirit to write accurately of what the Saviour had told them.

- **Philippians 1:3**

"I thank my God upon every remembrance of you,"

As Paul wrote from prison, he remembered his genuine Christians at Philippi and was thankful to God for every remembrance of them.

- **1 Thessalonians 3:6**

"But now when Timotheus came from you unto us, and brought us good tidings of your faith and charity, and that ye have good remembrance of us always, desiring greatly to see us, as we also *to see* you:"

Timothy brought back the news to Paul that the true Christians at Thessalonica had good remembrance of him and greatly wanted to see him once again.

- **2 Peter 1:15**

"Moreover I will endeavour that ye may be able after my decease to have these things always in remembrance."

Peter wanted his readers to remember his teachings to them after he went to Heaven.

1 Corinthians 4:18

"Now some are puffed up, as though I would not come to you."

Some of those in the church at Corinth were "*puffed up.*"

THE MEANING OF THE GREEK WORD, "PHUSIOO"

The Greek Word for "*puffed up*" is PHUSIOO. Some of the meanings of this Greek Word are:

"1) to make natural, to cause a thing to pass into nature; 2) to inflate, blow up, to cause to swell up; 2a) to puff up, make proud; 2b) to be puffed up, to bear one's self loftily, be proud."

Some of these genuine Christians at Corinth were puffed up. They looked down their noses at people, so to say. Apparently, they didn't want Paul to come to visit them. Perhaps they thought that Paul didn't want to come to them either.

1 Corinthians 4:19

"But I will come to you shortly, if the Lord will, and will know, not the speech of them which are puffed up, but the power."

Paul said, "*if the Lord will,*" I will come to visit the church at Corinth. When he would arrive, he would come with God's power and deal with those who are "*puffed up.*" Paul wanted to straighten up the terrible conditions that were to be found in that church.

Verses On Power
- **Romans 1:16**

"For I am not ashamed of the gospel of Christ: for it is the power of God unto salvation to every one that believeth; to the Jew first, and also to the Greek."

The Gospel of the Lord Jesus Christ is God's power to bring those who accept it salvation and eternal life.

- **Romans 15:13**

"Now the God of hope fill you with all joy and peace in believing, that ye may abound in hope, through the power of the Holy Ghost."

God the Holy Spirit has all the power of the Godhead. He indwells every genuine Christian and makes His power available to those who allow Him to control them.

- **1 Corinthians 1:18**
"For <u>the preaching of the cross</u> is to them that perish foolishness; but <u>unto us which are saved it is the power of God</u>."

The Biblical and accurate preaching about what took place on the cross of Calvary is God's Divine power at work.

- **1 Corinthians 1:24b**
"<u>Christ the power of God</u>, and the wisdom of God."

The Lord Jesus Christ is God the Son and has all the power of the Godhead.

- **1 Corinthians 2:5**
"That <u>your faith should</u> not <u>stand</u> in the wisdom of men, but <u>in the power of God</u>."

The faith of true Christians must stand in the power of God rather than in their own limited wisdom.

- **2 Corinthians 4:7**
"But we have this treasure in earthen vessels, that <u>the excellency of the power may be of God, and not of us</u>."

God the Holy Spirit indwells all genuine Christians and permits His power to be manifested in their bodies of clay.

- **2 Corinthians 12:9b**
"Most gladly therefore will <u>I rather glory in my infirmities, that the power of Christ may rest upon me</u>."

When Paul had infirmities and weaknesses, God's power was still there to uplift him and give him victories.

- **Ephesians 6:10**
"Finally, my brethren, <u>be strong in the Lord, and in the power of his might</u>."

When Paul was in a Roman prison, he urged the true Christians in Ephesus to be strong in God's mighty power.

1 Corinthians 4:20

"For the kingdom of God *is* not in word, but in power."

This is very true. The power of God is what makes a person become a genuine Christian once they put true faith in the Lord Jesus Christ as their Saviour. This is necessary for every sinner to be born-again by God the Holy Spirit. This is accomplished once genuine faith in the Saviour is exercised.

- **1 Corinthians 6:19-20**

"What? know ye not that your body is the temple of the Holy Ghost *which is* in you, which ye have of God, and ye are not your own? For ye are bought with a price: therefore glorify God in your body, and in your spirit, which are God's."

The indwelling power of the Spirit of God–that's Who should manifest Himself in the true Christians by the things that they do. If God is with them, who can be effectively against them. He's a powerful God. Let Him do the work. Let their prayer and supplication be with thanksgiving. They should pray for these things to happen so that the Lord's power might work through them. As Paul said: *"therefore will I rather glory in my infirmities, that the power of Christ may rest upon me."*

1 Corinthians 4:21

"What will ye? shall I come unto you with a rod, or in love, and *in* the spirit of meekness?"

Paul asked the church at Corinth if he should come to them with three possible attitudes: (1) with a rod; (2) in love; or (3) in the spirit of meekness. He gave them these three choices.

Verses On The Rod

- **Psalms 23:4**

"Yea, though I walk through the valley of the shadow of death, I will fear no evil: for thou *art* with me; thy rod and thy staff they comfort me."

In this shepherd's verse, David said that His rod and staff comforted him. The shepherd's rod had a large crook on it to lift up any of his sheep that had fallen in some hole. The shepherd's rod was what he used to beat off the dangerous wolves that wanted to kill his sheep.

- **Psalms 89:32**

"Then will I visit their transgression with the rod, and their iniquity with stripes."

It is clear in this verse that this rod would punish transgression in terms of judgment.

- **Proverbs 10:13**

"In the lips of him that hath understanding wisdom is found: but a rod *is* for the back of him that is void of understanding."

In many cases, such as in this verse, the only thing a servant without understanding must be handled with is rod of correction.

- **Proverbs 22:15**

"Foolishness *is* bound in the heart of a child; *but* the rod of correction shall drive it far from him."

The Bible is clear that when needed, and only when needed, fathers and mothers must use the rod of correction to teach their children proper behavior and drive away bad behavior. It is sad that, today, corporal discipline of children by their parents is not acceptable, but it is very Scriptural!

- **Proverbs 29:15**

"The rod and reproof give wisdom: but a child left *to himself* bringeth his mother to shame."

The rod is the corporal punishment of the child, in the proper way, as well as spoken reproofs, which make the children learn wisdom. But children, left to themselves without any proper and needed correction, brings shame to their mother.

- **Revelation 2:27**

"And he shall rule them with a rod of iron; as the vessels of a potter shall they be broken to shivers: even as I received of my Father."

During the millennial reign of the Lord Jesus Christ upon this earth, He will bear strong with a rod of iron in order to bring peace.

- **Revelation 12:5**

"And she brought forth a man child, who was to rule all nations with a rod of iron: and her child was caught up unto God, and *to* his throne."

This is a reference to the previous verse, showing that the Lord Jesus Christ will rule all the nations with force as needed.

- **Revelation 19:15**

"And out of his mouth goeth a sharp sword, that with it he should smite the nations: and he shall rule them with a rod of iron: and he treadeth the winepress of the fierceness and wrath of Almighty God."

This is the third time in the book of Revelation that the Lord Jesus Christ is said to rule the nations with a rod of iron. They must obey the King of kings and Lord of lords.

1 Corinthians Chapter Five

1 Corinthians 5:1

"It is reported commonly *that there* is fornication among you, and such fornication as is not so much as named among the Gentiles, that one should have his father's wife."

We're going to deal with the subject of evil. How should evil be handled in a local church? The world doesn't have any standards. The world may be standard-less, without standards, as far as evil is concerned. The Bible has standards. Local churches must have standards as well.

Now this, having his father's wife, is termed fornication, here by the scriptures. Usually that term is referring to sexual relations on the part of unmarried people, but this situation here is a person, a man, having his father's wife, which is by definition, incest today. Now we have incest all over the world. The world is full of it. The world has no standards. It's having ungodly relations, one with another, with a close family tie. I'd like to read from an article, called "Incest, the Family Secret" which gives statistics about incest in the world today. This was in the local church. They didn't deal with it properly. Many local churches today don't deal properly with sin and this is a terrible thing. This is from that article:

> *"Of the known sexual abuse, seventy-five percent is committed by the children's own parents. The victims are usually girls between eight and twelve, with twenty percent under seven. There are also many young boys abused by both men and women. One girl out of four and one boy out of ten will be sexually assaulted at least once by the age of eighteen. And for those trapped in the nightmare of incest, the average period of abuse is seven years. The hurt and long-term effects are understandingly alarming.*

> *In recent studies, seventy percent of the prison inmates and ninety percent of the prostitutes interviewed, had been molested as children."*

This is sexual molestation of children. About a month or two ago, someone called on the telephone and asked: "*Is incest prohibited in scripture?*" I went to the book of Leviticus, chapter eighteen, and there, incest is very clearly prohibited.

- **Leviticus 18:6-18**

"None of you shall approach to any that is near of kin to him, to uncover their nakedness: I am the LORD. The nakedness of thy father, or the nakedness of thy mother, shalt thou not uncover: she is thy mother; thou shalt not uncover her nakedness. The nakedness of thy father's wife shalt thou not uncover: it is thy father's nakedness. The nakedness of thy sister, the daughter of thy father, or daughter of thy mother, whether she be born at home, or born abroad, even their nakedness thou shalt not uncover. The nakedness of thy son's daughter, or of thy daughter's daughter, even their nakedness thou shalt not uncover: for theirs is thine own nakedness. The nakedness of thy father's wife's daughter, begotten of thy father, she is thy sister, thou shalt not uncover her nakedness. Thou shalt not uncover the nakedness of thy father's sister: she is thy father's near kinswoman. Thou shalt not uncover the nakedness of thy mother's sister: for she is thy mother's near kinswoman. Thou shalt not uncover the nakedness of thy father's brother, thou shalt not approach to his wife: she is thine aunt. Thou shalt not uncover the nakedness of thy daughter in law: she is thy son's wife; thou shalt not uncover her nakedness. Thou shalt not uncover the nakedness of thy brother's wife: it is thy brother's nakedness. Thou shalt not uncover the nakedness of a woman and her daughter, neither shalt thou take her son's daughter, or her daughter's daughter, to uncover her nakedness; for they are her near kinswomen: it is wickedness. Neither shalt thou take a wife to her sister, to vex her, to uncover her nakedness, beside the other in her life time."

In other words, to have a marital relationship with close relatives, this is "*incest.*" We have laws today so that marriage between close relatives and amongst close relatives, is prohibited. The Scripture is very clearly against this as well.

In 1 Corinthians 5:1, this sexual relationship between close relatives was going on in the church at Corinth. This was a prohibited
sexual relationship according to the Old Testament Scriptures. As seen in 1 Corinthians 5, it is prohibited in the New Testament as well.

These are prohibitions in God's Word and this was, as it says, commonly reported. Paul had heard of this scandal at the local church at Corinth, commonly, by many people. Many voices had spoken these things in his ears, "fornication among you, and such fornication as is not so much as named among the Gentiles." The Gentiles were not as wicked and filthy in the city of Corinth, even as these that were in the church.

The word *'fornication'* occurs thirty-two times in the Scriptures. Twenty-eight of the times it is found in the New Testament.

THE MEANING OF THE GREEK WORD, "PORNEIA"

The Greek Word for "fornication" is PORNEIA. Some of the meanings of that Greek Word are:

"1) illicit sexual intercourse; 1a) adultery, fornication, homosexuality, lesbianism, intercourse with animals, etc.; 1b) sexual intercourse with close relatives; Lev. 18; 1c) sexual intercourse with a divorced man or woman; Mk. 10:11,12; 2) metaph. the worship of idols; 2a) of the defilement of idolatry, as incurred by eating the sacrifices offered to idols."

Verses On Fornication

- **Acts 15:20b**

". . . that they abstain from pollutions of idols, and *from* fornication, and *from* things strangled, and *from* blood."

These four things were to be abstained from by believers that were Gentiles or Jews, regardless of what it would be. The same is true in Acts 15:29, where it is repeated.

- **Acts 21:25**
  "As touching the Gentiles which believe, we have written and concluded that they observe no such thing, save only that they keep themselves from *things* offered to idols, and from blood, and from strangled, and from fornication."

There should be a separation by true Christians from all these sins mentioned.

- **Romans 1:29**
  "Being filled with all unrighteousness, fornication, wickedness, covetousness, maliciousness; full of envy, murder, debate, deceit, malignity; whisperers,"

These words in this verse in Romans are talking about the many sins of the ancient Gentile world.

As you can see from the definition of the Greek Word for *"fornication,"* this Greek Word, PORNEIA, has many meanings:

> *"1) illicit sexual intercourse; 1a) adultery, fornication, homosexuality, lesbianism, intercourse with animals, etc.; 1b) sexual intercourse with close relatives; Lev. 18; 1c) sexual intercourse with a divorced man or woman; Mk. 10:11,12; 2) metaph. the worship of idols; 2a) of the defilement of idolatry, as incurred by eating the sacrifices offered to idols."*

- **1 Corinthians 6:13c**
  "Now the body *is* not for fornication, but for the Lord; and the Lord for the body."

You might wonder why are we talking about fornication to genuine Christians? Paul preached against it because it was necessary in his day. It is even more important today. Churches need to preach against it because it is being practiced in Christian schools and churches today all too frequently. The Word of God is crystal clear on this subject. Every young man and young woman who are in our local church and who are listening to our services on the Internet must guard against this wicked sin.

- **1 Corinthians 6:18**
  "Flee fornication. Every sin that a man doeth is without the body; but he that committeth fornication sinneth against his own body."

God commands true Christians, and all others, to run away from it speedily. Don't get near the temptation.

- **1 Corinthians 10:8**

"<u>Neither let us commit fornication</u>, as some of them committed, and fell in one day three and twenty thousand." Paul illustrates this great sin from the Old Testament Israelites. Those who committed this sin were slain by the Lord–this included twenty-three thousand people. Can you imagine how many would be slain by the Lord today if he would slay all the fornicators in the world? It would number many millions in the United States of America alone and many, many more millions around the world.

- **2 Corinthians 12:21**

"*And* lest, when I come again, my God will humble me among you, and *that* I shall bewail many which have sinned already, and <u>have not repented of</u> the uncleanness and <u>fornication</u> and lasciviousness which they have committed." Paul is speaking about those in Corinth at the time. These genuine Christians had sinned in this manner yet showed no repentance of any kind for it. This man, who committed fornication and incest with his own father's wife, we read in 2 Corinthians, repented of it and came back to the Lord and to the Corinthian church.

- **Ephesians 5:3**

"<u>But fornication</u>, and all uncleanness, or covetousness, <u>let it not be once named among you, as becometh saints</u>;" This sin shouldn't be found at all in the lives of true Christians or in any other people either.

- **Colossians 3:5**

"<u>Mortify therefore your members</u> which are upon the earth; <u>fornication</u>, uncleanness, inordinate affection, evil concupiscence, and covetousness, which is idolatry:" All these sins listed above, including fornication, should be put to death in the lives of all genuine Christians, especially.

- **1 Thessalonians 4:3**

"For <u>this is the will of God</u>, *even* your sanctification, <u>that ye should abstain from fornication</u>:" God says, he wants true Christians to be set apart, sanctified and holy. God teaches them to abstain from fornication. This abstaining should be practiced by all people, but the non-Christians are not guided by God and His Words. They do what they want to do–including all sorts of sins and iniquities.

- **Jude 1:7**

"Even <u>as Sodom and Gomorrha</u>, and the cities about them in like manner, <u>giving themselves over to fornication, and going after strange flesh, are set forth for an</u> example, suffering the vengeance of eternal fire."

The Old Testament cities of Sodom and Gomorrha had to be destroyed by God because of their fornication and many other sins.

Verses On Lust
- **Ephesians 2:1-3**

"And you *hath he quickened*, who were dead in trespasses and sins; Wherein in time past ye walked according to the course of this world, according to the prince of the power of the air, the spirit that now worketh in the children of disobedience: Among whom also we all had our conversation in times past in the lusts of our flesh, fulfilling the desires of the flesh and of the mind; and were by nature the children of wrath, even as others."

If lusts were practiced by any genuine Christians in the past, let it be kept 100% in the past, but never in the present or future.
- **1 Peter 4:3**

"For the time past of our life may suffice us to have wrought the will of the Gentiles, when we walked in lasciviousness, lusts, excess of wine, revellings, banquetings, and abominable idolatries:"

The Apostle Peter also wrote that these Gentiles, before they became true Christians, practiced lusts as well.

1 Corinthians 5:2

"And ye are puffed up, and have not rather mourned, that he that hath done this deed might be taken away from among you."

Those genuine Christians in the church at Corinth were puffed up and headstrong. They should have mourned and put this incestuous man out of the church membership immediately. The sinning man's sin was wicked, and the church was wicked by putting up with this incest rather than dismissing the sinner.

The church that will not put away such a man who is committing this sin, not mourning for it, but is puffed up and proud of it, might be just as wrong, or more wrong than the sinful person. There are churches all over this country that permit known sin in their membership or attenders. I can think of three cases of this thing among people in Baptist churches.

Three Cases Of Christians' Incest Without Penalty

Case #1 I know of one man who committed the sin of sexual incest with both of his two daughters. He was a member of a Baptist church. Now I know of this first-hand from one of the daughters who was a victim of her father's sexual incest. His church did not do anything to this member. They only said that the sinner should just sit in the back of the church for a while, instead of going to a regular seat. That's all they did.

Case #2 I think of a second incident. There was a man who was an assistant pastor who committed sexual incest with one of his daughters. But there was no judgment against him. This was a fundamental Baptist church. This wasn't some modernistic group. Here they were, in this church, and here was this young pastor, reading Scripture as if nothing was wrong.

Case #3 There was a third example that I know about. It concerned an older gentleman who committed sexual incest with his daughters, but nothing was ever done about it in punishment.

I'm sure these things are happening today, as in the time of 1 Corinthians, and probably, in many instances, nothing whatsoever is done about it. Paul said, in verse two, that the Corinthian church was puffed up and gloating about this thing. They should have mourned about the sin and put the man out of the church.

Verses On Evil
- **Psalms 97:10**

"Ye that love the LORD, hate evil: he preserveth the souls of his saints; he delivereth them out of the hand of the wicked."
Genuine Christians should hate all kinds of evil.

- **Proverbs 8:13**

"The fear of the LORD is to hate evil: pride, and arrogancy, and the evil way, and the froward mouth, do I hate."
The Corinthian church was not hating evil.

- **Amos 5:15**

"Hate the evil, and love the good, and establish judgment in the gate: it may be that the LORD God of hosts will be gracious unto the remnant of Joseph."
God wants us to love that which is good, hate that which is evil.

- **Hebrews 1:8-**9

"But unto the Son he saith, Thy throne, O God, is for ever and ever: a sceptre of righteousness is the sceptre of thy kingdom. Thou hast loved righteousness, and hated iniquity; therefore God, even thy God, hath anointed thee with the oil of gladness above thy fellows."

This is referring to the Lord Jesus Christ. He loved righteousness and hated iniquity. If the Saviour hated evil and iniquity, so should every genuine Christian.

1 Corinthians 5:3

"For I verily, as absent in body, but present in spirit, have judged already, as though I were present, concerning him that hath so done this deed,"

It is interesting that Paul, though absent from them in the body, was with them in spirit. This applies to our many listeners to our church services over SermonAudio.Com.

Paul had already come to a conclusion about the incest that this man had committed against his own father's wife. He concluded that this was sin. The church should recognize this as sin and put the man out of the church until he repented. Paul did not have to be present to render judgment. Some things you can judge from afar.

I think of an instance where a Baptist church had a problem with their assistant pastor. This is a different church than the one I mentioned earlier. There was a woman choir director with whom the assistant pastor had sexual relations. They had a so-called confession service where only the lady fornicator was present and spoke. The assistant pastor didn't even make an appearance. After she spoke, the whole church paraded up there and shook hands with her. That's all the church did with this adulterous activity in their church.

1 Corinthians 5:4

"In the name of our Lord Jesus Christ, when ye are gathered together, and my spirit, with the power of our Lord Jesus Christ,"

Apparently the church was going to gather together to decide on what to do with this incestuous man. They were to meet, and Paul was going to be there in spirit, though not in body. They were gathering with the mighty power of the Lord Jesus Christ Who would help them in their decisions. It was in this local church that their decision about this sinning member should be made.

In the church at Corinth, as in our own Bible For Today Baptist Church in Collingswood, New Jersey, the Lord Jesus Christ and His power should be manifest in all of the services and undertakings. Problems that might come up must be solved properly and without delay.

Paul wanted this trial to be done openly and in a decent manner by the entire church when they were gathered together by the power of the Lord Jesus Christ. Church discipline should not be done by fleshly power, but by God's leading and authority.

Verses On The Church Gathered Together
- **Matthew 18:20**

"For where two or three are gathered together in my name, there am I in the midst of them."

No matter how small the local Bible-believing churches were in Biblical times or in our own times, the Lord Jesus Christ has promised to be there in the midst of them. He is God the Son Who is omnipresent, omniscient, and omnipotent. These three Divine attributes enable Him to be with meetings of Bible-believing churches.

- **Acts 14:27**

"And when they were come, and had gathered the church together, they rehearsed all that God had done with them, and how he had opened the door of faith unto the Gentiles."

This church was gathered together for Paul and his helpers to give them a report of how God opened the door for Gentiles to trust the Lord Jesus Christ and be saved.

- **Acts 20:8**

"And there were many lights in the upper chamber, where they were gathered together."

Paul was at Philippi where he preached a lengthy sermon where the people were gathered together. It was in the next verse where Eutychus was sound asleep, fell down from an upper chamber and died, but Paul raised him up again.

1 Corinthians 5:5

"To deliver such an one unto Satan for the destruction of the flesh, that the spirit may be saved in the day of the Lord Jesus."

Paul's wish was that the Corinthian church should deliver this sinning man *"unto Satan,"* so his flesh would have no power to sin in this or any other manner; his spirit would be the victorious part of his body from then on until the Lord Jesus Christ would return or until the man died. Now this is a very interesting verse—to deliver such a one to Satan? Satan can be a powerful evil influence in a person's life as he was in Job's life and others although Job didn't sin.

Satan can do a lot of damage. He caused a lot of damage to Job. He lost all of his animals. He lost all of his children. He lost all of his servants. He almost lost his wife. He lost the fellowship of his wife. He lost many of his friends.

Verses On Satan

- **1 Timothy 1:20**

"Of whom is Hymenaeus and Alexander; <u>whom I have delivered unto Satan</u>, that they may learn not to blaspheme."

Here's another place where Paul delivered people "*unto Satan.*" Perhaps he wants them to know how evil Satan is so they will not be evil like him. Paul wanted these two men to learn not to blaspheme the Lord, as Satan does, so as not to imitate his evil ways.

- **Acts 5:3**

"But Peter said, Ananias, <u>why hath Satan filled thine heart to lie to the Holy Ghost</u>, and to keep back part of the price of the land?"

Satan filled the heart of Ananias to lie to the Holy Spirit. This is a very serious example of Satan's power, even to a professing Christian.

- **2 Corinthians 12:7-9**

"And lest I should be exalted above measure through the abundance of the revelations, <u>there was given to me a thorn in the flesh, the messenger of Satan to buffet me</u>, lest I should be exalted above measure. For this thing I besought the Lord thrice, that it might depart from me. And he said unto me, My grace is sufficient for thee: for my strength is made perfect in weakness. Most gladly therefore will I rather glory in my infirmities, that the power of Christ may rest upon me."

Satan worked against Paul himself to give him a thorn in the flesh in order to buffet him. Satan has the power to harm and buffet even genuine Christians, like Paul.

- **2 Timothy 2:24-26**

"And the servant of the Lord must not strive; but be gentle unto all men, apt to teach, patient, In meekness instructing those that oppose themselves; if God peradventure will give them repentance to the acknowledging of the truth; And <u>that they may recover themselves out of the snare of the devil, who are taken captive by him at his will</u>."

In these verses, you can see the power of Satan to snare some people and take them captive to his evil ways. This is a serious warning and danger!

- **Revelation 2:10**
"Fear none of those things which thou shalt suffer: behold, the devil shall cast some of you into prison, that ye may be tried; and ye shall have tribulation ten days: be thou faithful unto death, and I will give thee a crown of life."

The Apostle John is speaking to the church at Smyrna, which is one of the seven churches of Asia Minor spoken of in Revelation 2 and 3. They were told that the Devil would cast some of these genuine Christians into prison. They were told to be faithful unto death so that they might receive the crown of life.

Paul was cast into prison as were many true Christians in his days because of their preaching about the Person and Work of the Lord Jesus Christ. In many countries even today, true Christians are imprisoned and even killed.

1 Corinthians 5:6

"Your glorying is not good. Know ye not that a little leaven leaveneth the whole lump?"

There should be no glorying, especially with the man who committed incest. Sin acts like leaven. When you put even a little leaven into bread dough, it will spread that leaven throughout the dough. So if sin is present in the church and it is not dealt with as well. It is like cancer which grows and spreads throughout a person's body.

Verses On Leaven

- **Exodus 12:15**
"Seven days shall ye eat unleavened bread; even the first day ye shall put away leaven out of your houses: for whosoever eateth leavened bread from the first day until the seventh day, that soul shall be cut off from Israel."

That is a very strong verse against leaven. As they were about to leave Egypt, in the Passover feast, God said get rid of leaven. That means God didn't want it. It's evil, it's wrong, and that's clear.

- **Exodus 12:20**
"Ye shall eat nothing leavened; in all your habitations shall ye eat unleavened bread."

God looked on leaven as a poison that Israelites should not eat.

- **Exodus 34:25**
"Thou shalt not offer the blood of my sacrifice with leaven; neither shall the sacrifice of the feast of the Passover be left unto the morning."

No leaven with their blood sacrifices. It's considered poison to the Lord.

- **Matthew 13:33**
"Another parable spake he unto them; The kingdom of heaven is like unto leaven, which a woman took, and hid in three measures of meal, till the whole was leavened."

Once poisonous unbiblical doctrines enter a church's ministry, it permeates the entire church until all is unbiblical.

- **Matthew 16:6**
"Then Jesus said unto them, Take heed and beware of the leaven of the Pharisees and of the Sadducees."

Their leaven was false and unscriptural doctrines which the Lord Jesus Christ warned people about.

- **Matthew 16:11**
"How is it that ye do not understand that I spake it not to you concerning bread, that ye should beware of the leaven of the Pharisees and of the Sadducees?"

The listeners didn't understand what the Lord Jesus Christ was talking about. They thought it was concerning the leaven in bread, but the Lord Jesus Christ meant to beware of the false doctrines and teachings of both the Pharisees and the Sadducees. So we, today, must beware of the false doctrines of many different groups such as the Seventh Day Adventists, the Jehovah Witnesses, Christian Science, and all the other false doctrinal groups and churches.

- **Luke 12:1c**
"Beware ye of the leaven of the Pharisees, which is hypocrisy."

The Lord Jesus Christ warned against the false teachings of the Pharisees.

- **Galatians 5:9**
"A little leaven leaveneth the whole lump."

Does God want our churches to be leavened and poisoned? No. False doctrinal leaven spreads throughout a church once it is tolerated. It is contagious like many diseases. It is contagious like TB, AIDS, and many others.

1 Corinthians 5:7

"Purge out therefore the old leaven, that ye may be a new lump, as ye are unleavened. For even Christ our Passover is sacrificed for us:"

Paul ordered the Corinthian church to purge out the old leaven, meaning that they should remove the incestuous man from their church membership. In doing so, they will be unleavened, that is, not poisoned by this wicked sinner.

They finally got around to the scriptural situation and purged this sinful man out of the membership. He was not permitted to return until he repented. This man was a leaven-poison in their midst. Having done that, that church would be "*unleavened*" once again.

When Paul reminded them that "*Christ our passover is sacrificed for us,*" he reminded them that there was to be no leaven at the original Passover feast. The Lord Jesus Christ is the genuine Christians' Passover who died for their sins and the sins of the entire world. The Passover is mentioned 75 times in the King James Bible. Here are a few of the verses.

Verses On Passover

- **Exodus 12:11**

"And thus shall ye eat it; *with* your loins girded, your shoes on your feet, and your staff in your hand; and ye shall eat it in haste: it *is* the LORD'S Passover."

That's the first usage of the word, "*Passover*" in Scripture. There were specific details to be followed when eating the Lord's Passover.

- **Exodus 34:25**

"Thou shalt not offer the blood of my sacrifice with leaven; neither shall the sacrifice of the feast of the Passover be left unto the morning."

No leaven was to be in the sacrifices of Israel.

- **John 18:39**

"But ye have a custom, that I should release unto you one at the Passover: will ye therefore that I release unto you the King of the Jews?"

The Romans released a man full of leaven poison named Barabbus who had committed murder; the Romans led the Lord Jesus Christ away to be crucified.

The words "*for us*" in 1 Corinthians 5:7 have been omitted from the Gnostic Critical Greek text used in the Westcott and Hort Greek text, the Nestle-Aland Greek text, and the United Bible Society's Greek text. It is omitted in every Bible version that follows the Gnostic false Greek text. This includes the ASV, the NASV, the NIV, the RSV, the ESV, and many, many others.

The key doctrinal Words in this verse are "Christ our Passover is sacrificed **for us**." This teaches a substitutionary sacrifice that the Lord Jesus Christ made for every person who ever lived. In that phrase, "*for us,*" it is important to note that there are two Greek Words used for our English word "for." One is ANTI which means "*instead of us,*" or "*in place of us.*" The Greek Word used in 1 Corinthians 5:7 and in many other places where Christ's substitutionary death for the sins of the world is taught, is the Greek Word HYPER. This Word, in addition to meaning only *"instead of or in place of,"* adds another element of the substitutionary death of the Lord Jesus Christ adds the additional meaning of "f*or the benefit of."*

I was listening to Chuck Swindoll on the radio when he was the President of Dallas Theological Seminary. He quoted 1 Corinthians 5:7 from the NASV which omits "***for us***." Without this prepositional phrase, you don't know the Divine purpose of the sacrifice of the Lord Jesus Christ on the cross.

Verses On "For You" Or "For Us"

Let's take a look at some verses about the substitutionary work of the Lord Jesus Christ Who died "*for us*" meaning for the whole world. This word "***for us***" is very important.

1 Corinthians 11:24

"And when he had given thanks, he brake *it*, and said, Take, eat: this is <u>my body, which is broken for you</u>: this do in remembrance of me."

The Lord's Supper is a picture of the Lord Jesus Christ's body which was broken on the cross, taking on Himself the sins of the world for any who truly trust Him as their Saviour.

- **Romans 5:8**

"But God commendeth his love toward us, in that, while we were yet sinners, <u>Christ died for us</u>."

Again, the Saviour died in the place of and for the benefit of all those in the world.

- **Romans 8:32**

"He that spared not his own Son, but <u>delivered him up for us all</u>, how shall he not with him also freely give us all things?"

God's deliverance from sin is for all those who become genuine Christians by faith in the Saviour.

- **2 Corinthians 5:21**

"For <u>he hath made him *to be* sin for us</u>, who knew no sin; that we might be made the righteousness of God in him."

The Lord Jesus Christ was made sin for every person that they might have eternal life if they truly believed in that Saviour.

- **Galatians 3:13**

"<u>Christ</u> hath redeemed us from the curse of the law, <u>being made a curse for us</u>: for it is written, Cursed *is* every one that hangeth on a tree:"

The Saviour was made a curse for all people so that they wouldn't be cursed if they truly trust Him.

- **Ephesians 5:2**

"And walk in love, as Christ also hath loved us, and <u>hath given himself for us</u> an offering and a sacrifice to God for a sweetsmelling savour."

The Saviour gave Himself on the cross for the whole world to provide eternal life to those who genuinely trust Him as their Saviour.

- **1 Thessalonians 5:10**

"<u>Who died for us</u>, that, whether we wake or sleep, we should live together with him."

He didn't have to die for His own sins because He had no sins. He died for the sins of the world. By sincerely trusting the Saviour, a person's sins have been paid for.

- **Titus 2:14**

"<u>Who gave himself for us</u>, that he might redeem us from all iniquity, and purify unto himself a peculiar people, zealous of good works."

The Lord Jesus Christ gave Himself for every person in the world in order to offer redemption for those who sincerely accept Him as their Saviour.

- **1 Peter 2:21**

"For even hereunto were ye called: because <u>Christ also suffered for us</u>, leaving us an example, that ye should follow his steps:"

Again, the Lord Jesus Christ suffered on Calvary for every one in the world so they could by true faith in Him receive eternal life.

- **1 Peter 4:1**

"Forasmuch then as <u>Christ hath suffered for us in the flesh</u>, arm yourselves likewise with the same mind: for he that hath suffered in the flesh hath ceased from sin;"

The Saviour suffered on the cross for every person in the world in order to enable them to receive everlasting life, provided they exercise genuine faith in Him.

The substitutionary work of the Lord Jesus Christ is very important in Scripture, as you can see through all these verses. For the Gnostic Critical Greek text and all the translations that follow this Greek text and leave out these two words, "**for us**," a serious heresy is committed. It totally destroys the Biblical Gospel of God clearly taught in the Bible.

1 Corinthians 5:8

"Therefore let us keep the feast, not with old leaven, neither with the leaven of malice and wickedness; but with the unleavened bread of sincerity and truth."

God does not want genuine Christians to harbor the poisonous leaven of malice and wickedness such as the Corinthian church was doing with this incestuous man. God wants sound churches to have only unleavened or non-poisonous people who have sincerity and truth.

> **THE MEANING OF THE GREEK WORD, "KAKIA"**
>
> The Greek Word for *"malice"* is KAKIA. Some of the meanings of this Greek Word are: *"1) malignity, malice, ill-will, desire to injure; 2) wickedness, depravity; 2a) wickedness that is not ashamed to break laws; 3) evil, trouble."*

Verses On Malice

- **1 Corinthians 14:20**

"Brethren, be not children in understanding: howbeit <u>in malice be ye children</u>, but in understanding be men."

Be like a little child with malice. Little children don't understand malice nor practice it. Neither should genuine Christians.

- **Ephesians 4:31**

"Let all bitterness, and wrath, and anger, and clamour, and evil speaking, <u>be put away from you, with all malice</u>:"

True Christians should put malice away from them.

- **Colossians 3:8**

"But now ye also <u>put off</u> all these; anger, wrath, <u>malice</u>, blasphemy, filthy communication out of your mouth."

One of the things genuine Christians at Colosse, and Christians today, should put away from themselves, is malice.

- **Titus 3:3**

"For <u>we ourselves also were sometimes</u> foolish, disobedient, deceived, serving divers lusts and pleasures, <u>living in malice</u> and envy, hateful, *and* hating one another."

This was Paul's past life before becoming a true Christian. He was living in malice towards many people, especially real Christians.

- **1 Peter 2:1**
  "Wherefore laying aside all malice, and all guile, and hypocrisies, and envies, and all evil speakings,"

Malice should be laid aside and no longer practiced by genuine Christians.

Verses On Wickedness

- **Mark 7:21-22**
  "For from within, out of the heart of men, proceed evil thoughts, adulteries, fornications, murders, Thefts, covetousness, wickedness, deceit, lasciviousness, an evil eye, blasphemy, pride, foolishness:"

Right from inside the hearts of people comes wickedness. True Christians should know its source and avoid it.

- **Romans 1:29**
  "Being filled with all unrighteousness, fornication, wickedness, covetousness, maliciousness; full of envy, murder, debate, deceit, malignity; whisperers,"

This was the condition of the godless, unsaved Gentile world of old.

- **1 John 5:19**
  "*And* we know that we are of God, and the whole world lieth in wickedness."

God considers the whole unregenerate world to be lying in the state and practice of wickedness.

Verses On Sincerity

- **Joshua 24:14**
  "Now therefore fear the LORD, and serve him in sincerity and in truth: and put away the gods which your fathers served on the other side of the flood, and in Egypt; and serve ye the LORD."

The word, "sincerity" comes from two Latin words, "sin" (without) and "ceras" (wax). When glasses or plates were broken, they repaired them with wax. When you bought a glass or a plate, you wanted them "*without wax*," that is, without any cracks that had to be patched with wax. Sincerity would indicate purity without any falseness or fabrication involved.

- **2 Corinthians 1:12**

"For our rejoicing is this, the testimony of our conscience, that <u>in simplicity and godly sincerity</u>, not with fleshly wisdom, but by the grace of God, we have had our conversation in the world, and more abundantly to you-ward."

The church at Corinth found Paul to have been with them with godly sincerity.

- **2 Corinthians 2:17**

"For we are not as many, which corrupt the word of God: but <u>as of sincerity</u>, but as of God, in the sight of God <u>speak we in Christ</u>."

Paul spoke to the Corinthian church in sincerity. He wasn't as the many who corrupt the Words of God. The Gnostic Critical Greek New Testament texts corrupt God's Words. Dr. Jack Moorman has written two books which show the places where the New Testament Greek Words have been changed in over 8,000 places. In another book, he illustrates 356 doctrinal passages that alter God's truth. Yet these false Gnostic and Critical Greek texts have been the foundation for over 99% of the modern Bible versions such as the ASV, NASV, NIV, RSV, ESV and many, many others in English, as well as in modern foreign languages.

- **Ephesians 6:24**

"Grace *be* with <u>all them that love our Lord Jesus Christ in sincerity</u>. Amen."

Love for the Lord Jesus Christ must be sincere love, not false or deceptive love.

- **Titus 2:6-7**

"<u>Young men</u> likewise exhort to be sober minded. In all things shewing thyself a pattern of good works: <u>in doctrine *shewing*</u> uncorruptness, gravity, <u>sincerity</u>,"

The preacher, Titus, there on the isle of Crete, was to show himself to the young people, as a pattern of doctrinal sincerity.

Verses On Truth

- **Isaiah 59:14-15**

"And judgment is turned away backward, and justice standeth afar off: for <u>truth is fallen in the street</u>, and equity cannot enter. Yea, <u>truth faileth</u>; and he *that* departeth from evil maketh himself a prey: and the LORD saw *it*, and it displeased him that *there was* no judgment."

In Isaiah's day, truth was fallen in the street. Without truth, lies and falseness prevail.

- **Jeremiah 9:3**

"And they bend their tongues *like* their bow *for* lies: but they are not valiant for the truth upon the earth; for they proceed from evil to evil, and they know not me, saith the LORD."

In our country there is an abundance of lies. The so-called main stream media is filled with the lies of fake news. The Bible is filled with truth, but, sad to say, many reject the truth of the Bible and the Saviour. In my preaching and living, I seek to be *"valiant for the truth"* of the Words of God.

- **John 1:14**

"And the Word was made flesh, and dwelt among us, (and we beheld his glory, the glory as of the only begotten of the Father,) full of grace and truth."

The Lord Jesus Christ was full of both grace and truth.

- **John 4:24**

"God *is* a Spirit: and they that worship him must worship *him* in spirit and in truth."

Those who are genuine Christians must worship in truth. We must worship by following the Words of God. We follow the Received Greek text on which the King James Bible is based. The Gnostic Greek text and the Bible versions based upon them are filled with doctrinal, historical errors.

- **John 8:32**

"And ye shall know the truth, and the truth shall make you free."

That's why I urge all of our church attenders both here and on the Internet to read the Bible through each year. This can be done by reading 85 verses each day. I have a tract that gives the daily reading schedule. We also have available my reading from Genesis through Revelation on MP3 disc that you can get; LISTEN to the Bible being read to you at 85 verses per day. After the truth of the Bible is found, there must be a willingness to follow that truth and live by it.

- **John 8:44**

"Ye are of *your* father the devil, and the lusts of your father ye will do. He was a murderer from the beginning, and abode not in the truth, because there is no truth in him. When he speaketh a lie, he speaketh of his own: for he is a liar, and the father of it."

Satan is a liar and there is no truth in him. He told a lie to Eve early in human history and she believed it.

- **John 14:6**
"<u>Jesus saith</u> unto him, <u>I am</u> the way, <u>the truth</u>, and the life: no man cometh unto the Father, but by me."

The *"Truth"* is one of the many titles of the Lord Jesus Christ Who was the Author of every Word of God in both the Old and the New Testaments. True Christians should follow His Words of truth.

- **John 17:17**
"<u>Sanctify them through thy truth: thy word is truth</u>."

The Lord Jesus Christ is praying to God the Father. God's Words are truth. That's why genuine Christians should read and practice God's Words, day by day by day.

- **1 Corinthians 13:6**
"Rejoiceth not in iniquity, but <u>rejoiceth in the truth</u>;"

Even if the truth hurts, we should rejoice in it and conform to it.

Galatians 4:16
"<u>Am I therefore become your enemy, because I tell you the truth</u>?"

Preachers, sometimes, beget many enemies because they tell the truth of the Words of God. Our speech should be in truth, and our worship should be in truth.

- **Ephesians 6:14**
"<u>Stand therefore, having your loins girt about with truth</u>, and having on the breastplate of righteousness;"

Truth and the Words of God must be a part of the bodies of every true Christian.

- **2 Timothy 2:15**
"Study to shew thyself approved unto God, a workman that needeth not to be ashamed, <u>rightly dividing the word of truth</u>."

Genuine Christians must rightly divide God's Words of truth. This is why our church takes a dispensational method of understanding the Bible. Here's a summary of the seven Bible dispensations.

The Seven Dispensations In The Bible

1. <u>**The dispensation of innocence**</u> (Genesis 1:28-30; 2:15-17) The time when Adam and Eve were in the garden of Eden.

2. **The dispensation of conscience** (Genesis 3:6-8:22) It lasted about 1,656 years from Adam and Eve's eviction from the Garden of Eden until the flood of Noah.
3. **The dispensation of human government** (Genesis 8) It lasted about 325 years from after the flood to the tower of Babel.
4. **The dispensation of promise** (Genesis 12:1--Exodus 19:25) It lasted about 430 years from the call of Abraham to Israel's exodus from Egypt.
5. **The dispensation of law** (from Exodus to the death of Christ) It lasted about 1500 years.
6. **The dispensation of grace** (from the death of Christ until He returns in the Rapture into the clouds for all genuine Christians.) It has lasted over 2000 years, and no one knows when it will end.
7. **The dispensation of the millennial Kingdom of Christ.** It will last for 1,000 years from the time of Christ's coming back to earth to set up His Kingdom until the 1,000 years are over.

- **2 Timothy 3:7**

"Ever learning, and <u>never able to come to the knowledge of the truth</u>."

This verse describes some people, including some professors, all apostate ministers, all liberals, and many others. It is very sad when "learning" gets in the way of God's truth found in the Bible.

- **2 Timothy 4:4**

"And <u>they shall turn away *their* ears from the truth</u>, and shall be turned unto fables."

That's the situation that prevails today. It is a very sad thing that this is happening and has happened for many, many years in the past.

1 Corinthians 5:9

"I wrote unto you in an epistle not to company with fornicators:"

It is clear that Paul's and God's orders were that genuine Christians should not keep in close company with fornicators. That applies to all genuine Christians today as well.

Here is the meaning of "fornication" or PORNEIA which was given earlier in this book.

THE MEANING OF THE GREEK WORD, "PORNEIA"

The Greek Word for "fornication" is PORNEIA. Some of the meanings of that Greek Word are:

"1) illicit sexual intercourse; 1a) adultery, fornication, homosexuality, lesbianism, intercourse with animals, etc.; 1b) sexual intercourse with close relatives; Lev. 18;1c) sexual intercourse with a divorced man or woman; Mk. 10:11,12; 2) metaph. the worship of idols; 2a) of the defilement of idolatry, as incurred by eating the sacrifices offered to idols."

Notice the extensive meanings of this word. It is not confined to sexual relations between unmarried people, but has many other important meanings.

Verses On Fornication

- **Galatians 5:19**

"Now <u>the works of the flesh are manifest</u>, which are *these*; Adultery, <u>fornication</u>, uncleanness, lasciviousness,"

Fornication is one of the many works of the flesh. The flesh is present in not only the non-Christians but also in all true Christians. As such, it must be realized and kept in check by all genuine Christians.

- **Ephesians 5:3**

"But <u>fornication</u>, and all uncleanness, or covetousness, <u>let it not be once named among you, as becometh saints</u>;"

This was a horrendous thing to have, right in the first-century in Corinth, and Paul dealt with it here.

- **1 Thessalonians 4:3**

"For <u>this is the will of God</u>, *even* your sanctification, <u>that ye should abstain from fornication</u>:"

This sin is rampant in the United States and all over the world, both on the part of non-Christians and, sad to say, on the part of many genuine Christians, young and old, in our own country. It is indeed a sexual plague seen all around us in every direction.

1 Corinthians 5:10

"**Yet not altogether with the fornicators of this world, or with the covetous, or extortioners, or with idolaters; for then must ye needs go out of the world.**"

It is not possible for true Christians to separate from all people in this non-Christian world who are fornicators, covetous, extortioners, or idolaters. That would be impossible. For this to happen, genuine Christians would have to leave this world. They have contact with postmen, doctors, dentists, store owners, policemen, school teachers, and many other people who make no profession of being true Christians. But this verse tells genuine Christians what to do while living in this world.

1 Corinthians 5:11

"**But now I have written unto you not to keep company, if any man that is called a brother be a fornicator, or covetous, or an idolater, or a railer, or a drunkard, or an extortioner; with such an one no not to eat.**"

Paul and God are calling for separation from the company of any genuine Christian who is either a fornicator, covetous, an idolater, a railer, a drunkard, an extortioner, or other similar sins. In fact, they are not even to eat with them. They should not even go to Wendy's with them. It is a part of what we call secondary separation.

Verses On Primary And Secondary Biblical Separation

- 2 Corinthians 6:14

"Be ye not unequally yoked together with unbelievers: for what fellowship hath righteousness with unrighteousness? and what communion hath light with darkness?"

This verse speaks of primary separation from unbelievers, unrighteousness, and darkness. This would apply to genuine Christians who should not have fellowship with such groups as the National and World Councils of Churches or any religious modernists, liberals, or apostates. There must be a Biblical separation from all such groups and individuals.

- 2 Thessalonians 3:14

"And if any man obey not our word by this epistle, note that man, and <u>have no company with him</u>, that he may be ashamed."

True Christians who walk with the Lord should separate from genuine Christians who are disobedient to Biblical teachings.

Some Biblical churches may not want to follow this teaching because they might lose some of their church members, but that reason, or any other reason, should never be an excuse for disobeying the Words of God.

- **Galatians 6:1**

"Brethren, <u>if a man be overtaken in a fault</u>, ye which are spiritual, restore such an one in the spirit of meekness; considering thyself, lest thou also be tempted."

Those true Christians who are walking in the power of the Holy Spirit of God should seek to restore any genuine Christian who has been overtaken in a fault, of whatever kind it might be. In that way, that being dismissed.

Until there is restoration of such a sinning true Christian, there should be a dismissal from the church until such restoration can be effected, lest his fault might work like leaven and permeate the church.

1 Corinthians 5:12

"For what have I to do to judge them also that are without? do not ye judge them that are within?"

So, Paul says, I don't judge them that are without, those that are outside of Christ. Do you not judge them that are within the church? That's what you should do. God's going to judge those that are outside of Christ. That's not up to the church to do that but those that are within. There's got to be a meeting of the minds. There's got to be a judgment, and if someone is inside of a local church, it's better for that church to get rid of that sin until the sinner repents, so as not to become like poison leaven to adversely influence the local church. This is what was done by the church at Corinth. After this man's restoration, he was brought back into the membership.

1 Corinthians 5:13

"But them that are without God judgeth.

Therefore put away from among yourselves that wicked person."

Those who are not genuine Christians, God will judge at the Great White Throne Judgment seat. The Corinthian church was told by Paul and the Lord Jesus Christ Who wrote this book that they must put away from among themselves this wicked person until he was restored. Then, and only then, should he be returned to the church membership. This is exactly what happened at the church in Corinth.

Verses On Putting Way
- **Genesis 35:2**

"Then Jacob said unto his household, and to all that *were* with him, Put away the strange gods that *are* among you, and be clean, and change your garments:"

In this verse, the putting away referred to the strange gods that they were worshipping. Jacob told his household to get rid of all their strange gods and idols.

- **Deuteronomy 22:24**

"Then ye shall bring them both out unto the gate of that city, and ye shall stone them with stones that they die; the damsel, because she cried not, *being* in the city; and the man, because he hath humbled his neighbour's wife: so thou shalt put away evil from among you."

The Israelites obeyed God's Words and put away by stoning both the man and the woman who had committed the sin of fornication and adultery.

- **Joshua 24:14**

"Now therefore fear the LORD, and serve him in sincerity and in truth: and put away the gods which your fathers served on the other side of the flood, and in Egypt; and serve ye the LORD."

In this case, Joshua told these idolaters to put away and get rid of these gods that their fathers had served.

- **1 Samuel 7:3**

"And Samuel spake unto all the house of Israel, saying, If ye do return unto the LORD with all your hearts, *then* put away the strange gods and Ashtaroth from among you, and prepare your hearts unto the LORD, and serve him only: and he will deliver you out of the hand of the Philistines."

Samuel was saying that if they really wanted to serve the Lord with all their hearts, they should then put away these strange gods and Ashtaroth from among them. Just throw them away!

- **Judges 10:16**
"And they put away the strange gods from among them, and served the LORD: and his soul was grieved for the misery of Israel."

The people in the days of the judges were faithful to God's commands and put away their strange gods.

- **Isaiah 1:16**
"Wash you, make you clean; put away the evil of your doings from before mine eyes; cease to do evil;"

The prophet Isaiah spoke clearly about the people around him to put away the evil that they were committing and cease doing it.

- **Ephesians 4:31**
"Let all bitterness, and wrath, and anger, and clamour, and evil speaking, be put away from you, with all malice:"

This entire verse from Paul to the church at Ephesus dealt with a command to put away from all six of these sins mentioned in this verse. In fact, they are commanded not even to eat with such a one. Eating with such a sinful genuine Christian might convey that you put your approval on this person. Therefore, put them away.

1 Corinthians Chapter Six

1 Corinthians 6:1

"Dare any of you, having a matter against another, go to law before the unjust, and not before the saints?" This verse has to do with Corinthian genuine Christians, going to law, with one another before the unjust, wicked, and non-Christian Corinthian judges. I believe this chapter is for the local churches, including the churches at Corinth, Ephesus, Colosse, and other churches then and now. If any true Christian has a matter against another in the local church, they should let their local church handle it.

That's why, in chapter five, Paul wrote that the local church should take care of such matters and ask the incestuous man not to return to the church until he changes his ways. This is a good example of the local church dealing with their own matters of judgment.

Verses On Unjust

- **Matthew 5:45**

"That ye may be the children of your Father which is in heaven: for he maketh his sun to rise on the evil and on the good, and <u>sendeth rain on the just and on the unjust</u>."

God sends His rain on both the just and unjust. He provides for both groups.

- **Acts 24:15**

"And have hope toward God, which they themselves also allow, that <u>there shall be a resurrection of the dead, both of the just and unjust</u>."

Both the just and the unjust will face resurrections, but their destinies are far different–a good destiny for those who are saved, but a very bad destiny for the unsaved people.

- **1 Peter 3:18**
"For Christ also hath once suffered for sins, the just for the unjust, that he might bring us to God, being put to death in the flesh, but quickened by the Spirit:"

The Lord Jesus Christ suffered as the Just and sinless One to pay for the sins of all the unjust people in the world.

- **2 Peter 2:9**
"The Lord knoweth how to deliver the godly out of temptations, and to reserve the unjust unto the day of judgment to be punished:"

God is going to punish the unjust. When matters deal with members in local churches, those churches should be in charge of choosing correct consequences.

1 Corinthians 6:2

"Do ye not know that the saints shall judge the world? and if the world shall be judged by you, are ye unworthy to judge the smallest matters?"

The genuine Christians are saints. They will be with the Lord Jesus Christ when He judges the world at the Great White Throne Judgment. If they will be with the Saviour when He judges both the saved and the lost, can't they fairly judge the smallest matters that come before them when they are on earth?

Verses On Judging

- **Revelation 19:11-12**
"And I saw heaven opened, and behold a white horse; and he that sat upon him *was* called Faithful and True, and in righteousness he doth judge and make war. His eyes *were* as a flame of fire, and on his head *were* many crowns; and he had a name written, that no man knew, but he himself."

The Lord Jesus Christ will judge people in righteousness.

- **Revelation 19:14**
"And the armies *which were* in heaven followed him upon white horses, clothed in fine linen, white and clean."

The armies that followed the Lord Jesus Christ are the true Christians who will be with Him when He judges, both at the judgment of the lost, and at the judgment of the genuine Christians.

1 Corinthians 6:3

"Know ye not that we shall judge angels? how much more things that pertain to this life?"

The genuine Christians will be with the Lord Jesus Christ when He judges the fallen angels. Since this is so, why should they not judge things that occur in their local churches?

Verses On Angels
- **Genesis 6:1-2**

"And it came to pass, when men began to multiply on the face of the earth, and daughters were born unto them, That the sons of God saw the daughters of men that they *were* fair; and they took them wives of all which they chose."

From the verses in Job (Job 1:6; 2:1; and 38:7), the sons of God appear to be angels that were in the presence of the Lord in Heaven. These "*sons of God*" in this verse were apparently fallen angels who had sinned against the Lord. In these verses in Genesis 6, these "*sons of God,*" I believe, were fallen angels who wickedly cohabited with the women on this earth.

- **Genesis 6:4-5**

"There were giants in the earth in those days; and also after that, when the sons of God came in unto the daughters of men, and they bare *children* to them, the same *became* mighty men which *were* of old, men of renown. And GOD saw that the wickedness of man *was* great in the earth, and *that* every imagination of the thoughts of his heart *was* only evil continually."

The result of this angel cohabitation with the daughters of men were giants, or NEPHALIM ("*fallen ones.*") The children that were born were a mixture of angels and human beings. Because of the creation of these monsters, God had to destroy all the people on the earth except eight. Noah, his three sons, and their wives went into the ark that Noah had built and were spared the death that fell upon every creature then living on the earth.

- **Matthew 25:41**

"Then shall he say also unto them on the left hand, Depart from me, ye cursed, into everlasting fire, prepared for the devil and his angels:"

Hell was prepared for the devil and his angels. It was not primarily built for those who reject the Lord Jesus Christ as their

Saviour, but they will go to this prepared Devil's place for all eternity.

- **Romans 8:38-39**
"For I am persuaded, that <u>neither</u> death, nor life, nor <u>angels</u>, nor principalities, nor powers, nor things present, nor things to come, Nor height, nor depth, nor any other creature, <u>shall be able to separate us from the love of God, which is in Christ Jesus our Lord</u>."

None of the above things, including angels, can separate true Christians from the love of God which is in the Lord Jesus Christ.

- **1 Corinthians 11:10**
"For this cause <u>ought the woman to have power on *her* head because of the angels</u>."

The women should have long hair and be in obedience to their own husbands lest the angels try to repeat what happened in Genesis 6. The women that we see in chapter eleven verses 14 & 15 should have longer hair than the men. The men should not have long hair.

- **Colossians 2:18**
"Let no man beguile you of your reward in a voluntary humility and <u>worshipping of angels</u>, intruding into those things which he hath not seen, vainly puffed up by his fleshly mind,"

There should be no worship of angels.

- **2 Peter 2:4**
"For <u>if God spared not the angels that sinned</u>, but cast *them* down to hell, and delivered *them* into chains of darkness, to be reserved unto judgment;"

I believe this verse refers to the angels that sinned mentioned in Genesis chapter 6.

- **Jude 1:6**
"And <u>the angels which kept not their first estate</u>, but left their own habitation, he hath reserved in everlasting chains under darkness unto the judgment of the great day."

These fallen angels are reserved in everlasting chains. It might refer again to their sin in Genesis, chapter 6.

- **Revelation 12:7**
"And there was war in heaven: <u>Michael and his angels fought against the dragon</u>; and <u>the dragon fought and his angels</u>,"

1 Corinthians 6:4

"If then ye have judgments of things pertaining to this life, set them to judge who are least esteemed in the church."

Genuine Christians in the local church, though they might not be highly qualified in various ways. , should be able to deal properly with conflicts in the local church. They should not have to take these matters before the heathen courts and judges.

Verses On High And Low Estimation
- **1 Samuel 18:23**

"And Saul's servants spake those words in the ears of David. And David said, Seemeth it to you *a* light *thing* to be a king's son in law, seeing that I am a poor man, and lightly esteemed?"

David said that, in his humble opinion, he was a poor man and lightly esteemed.

- **Luke 16:15**

"And he said unto them, Ye are they which justify yourselves before men; but God knoweth your hearts: for that which is highly esteemed among men is abomination in the sight of God."

Many things might be highly esteemed by men, but, at the same time, be an abomination in the sight of God.

1 Corinthians 6:5

"I speak to your shame. Is it so, that there is not a wise man among you? no, not one that shall be able to judge between his brethren?"

Paul is shaming the church at Corinth. He can't understand why they don't have any genuine Christian men who are wise enough to judge correctly between two true Christians in their membership. They were wrong in going to the heathen courts in this case. It is the Lord Jesus Christ who is made unto these Christians "*wisdom*." He can give to this church the wisdom to judge righteously.

1 Corinthians 6:6

"But brother goeth to law with brother, and that before the unbelievers."

Paul explains the situation exactly. Genuine Christians are going to law against each other before unbelievers. This is not to be done in regard to issues that concern two true Christians who are members of the same local church. It should be handled by the church itself, unlike what the Corinthian church had done with the incestuous man.

There is a problem, however, if these two genuine Christians live in different towns and are not in the same local church. They could not handle any problem that they might have in this same manner because they might be separated, perhaps by many miles, or even in a foreign country. That is an entirely different problem that should be handled in an entirely different manner and discussed clearly between the two parties.

1 Corinthians 6:7

"Now therefore there is utterly a fault among you, because ye go to law one with another. Why do ye not rather take wrong? why do ye not rather *suffer yourselves to* be defrauded?"

Again, Paul berates the church at Corinth, saying there is utterly a fault among them. The solution, if the situation cannot be handled properly in their local church, is to take the wrong that one genuine Christian did to the other one and be defrauded.

Though this course of action is often very hard to take, that is what God, in His Word, expressly suggests to a true Christian who is facing the loss of a large sum of money, or of some valuable possession. But the answer is, in some cases, just "*take wrong.*"

1 Corinthians 6:8

"Nay, ye do wrong, and defraud, and that *your* brethren."

The genuine Christian who is defrauding and stealing from his fellow Christian, in this situation, is doing wrong. He or she is to be condemned in this action, whatever the sum of money or worth of the property.

Some people do defraud. As an illustration, I remember my father-in-law loaned a preacher $350.00. The preacher said he would pay him back. Later this preacher told my father-in-law that he was really hard up, so he never paid him back. My father-in-law took the wrong and lost all the loan money. This preacher never, never, never gave that money back. This preacher left this church and went to another. You might think that, when he saved up some money, he would have returned the loan. But this never happened. The man never wrote or spoke to the one who loaned him money. **1 Corinthians 6:9**

"Know ye not that the unrighteous shall not inherit the kingdom of God? Be not deceived: neither fornicators, nor idolaters, nor adulterers, nor effeminate, nor abusers of themselves with mankind,"

Paul lists five groups of people who are unrighteous. All five of these who continue in this wickedness will not be allowed in the kingdom of God and salvation. Here are the five sinful actions that the unrighteous continue to live in:

1. **Fornicators**
2. **Idolaters**
3. **Adulterers**
4. **Effeminate**
5. **Abusers of themselves with mankind**

None of the people who live in these sins will enter into the kingdom of God or Heaven. Though most of us are familiar with the meaning of the first three of these sins (fornicators, idolaters, and adulterers), but let's look at the last two sins (effeminate, and abusers of themselves with mankind).

THE MEANING OF THE GREEK WORD, "MALAKOS"

The Greek Word for *"effeminate"* MALAKOS means:
"1) soft, soft to the touch; 2) metaph. in a bad sense; 2a) effeminate; 2a1) of a catamite; 2a2) of a boy kept for homosexual relations with a man; 2a3) of a male who submits his body to unnatural lewdness; 2a4) of a male prostitute."

MEANING OF THE GREEK WORD, "ARSENOKOITES"

> The Greek Word for *"abusers of themselves with mankind"* is ARSENOKOITES. Some of the meanings of this Greek Word are:
> *"1) one who lies with a male as with a female, sodomite, homosexual."*

Part of verse nine warns the Corinthian church to *"Be not deceived:"* Since it is the Greek present tense prohibition, it means to *"stop being deceived."* Apparently some true Christians in this church were being deceived in some ways by those who were committing any of these five sins.

1 Corinthians 6:10

"Nor thieves, nor covetous, nor drunkards, nor revilers, nor extortioners, shall inherit the kingdom of God."

Here are five more sins listed which, if continually practiced as a way of life, would indicate that those who practice them are lost and are not a part of the kingdom of God and do not have genuine salivation.

6. Thieves
7. Covetous
8. Drunkards
9. Revilers
10. Extortioners

Each one of these additional five sins is familiar to most people in our world today. God is against them all and so should genuine Christians be against them and never practice them.

1 Corinthians 6:11

"And such were some of you: but ye are washed, but ye are sanctified, but ye are justified in the name of the Lord Jesus, and by the Spirit of our God."

Notice the word, *"such."* This includes all of these ten sins mentioned in the preceding verses. The beautiful part about this verse is when Paul says that *"such **WERE** some of you."* The Greek Word for "were" is in the Greek imperfect tense. It means these people were continually living in these ten sins.

These sins were in their past, but now they have been washed by true faith in the Lord Jesus Christ through His blood offering on Calvary, sanctified in His Name, and by God the Holy Spirit. The lives of these genuine Christians had been **CHANGED** by the power of God!

Verses On Wash

- **Titus 3:5**

"Not by works of righteousness which we have done, but according to his mercy he saved us, by the washing of regeneration, and renewing of the Holy Ghost;"

Regeneration and new-birth by genuine faith in the Lord Jesus Christ results in a washing and a cleansing by the Saviour.

- **Revelation 1:5**

"And from Jesus Christ, *who is* the faithful witness, *and* the first begotten of the dead, and the prince of the kings of the earth. Unto him that loved us, and washed us from our sins in his own blood,"

Though John MacArthur wrongly interprets "*blood*" to mean only "*death,*" it is His blood that washes the genuine Christians from their sins once they accept Him as their Saviour by true faith.

- **Revelation 7:14**

"And I said unto him, Sir, thou knowest. And he said to me, These are they which came out of great tribulation, and have washed their robes, and made them white in the blood of the Lamb."

It is the blood of the Lamb of God that washes the genuine Christians.

Verses On Sanctification

- **John 17:17**

"Sanctify them through thy truth: thy word is truth."

The Words of God are the truth that can sanctify and set apart the true Christians. This is why I urge ever genuine Christian to read their Bibles from Genesis through Revelation every year. This can be done by reading 85 verses each day of the year. I have a YEARLY BIBLE READING SCHEDULE that shows how this can be done and also two MP3's in which (1) I read the Bible day by day and (2) I make brief comments on the 85 verses each day.

- **Acts 26:18**

"To open their eyes, *and* to turn *them* from darkness to light, and *from* the power of Satan unto God, that they may receive forgiveness of sins, and inheritance among them which are sanctified by faith that is in me."

Biblical sanctification is in three tenses for every genuine Christian:
1. **Past sanctification from the penalty of sin**
2. **Present sanctification from the power of sin**
3. **Future sanctification from the presence of sin**
- **1 Corinthians 1:30**

"But of him are ye in Christ Jesus, who of God is made unto us wisdom, and righteousness, and sanctification, and redemption:"

Every true Christian who is in Christ has been given positional sanctification before God.
- **Ephesians 5:26**

"That he might sanctify and cleanse it with the washing of water by the word,"

The Word of God sanctifies and cleanses genuine Christians who read God's Words and obey these Words each day.
- **1 Thessalonians 5:23**

"And the very God of peace sanctify you wholly; and *I pray God* your whole spirit and soul and body be preserved blameless unto the coming of our Lord Jesus Christ."

God wants all true Christians to be sanctified in their spirits, souls, and bodies.
- **Hebrews 10:10**

"By the which will we are sanctified through the offering of the body of Jesus Christ once *for all*."

The offering on Calvary's cross by the Lord Jesus Christ positionally sanctifies and sets apart all genuine Christians.

Verses On Justification
- **Acts 13:39**

"And by him all that believe are justified from all things, from which ye could not be justified by the law of Moses."

True Christians are declared to be justified from all things when they genuinely trust the Lord Jesus Christ as their Saviour.
- **Romans 3:24**

"Being justified freely by his grace through the redemption that is in Christ Jesus:"

Justification is free to those who have been redeemed by trusting

the Lord Jesus Christ as their Saviour.
- **Romans 5:1**
"Therefore <u>being justified by faith, we have peace with God through our Lord Jesus Christ</u>:"

Genuine faith in the Lord Jesus Christ as Saviour brings positional justification and peace with God.

1 Corinthians 6:12

"All things are lawful unto me, but all things are not expedient: all things are lawful for me, but I will not be brought under the power of any."

Paul is writing to genuine Christians. Though things might be lawful, they are not always expedient and a don't provide a good testimony for the Lord Jesus Christ.

Verses On Expedient
- **John 11:50**
"Nor consider that <u>it is expedient for us</u>, that one man should die for the people, and that the whole nation perish not."

It was expedient for the Jewish leaders that the Lord Jesus Christ should die rather than many in the Jewish nation perish.

- **John 16:7**
"Nevertheless I tell you the truth; <u>It is expedient for you that I go away: for if I go not away</u>, the Comforter will not come unto you; but if I depart, I will send him unto you."

It was expedient that the Lord Jesus Christ go to Heaven so He could send the true Christians God the Holy Spirit.

- **John 18:14**
"Now Caiaphas was he, which gave counsel to the Jews, that <u>it was expedient that one man should die for the people</u>."

Caiaphas believed it was expedient that one Man should die in the Jews' place.

- **1 Corinthians 10:23**
"All things are lawful for me, but <u>all things are not expedient</u>: all things are lawful for me, but all things edify not."

Paul agreed that all things were not expedient.

In this verse twelve, Paul did not want to be brought under the power or enslaved by anything. Some things that enslave people by their power are such things as: (1) nicotine, such as in tobacco from cigarettes or cigars; (2) caffeine, such as in coffee and tea; (3) alcohol; drugs of all kinds; (4) sexual enslavement that leads to adultery, fornication, male homosexuality, lesbianism, and many other empowering substances and even mental thoughts.

> **THE MEANING OF THE GREEK WORD, "EXOUSIAZO"**
>
> The Greek Word for *"power"* here is EXOUSIAZO. Some of the meanings of that Greek Word are:
>
> *"1) to have power or authority, use power; 1a) to be master of any one, exercise authority over one; 1b) to be master of the body; 1b1) to have full and entire authority over the body; 1b2) to hold the body subject to one's will; 1c) to be brought under the power of anyone."*

1 Corinthians 6:13

"Meats for the belly, and the belly for meats: but God shall destroy both it and them. Now the body is not for fornication, but for the Lord; and the Lord for the body."

Both food and the stomachs where food is sent will pass away. They are not permanent. Neither of these are eternal. The Lord Jesus Christ said it in Matthew 4:4 and in other verses as well.

- **Matthew 4:4**

"But he answered and said, It is written, <u>Man shall not live by bread alone</u>, but by every word that proceedeth out of the mouth of God."

Paul continues by saying that the bodies of genuine Christians are not for fornication but for the Lord, and the Lord is for their bodies. Once people become true Christians, their bodies are to be used for their Saviour, the Lord Jesus Christ. The sins of the old life must be forsaken and removed in order to glorify the Lord Jesus Christ.

Verses On Fornication
- **1 Corinthians 10:8**

"<u>Neither let us commit fornication, as some of them committed</u>, and fell in one day three and twenty thousand."

God judged the Israelites for this sin of fornication, slaying

23,000 of Israel.
- **Ephesians 5:3**
"But <u>fornication</u>, and all uncleanness, or covetousness, <u>let it not be once named among you</u>, as becometh saints;"

This is a sin that was prevalent at Corinth, and it is a sin that is prevalent today. Our young people are committing fornication in high schools, grade schools, colleges and graduate schools.
- **1 Thessalonians 4:3**
"For this is the will of God, even your sanctification, that <u>ye should abstain from fornication</u>:"

Genuine Christians should abstain from the sin of fornication.
- **Jude 1:7**
"Even as <u>Sodom and Gomorrha</u>, and the cities about them in like manner, <u>giving themselves over to fornication</u>, and going after strange flesh, are set forth for an example, suffering the vengeance of eternal fire."

God punished Sodom and Gomorrha for fornication and homosexuality as well.

Verses On Body
- **Daniel 3:28**
"Then Nebuchadnezzar spake, and said, Blessed be the God of Shadrach, Meshach, and Abednego, who hath sent his angel, and delivered his servants that trusted in him, and have changed the king's word, and <u>yielded their bodies, that they might not serve nor worship any god, except their own God</u>."

Shadrach, Meshach, and Abednego did not want to yield their bodies to the false deities and images, but to the Lord alone.
- **Romans 6:12**
"<u>Let not sin therefore reign in your mortal body</u>, that ye should obey it in the lusts thereof."

The sin nature should not rule in the bodies of true Christians.
- **Romans 8:13**
"For if ye live after the flesh, ye shall die: but if ye through the Spirit do <u>mortify the deeds of the body</u>, ye shall live."

Genuine Christians should reject the sins of their flesh.
- **1 Corinthians 6:19**
"What? know ye not that <u>your body is the temple of the Holy Ghost which is in you, which ye have of God</u>, and ye are not your own?"

The bodies of all true Christians are not their own, but they must be used for the Lord Jesus Christ and His ministries.

- **1 Corinthians 9:27**

"But <u>I keep under my body, and bring it into subjection</u>: lest that by any means, when I have preached to others, I myself should be a castaway."

Paul controlled his body lest he should be laid on the shelf by the Lord Jesus Christ and unable to serve Him. This happens to some pastors, deacons, and church officials all too often.

- **2 Corinthians 5:10**

"For we must all appear before the judgment seat of Christ; that every one may <u>receive the things done in his body</u>, according to that he hath done, whether it be good or bad."

At the judgment seat of Christ, all genuine Christians will have to answer for the things done in their bodies, whether good or bad.

- **Philippians 1:20c**

". . . so now also <u>Christ shall be magnified in my body</u>, whether it be by life, or by death."

It's by the bodies of all true Christians that the Lord Jesus Christ should be magnified.

- **1 Thessalonians 5:23**

"And the very God of peace sanctify you wholly; and <u>I pray God your whole spirit and soul and body be preserved blameless</u> unto the coming of our Lord Jesus Christ."

God wants the bodies of all genuine Christians to be pure and clean, blameless until the Lord Jesus Christ returns in the Rapture to take them Home to Heaven in glorified bodies.

1 Corinthians 6:14

"And God hath both raised up the Lord, and will also raise up us by his own power."

True Christians will be raised bodily just as the Lord Jesus Christ was raised bodily from death.

Verses On The Bodily Resurrection
Of All Genuine Christians

- **John 6:39-40**

"And this is the Father's will which hath sent me, that of all which he hath given me I should lose nothing, but should raise it up again at the last day. And this is the will of him that sent me, that <u>every one which seeth the Son, and believeth on him, may have everlasting life: and I will raise him up at the last day</u>."

The Lord Jesus Christ promised the bodily resurrection of all true Christians. Bodily resurrection is a Christian doctrine.

- **John 6:44**

"No man can come to me, except the Father which hath sent me draw him: and I will raise him up at the last day."
All those who are drawn to the Lord Jesus Christ and regenerated by Him will be raised again bodily.
- **2 Corinthians 4:14**
"Knowing that he which raised up the Lord Jesus shall raise up us also by Jesus, and shall present us with you."

In the Gnostic, Critical Greek translations such as the NASV, the NIV, the RSV, and many others, there is a doctrinal heresy taught. They have "*raised up **WITH** Jesus*" rather than "***BY***" Jesus. The word, "*with*" Jesus would imply they would be raised up at the same time the Lord Jesus Christ was raised up. If so, Jesus would still be in the grave and never was raised yet. The Gnostics, whose false Greek text these (and most of the other) versions use, did not believe the Lord Jesus Christ could raise up anyone; they believe He was just a sinful human being with no power to raise up anyone.

1 Corinthians 6:15

"Know ye not that your bodies are the members of Christ? shall I then take the members of Christ, and make them the members of an harlot? God forbid."

The bodies of all genuine Christians are defined by God's Words as being the members of Christ. Every true Christian is also a member one with another. Bodies have members. If genuine Christians are members of Christ, they are members of the Body of Christ. This includes every true Christian who has lived from the day of Pentecost until the Rapture.

Some Baptist churches, and others, do not hold to this Biblical doctrine. One of the sources of this false doctrine is the Maranatha Baptist Seminary in Watertown, Wisconsin. The teachers, former and present, and many of their graduates, believe that only their own kind of local Baptist churches are the "*body of Christ.*" Every other kind of Baptist churches and all the other denominations, even if they are genuine Christians, are only in the "*family of God*" but not in "*the body of Christ.*" One of the most vocal leaders in this heretical view of the "*body of Christ*" is Dr. Thomas Strouse, who is the pastor of a Baptist church in Connecticut. Though Dr. Strouse, a former professor at Maranatha Baptist College, is in agreement with many of the doctrines we hold to, for which I am glad, I believe strongly that he is wrong in this area.

We should not take any true Christians who are in the "*body of Christ"* and make them members of a prostitute. All such fornication and adultery is a grievous sin in the eyes of God.

1 Corinthians 6:16

"What? know ye not that he which is joined to an harlot is one body? for two, saith he, shall be one flesh."

The sinful joining of a man with a harlot makes them one body. This must be avoided. It makes them one body, just as properly joining a man and a woman into a marital union makes them one flesh. That union is Biblical, the other is forbidden.

Verses On Married Love
- **Hebrews 13:4**

"Marriage is honourable in all, and the bed undefiled: but whoremongers and adulterers God will judge."
Marriage and married love is honorable in all, but whoremongers and adulterers will be judged by God.

- **Genesis 2:24**

"Therefore shall a man leave his father and his mother, and shall cleave unto his wife: and they shall be one flesh."
The sexual union on the part of a husband and his wife makes them one flesh in the eyes of God.

- **Matthew 19:5-6**

"And said, For this cause shall a man leave father and mother, and shall cleave to his wife: and they twain shall be one flesh? Wherefore they are no more twain, but one flesh. What therefore God hath joined together, let not man put asunder."
This is the marriage union that is God's standard. It should be permanent, though sadly, many couples dissolve their marriages in disobedience to this command.

- **Ephesians 5:31**

"For this cause shall a man leave his father and mother, and shall be joined unto his wife, and they two shall be one flesh."
God considers the marriage union of a man and a woman to be joined in one flesh. Notice the various Greek meanings of *"joined."* It indicates a permanence in marriage.

THE MEANING OF THE GREEK WORD, "KOLLAO"

> The Greek Word for *"joined"* is KOLLAO. Some of the meanings of that Greek Word are:
>
> *"1) to glue, to glue together, cement, fasten together; 2) to join or fasten firmly together; 3) to join one's self to, cleave to."*

1 Corinthians 6:17

"But he that is joined unto the Lord is one spirit."

The word for "joined" is the same Greek Word, KOLLAO, which is defined above. All genuine Christians are one spirit united with the Lord Jesus Christ for all eternity. Though they may sin and lose their fellowship with the Lord, it is impossible for them to lose their salvation. On eternal security, we differ with such groups as the Methodists, holiness groups, and many others who believe true Christians are able to lose their salvation and be un-joined with their Saviour. No, true Christians are joined, permanently glued, and fastened together unto the Lord Jesus Christ in one Spirit.

1 Corinthians 6:18

"Flee fornication. Every sin that a man doeth is without the body; but he that committeth fornication sinneth against his own body."

This is a very clear command for genuine Christians to flee from the sin of fornication. The Greek Word for *"flee"* is in the Greek present tense which means continually and always flee from this sin and wickedness.

> **THE MEANING OF THE GREEK WORD, "PHEUGO"**
>
> The Greek Word for *"flee"* is "PHEUGO." Some of the meanings of this Greek Word are:
>
> *"1) to flee away, seek safety by flight; 2) metaph. to flee (to shun or avoid by flight) something abhorrent, esp. vices; 3) to be saved by flight, to escape safely out of danger; 4) poetically, to flee away, vanish"*

When a genuine Christian, or anyone else gets into a close proximity of sin, the temptation to yield to this sin is very great. What should be done in this situation? God has a remedy right here in this verse. He orders that these people use the two legs that they have and run as fast as possible in the other way. That's God's remedy. That's what "*flee*" means.

That's exactly what Joseph did in Genesis 39:7-13. He was a servant in Potiphar's house in Egypt. One day, Potiphar's wife asked him to commit fornication with her. He refused and took the Biblical way out of this temptation and fled away from her. Unfortunately, because of his refusal to this wicked fornication, the woman lied to the authorities, and said Joseph tried to rape her. The authorities believed the lying woman and put Joseph into prison. He paid a price for standing for God's moral code.

God tells genuine Christians to continuously flee from the sin of fornication. Stay away from it, no matter what someone says! Because "*he that committeth fornication sinneth against his own body.*" True Christians should use their bodies for the Lord Jesus Christ, not for sin!

1 Corinthians 6:19

"What? know ye not that your body is the temple of the Holy Ghost which is in you, which ye have of God, and ye are not your own?"

The bodies of genuine Christians are the temples of God the Holy Spirit, Who indwells them. They are not their own to be used in any sinful ways whatever. They are to be used for the Lord Jesus Christ. They must not defile God's temples. The temple is a holy place and is not to be used for unholiness and sin. God the Holy Spirit never leaves the bodies of true Christians, no matter what various churches falsely teach on this matter. They have the indwelling Holy Spirit from God the Father the minute they truly trust the Lord Jesus Christ as their Saviour.

Old Testament Verses On Temples
- **Psalms 11:4**

"The LORD is in his holy temple, the LORD'S throne is in heaven: his eyes behold, his eyelids try, the children of men."
The earthly temple was where the Lord dwelt in the Old Testament. His presence was there as well as everywhere in His omnipresence. Today, He also dwells in the bodies of all genuine Christians.
- **Psalms 48:9**

"We have thought of thy lovingkindness, O God, in the midst of thy temple."
This is speaking of the Jewish temple of the Old Testament.

- **Isaiah 6:1**

"In the year that king Uzziah died <u>I saw also the Lord</u> sitting upon a throne, high and lifted up, and <u>his train filled the temple</u>."

This was the temple in the Old Testament time. There were many temples of other nations. This was Solomon's temple.

- **Habakkuk 2:20**

"But <u>the LORD is in his holy temple</u>: let all the earth keep silence before him."

The Lord dwelled in His Old Testament temple.

New Testament Verses On Temples
- **1 Corinthians 3:16-17**

"<u>Know ye not that ye are the temple of God, and that the Spirit of God dwelleth in you</u>? If any man defile the temple of God, him shall God destroy; for the temple of God is holy, which temple ye are."

The true Christians' bodies are the temple of God today. They are indwelled by God the Holy Spirit.

- **2 Corinthians 6:16**

"And what agreement hath the temple of God with idols? for <u>ye are the temple of the living God; as God hath said, I will dwell in them</u>, and walk in them; and I will be their God, and they shall be my people."

This verse affirms that all genuine Christians are the temple of the living God.

1 Corinthians 6:20

"For ye are bought with a price: therefore glorify God in your body, and in your spirit, which are God's."

This verse refers to genuine Christians as being bought with the price of the Lord Jesus Christ's dying for them and shedding His righteous blood for their sins. Because of this, they should glorify God in their bodies and in their spirits which belong to God.

Verses On Being Bought Or Redeemed By Christ
- **2 Peter 2:1**

"But there were false prophets also among the people, even as there shall be false teachers among you, who privily shall bring in damnable heresies, even <u>denying the Lord that bought them</u>, and bring upon themselves swift destruction."

According to this verse, the Lord Jesus Christ "*bought*" even the ones who never receive Him and are lost. They won't trust him or accept him, but at least he made **provision** for their sins; they must avail themselves of this provision by sincerely trusting the Lord Jesus Christ as their Saviour. Otherwise, they are still doomed to spend all eternity in the Lake of Fire in Hell.

John MacArthur is in serious error by his false teaching that "blood" does not mean "blood" but only "death." He is wrong. Death is death and blood is blood. The Lord Jesus Christ died for the sins of the world; at His death, He shed His blood. It is the shedding of His blood that was the price that was paid for the forgiveness of all those who trust in Him sincerely.

- **Galatians 3:13**
"<u>Christ hath redeemed us from the curse of the law</u>, being made a curse for us: for it is written, Cursed is every one that hangeth on a tree:"

The Lord Jesus Christ redeemed genuine Christians from the curse of the law of Moses. He bought them with His own death and the shedding of His blood.

- **Titus 2:14**
"<u>Who gave himself for us, that he might redeem us</u> from all iniquity, and purify unto himself a peculiar people, zealous of good works."

True Christians are redeemed by the Lord Jesus Christ.

- **1 Peter 1:18-19**
"Forasmuch as ye know that ye were not <u>redeemed</u> with corruptible things, as silver and gold, from your vain conversation received by tradition from your fathers; But <u>with the precious blood of Christ</u>, as of a lamb without blemish and without spot:"

Silver and gold can never buy redemption for people. People can be redeemed by the precious blood of Christ by sincerely trusting Him as their Saviour.

- **Revelation 5:9**
"And they sung a new song, saying, <u>Thou art worthy</u> to take the book, and to open the seals thereof: <u>for thou wast slain, and hast redeemed us to God by thy blood</u> out of every kindred, and tongue, and people, and nation;"

This verse refers to two separate acts: (1) The Lord Jesus Christ was slain. (2) He redeems those people who trust Him as their Saviour because of the shedding of His blood on the cross.

Verses On Glorify

- **Psalms 50:15**
"And call upon me in the day of trouble: I will deliver thee, and <u>thou shalt glorify me</u>."

We are not to glorify ourselves, but genuine Christians are to

glorify the Lord.
- **Matthew 5:16**
  "Let your light so shine before men, that they may see your good works, and <u>glorify your Father which is in heaven</u>."

True Christians should maintain good works that will glorify their Heavenly Father.

- **John 16:13-14**
  "Howbeit when he, <u>the Spirit of truth</u>, is come, he will guide you into all truth: for he shall not speak of himself; but whatsoever he shall hear, that shall he speak: and he will shew you things to come. He <u>shall glorify me</u>: for he shall receive of mine, and shall shew it unto you."

God the Holy Spirit will always glorify the Lord Jesus Christ. That is one of His many ministries.

- **John 21:19**
  "<u>This spake he, signifying by what death he should glorify God</u>. And when he had spoken this, he saith unto him, Follow me."

The Lord Jesus Christ told Peter how he was to die and by that death, he would glorify God.

- **Romans 15:6**
  "<u>That ye may with one mind and one mouth glorify God, even the Father of our Lord Jesus Christ</u>."

Genuine Christians are told by God that they should glorify God with one mind and one mouth.

- **Romans 15:9**
  "And <u>that the Gentiles might glorify God for his mercy</u>; as it is written, For this cause I will confess to thee among the Gentiles, and sing unto thy name."

Gentiles who have become true Christians should glorify God for His mercy.

- **1 Peter 4:16**
  "Yet <u>if any man suffer as a Christian</u>, let him not be ashamed; but <u>let him glorify God on this behalf</u>."

When genuine Christians suffer for their beliefs and Godly actions, they should not be ashamed, but should glorify God in it all.

1 Corinthians Chapter Seven

1 Corinthians 7:1

"Now concerning the things whereof ye wrote unto me: It is good for a man not to touch a woman."

These beginning verses in this chapter give us God's teachings on Biblical Christian marriage between husband and wife.

Beginning this important theme, God says, "*It is **good** for a man not to **touch** a woman.*" Before this verse can be clearly understood, it is needful to understand the meaning of two Greek Words used in this verse: (1) the meaning of the Greek Word for "*good,*" and (2) the meaning of the Greek Word for "*touch.*"

THE MEANING OF THE GREEK WORD, "KALOS"

The Greek Word for "*good*" is KALOS. Some of the meanings of that Greek Word are:

"1) beautiful, handsome, excellent, eminent, choice, surpassing, precious, useful, <u>suitable, commendable, admirable</u>; 1a) beautiful to look at, shapely, magnificent; 1b) good, excellent in its nature and characteristics, and therefore well adapted to its ends; 1b1) genuine, approved; 1b2) precious' 1b3) joined to names of men designated by their office, competent, able, such as one ought to be; 1b4) praiseworthy, noble; 1c) beautiful by reason of purity of heart and life, and hence praiseworthy; 1c1) morally good, noble; 1d) honourable, conferring honour; 1e) affecting the mind agreeably, comforting and confirming."

> **THE MEANING OF THE GREEK WORD, "HAPTOMAI"**
>
> The Greek Word for *"touch"* is HAPTOMAI. Some of the meanings of that Greek Word are:
>
>> *"1) to fasten one's self to, adhere to, cling to; 1a) to touch; 1b) <u>of carnal intercourse with a women or cohabitation</u>; 1c) of levitical practice of having no fellowship with heathen practices. Things not to be touched appear to be both women and certain kinds of food, so celibacy and abstinence of certain kinds of food and drink are recommended. 1d) to touch, assail anyone."*

What God is teaching us in this verse is that it is suitable, commendable, and admirable if a genuine Christian man wants to remain unmarried and have no sexual relations with a woman in marriage. In other words, non-marriage is not sinful. It is all right if this true Christian man wishes to remain single.

1 Corinthians 7:2

"Nevertheless, to avoid fornication, let every man have his own wife, and let every woman have her own husband."

> **THE MEANING OF THE GREEK WORD, "PORNEIA"**
>
> The Greek Word for *"fornication"* is PORNEIA. Some of the meanings of this Greek Word are:
>
>> *"1) illicit sexual intercourse; 1a) adultery, fornication, homosexuality, lesbianism, intercourse with animals, etc.; 1b) sexual intercourse with close relatives; Lev. 18; 1c) sexual intercourse with a divorced man or woman; Mk. 10:11,12; 2) metaph. the worship of idols; 2a) of the defilement of idolatry, as incurred by eating the sacrifices offered to idols."*

Though the Greek Word for *"fornication"* has other very serious meanings such as: (1) adultery; (2) homosexuality; (3) lesbianism; (4) bestiality; (5) incest, and others, the meaning here is *"illicit sexual intercourse."* To avoid this sin, every man should have his own wife and every woman should have her own husband. There should be a Biblical marriage. The Greek Word for "*have*" is in the Greek present tense. This means that this man and woman should have each other continuously in their marriage.

1 Corinthians 7:3

"Let the husband render unto the wife due benevolence: and likewise also the wife unto the husband."

The verbs "*render*" for the husband and "*due benevolence*" for the wife are both in the Greek present tenses. Both the husband and the wife are to continuously reciprocate in the sexual relations. Both of them should give due regard to one another's sexual needs throughout their marriage. There should be no refusals in this area on either's part. Both husbands and wives should be informed about this and willing to obey God's order in genuine Christian marriage.

The sexual immorality in the city of Corinth in the days when the Bible was written was rampant as it is in many of our cities and towns in the United States today. God's will in married love is to be followed rather than the dictates of the world which is filled with a host of sexual perverts!

1 Corinthians 7:4

"The wife hath not power of her own body, but the husband: and likewise also the husband hath not power of his own body, but the wife."

When genuine Christians get married, they must share the authority of their bodies with their mate. The husband does not have exclusive use of his body, but must share it with his wife. Likewise, the wife does not have exclusive use of her body, but must share it with her husband. This refers to their sexual relations. Since the two Greek Words for "*power*" are both in the Greek present tense, it means that this sharing of each others' bodies must be continuous. Before they were married, their bodies were their own. After their marriage, their bodies must be shared with their married mate.

The expression is often used when two people are married, that they refer to it as giving each other's "*hand*" in marriage. What is also the case, from God's commands in this verse regarding true Christian marriage, when marriage takes place, the genuine Christians who are part of the marriage also give their "*bodies*" to one another to be shared with one another.

> **THE MEANING OF THE GREEK WORD, "EXOUSIAZO"**
>
> The Greek verb for "*power*" is EXOUSIAZO. Some of the meanings of this Greek Word are:
>
> "*1) to have power or authority, use power; 1a) to be master of any one, exercise authority over one; 1b) to be master of the body; 1b1) <u>to have full and entire authority over the body</u>; 1b2) to hold the body subject to one's will; 1c) to be brought under the power of anyone.*"

1 Corinthians 7:5

"Defraud ye not one the other, except it be with consent for a time, that ye may give yourselves to fasting and prayer; and come together again, that Satan tempt you not for your incontinency."

The Greek verb for "*defraud*" or rob one another in married love relations is in the Greek present tense. Since it is a negative, Greek grammar means to stop an action already in progress. These genuine Christian husbands and wives were to stop robbing or refusing each other married love which they had been doing.

There are only five things that stop their married love relations:
1. <u>It must be with consent of both mates</u>.
2. <u>It must be only for a short time</u>.
3. <u>It must be for a proper purpose</u>.
4. <u>It must be resumed once again</u>.
5. <u>It must prevent Satan's temptations for being apart</u>.

Here are some notes on the Greek Words involved in this verse and in these five things above.
1. "*Consent*" is SUMPHONOS meaning "*harmonious, agreeing, and accordant.*"
2. "*For a time*" is KAIROS meaning "*a limited period of time.*"
3. "*That ye may give yourselves*" is SCHOLAZO meaning "*to have leisure for a thing*" such as for "*Fasting and Prayer*" or some other proper reason.

4. *"Come together again"* is SUNERCHOMAI resume *"conjugal cohabitation."*
5. *"That Satan tempt you not"* Tempt is PEIRAZO which is continuously (Greek present tense) to *"solicit to sin."* *"For your incontinency"* the Greek Word is AKRASIA meaning *"want of self-control."*

1 Corinthians 7:6

"But I speak this by permission, and not of commandment."

Is verse not God's Word? Yes, it's God's Word. but Paul speaks it by God's permission. The Lord Jesus Christ took Paul to the backside of the desert in Arabia for three years and taught him many Bible doctrines like He had taught His other apostles while He was here on earth. Paul was writing this letter to the genuine Christians at Corinth under the guidance and leadership of God the Holy Spirit. What Paul wrote here is just as much Scripture as if the Lord Jesus Christ told him exactly this particular thing. Many people might say, *"Paul wrote it by permission, therefore I don't have to obey it."* Yes, you do have to obey it because it's in the Bible. It's God's Word. It's given by the inspiration of God yet not a specific commandment.

1 Corinthians 7:7

"For I would that all men were even as I myself. But every man hath his proper gift of God, one after this manner, and another after that."

As far as Paul's opinion either in marriage or as a widower, he would like men to be as he is. Since he was a member of the Jewish Sanhedrin, he would have been married. Apparently his wife died, and he is now a widower and has not re-married. This is the plan he would like to see all men follow if they have the proper gift from God.

As far as both pastors and deacons, they are required to be married and have children (1 Timothy 3:2; 3:12). As for other men, they must be led of the Lord as to marriage and undertake what God's gift is for them.

1 Corinthians 7:8

"I say therefore to the unmarried and widows, It is good for them if they abide even as I."

Here are listed by Paul two classifications: (1) the unmarried, and (2) the widows or widowers, implied. When Paul says "*even as I,*" He put himself in one or the other of these two categories. I believe he is a widower whose wife had died. I believe he was formerly married as I explained in the previous verse, because he was a member of the Jewish Sanhedrin whose members were all married. Paul said that would be good for them if God has given them that gift. Both the unmarried and the widowers would have to decide for themselves what they should do in these circumstances.

1 Corinthians 7:9

"But if they cannot contain, let them marry: for it is better to marry than to burn."

THE MEANING OF THE GREEK WORD, "EGCRATEOUOMAI"

The Greek Word for *"contain"* is EGCRATEUOMAI. Some of the meanings for that Greek Word are:

"1) to be self-controlled, continent; 1a) to exhibit self-government, conduct, one's self temperately; 1b) in a figure drawn from athletes, who in preparing themselves for the games abstained from unwholesome food, wine, and sexual indulgence."

This verb, "*contain,*" is in the Greek present tense and means a continuous action. If genuine Christians cannot control their passion, lust, and sexual indulgence, by all means let them marry. It is better to marry than to "*burn.*"

THE MEANING OF THE GREEK WORD, "PUROO"

The Greek Word for *"burn"* is PUROO. Some of the meanings of that Greek Word are:

"1) to burn with fire, to set on fire, kindle; 1a) to be on fire, to burn; 1a1) to be incensed, indignant; 1b) make to glow; 1b1) full of fire, fiery, ignited; 1b1a) of darts filled with inflammable substances and set on fire; 1b2) melted by fire and purged of dross."

It is in the Greek present tense and signifies a continuous action. In this context, it means to burn with lust and sexual passion. That burning and passion might be in thought, word or deed. It's better for true Christians to marry other Christians rather than to burn in lust. Fornication must be always avoided.

1 Corinthians 7:10

"And unto the married I command, yet not I, but the Lord, Let not the wife depart from her husband:"

Paul gives a command here. It is in the Greek present tense "*Let not the wife depart,*" this is a negative in the Greek present tense. As such, it means to stop an action already in progress. He is saying that those who are married should stop letting their wives depart from their husbands. Evidently, some in the church at Corinth were doing this. Genuine Christians should remain married and the wife or husband should not separate from one another. They are to stay together until death parts them, regardless of how differences and arguments might prevail. Patch things up quickly, and go on together in the Lord Jesus Christ.

1 Corinthians 7:11

"But and if she depart, let her remain unmarried, or be reconciled to her husband: and let not the husband put away his wife."

The Greek Word for "depart" is in the Greek Aorist tense. Being a negative prohibition in that tense, it means not to even begin this action of departure from her husband.

The true Christian wife should not leave her husband. Nor, by application, the genuine Christian husband should not leave his wife. If this happens, there are only two alternatives. (1) The first alternative is for the wife to remain unmarried for the rest of her life. (2) The second alternative is for the wife to patch things up with her husband and be reconciled to him. These alternatives would apply to the husbands as well.

The Christian husband should not put away and divorce his wife. Christian marriage is for life and is not to be interrupted by a divorce. Though this might be difficult to follow, it is God's will and God's command. It must be followed.

The husband should never put away or divorce his wife. The husband must stick with that woman as long as they both shall live. She may be hard to live with, but these two genuine Christians must stay together come what may. Apparently these difficulties were present in the Corinthian church, and Paul told them to follow God's program and will in their marriages.

1 Corinthians 7:12
"But to the rest speak I, not the Lord: If any brother hath a wife that believeth not, and she be pleased to dwell with him, let him not put her away."

This is Paul's opinion in this situation. If a genuine Christian has an unbelieving wife, and she wants to continue being married to him, he should not put her away in divorce. This verb for "putting away" is in the Greek present tense. Since it is a negative, it means to stop an action already in progress. The man is to stop putting his wife away in divorce. Probably many in Corinth were doing this and God says "Stop it!" Apparently, when they married, neither of them were true Christians. Then, the husband became a Christian. Genuine Christians are not to marry non-Christians, but this is a different situation.

1 Corinthians 7:13
"And the woman which hath an husband that believeth not, and if he be pleased to dwell with her, let her not leave him."

This principal is the same for a woman who apparently became a genuine Christian after both of them were originally unbelievers. If this non-Christian husband really wants to remain married to her, she should stop wanting to put him away in divorce. This verb is also in the Greek present tense and with the negative, it means she should stop any action like this. Possibly many women at Corinth were putting away their non-Christian husbands when they became true Christians.

1 Corinthians 7:14
"For the unbelieving husband is sanctified by the wife, and the unbelieving wife is sanctified by the husband: else were your children unclean; but now are they holy."

In the case where both husband and wife were not genuine Christians when they married and one of them becomes a true Christian, if the non-Christians wants to remain, let he or she remain because the Christian mate, will be able to have a healthy effect on the non-Christian mate, possibly being able to lead the mate to salvation by genuine faith in Christ. In the same way, the true Christian mate might also be able to lead their children to know the Lord Jesus Christ as their Saviour. This explains the reason for the non-Christian to be allowed to stay with the mate who has become a genuine Christian after their marriage.

1 Corinthians 7:15

"**But if the unbelieving depart, let him depart. A brother or a sister is not under bondage in such cases: but God hath called us to peace.**"

If the unbelieving non-Christian, whether the husband or wife, wants to leave the marriage, the genuine Christian is to let them depart. The true Christian is not under any obligation to do battle and try to force them to remain. God has called genuine Christians to peaceful actions rather than to fight for this unbelieving person to remain in the marriage.

The expression "*not under bondage*" is used by many to believe that this dissolves the marriage so that the true Christian mate can re-marry. No, the Bible is clear that genuine Christian marriage is for life and until the mate dies. The Greek Word for "*bondage*" is DOULOO. It refers to the fact that the true Christian mate is not enslaved to the one who wants to depart the marriage. They are not required to fight and force the non-Christian to remain in the marriage.

1 Corinthians 7:16

"**For what knowest thou, O wife, whether thou shalt save thy husband? or how knowest thou, O man, whether thou shalt save thy wife?**"

This refers to the circumstances mentioned in the preceding verses where both mates were non-Christians at the beginning of the marriage and then one became a genuine Christian. The true Christian wife should endeavor to help her non-Christian husband to become a true Christian. Likewise, the genuine Christian husband should seek to help his wife to become a Christian. God might work out this miracle in their marriage for His glory and praise.

1 Corinthians 7:17

"**But as God hath distributed to every man, as the Lord hath called every one, so let him walk. And so ordain I in all churches.**"

God does not give the same gifts to everyone, but as He has called genuine Christians, and given them certain gifts and abilities, so they should continue to walk and live according to the gifts God has given them. When we walk, we take one step at a time. Some gifts are given to genuine Christians in order for them to marry. To other true Christians, God has given the gift to remain single. Paul made this clear to all the churches that he established.

1 Corinthians 7:18

"Is any man called being circumcised? let him not become uncircumcised. Is any called in uncircum-cision? let him not be circumcised."

When any man who is circumcised is called by the Lord and genuinely receives the Lord Jesus Christ as his Saviour, let him not undergo the specialized surgery to make it look like he was never circumcised. This was done when circumcised Jews were being persecuted. They tried to hide this by this special surgery. Likewise, if any man who is not circumcised comes to know the Lord Jesus Christ as his Saviour, he should not be circumcised. These men should stay as they are when becoming genuine Christians.

1 Corinthians 7:19

"Circumcision is nothing, and uncircumcision is nothing, but the keeping of the commandments of God."

God had circumcision for the Jews. That was the sign for the Jewish nation and Abraham was given that sign and from then on, that was the sign of being a part of the children of Abraham. But under the dispensation of grace, circumcision is no longer required of genuine Christians whether they are Jews or Gentiles. The only thing that is true of either circumcision or uncircumcision is the keeping of God's commandments. God is very concerned that true Christians in the age of grace keep all of the things He has given them in His Words. In order to keep what God wants them to keep, they must have the right Bible, which in English is the King James Bible, in order to know what God expects them to obey.

1 Corinthians 7:20

"Let every man abide in the same calling wherein he was called."

God says, in this verse, that those who have become genuine Christians, whether they were formerly Jews or Gentiles, they were to continue in the same physical condition as they were in before becoming true Christians. The verb "*abide*" (MENO) is in the Greek present tense which means they were to continue to abide in that same state of calling. If they were circumcised before, keep that state. If they were uncircumcised before becoming genuine Christians, let them stay the same way physically.

1 Corinthians 7:21

"Art thou called being a servant? care not for it: but if thou mayest be made free, use it rather."

The word "*call*" is used four different times in these verses--verses 21, 22, 22 and again in 24. In this verse, it refers to a servant who is called. A person is called by the Gospel of the Lord Jesus Christ.

- **Matthew 11:28**

"Come unto me, all ye that labour and are heavy laden, and I will give you rest."

When the Lord Jesus Christ said "*come unto me*," that is His **call** to the people. Those who have trusted the Lord Jesus Christ as their Saviour, have been spiritually "called." It is up to whose who are called to accept that calling by Him and receive Him as their Saviour.

The Greek Word for "call" in this verse is MELO. Since it is in the Greek present tense prohibition, it means to stop an action already in progress. They were "*caring*" or worrying about their being servants. God told them to stop their worrying! If these people who are genuine Christians are bondmen or slaves (DOULOS), they shouldn't be overly concerned about it. If they could be free, they should use their freedom for the Lord Who has saved them.

1 Corinthians 7:22

"For he that is called in the Lord, being a servant, is the Lord's freeman: likewise also he that is called, being free, is Christ's servant."

Once again, this being "*called in the Lord*," does not only mean that the Gospel of Christ was explained to a person, but it means they have accepted this call and genuinely trusted the Lord Jesus Christ as their Saviour. If becoming a genuine Christian when a servant or slave, you are free in the Lord. If becoming a true Christian when being free, you are the Lord Jesus Christ's servant. It's a wonderful thing to be free from the penalty and bondage of sin and be free in the Lord.

- **John 8:32**
  "And ye shall know the truth, and <u>the truth shall make you free</u>."

Trusting the Lord Jesus Christ, who is the Truth, makes a person free from the enslaving power of Satan.

- **John 8:36**
  "<u>If the Son therefore shall make you free, ye shall be free indeed</u>."

Only by genuinely trusting the Lord Jesus Christ, God's Son, can a person be really free from Satan's power, from God's judgment, and from the everlasting Lake of Fire in Hell. Being free means a person is no longer a servant or slave to the Devil.

> **THE MEANING OF THE GREEK WORD, "DOULOS"**
>
> The Greek Word for *"servant"* is DOULOS. Some of the meanings of this Greek Word are:
>
> *"1) a slave, bondman, man of servile condition; 1a) a slave; 1b) metaph., <u>one who gives himself up to another's will</u>, those whose service is used by Christ in extending and advancing His cause among men; 1c) devoted to another to the disregard of one's own interests;*
>
> *2) a servant, attendant."*

When the Lord Jesus Christ gives people salvation by a genuine faith in Him and in His finished work on the cross, they are free. Not free from physical slavery or bondage, but free spiritually from the bondage of the world, the flesh, and the Devil.

1 Corinthians 7:23

"Ye are bought with a price; be not ye the servants of men."

Paul is writing to genuine Christians in the church at Corinth. They were saved, born-again because they truly trusted in the Lord Jesus Christ as their Saviour and were bought by the shedding of His blood on the cross at Calvary.

> **THE MEANING OF THE GREEK WORD, "AGORAZO"**
>
> The Greek Word for *"bought"* is AGORAZO. Some of the meanings of this Greek Word are:
>
> *"1) <u>to be in the market place</u>, to attend it; 2) to do business there, buy or sell;*

> *3) of idle people: to haunt the market place, lounge there."*

THE MEANING OF THE GREEK WORD, "TIME"

The Greek Word for *"price"* is TIME. Some of the meanings of that Greek Word are:

> *"1) a valuing by which the price is fixed; 1a) of the price itself; 1b) of the price paid or received for a person or thing bought or sold; 2) honour which belongs or is shown to one; 2a) of the honour which one has by reason of rank and state of office which he holds; 2b) deference,"*

These true Christians were bought off the slave market of Satan by the price of Christ's sinless and atoning blood at Calvary.

1 Peter 1:18
"Forasmuch as ye know that <u>ye were not redeemed with corruptible things, as silver and gold,</u> from your vain conversation received by tradition from your fathers; <u>But with the precious blood of Christ, as of a lamb without blemish and without spot</u>:"

The price was not by silver or gold, but by the precious blood of the Lord Jesus Christ as of a Lamb without blemish.

After this truth is stated, Paul tells these genuine Christians to stop being the servants of men. This is the meaning because this Greek verb (GINOMAI) is in the Greek present tense which means to stop the action that is presently going on. They were to stop serving men, their actions, and their sins.

1 Corinthians 7:24

"Brethren, let every man, wherein he is called, therein abide with God."

Paul is speaking once again about those genuine Christians who were called by the Lord to be saved and who accepted the invitation and received the Lord Jesus Christ as their Saviour. Every true Christian should abide and stay in that faith and doctrine that is clearly taught in the Words of God found in true and faithful Bibles like the English King James Bible. Stay away from inferior and false so-called "bibles" which are founded on the erroneous Gnostic and Critical New Testament Greek Texts and false Hebrew and Aramaic Hebrew texts.

These very false English versions (as well as most of the foreign language Bibles) should be avoided and a person should not abide in them. Such false English versions are the RSV, ASV, NASV, NIV, NRSV, ESV and many, many others. Their New Testaments have 8,000 differences from the proper Traditional Greek text. This amounts to a total of 356 doctrinal passages, as Dr. Jack Moorman has detailed in two of his excellent research books on this.

1 Corinthians 7:25

"Now concerning virgins I have no commandment of the Lord: yet I give my judgment, as one that hath obtained mercy of the Lord to be faithful."

Paul is writing about those who have never been married. He has not received anything from the Lord on this subject, but gives his own opinion on it. Paul obtained God's mercy to be faithful in all things. This does not mean that this verse is not God's Word. It was written under the inspiration of God as part of God's Words given by the Spirit of God.

1 Corinthians 7:26

"I suppose therefore that this is good for the present distress, I say, that it is good for a man so to be."

By the "*present distress,*" Paul is no doubt referring to the severe persecution of genuine Christians at that time. Because of those severe problems, it would be better for single men not to marry, but to be faithful, pure, and unmarried. The same would be true of the true Christian women in that time of trouble and persecution.

Paul was writing this about 59 A.D. About eleven years later (70 A.D.) Emperor Titus would come to Jerusalem and destroy much of the city. Even before that time, conditions were very difficult for the genuine Christians.

Conditions in the USA today are looking perilous as well. There are reports of at least 36 prison camps intended for genuine Christians and others who will resist the orders of a socialist-communist state which many radicals wish to bring to the United States of America.

1 Corinthians 7:27

"Art thou bound unto a wife? seek not to be loosed. Art thou loosed from a wife? seek not a wife."

Paul speaks here about those genuine Christian men in the church at Corinth who are bound in marriage to their wives. They are not to seek to be loosed from their wives by way of divorce.

On the other hand, true Christian men who have been loosed from a wife due to her death, they are to stop trying to seek another wife and remarry. The Greek verb for "*seek*" (ZETEO) is in the Greek present tense. Since it is a prohibition, the meaning is to stop an action already being taken. They are to stop their seeking of another genuine Christian wife. This order was because of the persecution by the Roman Emperor Titus coming in 70 A.D. and much of it was already evident.

1 Corinthians 7:28

"But and if thou marry, thou hast not sinned; and if a virgin marry, she hath not sinned. Nevertheless such shall have trouble in the flesh: but I spare you."

Even in the difficult times that were approaching the genuine Christian men of Paul's day, if their wife dies, they can marry. They have not sinned in doing this. And if a woman who is a virgin and never had a husband before, marry, she has not sinned, but, because of the very serious times which were upon them in that day, she would have trouble in the flesh.

1 Corinthians 7:29

"But this I say, brethren, the time is short: it remaineth, that both they that have wives be as though they had none;"

As I have said before, Paul is writing this in about 59 A.D. Just eleven years later, in 70 A.D., the Titans would come to destroy the temple of Jerusalem. There would be great distress and persecution of genuine Christians. Many would be put in jail and others executed. Because the wives would either be snatched by some wicked soldier and taken away, or they might even be put to death, leaving their husbands without any wife at all. In wartime, those in power separate husbands and wives, putting them in separate jails. That also would be as if these husbands had no wives.

1 Corinthians 7:30

"And they that weep, as though they wept not; and they that rejoice, as though they rejoiced not; and they that buy, as though they possessed not;"

When these troublesome times would be upon them, all things would be changed. Weeping would not be the same. Rejoicing would not be the same. Those who would buy things, it would be as though they would not be able to enjoy the things they purchased. It would be as though the thing they just bought would not be used because they were either in prison, or unable to make use of it.

1 Corinthians 7:31

"And they that use this world, as not abusing it: for the fashion of this world passeth away."

While living in this world, there are many things that true Christians need. They need food, shelter, employment, and many other things, but they should never be so enchanted with this old world that they become attached to it and follow it's evil and sinful ways. The fashions and schemes of the world as well as the world itself will one day pass away. It is not permanent and fixed.

- 1 John 2:15-16

"<u>Love not the world</u>, neither the things that are in the world. If any man love the world, the love of the Father is not in him. For <u>all that is in the world</u>, the lust of the flesh, and the lust of the eyes, and the pride of life, <u>is not of the Father</u>, but is of the world. <u>And the world passeth away</u>, and the lust thereof: but he that doeth the will of God abideth for ever." The Greek Word for "love" is in the Greek present tense. Since it is a prohibition, it means to "*stop loving the world.*" The genuine Christians to whom John was writing were loving this sinful world. John told them to "Stop it!" That includes the lust of the flesh and eyes as well as the pride of life.

The entire "*fashion*" of this world will one day pass away and be forever in the past. For this reason, genuine Christians are not to abuse or compromise with the wicked things of this ungodly world.

THE MEANING OF THE GREEK WORD, "SCHEMA"

The Greek Word for "*fashion*" is SCHEMA. Some of the meanings of this Greek Word are:

"1) *the habitus, as* <u>*comprising*</u>

> *everything in a person which strikes the senses, the figure, bearing, discourse, actions, manner of life etc."*

The Greek Word for *"fashion"* refers to "*everything in a person which strikes the senses.*" Do you like to be fashionable? Is your car fashionable? Is your house fashionable? Is your hat fashionable? Is your dress, your shoes, your clothes, your suit? The *"fashion"* of this world passes away. You can't keep up with fashion. It changes. Skinny ties, big ties, big collars, little collars. You can't keep up with it. Hats and everything else.

The Greek Word for *"fashion"* refers to everything that strikes the senses. We have five senses: seeing, hearing, smelling, touching and tasting. Those are the five senses. It includes the words used, the actions, the manner of life, and many other things.

The fashions in when the Lord Jesus Christ was on earth were different than those in our days and probably in future days. Some things in the past look strange to us today such as old-fashioned cars, old-fashioned trucks, old-fashioned hats, and many other old things. All these things, and things in the future, will all pass away.

1 Corinthians 7:32

"But I would have you without carefulness. He that is unmarried careth for the things that belong to the Lord, how he may please the Lord:"

Paul wanted the true Christians at Corinth to be *"without carefulness."*

> **THE MEANING OF THE GREEK WORD, "AMERIMNOS"**
> The Greek Word for *"carefulness"* is AMERIMNOS. Some of the meanings of this Greek Word are:
> **"1) free from anxiety, free from care."**

He says something about the genuine Christians who are not married. They *"care"* about things. This Greek Verb is the root of the previous Word for *"carefulness."*

> **THE MEANING OF THE GREEK WORD, "MERIMNAO"**
> The Greek Word here for *"care"* is MERIMNAO. Some of the meanings of this Greek Word are:
> *"1) to be anxious; 1a) to be troubled*

> *with cares; 2) <u>to care for, look out for</u> (a thing); 2a) to seek to promote one's interests; 2b) <u>caring or providing for</u>."*

Those genuine Christians, who are not married, care for, look out for, and provide for the things that belong to the Lord Jesus Christ and how they may please Him. That's what **should** be true of true Christians who are unmarried, but, sad to say, many, many singles do not serve their Saviour and don't seem to want to please Him above all other things.

1 Corinthians 7:33

"But he that is married careth for the things that are of the world, how he may please his wife."

By way of contrast, a genuine Christian man who is married is concerned about the world around him and how he may please his wife and his children when they are born. If he doesn't provide for his own, he is worse than an infidel (1 Timothy 5:8). Husbands can be in fellowship with the Lord Jesus Christ as much as possible, but they've got to spend time with their wives, with their families, for making a living, and so on. Paul, I believe, was married, and then his wife died. I think he was a widower and on his own. He could be a missionary, he could go at the drop of a hat, he could be beaten, and he was, he could be stoned, and he was, and ship wrecked and he was, without dragging his wife and family along. That would be horrible for the family. So, God gave Paul the gift to remain as a single widower and not to marry again. You true Christian men who are married, I hope you are pleasing your wives while pleasing the Lord Jesus Christ, putting Him in first place always.

THE MEANING OF THE GREEK WORD, "ARESKO"

The Greek Word for *"please"* is ARESKO. Some of the meanings of that Greek Word are:

> *"1) to please; 2) to strive to please; 2a) to accommodate one's self to the opinions, desires and interests of others."*

1 Corinthians 7:34

"**There is difference also between a wife and a virgin. The unmarried woman careth for the things of the Lord, that she may be holy both in body and in spirit: but she that is married careth for the things of the world, how she may please her husband.**"

Paul explains some of the differences between a genuine Christian woman who is married and a genuine Christian woman who is unmarried.

1. The genuine Christian woman who is unmarried. She should care for the things of the Lord that she might be holy in her body and in her spirit. Some of the meanings for the Greek Word for *"care"* (MERIMNAO) is explained above in verse 32. Since it is in the Greek present tense, it means a continuous care in the positive sense of this word.

> "*1) to be anxious; 1a) to be troubled with cares; 2) to care for, look out for (a thing); 2a) to seek to promote one's interests; 2b) caring or providing for.*"

That does not mean that marriage is "unholy." It means that she can be set apart completely for the Lord Jesus Christ and His ministries without needing to care for the many responsibilities toward her husband, her children, and in the many other things that are involved in Christian marriage. She could be used completely for the Lord's work. She could be a missionary. She could type. She could work in a job of interest. She does not have to please a husband because she does not have one.

2. The genuine Christian woman who is married

However, the woman who is married cares for the things that are going on in the world and how she may please her husband. Marriage is not easy; Once you enter marriage, you're in a learning experience. This learning goes on day in and day out, week in and week out, month in and month out, and year in and year out. There is no end of learning in the marriage experience.

How should the wives please their husbands? There are many areas in her husband-pleasing life which go on throughout the marriage. One of the reasons for marriage break-ups is when wives do not care about pleasing their husbands. How can wives please their husbands? Some of the ways are by cooking, sewing, making the beds, washing windows, and many other things.

Paul was not against marriage. He explains this in Hebrews.
- **Hebrews 13:4**
"<u>Marriage is honourable</u> in all, and the bed undefiled: but whoremongers and adulterers God will judge."

Marriage is honorable for everyone, including all the Roman Catholic priests of today, the Pope of Rome, and all the Catholic nuns.

1 Corinthians 7:35

"And this I speak for your own profit; not that I may cast a snare upon you, but for that which is comely, and that ye may attend upon the Lord without distraction."

Paul was very clear as to his purpose in speaking to the genuine Christians in the Corinthian church. He did not want to cast a snare. He wanted their lives to be comely and respectful. The special purpose of his writing was that, whether true Christians are married or unmarried, they may serve the Lord Jesus Christ without anything that would discourage this service for Him.

Paul did not want to bring a snare to these true Christians, whether married or unmarried.

THE MEANING OF THE GREEK WORD, "BROCHOS"

The Greek Word for "*snare*" is BROCHOS. Some of the meanings of that Greek Word are:

> "*1) a noose, slip-knot, <u>by which any person or thing is caught</u>, or fastened, or suspended; 2) to throw a noose upon one, a figure borrowed from war or the chase so that by craft or by force one is bound to some necessity, to constrain him to obey some command.*"

---

1 Corinthians 7:36

"But if any man think that he behaveth himself uncomely toward his virgin, if she pass the flower of her age, and need so require, let him do what he will, he sinneth not: let them marry."

Paul writes about any man who is going with an unmarried woman and continues (Greek present tense) to think that he is continuing to act (Greek present tense) uncomely or unbecomingly toward this unmarried woman. This is not good and could lead to sin on his part. This woman has passed the prime of her life (UPERAKMOS). If she wants and needs to marry, the man can do what he wishes and can marry her. There is no sin involved in this at all.

1 Corinthians 7:37

"Nevertheless he that standeth stedfast in his heart, having no necessity, but hath power over his own will, and hath so decreed in his heart that he will keep his virgin, doeth well."

If this genuine Christian man stands firm and steadfast in his heart, has no necessity to marry, has control over his own will and sexual desires, has settled in his heart to keep pure and guard this unmarried true Christian woman, without marrying her, keeping her only as a friend, without marrying her, he does very well.

1 Corinthians 7:38

"So then he that giveth her in marriage doeth well; but he that giveth her not in marriage doeth better."

In view of the present stress they were living under, with only eleven years before the terrible war with the Roman emperor Titus, here are his two conclusions for a genuine Christian man to weigh:

(1) If he marries this genuine Christian woman, he does well.

(2) If he does not marry her, he does better.

There is a false teaching that is being promoted by Bill Gothard and others in our days. He teaches that his staff and all other true Christians should stay single in the present days. He himself has been single all of his life, yet he seems to be an authority on marriage. Figure that out if you can! He teaches that this should be true of other genuine Christians. His father taught him this heresy, which he has been passing on to his audiences in his meetings, wherever they are held.

He urges young ladies on his staff to remain single. He tells them that if they can remain single until they are thirty, he will give them one of two things, either an automobile, a vacation in the Bahamas, or some other thing like that. In his mind, singleness is prime. That is wrong and unscriptural. Singleness is only for those who have a gift for this state and personally desire it. It is not for everyone.

1 Corinthians 7:39

"The wife is bound by the law as long as her husband liveth; but if her husband be dead, she is at liberty to be married to whom she will; only in the Lord."

The law of Moses was very clear that marriage between two genuine Christians is until one of them dies. This was the Biblical standard for all the Jews in the Old Testament era. This standard of marriage for life is not confined to the Old Testament. Though this standard is violated today by many true Christian couples, it is still God's clear standard that should be followed by them all. Though the verse mentions only the "wife," I believe, by application, it applies to the husband as well. If death occurs with either of the members of the marriage, the other member can marry again, but *"only in the Lord."* This would indicate that the prospective spouse should only be a genuine Christian person.

Verses In The New Testament On Marriage Until Death
- **Matthew 19:5-6**

"And said, For this cause shall a man leave father and mother, and shall cleave to his wife: and they twain shall be one flesh? Wherefore they are no more twain, but one flesh. <u>What therefore God hath joined together, let not man put asunder.</u>"

No authority of man should dissolve true Christian marriages.
- **Mark 10:6-9**

"But from the beginning of the creation God made them male and female. For this cause shall a man leave his father and mother, and cleave to his wife; And they twain shall be one flesh: so then they are no more twain, but one flesh. <u>What therefore God hath joined together, let not man put asunder.</u>"

This is what Matthew has also stated in the verse above. Because of genuine Christian couples breaking this Biblical standard, as a Pastor, I do not like to marry true Christian couples, or any couples.

When I was a Navy Chaplain for five years on active duty, I was called upon to marry various Navy couples. The first couple I married were only together for a month or two and then divorced. I stopped marrying Navy personnel.

After the active duty service, I married a relative of mine whose marriage ended up in divorce. Only one time after that I married a genuine Christian couple who also divorced one another. I did have a few marriages that have remained, for which I am grateful to the Lord, but for many years, I have turned down requests for marriage, because I do not want to be a party to marriages that only last for a while and then are broken up.

- **Romans 7:2-3**
"<u>For the woman which hath an husband is bound by the law to her husband so long as he liveth</u>; but if the husband be dead, she is loosed from the law of her husband. So then <u>if, while her husband liveth, she be married to another man, she shall be called an adulteress</u>: but if her husband be dead, she is free from that law; so that she is no adulteress, though she be married to another man."

Many pastors today say that adultery on the part of one of the marriage partners breaks the marriage and can Biblically end up in divorce. This is heresy! All the Bible verses are clear that only death can break the bonds of genuine Christian marriage. I realize that I part company with many preachers and pastors on this. I know I am in the minority by taking this view, but I can take no other view because the Bible says that genuine Christian marriages last until the death of one of the mates.

1 Corinthians 7:40

"But she is happier if she so abide, after my judgment: and I think also that I have the Spirit of God."

Paul's opinion was that the wife would be happier if she abides without remarrying. This might be his position because of the stressful times that were then upon the true Christian church, or it might be at all times, provided that she has the gift of remaining unmarried. If she chooses to remain unmarried, she might be able to serve the Lord in various ways while remaining unmarried. She can still serve the Lord in that way. The rule is, serve the Lord without distraction and that's the most important thing. So the decision, upon the death of either the husband or the wife, must be made by the parties effected so they can continue to serve the Lord without any distraction.

1 Corinthians Chapter Eight

1 Corinthians 8:1

"Now as touching things offered unto idols, we know that we all have knowledge. Knowledge puffeth up, but charity edifieth."

It is totally against God's Words to make knowledge an idol. It is true that it's good to have sufficient knowledge, in staying away from idols. However, making knowledge the most important thing for true Christians to seek is a serious flaw. Knowledge, if not restrained, can puff people up.

THE MEANING OF THE GREEK WORD, "PHUSIOO"

The Greek Word for *"puff up"* is PHUSIOO. Some of the meanings of that Greek Word are:

"1) to make natural, to cause a thing to pass into nature; 2) to inflate, blow up, to cause to swell up; 2a) to puff up, make proud; 2b) to be puffed up, to bear one's self loftily, be proud."

Genuine Christians must be very careful not to walk around inflated like a blow fish. They should be surrounded by Bible *"charity"* or love. If this is the case, they, and those around them, will be able to edify themselves and other true Christians should ask the Lord to give them this gift of love and how to use it.

THE MEANING OF THE GREEK WORD, "OIKODOMEO"

The Greek Word for *"edification"* is OIKODOMEO. Some of the meanings of this Greek Word are:

"1) to build a house, erect a building; 1a) to build (up from the foundation); 1b) to restore by building, to rebuild, repair; 2) metaph; 2a) to found, establish; 2b) to promote growth in Christian wisdom, affection, grace, virtue, holiness, blessedness; 2c) to grow in wisdom and piety."

Verses On Puff Up
- **1 Corinthians 4:6**

"And these things, brethren, I have in a figure transferred to myself and to Apollos for your sakes; that ye might learn in us not to think of men above that which is written, <u>that no one of you be puffed up for one against another</u>."

In other words, no genuine Christians are supposed to puff themselves up against other true Christians.

- **1 Corinthians 4:18-19**

"Now some are puffed up, as though I would not come to you. But I will come to you shortly, if the Lord will, and <u>will know, not the speech of them which are puffed up, but the power</u>."

Some of the genuine Corinthians at Corinth were puffed up, thinking that Paul would not come to them. He would visit them soon if the Lord willed it. When he would arrive, his speech would be in the power of God the Holy Spirit. His would not be puffed up speech.

- **1 Corinthians 5:2**

"And <u>ye are puffed up</u>, and have not rather mourned, that he that hath done this deed might be taken away from among you."

Paul is referring to the wicked deed of incest that was performed by one of their members. They did not mourn over it, nor want him removed from the church. They were puffed up about it instead.

- **1 Corinthians 13:4**

"Charity suffereth long, and is kind; charity envieth not; <u>charity</u> vaunteth not itself, <u>is not puffed up</u>,"

Genuine Christian love is never puffed up.

- **Colossians 2:18**

"Let no man beguile you of your reward in a voluntary humility and worshipping of angels, intruding into those things which he hath not seen, <u>vainly puffed up by his fleshly mind</u>,"

Genuine Christians should not lose their rewards by the worship of angels, being interest in unseen things, or having an arrogant mind-set.

Verses On Knowledge
- **Genesis 2:9**

"And out of the ground made the LORD God to grow every tree that is pleasant to the sight, and good for food; the tree of life also in the midst of the garden, and <u>the tree of knowledge of good and evil</u>."

Satan called the forbidden garden-of-Eden tree a tree of the knowledge about good and evil. Failing to keep God's Words about this tree was the wrong way to acquire godly knowledge.

- **Genesis 2:17**

"But <u>of the tree of the knowledge of good and evil, thou shalt not eat of it: for in the day that thou eatest thereof thou shalt surely die</u>."

Adam and Eve both ate this forbidden fruit by using their own false *"knowledge"* and suffered God's judgment, not only upon them, but also upon every other human being that would ever be born. Their spiritual death followed instantly. Their physical death was assured for them and every other man, woman, and child to be born on this earth.

- **Proverbs 1:7**

"<u>The fear of the LORD is the beginning of knowledge</u>: but fools despise wisdom and instruction."

According to this verse, no person on earth has what God calls godly *"knowledge"* until they have come to realize the *"fear of the LORD,"* respecting Him and genuinely trusting His Son as their Saviour. All the other so-called *"knowledge"* that humans follow is not godly and true *"knowledge."*

- **Proverbs 2:6**

"For <u>the LORD giveth</u> wisdom: out of his mouth cometh <u>knowledge</u> and understanding."

Here again, the LORD is the One Who gives true wisdom, knowledge, and understanding.

- **Proverbs 15:2**

"<u>The tongue of the wise useth knowledge aright</u>: but the mouth of fools poureth out foolishness."

Only the *"wise"* can use knowledge in the right way. Fools' mouths pour out foolishness.

- **Isaiah 47:10**

"For thou hast trusted in thy wickedness: thou hast said, None seeth me. <u>Thy wisdom and thy knowledge, it hath perverted thee</u>; and thou hast said in thine heart, I am, and none else beside me."

Those who trust in their own wickedness have been perverted. Their self-exaltation knows no bounds.

- **Daniel 12:4**

"But thou, O Daniel, shut up the words, and seal the book, even to the time of the end: many shall run to and fro, and <u>knowledge shall be increased</u>."

Knowledge about many earthly things is increasing daily, but the true knowledge of God the Father and of the Lord Jesus Christ has been diminishing day by day since the beginning of God's creation.

- **Habakkuk 2:14**
  "For the earth shall be filled with the knowledge of the glory of the LORD, as the waters cover the sea."

This will be fulfilled during the millennial reign of the Lord Jesus Christ which will take place after the seven-year Tribulation period. There will be true knowledge rather than much false "*knowledge*"that is around today.

- **Romans 10:2**
  "For I bear them record that they have a zeal of God, but not according to knowledge."

Zeal is merely enthusiasm which the Jews had, but they possessed little or no knowledge of the Words of God and His will.

- **Romans 11:33**
  "O the depth of the riches both of the wisdom and knowledge of God! how unsearchable are his judgments, and his ways past finding out!"

God's wisdom and knowledge is perfect. It is found for us in the Words of God. In English, His revealed knowledge is found in the pages of the King James Bible.

- **Ephesians 3:19**
  "And to know the love of Christ, which passeth knowledge, that ye might be filled with all the fulness of God."

The love of the Lord Jesus Christ for all the wicked sinners in the world from the beginning of Adam and Eve surpasses all human knowledge. It is truly unfathomable!

- **2 Timothy 3:7**
  "Ever learning, and never able to come to the knowledge of the truth."

Despite much human learning, many people who have hardened their minds and hearts against the Lord Jesus Christ will never come to the knowledge of Him Who is "*the Way, the Truth, and the Life*" (John 14:6).

- **2 Peter 3:18**
  "But grow in grace, and in the knowledge of our Lord and Saviour Jesus Christ. To him be glory both now and for ever. Amen."

Genuine Christians should not remain spiritual babies, but they should spiritually grow and develop by daily reading and following the Words of God found in the Bible.

Verses On Charity or Love
- **1 Corinthians 13:1-2**

"Though I speak with the tongues of men and of angels, and have not charity, I am become as sounding brass, or a tinkling cymbal. And though I have the gift of prophecy, and understand all mysteries, and all knowledge; and though I have all faith, so that I could remove mountains, <u>and have not charity, I am nothing</u>."

Without sincere and godly charity or love, all these fine things listed above in his verse make true Christians spiritually empty.

- **1 Corinthians 13:4**

"<u>Charity suffereth long, and is kind; charity envieth not; charity vaunteth not itself, is not puffed up</u>,"

These five things show what true Christian charity or love is not.

- **1 Corinthians 13:8**

"<u>Charity never faileth</u>: but whether there be prophecies, they shall fail; whether there be tongues, they shall cease; whether there be knowledge, it shall vanish away."

These temporary sign gifts mentioned here all ceased in 90 to 100 A.D. when the Bible was completed. But charity or love will never cease, but goes on upon earth and even into eternity.

- **2 Timothy 3:10**

"But <u>thou hast fully known my</u> doctrine, manner of life, purpose, faith, longsuffering, <u>charity</u>, patience,"

Pastor Timothy, who traveled with Paul on many journeys, fully knew and understood Paul's Christian charity and love.

- **1 Peter 4:8**

"And <u>above all things have fervent charity among yourselves</u>: for <u>charity shall cover the multitude of sins</u>."

Genuine Christians, even though they might differ on some things, should have fervent charity and love for each other because charity and love does not agree with their sins, but overlooks them and maintains an understanding of them.

- **Revelation 2:19**

"<u>I know thy works, and charity</u>, and service, and faith, and thy patience, and thy works; and the last to be more than the first."

The Lord Jesus Christ told the church at Ephesus that He was aware of their works of charity and love.

1 Corinthians 8:2
"And if any man think that he knoweth any thing, he knoweth nothing yet as he ought to know."

Here is probably a true Christian who thinks he knows something about a topic. It appears that he is boasting. In reality, he knows nothing when compared to what he ought to know. These kinds of people should not have such a boastful attitude about what they know. They look down on others as being uninformed, misinformed, or totally ignorant of some topic.

Verses On Boasting
- **1 Kings 20:11**

"And the king of Israel answered and said, Tell him, <u>Let not him that girdeth on his harness boast himself as he that putteth it off</u>."

Wait until the battle is over before you boast about how you're going to win that battle.

- **2 Chronicles 25:19**

"Thou sayest, Lo, <u>thou hast smitten the Edomites; and thine heart lifteth thee up to boast</u>: abide now at home; why shouldest thou meddle to thine hurt, that thou shouldest fall, even thou, and Judah with thee?"

Just because you won a battle, don't boast about it. Instead, just thank the Lord Who enabled you to be victorious.

- **Psalms 49:6**

"They that trust in their wealth, and <u>boast themselves in the multitude of their riches</u>;"

Riches won't go to heaven with people who have them. There should be no boasting, regardless of how wealthy you might be. Genuine Christians should be thankful for the Lord's supply for their needs without any boasting.

- **Psalms 97:7**

"<u>Confounded be all they that</u> serve graven images, that <u>boast themselves of idols</u>: worship him, all ye gods."

We don't boast of idols. Idolatry is wrong. You shouldn't boast of them. Idols should never be made or worshipped by true Christians. They should never take the place of the Almighty Creator God of the Bible.

- **Proverbs 25:14**

"Whoso <u>boasteth himself of a false gift</u> is like clouds and wind without rain."

Whether genuine Christians have true gifts or false gifts, there should be no boasting of any kind. False gifts are like beautiful clouds without any water in them.

- **Proverbs 27:1**
  "Boast not thyself of to morrow; for thou knowest not what a day may bring forth."

Tomorrow is yet future. No one knows what might take place on the next day. Therefore, there should be no boasting about what might happen tomorrow.

- **Romans 1:30**
  "Backbiters, haters of God, despiteful, proud, boasters, inventors of evil things, disobedient to parents,"

Many of the Gentiles mentioned in Romans chapter one who lived in the early years of God's creation were boasters as well as the other sins listed in this verse.

- **Ephesians 2:8-9**
  "For by grace are ye saved through faith; and that not of yourselves: it is the gift of God: Not of works, lest any man should boast."

If anyone could be saved and go to Heaven by their own works and good deeds, they might do a little boasting. But since salvation is by God's grace alone without any deeds, there should be no boasting about a person's deeds that brought them eternal life.

- **2 Timothy 3:2**
  "For men shall be lovers of their own selves, covetous, boasters, proud, blasphemers, disobedient to parents, unthankful, unholy,"

Paul told Pastor Timothy that there would be boasters in the latter days. We're in those days, and there is much boasting by many people in these days.

- **James 3:5**
  "Even so the tongue is a little member, and boasteth great things. Behold, how great a matter a little fire kindleth!"

Genuine Christians should never use their tongues to boast about the things that they have accomplished. They should be thankful, not boastful.

1 Corinthians 8:3

"But if any man love God, the same is known of him."

Only those who are genuine Christians--who have (1) realized they are sinners in God's eyes; (2) realized that the Lord Jesus Christ died for their sins as their Substitute; and (3) truly believed on and trusted the Lord Jesus Christ as their Saviour–really have the ability to *"love God"* truly, properly, and Biblically.

If these people are true Christians, they are recognized and known of God to be His genuine children. He is able to know them because He has omniscience and is all-knowing. This Divine attribute of omniscience is possessed by all three Members of the Divine Trinity including God the Father, God the Son, and God the Holy Spirit. Some hold the heretical and false belief that the Lord Jesus Christ did not possess this attribute while He was on the earth. That is in total and severe error.

Verses On Christ Knowing His Genuine Christians
- **John 10:14**
"I am the good shepherd, and <u>know my sheep</u>, and am known of mine."

Because of His omniscience, the Lord Jesus Christ knows those whom He has saved. He cares for them as well.

- **John 10:27**
"My sheep hear my voice, and <u>I know them</u>, and they follow me:"

Those who follow the Lord Jesus Christ are those who are genuine Christians.

1 Corinthians 8:4

"As concerning therefore the eating of those things that are offered in sacrifice unto idols, we know that an idol is nothing in the world, and that there is none other God but one."

Paul brought up to the true Christians in Corinth about eating things that had been offered to idols. Perhaps some were doing this. Buddhists, Shintoists, Hindus, Roman Catholics, and many other groups use idols in some way or another. In fact, research has mentioned that Hindus have 300 million false idol gods.

Verses On Idols
- **Psalms 115:4-7**
"<u>Their idols are silver and gold, the work of men's hands</u>. <u>They have mouths</u>, but they speak not: <u>eyes</u> have they, but they see not: They have <u>ears</u>, but they hear not: <u>noses</u> have they, but they smell not: They have <u>hands</u>, but they handle not: <u>feet</u> have they, but they walk not: <u>neither speak they through their throat</u>."

This verse shows that idols cannot do anything that human beings can do. That's because man made the idols, but God Himself creates human beings.

- **Psalms 135:15-17**
"<u>The idols of the heathen are silver and gold, the work of men's hands</u>. They have <u>mouths</u>, but they speak not; <u>eyes</u> have they, but they see not; They have <u>ears</u>, but they hear not; <u>neither is there any breath in their mouths</u>."

The Psalmist repeats many of the things written in the preceding verses, and adds that they have <u>no breath</u>. Idol worship is ungodly and totally unscriptural.

- **Ezekiel 14:3**
"Son of man, these men have <u>set up their idols in their heart</u>, and put the stumblingblock of their iniquity before their face: should I be enquired of at all by them?"

People may have idols that can be seen, but may also have idols in their hearts.

- **Ezekiel 14:6**
"Therefore <u>say unto the house of Israel</u>, Thus saith the Lord GOD; <u>Repent, and turn yourselves from your idols</u>; and turn away your faces from all your abominations."

Not only were the heathen worshipping idols, but even God's earthly people, Israel, also were practicing this sin, even though it was clearly condemned in God's Ten Commandments and in many other places in the Old Testament.

- **Ezekiel 20:7**
"Then said I unto them, Cast ye away every man the abominations of his eyes, and <u>defile not yourselves with the idols of Egypt</u>: I am the LORD your God."

The idols of Egypt, and all other idols, defile those who worship them.

- **Hosea 4:17**
"<u>Ephraim is joined to idols: let him alone</u>."

This Old Testament principle teaches people that they should not have fellowship with those who have joined themselves to idols.

- **Acts 15:20**
"But that we write unto them, that they <u>abstain from pollutions of idols</u>, and from fornication, and from things strangled, and from blood."

Some of the Old Testament regulations were brought over into the New Testament as well. Abstaining from idols is one thing that has been brought over to the age of grace.

- **Acts 15:29**
"<u>That ye abstain from meats offered to idols</u>, and from blood, and from things strangled, and from fornication: from which if ye keep yourselves, ye shall do well. Fare ye well."

This repeats the command in the verse preceding. It is very important, being mentioned two times.

- **Acts 17:16**
"Now <u>while Paul waited for them at Athens</u>, his spirit was stirred in him, when <u>he saw the city wholly given to idolatry</u>."
Paul saw the entire city of Athens, Greece, totally given over to the sin of idolatry.
- **1 Corinthians 5:11**
"But now I have written unto you <u>not to keep company, if any man that is called a brother be</u> a fornicator, or covetous, or <u>an idolater</u>, or a railer, or a drunkard, or an extortioner; with such an one no not to eat."
It's one thing to have non-Christians guilty of these sins and many others, but genuine Christians are not to keep company and have fellowship with such people.
- **1 Corinthians 10:7**
"<u>Neither be ye idolaters</u>, as were some of them; as it is written, The people sat down to eat and drink, and rose up to play."
This is a very clear-cut command. It is clearly condemned.
- **1 Corinthians 10:14**
"Wherefore, my dearly beloved, <u>flee from idolatry</u>."
True Christians are to run away from any form of idolatry as fast as they can.
- **1 Corinthians 12:2**
"Ye know that <u>ye were Gentiles, carried away unto these dumb idols</u>, even as ye were led."
Dealing with dumb idols in the past is one thing. It should never be continued in the present by genuine Christians.
- **2 Corinthians 6:16-17a**
"And <u>what agreement hath the temple of God with idols</u>? for ye are the temple of the living God; as God hath said, I will dwell in them, and walk in them; and I will be their God, and they shall be my people. Wherefore come out from among them, and be ye separate, saith the Lord,"
The bodies of true Christians are God's temple here on earth. God's temples are never to have fellowship with the many idols of this earth. They are to come out from them and be separate.
- **Galatians 5:20**
"<u>Idolatry</u>, witchcraft, hatred, variance, emulations, wrath, strife, seditions, heresies,"
Idolatry is one of the works of the wicked, sinful, and ungodly flesh that even genuine Christians possess.
- **Ephesians 5:5**
"For this ye know, that no whoremonger, nor unclean person, <u>nor covetous man, who is an idolater</u>, hath any inheritance in the kingdom of Christ and of God."

Covetousness is a form of idolatry because it longs for, and in a sense, worships the things that can be seen.
- **Colossians 3:5**
  "Mortify therefore your members which are upon the earth; fornication, uncleanness, inordinate affection, evil concupiscence, and <u>covetousness, which is idolatry</u>:"

Paul repeats this same thing as he writes from a Roman prison to the true Christians at both Ephesus and Colosse that they should put to death their idolatrous covetousness.
- **1 Thessalonians 1:9**
  "For they themselves shew of us what manner of entering in we had unto you, and how <u>ye turned to God from idols</u> to serve the living and true God;"

The first step is for non-Christians to turn to God and become true Christians. After that, they can see the error of idols and turn from them.
- **1 Peter 4:3**
  "For <u>the time past of our life may suffice us to have wrought</u> the will of the Gentiles, when we walked in lasciviousness, lusts, excess of wine, revellings, banquetings, and <u>abominable idolatries</u>:"

What's evil in the past is still evil in the present and future. It should be forsaken, including abominable idolatries.
- **1 John 5:21**
  "Little children, <u>keep yourselves from idols</u>. Amen."

That's a clear prohibition against idols, whether for new Christians or genuine older Christians. Keep away from these idols!
- **Revelation 9:20**
  "And the rest of the men which were not killed by these plagues yet <u>repented not</u> of the works of their hands, <u>that they should not worship devils, and idols of gold, and silver, and brass, and stone, and of wood</u>: which neither can see, nor hear, nor walk:"

Despite all of God's pouring out His wrath during this Tribulation period, many of those whom God was punishing still maintained their idolatry.
- **Revelation 21:8**
  "<u>But the fearful, and unbelieving</u>, and the abominable, and murderers, and whoremongers, and sorcerers, <u>and idolaters</u>, and all liars, <u>shall have their part in the lake which burneth with fire and brimstone</u>: which is the second death."

Those people who have rejected the Lord Jesus Christ as their only Saviour and, instead, have committed all these sins, will end up in the eternal fires of Hell.

1 Corinthians 8:5
"For though there be that are called gods, whether in heaven or in earth, (as there be gods many, and lords many,)"

Just look at some of those who are "*called gods.*" Articles tell us that there are 330,000,000 (three hundred and thirty million) gods that Hindus alone worship in addition to the many other false religions of the world. Major numbers of gods does not make these gods real and true. Any other God but the God of the Bible is a false god and should never be worshipped or followed.

1 Corinthians 8:6
"But to us *there is* but one God, the Father, of whom are all things, and we in him; and one Lord Jesus Christ, by whom are all things, and we by him."

There is only one true God Who is revealed in three co-equal Persons: God the Father, God the Son, and God the Holy Spirit. Notice, "*of whom are all things*" and also "*by whom are all things.*" The Triune God is the Creator of all things. His creation is believed by very few today and denied by very many. The falsehood and lie of the theories of evolution are substituted for God's creation by BILLIONS of people today, including most of the "Christian" churches and religions. Those who reject the Creator and His creation teach and preach evolution. They believe that life, animals, fish, the stars, and planets all came from some sort of explosion or some other false source.

Verses On God's Creation
- **Genesis 1:1-3**

"In the beginning God created the heaven and the earth. And the earth was without form, and void; and darkness was upon the face of the deep. And the Spirit of God moved upon the face of the waters. And God said, Let there be light: and there was light."

All three Persons of the Godhead had a part in the creation of all things:
      (1) God the Father ("*God created*");
      (2) God the Son –the LOGOS ("*God said*"; and
      (3) God the Holy Spirit ("*the Spirit of God moved.*")

- **Genesis 1:21**
"And <u>God created great whales, and every living creature that moveth, which the waters brought forth abundantly, after their kind, and every winged fowl after his kind</u>: and God saw that it was good."

These creations by the God of the Bible were done only by Him. No matter how you might phrase it, the evolutionary liars could never fulfill these tasks, nor the many other things from God's miraculous creation. Though many of the world's millions of pro-evolutionists believe in their fairy tale, there's not any indisputable proof for it.

- **Colossians 1:16-17**
"For <u>by him were all things created, that are in heaven, and that are in earth, visible and invisible, whether they be thrones, or dominions, or principalities, or powers: all things were created by him, and for him</u>: And he is before all things, and by him all things consist."

Here's another list of God's marvelous creations by the Lord Jesus Christ, God the Father, and God the Holy Spirit.

- **Hebrews 1:2**
"Hath in these last days spoken unto us by <u>his Son</u>, whom he hath appointed heir of all things, <u>by whom also he made the worlds;</u>"

The Lord Jesus Christ, together with the two other members of the Trinity created all things.

- **1 Peter 4:19**
"Wherefore let them that suffer according to the will of God <u>commit the keeping of their souls to him in well doing, as unto a faithful Creator</u>."

God is not only the Creator, but He is a faithful Creator.

- **Genesis 1:27**
"<u>So God created man in his own image</u>, in the image of God created he him; <u>male and female created he them</u>."

God created one male (Adam) and one female (Eve). He intended them to produce children to replenish the earth. He never approved of either sinful male homosexuality, sinful female lesbianism, or sinful bestiality, all of which are practiced today.

- **Psalms 148:5**
"Let them praise the name of <u>the LORD</u>: for he <u>commanded, and they were created</u>."

The heavens were all created merely by God's powerful command.

- **Ecclesiastes 12:1**
"<u>Remember now thy Creator in the days of thy</u> youth, while the evil days come not, nor the years draw nigh, when thou shalt say, I have no pleasure in them;"

Genuine Christians should remember their Creator in the days of their youth.

- **Isaiah 40:28**
"Hast thou not known? hast thou not heard, <u>that the everlasting God, the LORD, the Creator of the ends of the earth, fainteth not, neither is weary</u>? there is no searching of his understanding."

Isaiah has it right about the everlasting Creator God's creation extending to the ends of the earth.

- **Isaiah 45:18**
"For thus saith <u>the LORD that created the heavens; God himself that formed the earth and made it; he hath established it, he created it not in vain, he formed it to be inhabited</u>: I am the LORD; and there is none else."

This is a verse, along with many other verses, that showing God both created the heavens and made the earth and "*established*" it. Something that is "established" doesn't move. The Bible teaches that the earth–not the sun–is the center of the universe. This is called geocentricity (earth-centered). There are about ten, fifteen, or twenty verses in Scripture saying that the earth doesn't move, doesn't rotate, and doesn't revolve around the sun. All the heavenly bodies revolve around the earth. The earth is established. For many years in the past, this was taught by scientists. Then the scientists changed their position into the false heliocentricity (sun-centered) position.

- **Mark 10:6**
"<u>But from the beginning of the creation God made them male and female</u>."

God is the Creator of both the original male (Adam) and the original female (Eve).

- **John 1:3-4**
"<u>All things were made by him; and without him was not any thing made that was made</u>. In him was life; and the life was the light of men."

These verses are speaking about the Lord Jesus Christ's part in creation. All things were made by Him and without Him nothing was made. That's very clear statement about the creation of the world and all that is in it. When evolutionists say creation is false, they're blaspheming the Lord Jesus Christ and His work. His work is not only what He did on the cross of Calvary for the sins of the world, but it also includes His work as the Creator.

- **John 1:10-12**
  "<u>He was in the world, and the world was made by him</u>, and the world knew him not. He came unto his own, and his own received him not. But as many as received him, to them gave he power to become the sons of God, even to them that believe on his name:"

The world was made by the Lord Jesus Christ, not by evolution. When evolution thrives, that's a blasphemy against the Lord Jesus Christ, the Creator, as well as God the Father and God the Holy Spirit.
- **Ephesians 3:9**
  "And to make all men see what is the fellowship of the mystery, which from the beginning of the world hath been hid in <u>God, who created all things by Jesus Christ</u>:"

These words which are underlined have all been omitted by the Gnostic Critical Greek text and by virtually 99% of all the modern English Bible versions which have followed this false and erroneous pagan text. The Gnostics did not believe the Lord Jesus Christ was God in the flesh, so He could not create anything. Therefore, they eliminated this verse and 355 other doctrinal New Testament passages.

1 Corinthians 8:7

"Howbeit *there is* not in every man that knowledge: for some with conscience of the idol unto this hour eat *it* as a thing offered unto an idol; and their conscience being weak is defiled."

Some of the genuine Christians at Corinth did not understand that eating things that had been offered to idols was wrong. This stumbles some people and it should be avoided. If eating foods offered to idols is practiced, their consciences are defiled.

Conscience is usually defined as the part of our human bodies that, if working properly, determines what is good and what is bad. It then commends the good and condemns the bad. If it is not working, people have nothing to give them this discernment.

Verses On Conscience
- **John 8:9**
  "And <u>they which heard it, being convicted by their own conscience</u>, went out one by one, beginning at the eldest, even unto the last: and Jesus was left alone, and the woman standing in the midst."

The consciences of the men who wanted to stone the woman who

committed adultery convicted them and they abandoned this stoning. The Lord Jesus Christ told them that he who is without sin, let him cast the first stone at her. That's when they went out, "*convicted by their own conscience.*" The men were all adulterers as well.
- **Acts 24:16**
  "And herein do I exercise myself, to have always a conscience void of offence toward God, and toward men."

That's what the conscience of every true Christian should be–void of offence toward God, and toward men.
- **1 Corinthians 10:25**
  "Whatsoever is sold in the shambles, that eat, asking no question for conscience sake:"

This food was not sold in the idol's temple, but in a food store where it is unknown whether or not it was offered to idols. If this is the case, genuine Christians could eat of that food without offending their consciences.
- **1 Corinthians 10:27**
  "If any of them that believe not bid you to a feast, and ye be disposed to go; whatsoever is set before you, eat, asking no question for conscience sake."

If a non-Christian invited true Christians to a feast, and they go, they can eat whatever is set before them, asking no question for conscience's sake.
- **1 Timothy 4:2**
  "Speaking lies in hypocrisy; having their conscience seared with a hot iron;"

Many of those who are not genuine Christians today speak lies and have their consciences inoperable because they were seared with a hot iron. That renders them without any feeling at all. That's the case with many apostate preachers today, whether Protestants, Roman Catholics, or Jewish rabbis as well. Their consciences are seared with a hot iron and have no feeling.

There are many other people who are using all sorts of filthy language and writing, listening to filthy and corrupt music, and committing all sorts of sexual immorality. Apparently, their consciences never bother them about these sinful practices.
- **2 Timothy 1:3**
  "I thank God, whom I serve from my forefathers with pure conscience, that without ceasing I have remembrance of thee in my prayers night and day;"

Paul was glad that he served God with a pure conscience rather than a seared conscience.

- **Titus 1:15**
"Unto the pure all things are pure: but <u>unto them that are defiled and unbelieving is nothing pure; but even their mind and conscience is defiled</u>."
Nothing is pure to the defiled and unbelieving. Both their minds and consciences are defiled.
- **Hebrews 9:14**
"<u>How much more shall the blood of Christ</u>, who through the eternal Spirit offered himself without spot to God, <u>purge your conscience from dead works to serve the living God</u>?"
There's purging, cleansing, and purifying of the consciences of true Christians, by the blood of the Lord Jesus Christ, from dead works to serve God.
- **Hebrews 13:18**
"Pray for us: for <u>we trust we have a good conscience, in all things willing to live honestly</u>."
This should be true of all genuine Christians so they can live honest lives which are pleasing to the Lord Jesus Christ.
- **1 Peter 3:16**
"<u>Having a good conscience; that</u>, whereas they speak evil of you, as of evildoers, <u>they may be ashamed that falsely accuse your good conversation in Christ</u>."
Though people might speak evil of true Christians falsely, the Christians should have a good conscience about it and not be too concerned. They should continue to faithfully follow the Words of God, regardless of who might disagree with them for doing it.

1 Corinthians 8:8

"But meat commendeth us not to God: for neither, if we eat, are we the better; neither, if we eat not, are we the worse."

Meat or food of any kind does not commend genuine Christians to God. They are no better in His eyes, if they eat, or if they eat not.

THE MEANING OF THE GREEK WORD, "PARISTEMI"
The Greek Word for *"commend"* is PARISTEMI. Some of the meanings of this Greek Word are:
"1) to place beside or near; 1a) to set at hand; 1a1) to present; 1a2) to proffer; 1a3) to provide; 1a4) to place a person or thing at one's disposal; 1a5) to present a person for another to see and question; 1a6) to present or show;

> 1a7) to bring to, bring near; 1a8) metaph. i.e to bring into one's fellowship or intimacy; 1b) to present (show) by argument, to prove; 2) to stand beside, stand by or near, to be at hand, be present; 2a) to stand by; 2a1) to stand beside one, a bystander; 2b) to appear; 2c) to be at hand, stand ready; 2d) to stand by to help, to succour; 2e) to be present;"

The whole idea of the verses, from seven to thirteen, is the question of eating meat offered to idols. Paul says it doesn't commend us to God if we eat, so these true Christians at Corinth are not to emphasize such eating or not eating.

Verses On Commending
- **Romans 5:8**

"But <u>God commendeth his love toward us, in that, while we were yet sinners, Christ died for us</u>."

God made His love stand close to all the sinners of the world because while every one of them were and are sinners, the Lord Jesus Christ died for their sins in their place. He died for all sinners, not merely only for the so-called "elect." This view is a serious heresy believed by many Christian denominations.

- **2 Corinthians 3:1**

"<u>Do we begin again to commend ourselves? or need we</u>, as some others, <u>epistles of commendation</u> to you, or letters of commendation from you?"

No genuine Christians should praise and exalt themselves. Nor do they need praise and commendation from others. I'm sure when Paul was a Pharisee, he bragged about himself in praise.

- **2 Corinthians 10:18**

"For <u>not he that commendeth himself is approved, but whom the Lord commendeth</u>."

For people to be approved, the Lord must commend them. Self-commendation won't do any good. There is a lot of braggadocio among some believers, some Christians, even some pastors. They talk about their great church, their great sermons, their great crowds, and many other things.

1 Corinthians 8:9

"But take heed lest by any means this liberty of yours become a stumblingblock to them that are weak."

This liberty mentioned in previous verses regarding eating of meat might stumble other genuine Christians.

Verses On Liberty

- **Psalms 119:45**

"And I will walk at liberty: for I seek thy precepts."

The psalmist was walking free and was seeking God's Words and commands.

- **Luke 4:18**

"The Spirit of the Lord is upon me, because he hath anointed me to preach the gospel to the poor; he hath sent me to heal the brokenhearted, to preach deliverance to the captives, and recovering of sight to the blind, to set at liberty them that are bruised,"

One of the reasons the Lord Jesus Christ came into the world was to set at liberty those who are bruised and in sin. They must receive Him as their Saviour to be made free in Him.

- **1 Corinthians 10:29**

"Conscience, I say, not thine own, but of the other: for why is my liberty judged of another man's conscience?"

Before I became a genuine Christian, I had a 15-piece dance band. If I continued to have this band, but it would stumble many other true Christians, so I got rid of it as soon as I thought it out.

- **1 Peter 2:16**

"As free, and not using your liberty for a cloke of maliciousness, but as the servants of God."

Just because genuine Christians have liberty in Christ, this liberty should never be used as a cloke of maliciousness.

Verses On Stumblingblock

- **Leviticus 19:14**

"Thou shalt not curse the deaf, nor put a stumblingblock before the blind, but shalt fear thy God: I am the LORD."

Putting a stumblingblock before the blind person is a sin. He couldn't see it and would probably fall and hurt himself.

- **Romans 14:13**

"Let us not therefore judge one another any more: but judge this rather, that no man put a stumblingblock or an occasion to fall in his brother's way."

> **THE MEANING OF THE GREEK WORD, "PROSKOMA"**
> The Greek Word for "stumbling block" is PROSKOMA. Some of the meanings of that Greek Word are:
>> *"1) a stumbling block; 1a) an obstacle in the way which if one strikes his foot against, he stumbles or falls; 1b) that over which a soul stumbles i.e., by which is caused to sin."*

Genuine Christians should not put stumbling blocks in each others' way. This should be guarded against, however difficult that might be.

- **1 Corinthians 1:23**

"But <u>we preach Christ crucified, unto the Jews a stumblingblock</u>, and unto the Greeks foolishness;"

The Jews stumbled at Paul's preaching to them about the Lord Jesus Christ Who was crucified for their sins.

1 Corinthians 8:10

"For if any man see thee which hast knowledge sit at meat in the idol's temple, shall not the conscience of him which is weak be emboldened to eat those things which are offered to idols;"

If those true Christians have knowledge about idols, yet eat in the idol's temple, those Christians who are spiritually weak may likely follow them and also eat the things offered to idols. This probably would turn out badly. If this be so, perhaps these knowledgeable Christians should never sit at meat in these heathen temples.

1 Corinthians 8:11

"And through thy knowledge shall the weak brother perish, for whom Christ died?"

It might be, if weak, yet genuine, Christians see other Christians eating meat offered to idols, they might perish (not in the sense of losing their salvation, but in the sense of losing their usefulness in service for the Lord Jesus Christ).

Verses On The Death Of Christ

- **Romans 5:6**

"For when we were yet without strength, in due time <u>Christ died for the ungodly</u>."

The Lord Jesus Christ died for the sins of every person who was ever born or whoever will be born in the future. God calls them the "*ungodly.*" It is a very serious heresy for the hyper-Calvinists to believe the falsehood and lie that the Lord Jesus Christ died exclusively for a tiny group of people that they call "*the elect.*"

- **Romans 5:8**
  "But God commendeth his love toward us, in that, <u>while we were yet sinners, Christ died for us</u>."

The Lord Jesus Christ died for the sins of all the sinners of the world, dying in their place. For those sinners who genuinely believe that He died for their sins, they are the recipients of salvation and eternal life.

- **Romans 14:15**
  "But if thy brother be grieved with *thy* meat, now walkest thou not charitably. <u>Destroy not him with thy meat, for whom Christ died</u>."

Genuine Christians should be very careful about getting, selfishly, too close to idols' meat. They must not destroy the faith of other Christians for whom the Lord Jesus Christ died.

- **1 Corinthians 15:3**
  "For I delivered unto you first of all that which I also received, how that <u>Christ died for our sins according to the scriptures</u>;"

The reason the Lord Jesus Christ died on the cross was to atone for and take the sins of the world in His own sinless body.

- **2 Corinthians 5:15**
  "And *that* <u>he died for all</u>, that they which live should not henceforth live unto themselves, but unto him which died for them, and rose again."

The Lord Jesus Christ "*died for all.*" This truth is discarded by those who believe in the heresy that the Lord Jesus Christ died exclusively for whom they call "*the elect*" rather than for ALL the sins of the ENTIRE WORLD!

- **1 Thessalonians 5:10**
  "<u>Who died for us</u>, that, whether we wake or sleep, we should live together with him."

Though Paul is speaking to the genuine Christians at Thessalonica, the "*us*" means that the Lord Jesus Christ died also for the sins of everyone else in all the world.

- **1 John 2:2**
  "And <u>he is the propitiation for our sins</u>: and not for ours only, <u>but also for *the sins of* the whole world</u>."

The Lord Jesus Christ provided propitiation not only for the sins of those true Christians to whom John was writing, but also for "*the sins of the whole world.*"

1 Corinthians 8:12

"But when ye sin so against the brethren, and wound their weak conscience, ye sin against Christ."

Only genuine Christians are "in the Body of Christ." They are so close to the Lord Jesus Christ, when a person sins against a genuine Christian That person sins against Christ Himself.

- **Acts 9:4**

"And he fell to the earth, and heard a voice saying unto him, Saul, Saul, why persecutest thou me?"

When Paul put genuine Christians in prison and agreed with putting them to death, the Lord Jesus Christ told Saul that he was persecuting Him.

- **1 Corinthians 6:15**

"Know ye not that your bodies are the members of Christ? shall I then take the members of Christ, and make them the members of an harlot? God forbid."

True Christians are the "*members of Christ.*" Should they not take these "*members of Christ*" and make them members of a harlot? That would be offending the Lord Jesus Christ Himself!

- **1 Corinthians 12:27**

"Now ye are the body of Christ, and members in particular."

Genuine Christians are "*the body of Christ*" and members of that body. They are united to Him.

1 Corinthians 8:13

"Wherefore, if meat make my brother to offend, I will eat no flesh while the world standeth, lest I make my brother to offend."

He doesn't make his brother sin against Christ, to offend and cause stumbling in any way, shape or form. There are many verses on offences and offending:

Verses On Offences

- **Psalms 119:165**

"Great peace have they which love thy law: and nothing shall offend them."

If true Christians love God's Words and law, "*nothing shall offend them.*" They will be able to overcome any hatred, jealousy, insult, or defamation if they are strongly attuned to the inerrant and infallible Words of God.

- **Proverbs 18:19**

"A brother offended is harder to be won than a strong city: and their contentions are like the bars of a castle."

When genuine Christians are offended, it is very hard to win them back. It's harder than taking over a strong city.
- **Ecclesiastes 10:4**
  "If the spirit of the ruler rise up against thee, leave not thy place; for yielding pacifieth great offences."

Now, if a ruler is against you, just stay put. Don't leave your place. Just stay in place. In so doing, you pacify great offences.
- **Matthew 11:6**
  "And blessed is he, <u>whosoever shall not be offended in me</u>."

True Christians are blessed and happy if they are never offended by people who speak out against the Lord Jesus Christ and them as being Christians.
- **Matthew 15:12**
  "Then came his disciples, and said unto him, Knowest thou that <u>the Pharisees were offended, after they heard this saying</u>?"

The Pharisees were offended over what the Lord Jesus Christ was teaching. They were apostate Jews who had resisted the Words of God. As such, they were offended by the Lord Jesus Christ.
- **Matthew 16:23**
  "<u>But he turned, and said unto Peter, Get thee behind me, Satan: thou art an offence unto me</u>: for thou savourest not the things that be of God, but those that be of men."

Peter was out of the will of God, being influenced by Satan. The Lord Jesus Christ told Satan to get behind Him because he was an offence to Him.
- **Matthew 26:31**
  "Then saith Jesus unto them, <u>All ye shall be offended because of me this night</u>: for it is written, I will smite the shepherd, and the sheep of the flock shall be scattered abroad."

The Lord Jesus Christ told his apostles that all of them would be offended in Him because He would be smitten by crucifixion.
- **Philippians 1:10**
  "That ye may approve things that are excellent; <u>that ye may be sincere and without offence till the day of Christ</u>;"

Paul, writing from a Roman prison, told the genuine Christians in Philippi to be sincere and without any offence until the Lord Jesus Christ would return for them in the Rapture and take them home to Heaven.
- **James 3:2**
  "For <u>in many things we offend all. If any man offend not in word, the same is a perfect man</u>, and able also to bridle the whole body."

In many things, true Christians might offend many people. If they don't offend by what they say, they are mature.
- **Romans 4:25**
"<u>Who was delivered for our offences</u>, and was raised again for our justification."

The Lord Jesus Christ was delivered to the cross of Calvary because of the sins and offences of the entire world of people.
- **Luke 7:23**
"And <u>blessed is he, whosoever shall not be offended in me</u>."

The Lord Jesus Christ said that genuine Christians who would not be offended in Him, would be blessed and happy.
- **Mark 4:17**
"And have no root in themselves, and so endure but for a time: afterward, <u>when affliction or persecution ariseth for the word's sake, immediately they are offended</u>."

When people have no root in the Lord and His Words, when affliction for God's Word's sake comes, they are offended.
- **Matthew 26:33**
"Peter answered and said unto him, <u>Though all men shall be offended because of thee, yet will I never be offended</u>."

Peter lied when he told the Lord Jesus Christ he would never be offended. In point of fact, Peter was offended in Him by denying he ever knew Him three different times.
- **Luke 7:23**
"<u>And blessed is he, whosoever shall not be offended in me</u>."

Genuine Christians or any other people would be blessed and happy if they would never be offended in the Lord Jesus Christ.

1 Corinthians Chapter Nine

1 Corinthians 9:1

"Am I not an apostle? am I not free? have I not seen Jesus Christ our Lord? are not ye my work in the Lord?"

In this verse, Paul is defending his apostleship. I'm sure that many genuine Christians at Corinth wondered if Paul was really an apostle. He saw the Lord Jesus Christ when He saved him on the way to Damascus to imprison Christians. The true Christians in that city were led to the Saviour by Paul the apostle. The word for *"apostle"* occurs nineteen times in the New Testament. Sixteen of these nineteen refer to the Apostle Paul. The word 'apostle' appears in the New Testament and out of those nineteen, sixteen refers to the apostle Paul.

Verses Calling Paul An Apostle

- **Romans 1:1**

"Paul, a servant of Jesus Christ, called to be an apostle, separated unto the gospel of God,"

The Lord Jesus Christ called Paul an apostle when He saved him.

- **Romans 11:13**

"For I speak to you Gentiles, inasmuch as I am the apostle of the Gentiles, I magnify mine office:"

Paul calls himself the apostle of the Gentiles.

- **1 Corinthians 1:1**

"Paul, called to be an apostle of Jesus Christ through the will of God, and Sosthenes our brother,"

Paul is named as an apostle by the will of God in his own writings.

- **1 Corinthians 15:9**

"For I am the least of the apostles, that am not meet to be called an apostle, because I persecuted the church of God."

In his humility, though he was an apostle, Paul calls himself the least of the apostles.

- **2 Corinthians 1:1**

"Paul, an apostle of Jesus Christ by the will of God, and Timothy *our* brother, unto the church of God which is at Corinth, with all the saints which are in all Achaia:"

Paul was an apostle by the will of God, not by the choice of any human being.

Verses On Paul Seeing The Lord Jesus Christ

Paul's testimony about his seeing the Lord Jesus Christ is in three places in the book of Acts. It is found in Acts 9, 22, and 26. He was on his way to Damascus to imprison Christians when the Saviour appeared unto him when he became a genuine Christian.

- **Acts 9:5**

"And <u>he said, Who art thou, Lord? And the Lord said, I am Jesus whom thou persecutest</u>: it is hard for thee to kick against the pricks."

Some of the apostate writers deny that this is true. They falsely claim that Paul was just dreaming or saw a vision, not a reality.

- **Acts 22:8**

"And I answered, <u>Who art thou, Lord</u>? And he said unto me, <u>I am Jesus of Nazareth</u>, whom thou persecutest."

The Lord Jesus Christ answered Paul when he asked "*Who art thou, Lord?*" He answered Paul, "*I am Jesus of Nazareth.*" The Lord Jesus Christ appeared in a light brighter than the sun at noonday.

- **Acts 26:15**

"And I said, <u>Who art thou, Lord? And he said, I am Jesus whom thou persecutest</u>."

This is the third time the Bible describes Paul's seeing the Lord Jesus Christ. Paul talked to Him, and He talked to Paul.

Paul continued in Corinth a year and six months ... teaching the Word of God among them. Notice what he was doing. Teaching the Word of God among them. That's what I believe the pastor's duty today is–teaching and preaching God's Words rather than majoring in topics and stories with very little Bible teaching involved. As some have said, "*Sermonettes make Christianettes.*" This is not what God wants.

1 Corinthians 9:2

"If I be not an apostle unto others, yet doubtless I am to you: for the seal of mine apostleship are ye in the Lord."

Paul wanted the genuine Christians at Corinth to know that he was an apostle unto them. He gave them the Gospel and led them to know the Lord Jesus Christ as their Saviour.

The Wrong Choice of Matthias As An Apostle

Peter and some early Christians used human methods to elect Matthias to take the place of Judas as an apostle. God's method

was for the Lord Jesus Christ Himself to choose the replacement for Judas, just as He chose the original twelve apostles.
- **Acts 1:20-26**
"For it is written in the book of Psalms, Let his habitation be desolate, and let no man dwell therein: and his bishoprick let another take. Wherefore of these men which have companied with us all the time that the Lord Jesus went in and out among us, Beginning from the baptism of John, unto that same day that he was taken up from us, must one be ordained to be a witness with us of his resurrection. And they appointed two, Joseph called Barsabas, who was surnamed Justus, and Matthias. And they prayed, and said, Thou, Lord, which knowest the hearts of all men, shew whether of these two thou hast chosen, That he may take part of this ministry and apostleship, from which Judas by transgression fell, that he might go to his own place. And they gave forth their lots; and the lot fell upon Matthias; and he was numbered with the eleven apostles."

Peter made up his own qualifications for being an apostle. Paul was a witness of the bodily resurrection of the Lord Jesus Christ. He saw Him and spoke with him, and the Lord Jesus also talked with Paul from Heaven's glory.

Many believe that Matthias was the true apostle who took the place of Judas the traitor. I do not believe that. I believe Matthias was an illegitimate apostle who was "elected" by the whims of Peter and the crowd. I believe Paul was the twelfth apostle to take the place of Judas. Matthias was elected by the people. Paul was chosen and called by the Lord Jesus Christ Who called all the other apostles. Men make mistakes in their choices and elections. The Lord Jesus Christ never makes mistakes.

The church at Corinth, founded by Paul, was an indication that he was an apostle, chosen by the Lord Jesus Christ Himself.

1 Corinthians 9:3

"Mine answer to them that do examine me is this,"
Paul had an answer to those who examined him.

> **THE MEANING OF THE GREEK WORD, "ANAKRINO"**
> The Greek Word for "*examine*" is ANAKRINO. Some of the meanings of this Greek Word are:
> > "1) examine or judge; 1a) to investigate, examine, enquire into, scrutinise, sift, question; 1a1) specifically in a forensic

> *sense of a judge to hold an investigation; 1a2) to interrogate, examine the accused or witnesses; 1b) to judge of, estimate, determine the excellence or defects of any person or thing.)"*

That Greek Word for "*examine*" is in the Greek present tense. As such, it means the examination is a continuous and unremitting action. Many have continued to deny the apostleship of Paul. He wrote fourteen books of the New Testament. These are more books than any other writer in the New Testament. God laid His hand upon Paul. Though he was an apostle, he was continuously examined and questioned about his apostleship.

1 Corinthians 9:4
"Have we not power to eat and to drink?"

Though this is not clear, perhaps Paul is continuing to put his eating and drinking in the context of the idols that were discussed in this book earlier. If this be true, Paul is saying that he has liberty to eat or drink things that may have been offered to idols and then sold in the stores of his day. Though it might not be wise in regard to weaker Christians, yet Paul had the power to do this. Paul might never do this because of possibly stumbling some genuine Christians, but at least he had the power, ability, and right to do these things.

1 Corinthians 9:5
"Have we not power to lead about a sister, a wife, as well as other apostles, and as the brethren of the Lord, and Cephas?"

Here is another power and right that Paul mentions. As an apostle, he has the power and right to be married. He mentions some of the other apostles who were married as "*the brethren of the Lord*" and Cephas who is the apostle Peter. Though others differ with me on this, I believe Paul was married and his wife had died before he did. He was a widower.

Paul was a member of the Jewish Sanhedrin. One of the qualifications of being a member of the Sanhedrin, the ruling body of the Jews of his day, was that every member had to be married. Another reason I believe he was a widower is the knowledgeable manner in which he covers marriage intimacy in 1 Corinthians 7:1-5.

Marriage is required in the Bible for all pastors-bishops-elders. It is also a Biblical requirement for all church deacons just like the pastors today. I believe as a requirement is that every deacon must be married. Every pastor-bishop-elder and ever deacon who is not married fails to meet the clear Biblical standards for these two Biblical church officers.

There is nothing wrong with marriage after the wives of pastors or deacons have died, provided a proper time for this second marriage is allowed.

Verses On Marriage

- **Mark 1:30**

"But <u>Simon's wife's mother lay sick of a fever</u>, and anon they tell him of her."

The apostle Peter had a wife, so Paul could have one also.

- **Luke 4:38**

"And he arose out of the synagogue, and entered into Simon's house. And <u>Simon's wife's mother was taken with a great fever</u>; and they besought him for her."

Three witnesses (Matthew, Mark, and Luke) all declared in their Gospels that Peter, (whom the Roman Catholic Church believes was the first Pope), was married.

- **Hebrews 13:4**

"<u>Marriage is honourable in all</u>, and the bed undefiled: but whoremongers and adulterers God will judge."

That includes priests, nuns, and popes as well as all preachers, and the lay people around the world. The Roman Catholic Church is contrary to the plain verses of the Bible like this one. Because of their being against marriage for their priests and nuns, many of their priests either have homosexual relations with other priests, or adulterous relations with nuns. Though this is well known, the Pope has made no penalties for such wickedness and sins.

1 Corinthians 9:6

"Or I only and Barnabas, have not we power to forbear working?"

Barnabas and Paul were both missionaries for the Lord Jesus Christ. They had the right not to work, but be supported by the churches. Yet both of them worked hard at their jobs to support themselves. They did not want to hurt their testimonies among the churches to whom they ministered.

Verses On The Apostles Working
- **Acts 18:1-3**

"After these things <u>Paul departed from Athens, and came to Corinth</u>; <u>And found</u> a certain Jew named <u>Aquila</u>, born in Pontus, lately come from Italy, with his wife Priscilla; (because that Claudius had commanded all Jews to depart from Rome:) and came unto them. And <u>because he was of the same craft, he abode with them, and wrought: for by their occupation they were tentmakers</u>."

Paul was a hard worker who made tents. This was a very difficult task. It involved working with tent-making materials such as leather or other materials. It involved sewing the materials together. I think that's why some pastors with small churches must work at some secular job to support their families; to support our family and our Bible For Today ministry, I taught English in the Philadelphia school district for nineteen years to classes who had many rowdy kids in them . . . eighteen years in junior high school and one year in senior high school.

- **Acts 20:31-38**

"Therefore watch, and remember, that by the space of three years I ceased not to warn every one night and day with tears. And now, brethren, I commend you to God, and to the word of his grace, which is able to build you up, and to give you an inheritance among all them which are sanctified. <u>I have coveted no man's silver, or gold, or apparel. Yea, ye yourselves know, that these hands have ministered unto my necessities, and to them that were with me. I have shewed you all things, how that so labouring ye ought to support the weak</u>, and to remember the words of the Lord Jesus, how he said, It is more blessed to give than to receive. And when he had thus spoken, he kneeled down, and prayed with them all. And they all wept sore, and fell on Paul's neck, and kissed him, Sorrowing most of all for the words which he spake, that they should see his face no more. And they accompanied him unto the ship."

Paul honored the Words of God and built up his followers with God's Words. He hadn't coveted anybody's silver. He was not a money-grabber as some pastors, TV-and-Internet speakers who live in million dollar homes. Paul was not selfish or greedy. That's one of the qualifications for pastors/bishops/elders mentioned in 1 Timothy 3:3. They should be ones who are *"not greedy of filthy lucre."*

1 Corinthians 9:7

"Who goeth a warfare any time at his own charges? who planteth a vineyard, and eateth not of the fruit thereof? or who feedeth a flock, and eateth not of the milk of the flock?"

Paul gives three illustrations why pastors, missionaries, or other genuine Christian workers should be cared for by those to whom they minister.

1. The Soldier. The soldier who goes to war to defend his country does not go to war at his own expense. His country hires him and pays his salary, pays for his family's housing, pays for any medical care, and many other things. I was a U.S. Navy Chaplain for five years on active duty. For all five of these years, the government paid my wages, provided an allowance for our house, an allowance for my uniforms, and many other things.

2. The Farmer. The farmer who plants a vineyard is able to eat the fruit of the grapes that grow in it. That is his reward for all the work it takes to care for the vineyard.

3. The Shepherd. The shepherd who feeds and takes care of his flock of sheep or his cattle, drinks the milk of those sheep or cattle.

Verses On True Christians Being Soldiers For Christ

- **2 Corinthians 10:3-4**

"For though we walk in the flesh, we do not war after the flesh: (For the weapons of our warfare <u>are not carnal, but mighty through God</u> to the pulling down of strong holds;)"

True Christians should realize that the Lord Jesus Christ expects them to use the weapons that He supplies, not the carnal, fleshly weapons of their own making.

- **1 Timothy 1:18-19**

"This charge I commit unto thee, son Timothy, according to the prophecies which went before on thee, <u>that thou</u> by them <u>mightest war a good warfare</u>; Holding faith, and a good conscience; which some having put away concerning faith have made shipwreck:"

The genuine Christian faith is pictured as a battle and a warfare. Those who think it is just a pink tea party do not understand the battles and the opposing armies. True Christians' warfare should be a "good" one at all times.

- **2 Timothy 2:3-4**
"Thou therefore <u>endure hardness, as a good soldier of Jesus Christ. No man that warreth entangleth himself with the affairs of this life</u>; that he may please him who hath chosen him to be a soldier."

The Lord Jesus is the Commander-in-Chief of all genuine Christians in their battles as good soldiers. They must fight for Him in all the battles that are against them in the power of the Holy Spirit Who indwells them.

All true Christians have three enemies: (1) the world; (2) their flesh; and (3) the Devil. Against all these three enemies, genuine Christians must do battle, not in their own strength, but in the power of God the Holy Spirit, the Lord Jesus Christ, and God the Heavenly Father–the Triune God.

- **1 Corinthians 9:26-27**
"<u>I therefore so run, not as uncertainly; so fight I</u>, not as one that beateth the air: But I keep under my body, and bring it into subjection: lest that by any means, when I have preached to others, I myself should be a castaway."

Paul speaks of his being in a fight. He doesn't do it in an uncertain manner, but in the certain power of God.

- **1 Timothy 6:12**
"<u>Fight the good fight of faith</u>, lay hold on eternal life, whereunto thou art also called, and hast professed a good profession before many witnesses."

Paul commands Pastor Timothy, there in the church at Ephesus, to fight the good fight for the faith, including the Words of God which specify the proper doctrines of that faith. This means that those true Christians today must have the proper and accurate Bible that is based on the preserved and inspired Words of the proper Hebrew, Aramaic, and Greek original languages. The King James Bible in English is such a Bible.

- **2 Timothy 4:7**
"<u>I have fought a good fight</u>, I have finished my course, I have kept the faith:"

In his last letter before the Roman government executed him, Paul told Pastor Timothy that he had fought a good fight during his entire ministry for the Lord Jesus Christ. This was a good pattern for Timothy and for all genuine Christians today.

1 Corinthians 9:8

"Say I these things as a man? or saith not the law the same also?"

Paul was not alone in his position that those who work for someone should be paid and supported by those for whom they work. This policy is not only taught in the New Testament, but is also found in the pages of the Old Testament as well.

1 Corinthians 9:9

"For it is written in the law of Moses, Thou shalt not muzzle the mouth of the ox that treadeth out the corn. Doth God take care for oxen?"

Here is one of the Old Testament verses that teaches that when a person or even an animal works, they should get a remuneration for this work. This is the fourth illustration of this principle. People should not muzzle the ox when he is treading out the corn. The ox has a right to eat some of the corn he is treading out.

- **Deuteronomy 25:4**

"Thou shalt not muzzle the ox when he treadeth out the corn."

The ox is working, and he should not be muzzled. He has a right to eat some of the corn as he is working. Paul asks the question: *"Doth God take care for oxen?"* The answer is *"Yes, He certainly does."*

- **Proverbs 12:10**

"A righteous man regardeth the life of his beast: but the tender mercies of the wicked are cruel."

Genuine Christians should follow this Old Testament principle and they take good care of any animals they might have, large or small.

1 Corinthians 9:10

"Or saith he it altogether for our sakes? For our sakes, no doubt, this is written: that he that ploweth should plow in hope; and that he that thresheth in hope should be partaker of his hope."

This principle was written for the sakes of true Christians as well as those Israelites in the Old Testament. The men who plow or thresh wheat should be partakers of the fruit of the plowing and threshing. Plowing is the 5th illustration of what Paul is teaching here and threshing is the 6th illustration of this principle of receiving a reward for the work that you do.

1 Corinthians 9:11

"If we have sown unto you spiritual things, is it a great thing if we shall reap your carnal things?"

Paul now illustrates his instruction in this verse by saying if he preaches and teaches the spiritual things of the Lord, isn't it easy to understand how he should reap some of the church's material things in the form of payment for this ministry?

The same is true of a genuine Christian evangelist. If he preaches and teaches the Gospel in a local church for a week or two weeks of meetings, should he not receive some payment for his faithful ministry to the churches to which he ministers?

The same can be said for true missionaries on the home or foreign fields. They preach and teach the Words of God to those to whom they minister. Why is it not reasonable that the people to whom they minister, or the mission board who sends them forth, provide money for them to live?

From my wife's and my observations while on the mission field of Africa, we noticed some (not all) missionaries who didn't seem to be working at all. They were playing ball and doing other secular things, but no things that were of eternal value. They seemed to be getting full-time-pay for part-time work.

1 Corinthians 9:12

"If others be partakers of *this* power over you, *are* not we rather? Nevertheless we have not used this power, but suffer all things, lest we should hinder the gospel of Christ.

Paul did not use the power of being paid by the churches, even though he deserved and could have used it, but he did not, lest it might hinder the cause of the Lord Jesus Christ in his day.

1 Corinthians 9:13

"Do ye not know that they which minister about holy things live of the things of the temple? and they which wait at the altar are partakers with the altar?"

This is the seventh illustration, of how it is absolutely essential, reasonable, and Scriptural, for those that work in holy things should be paid by the people to whom they minister. This was the case of those who ministered of holy things in the Old Testament.

Israel Gave 10% To The Lord And His Servants
- **Leviticus 27:30**
"And all the tithe of the land, whether of the seed of the land, or of the fruit of the tree, is the LORD'S: it is holy unto the LORD."

Holy things were given to the Lord. The Levities were the representatives of the Lord and received 10% of these gifts.

- **Leviticus 27:32**
"And concerning the tithe of the herd, or of the flock, even of whatsoever passeth under the rod, the tenth shall be holy unto the LORD."

This 10% was his portion given to the LORD in the Old Testament. In the New Testament, it is to be *"as God hath prospered"*(1 Corinthians 16:2) whether less or greater than 10% giving.

- **Numbers 18:21**
"And, behold, I have given the children of Levi all the tenth in Israel for an inheritance, for their service which they serve, even the service of the tabernacle of the congregation."

This was God's order for His Old Testament Levites for their service unto the LORD.

- **Numbers 18:26**
"Thus speak unto the Levites, and say unto them, When ye take of the children of Israel the tithes which I have given you from them for your inheritance, then ye shall offer up an heave offering of it for the LORD, even a tenth part of the tithe."

Again, God gave the Levites the tithes for their inheritance. Then they were to give back to the LORD the tenth of the tithe. The priests also had a certain portion of the offerings such as the heave offering and wave breast. (Exodus 29:27)

1 Corinthians 9:14

"Even so hath the Lord ordained that they which preach the gospel should live of the gospel."

This is the way God ordained it, not man. It is God's way of providing for faithful pastors, missionaries, and other Christian workers.

Verses On Preaching
- **Mark 16:15**
"And he said unto them, Go ye into all the world, and preach the gospel to every creature."

The Gospel of the Lord Jesus Christ is to be preached to all the world. The last twelve verses of Mark, including this verse, have been eliminated in the Gnostic Critical Greek texts of Sinaiticus and Vaticanus. Every single one of the other Greek texts have all 12 of these verses. Because of this, over 99% of the current English versions also omit these verses such as the ASV, NASV, NIV, RSV, NRSV, and ESV, to name only a few.
- **Luke 4:18a**
"The Spirit of the Lord is upon me, because he hath anointed me to preach the gospel to the poor;"

The Gospel is to be preached to the poor as well to all others.
- **Acts 16:10b**
". . . the Lord had called us for to preach the gospel unto them."

The Lord Jesus Christ called the apostles, and all genuine Christians as well, to preach the true Biblical Gospel to all people.
- **Romans 1:15**
"So, as much as in me is, I am ready to preach the gospel to you that are at Rome also."

Paul was a Gospel preacher. He preached the good news of the Lord Jesus Christ, how he died for the sins of the world, and how they must truly trust Him for their salvation.
- **Romans 10:15**
"And how shall they preach, except they be sent? as it is written, How beautiful are the feet of them that preach the gospel of peace, and bring glad tidings of good things!"

God says that those who preach the genuine Gospel of the Lord Jesus Christ have beautiful feet, that is, do a very needful task.
- **Romans 15:20**
"Yea, so have I strived to preach the gospel, not where Christ was named, lest I should build upon another man's foundation:"

Paul didn't want to preach the Gospel where it had already been preached, but wanted to spread it elsewhere.
- **1 Corinthians 1:17**
"For Christ sent me not to baptize, but to preach the gospel: not with wisdom of words, lest the cross of Christ should be made of none effect."

Paul was called by the Lord Jesus Christ to preach the Gospel in the power of the Holy Spirit, not in the wisdom of words.
- **1 Corinthians 9:16**
"For though I preach the gospel, I have nothing to glory of: for necessity is laid upon me; yea, woe is unto me, if I preach not the gospel!"

Paul would have a woe upon him if he did not preach the genuine Gospel of Christ.
- **Galatians 1:8-9**
"But <u>though we</u>, or an angel from heaven, <u>preach any other gospel</u> unto you than that which we have preached unto you, <u>let him be accursed</u>. As we said before, so say I now again, If any man preach any other gospel unto you than that ye have received, <u>let him be accursed</u>."

Paul warns about those who preach another or false Gospel as many do today. They will be accursed.

The genuine Gospel of the Lord Jesus Christ is both bad news and good news. It's bad news because it teaches that everyone in the world is lost and bound for an everlasting hell. It's good news because it teaches that the Lord Jesus Christ, on the cross, carried the sins of all the world in His own sinless body. It is important news, because it teaches the necessity of people to genuinely believe in the Lord Jesus Christ and sincerely trust Him as their Saviour in order to have everlasting life. It is a gross perversion of the Gospel to say that the Lord Jesus Christ died only for the "*elect*" rather than for the entire world, and that only the "*elect*" can go to Heaven and have everlasting life. John 3:16 clearly denies this false gospel!

1 Corinthians 9:15

"But I have used none of these things: neither have I written these things, that it should be so done unto me: for *it were* better for me to die, than that any man should make my glorying void."

Paul didn't want things to be done to him or for him. He wasn't selfish, but wanted to glory in the Lord alone.

1 Corinthians 9:16

"For though I preach the gospel, I have nothing to glory of: for necessity is laid upon me; yea, woe is unto me, if I preach not the gospel!"

Paul preached the true and Biblical gospel of the Lord Jesus Christ. It was a necessity. That is why the Lord Jesus Christ called Paul to be an apostle and an evangelist. He didn't get any glory for himself by preaching the Gospel. It was his joy. He had an urgency and a necessity to do this faithfully. If he did not preach the genuine Gospel, he had a woe against him, as to all those in our times who do not preach the Biblical Gospel.

Many preachers have taken the necessity out of their preaching. There's no necessity. There's no need. There's no power. There's no push. They just go through the motions.

1 Corinthians 9:17

"For if I do this thing willingly, I have a reward: but if against my will, a dispensation of the gospel is committed unto me."

Paul is preaching the genuine Gospel of the Lord Jesus Christ willingly. It is not against his will. Nobody but the Lord Jesus Christ saved him and called him into His service. No one forced him to do it. He surrendered his life and will to the Lord Jesus Christ.

Willingness is great. When the Lord Jesus Christ has the wills of genuine Christians, He has their whole selves. He has their whole beings. Proverbs 23:26a says: *"My son, give me thine heart."* When God has a true Christian's heart, He also has their lips, their eyes, their ears, their hands, their feet, and their minds, He has all of them. Paul served the Lord Jesus Christ willingly, because he was yielded to Him.

1 Corinthians 9:18

"What is my reward then? Verily that, when I preach the gospel, I may make the gospel of Christ without charge, that I abuse not my power in the gospel."

Paul's reward was that he could preach the Gospel without charge. He was definitely entitled for his needs being cared for from his faithful preaching, but he doesn't want to abuse his power in the Gospel. His reward is that he makes it without charge. He does not want to abuse his power.

Paul didn't want to charge the Corinthian church money for his preaching, although it is Biblical for other pastors, missionaries, and Christian workers to be paid for their services by those they serve. It was true in Paul's day and is true now.

1 Corinthians 9:19

"For though I be free from all men, yet have I made myself servant unto all, that I might gain the more."

Paul tells the church at Corinth six things about himself in order to gain more people for the Lord Jesus Christ.

Verses About Paul:
(1) Paul Was Born Free
- Acts 22:28

"And the chief captain answered, With a great sum obtained I this freedom. And <u>Paul said, But I was free born</u>." Though Paul was born free, yet he made himself servant unto all people in order that he may gain more to the cause of the Lord Jesus Christ and His everlasting life. He was sympathetic to the needs of both the servants and the free people to whom he ministers.

I remember the man who gave the charge at my ordination ceremony at the Berea Baptist Church in Berea, Ohio. He said to me, in that ordination ceremony:

"You must be able to be sympathetic to those to whom you minister. You must be able to look at them as they are looking up out of their hospital bed. You must be able to put yourself in their place and minister to them. All those who are sick, all those that have lost loved ones and those who have other difficulties, you seek to help them in spiritual matters and in other ways to the best of your ability."

1 Corinthians 9:20

"And unto the Jews I became as a Jew, that I might gain the Jews; to them that are under the law, as under the law, that I might gain them that are under the law;"

Paul explains two more types of people that he sought to win for the Lord Jesus Christ.

(2) To Jews, Paul Was As A Jew

Though Paul was now a genuine Christian, he became as a Jew to those who were not Christians, but still Jews. His mind thought like the Jew might think, so he might gain the Jews for the Lord Jesus Christ.

(3) To Those Under The Law, Paul Was As Under The Law

To those who were under the law of Moses, Paul became as under that law; he remembered how it was to be under the Mosaic system, so he could better seek them to trust in the Lord Jesus Christ as their Saviour.

1 Corinthians 9:21

"**To them that are without law, as without law, (being not without law to God, but under the law to Christ,) that I might gain them that are without law.**"

Paul mentioned a fourth kind of people that he sought to win to the Lord Jesus Christ.

(4) To Those Without Law, Paul Was As Without Law

This is the fourth category, of those who are without law, those who were Gentiles and had nothing to do with the law of Moses, or any law at all. It sounds like they were those who were absolutely lawless. Put yourself in Paul's position. This might mean those who were harlots, murderers, thieves, gangsters, gamblers, or a number of other lawless people. These would indeed be hard to win over to become genuine Christians, but Paul was willing to witness faithfully to them as well.

1 Corinthians 9:22

"**To the weak became I as weak, that I might gain the weak: I am made all things to all men, that I might by all means save some.**"

Here are groups five and six to whom Paul was willing to give the Gospel of the Lord Jesus Christ.

(5) To Those Who Are Weak, Paul Was As Weak

If you are a strong person, it's somewhat difficult to put yourself in a position of someone who is very weak. You might go to minister to someone who is very weak. Perhaps they are in bed, such as very old people who are confined to bed for the rest of their lives. Or perhaps they are not confined to bed, but are so weak they cannot even get up out of their chair without help. I hope, as Paul did, true Christians would be able to minister to those who are weak in their health.

(6) To All Other People, Paul Was As They Were

Some have taken this to mean that Paul or other genuine Christians may compromise their Biblical position of doctrinal and Biblical purity. No, I don't think that is what Paul is talking about at all. Don't be a sinner. You don't have to be a drunk to minister to drunks. You don't have to be a thief to minister to a thief, and so on.

In other words, Paul wanted to be made sympathetic to any condition he might find in people, without living in that condition

himself. Paul, by all means wanted to save some to become true Christians who receive the Lord Jesus Christ as their Saviour.
- **Luke 19:10**
"For the Son of man is come to seek and to save that which was lost."

The Lord Jesus Christ Himself came into this world and died on the cross for every person who ever lived in order, if they sincerely trust Him, they might become genuine Christians.

1 Corinthians 9:23

"And this I do for the gospel's sake, that I might be partaker thereof with you."

All that Paul was doing in dealing with all these different classes of people was for the Gospel's sake. Notice the last part of this verse: *"that I might be partaker thereof with you."* You might ask, *"In what sense did the Corinthian church partake of Paul's ministry?"* The answer is the true Christians in the church at Corinth, were partakers of Paul's ministry in every sense. They are joint-partners with him. They prayed for him as he went on his three missionary journeys and in other ways as well.

1 Corinthians 9:24

"Know ye not that they which run in a race run all, but one receiveth the prize? So run, that ye may obtain."

Every genuine Christian is in a spiritual race. In a large race, there are many runners. Paul urges the true Christians in Corinth to run faithfully to receive the prize that the Lord Jesus Christ can give them as race winners. The pronoun "ye" is plural. This seems to indicate that, if the runners are all running well, they will receive a prize. God is righteous in giving out prizes to faithful genuine Christian runners.

1 Corinthians 9:25

"And every man that striveth for the mastery is temperate in all things. Now they do it to obtain a corruptible crown; but we an incorruptible."

Genuine Christians should strive for the mastery in all things involving their ministry for the Lord Jesus Christ, their Saviour. To obtain this mastery, they must be temperate in their lives. That word, *"temperate"* refers to people who are self-controlled, and conduct themselves temperately.

Paul mentions one crown in this verse, the incorruptible crown. This is one of five crowns mentioned here. The others are the crown of righteousness, the crown of glory, the crown of rejoicing, and the crown of life.

Non-Christians look for corruptible crowns and awards as they strive in various contests in life. True Christians strive for awards and crowns that are incorruptible which last for eternity.

Verses On Two Other Crowns
- **2 Timothy 4:8**

"Henceforth there is laid up for me a crown of righteousness, which the Lord, the righteous judge, shall give me at that day: and not to me only, but unto all them also that love his appearing."

Genuine Christians who love the appearing of the Lord Jesus Christ at the Rapture of all true Christians will receive this crown from their Saviour.

- **James 1:12**

"Blessed is the man that endureth temptation: for when he is tried, he shall receive the crown of life, which the Lord hath promised to them that love him."

This crown will be given by the Lord Jesus Christ to those true Christians who love Him.

- **Revelation 2:10c**

". . . be thou faithful unto death, and I will give thee a crown of life."

This is another reason for genuine Christians to receive the crown of life. It is also given to those who are faithful to the Lord Jesus Christ, even if it means their death.

1 Corinthians 9:26

"I therefore so run, not as uncertainly; so fight I, not as one that beateth the air:"

Paul said that he was running in this race for the Lord Jesus Christ, his Saviour. As human runners, they must keep themselves in good shape physically. They can't run uncertainly either. They must know the track and the conditions they will be facing when they run. Running spiritually, the genuine Christian runners must follow all the Words of God so as not to go astray or violate some of God's running rules in His Bible Words. All the rules and cautions for true Christian runners are found in His Words in the Bible. They must make certain that they have the right Bible based on the proper Hebrew, Aramaic, and Greek Words properly translated, such as, in English, the King James Bible.

In this verse, Paul also said that he was not the kind of a fighter for the Lord Jesus Christ who merely beats the air. He has a real enemy, whether it's the world, the flesh, or the Devil. He follows the Words of God in his battles and so should all genuine Christians in their fights and battles as they seek to live to please the Lord Jesus Christ Who saved them.

1 Corinthians 9:27

"But I keep under my body, and bring it into subjection: lest that by any means, when I have preached to others, I myself should be a castaway."

Paul said that he kept in subjection his body, bringing it into subjection. The reason for this is that he did not want to become a castaway and never more to be useful to his Lord and Saviour, Jesus Christ. One of the ways Paul had to bring his body into subjection was to keep it under by very harsh treatment. Notice the Greek Word for *"keep under."*

THE MEANING OF THE GREEK WORD, "HUPOPIAZO"

The Greek Word for *"keep under"* is HUPOPIAZO. Some of the meanings of that Greek Word are:

> *"1) to beat black and blue, to smite so as to cause bruises and livid spots; 1a) like a boxer one buffets his body, handle it roughly, discipline by hardships; 2) metaph. 2a) to give one intolerable annoyance; 2a1) beat one out, wear one out; 2b) by entreaties; 3) that part of the face that is under the eyes."*

This would be a very difficult thing to do, but Paul was determined to discipline his body, even if it took strong means to bring it into subjection.

MEANING OF THE GREEK WORD, "DOULAGOGEO"

The Greek Word for *"subjection"* is DOULAGOGEO. Some of the meanings of this Greek Word are:

> *"1) to lead away into slavery, claim as one's slave; 2) to make a slave and to treat as a slave i.e. with severity, subject to stern and rigid discipline."*

This is a very strong word, showing that Paul subjected himself to *"stern and rigid discipline."* If he did not do this, he might become a *"castaway."*

In addition to what Paul had to do personally, he had to be controlled by God the indwelling Holy Spirit. His fruits are listed in these verses.

Galatians 5:22-23

"But the fruit of the Spirit is love, joy, peace, longsuffering, gentleness, goodness, faith, Meekness, temperance: against such there is no law."

One of the fruits of God the Holy Spirit Who indwells all genuine Christians is *"temperance."*

THE MEANING OF THE GREEK WORD, "EGKRATEIA"

The Greek Word for *"temperance"* is EGKRATEIA. Some of the meanings of this Greek Word are:

"1) self-control (the virtue of one who masters his desires and passions, esp. his sensual appetites)."

God the Holy Spirit was able to give Paul self-control when he yielded to Him. He is able to do this for genuine Christians today as well. Paul was concerned about keeping his body under control, lest after he had preached to others, he would become a useless *"castaway."*

THE MEANING OF THE GREEK WORD, "ADOKIMOS"

The Greek Word for *"castaway"* is ADOKIMOS. Some of the meanings of that Greek Word are:

"1) not standing the test, not approved; 1a) properly used of metals and coins; 2) that which does not prove itself such as it ought; 2a) unfit for, unproved, spurious, reprobate."

Paul did not want to be laid on the shelf and no longer be greatly used by the Lord Jesus Christ; he desired to be a faithful witness for Him in serving Him wherever He was led and in whatever ministry He had for him. He did not want to be disapproved and unfit any longer to be a faithful servant for the Lord.

The problem with so many pastors and Christian workers today is that they have become castaways and disapproved by the Lord. Many have been laid on the shelf and are no longer of any use for the Lord Jesus Christ. I'm thinking of one of my former pastors, Pastor Virgil Stoneking of the Haddon Heights Baptist

Church in Haddonfield, New Jersey. After it became known that he had committed adultery with a woman who was a member of his church, he thought nothing of it and wanted to continue pastoring this church as though nothing wrong had happened. There was a vote in the congregation about this, and the church wisely dismissed him as their Pastor. He had become a "*castaway.*"

1 Corinthians Chapter Ten

1 Corinthians 10:1

"Moreover, brethren, I would not that ye should be ignorant, how that all our fathers were under the cloud, and all passed through the sea;"

This is the reference, of course, to the Israelites. This whole chapter is talking about the Israelites' experiences. The Israelites were in Egypt. They crossed the Red Sea and went over into the wilderness; they wandered and then they came, finally, after forty years, into the land of Palestine. All were under the cloud. The Lord led them, everyone of the Israelites. They saw God's miracles. They saw his power. That didn't matter with some of them. They didn't even believe in Him. This is a picture for us. All were under the cloud, meaning they were under God's leading.

Verses On God's Leading Cloud

- **Exodus 13:21**

"And the LORD went before them by day in a pillar of a cloud, to lead them the way; and by night in a pillar of fire, to give them light; to go by day and night:"

The Israelites were led by God's cloud during their entire 40 years in the wilderness. When the cloud moved, Israel moved, following that cloud.

- **Exodus 14:19-20**

"And the angel of God, which went before the camp of Israel, removed and went behind them; and the pillar of the cloud went from before their face, and stood behind them: And it came between the camp of the Egyptians and the camp of Israel; and it was a cloud and darkness to them, but it gave light by night to these: so that the one came not near the other all the night."

The Egyptians tried to catch the fleeing Israelites. The cloud was light to the fleeing Israelites, but was darkness to the Egyptians so they couldn't see Israel.

- **Exodus 40:34**

"Then a cloud covered the tent of the congregation, and the glory of the LORD filled the tabernacle."

That cloud represented the presence of God, the glory of God which was called the shekinah glory.
- **Numbers 9:15**
"And on the day that the tabernacle was reared up the cloud covered the tabernacle, namely, the tent of the testimony: and at even there was upon the tabernacle as it were the appearance of fire, until the morning."

God's cloud was on the tabernacle by day and turned into the appearance of fire by night until morning.

Verses On Opening The Red Sea
- **Exodus 14:16**
"But lift thou up thy rod, and stretch out thine hand over the sea, and divide it: and the children of Israel shall go on dry ground through the midst of the sea."

The sea speaks of the Red Sea which is a large body of water. For the Israelites to go from Egypt to the wilderness where they abode for 40 years, they had to cross this Red Sea. This was not the "reed" sea, but the Red Sea which the Israelites crossed by a tremendous miracle of God.
- **Exodus 14:22**
"And the children of Israel went into the midst of the sea upon the dry ground: and the waters were a wall unto them on their right hand, and on their left."

Israel went right through that Red Sea with a wall of water on both sides of them. It was completely dry where the Israelites walked and they were completely safe. What a miracle!!
- **Exodus 14:28**
"And the waters returned, and covered the chariots, and the horsemen, and all the host of Pharaoh that came into the sea after them; there remained not so much as one of them."

When the Egyptian soldiers tried to go through the sea, they were all killed by the Lord. He spared His people, but destroyed their enemies and would-be murderers.
- **Psalms 78:13-14**
"He divided the sea, and caused them to pass through; and he made the waters to stand as an heap. In the daytime also he led them with a cloud, and all the night with a light of fire."

God made the waters stand up in a heap so His people could cross over in safety and in His Divine guidance.
- **Psalms 78:53**
"And he led them on safely, so that they feared not: but the sea overwhelmed their enemies."

God led Israel safely, but the sea drowned their enemies.

1 Corinthians Preaching Verse-By-Verse

- **Psalms 106:9**

"He rebuked the Red sea also, and it was dried up: so he led them through the depths, as through the wilderness."

God dried up the huge Red Sea and led His people safely through dry ground.

- **Psalms 136:13**

"To him which divided the Red sea into parts: for his mercy endureth for ever:"

Because of God's mercy, He divided the Red Sea into parts.

- **Psalms 136:15**

"But overthrew Pharaoh and his host in the Red sea: for his mercy endureth for ever."

Many of us genuine Christians have experienced our God's help and assistance to us throughout our lives. We thank Him for His leadership and help.

1 Corinthians 10:2

"And were all baptized unto Moses in the cloud and in the sea;"

They were baptized unto Moses in the cloud and in the sea. The word, "*baptize*" signifies to be brought under the surrounding influence of something. This took place both in God's special cloud that surrounded them, and the Red Sea which also surrounded them– so with water baptism by true Christians who are immersed in water after they became genuine Christians.

1 Corinthians 10:3

"And did all eat the same spiritual meat;"

God performed a miracle regarding the food the Israelites would eat in their 40 years of wandering in the wilderness. It was called manna. This is called here in this verse "*spiritual meat.*" All of the 600,000 men plus women and children ate this manna. It was not only for the leaders. God gave them special rules in eating it. It did not come on the Sabbath day (Saturday). On Friday, they were to collect enough manna for two days, for Saturday and Sunday. When some violated this rule, there was a judgment upon them.

1 Corinthians 10:4

"And did all drink the same spiritual drink: for they drank of that spiritual Rock that followed them: and that Rock was Christ."

Not only did God provide manna for for the Israelites (and quail on one occasion), but God also provided them water during their 40-year wilderness wandering. You and I know that you we go only so far without water. Without food, that's one thing, but without water, we have to replenish our systems and God provided that water for the Israelites. They drank water out of that *"spiritual Rock that followed them."* That Rock Who followed them was the Lord Jesus Christ. One of His titles is *"The Rock."* He followed them and provided water from various rocks they came to.

Verses On The Water Out Of The Rock
- **Exodus 17:6**

"Behold, I will stand before thee there upon the rock in Horeb; and thou shalt smite the rock, and there shall come water out of it, that the people may drink. And Moses did so in the sight of the elders of Israel."

Horeb is another word for Sinai. The rock was there. Now notice, it says in 1 Corinthians 10:4 above , it was the "*Rock that followed them:*" The Lord Jesus Christ was a Perfect Man Who was sent by God the Father from Heaven, to be born in a manger in Bethlehem. The Lord Jesus Christ was from all eternity past without beginning or end. He is the Messiah. He is God the Son. And He was that Rock Who followed these Israelites throughout their 40 years of wandering.

- **Numbers 20:8-12**

"Take the rod, and gather thou the assembly together, thou, and Aaron thy brother, and speak ye unto the rock before their eyes; and it shall give forth his water, and thou shalt bring forth to them water out of the rock: so thou shalt give the congregation and their beasts drink. And Moses took the rod from before the LORD, as he commanded him. And Moses and Aaron gathered the congregation together before the rock, and he said unto them, Hear now, ye rebels; must we fetch you water out of this rock? And Moses lifted up his hand, and with his rod he smote the rock twice: and the water came out abundantly, and the congregation drank, and their beasts also. And the LORD spake unto Moses and Aaron, Because ye believed me not, to sanctify me in the eyes of the children of Israel, therefore ye shall not bring this

congregation into the land which I have given them."
Moses and Aaron both disobeyed the Lord. Moses had a very mean and angry attitude when he spoke to the people of Israel. As a result, God they banned both of them from entering Canaan. He slew both of them very soon after this shameful and disobedient incident.

- **Deuteronomy 8:15**
  "Who led thee through that great and terrible wilderness, wherein were fiery serpents, and scorpions, and drought, where there was no water; who brought thee forth water out of the rock of flint;"

God led His people of Israel through the very dangerous serpents, scorpions, drought, and many other deadly things.

- **Psalms 105:39**
  "He spread a cloud for a covering; and fire to give light in the night."

God used a cloud of light to protect them safely from the following Egyptians, even during the dark of night.

- **Psalms 105:41**
  "He opened the rock, and the waters gushed out; they ran in the dry places like a river."

God helped the Israelites by giving them water out of the rocks and His manna for bread.

1 Corinthians 10:5

"But with many of them God was not well pleased: for they were overthrown in the wilderness."

With many of them he was not well pleased. In Numbers 13, God said send out some spies. Take a look at the people. Look at the land where I'm going to send you. The spies were sent out. One spy for every one of the twelve tribes. There were twelve spies. The spy who brought a good rep9rt was Caleb. They spied out the land and two spies brought a good report and said that Israel should enter the land. The other ten brought a bad report and did not want to enter Canaan because of the giants.

In Numbers 14:1-3, the congregation murmured against Moses. They wanted to go back to Egypt instead of following the Lord into the promised land. Joshua and Caleb told them not to rebel against the Lord. The congregation wanted to stone them because they wanted to follow the Lord and enter Canaan. God said He would smite them with pestilence, disinherit them, and make a nation greater and mightier than them.

Verses On Many Of Israel Who Were Disobedient
- **Numbers 14:22-23**

"Because <u>all those men which have seen my glory</u>, and my miracles, which I did in Egypt and in the wilderness, and have tempted me now these ten times, and <u>have not hearkened to my voice</u>; <u>Surely they shall not see the land</u> which I sware unto their fathers, neither shall any of them that provoked me see it:"

Though those Israelites who were protected by God, they disobeyed Him constantly and were forbidden from entering Canaan.
- **Numbers 14:29**

"<u>Your carcases shall fall in this wilderness</u>; and all that were numbered of you, according to your whole number, <u>from twenty years old and upward, which have murmured against me</u>,"

All those Israelites who wandered in the wilderness during these 40 years who were 20 years old and older, died in the wilderness and did not enter Canaan.
- **Numbers 14:31-34**

"But <u>your little ones, which ye said should be a prey, them will I bring in, and they shall know the land which ye have despised</u>. But as for you, your carcases, they shall fall in this wilderness. And <u>your children shall wander in the wilderness forty years, and bear your whoredoms, until your carcases be wasted in the wilderness</u>. After the number of the days in which ye searched the land, even forty days, each day for a year, shall ye bear your iniquities, even forty years, and ye shall know my breach of promise."

The men that brought a bad report about the land of Canaan, the Lord slew immediately with a plague. All the Israelites who were twenty years old and above died in the wilderness. Those who were nineteen years old and below were allowed to enter Canaan.

1 Corinthians 10:6

"Now these things were our examples, to the intent we should not lust after evil things, as they also lusted."

The wilderness wanderings by these Israelites are examples to those genuine Christians in the church at Corinth. They should never lust after the things these Israelites lusted after. They were bad examples which should never be followed. If true Christians today cannot learn from their and others' mistakes, they will be forced to repeat them. Genuine Christians today should learn to stay out of the sin, wickedness, and corruption committed by these Israelites of old so they may be blessed, honored, and led by the Lord Jesus Christ their Saviour.

1 Corinthians 10:7

"Neither be ye idolaters, as *were* some of them; as it is written, The people sat down to eat and drink, and rose up to play."

When Paul told these genuine Christians at Corinth about idolatry, he used a Greek present tense negative prohibition. This means to stop an action already in progress. He said to them, *"STOP being idolaters!"* In Greek, the phrase, "*it is written*" (GEGRAPTAI)," is in the perfect tense. It means that what is written in the past, will be preserved in the present, and on into the future. God wanted information about this sin of idolatry to be preserved in Hebrew in the past, the present, and into the future. Aaron sinned in encouraging the Israelites to commit idolatry.

Aaron's Sins While Moses Was On Mount Sinai
- **Exodus 32:2**
  "And <u>Aaron said unto them, Break off the golden earrings</u>, which are in the ears of your wives, of your sons, and of your daughters, <u>and bring them unto me</u>."

This was how Aaron was going to make an idol for Israel to worship. How pagan and crooked was Aaron the high priest!!

- **Exodus 32:4**
  "And <u>he received them</u> at their hand, <u>and fashioned it with a graving tool</u>, after <u>he had made it a molten calf</u>: and they said, <u>These be thy gods</u>, O Israel, which brought thee up out of the land of Egypt."

Pagan and godless Aaron just made this "idol-god" and lied when he said that this idol brought them out of Egypt before it was ever made. And the stupid Israelites believed him!

- **Exodus 32:6**
  "And they rose up early on the morrow, and offered burnt offerings, and brought peace offerings; and <u>the people sat down to eat and to drink, and rose up to play</u>."

Part of the *"play"* for these Israelites included the worshipping of this idol that Aaron made together with all the sensuous and sexual acts involved with this pagan idolatry.

1 Corinthians 10:8

"Neither let us commit fornication, as some of them committed, and fell in one day three and twenty thousand."

Paul again uses the Greek perfect tense when he told the true Christians at Corinth *"Neither let us commit fornication."* As in the verse before, this is a Greek present tense prohibition which means to stop an action already in progress. These genuine Christians at Corinth were committing fornication, and Paul said *"Stop it!!"* Because of this sin by the Israelites in the Old Testament, God slew 23,000 of them in one day by a plague.

Verses On Israel's Fornication Practices
- **Numbers 25:1**

"And Israel abode in Shittim, and the people began to commit whoredom with the daughters of Moab."

Israel intermarried, intermixed, and committed fornication with the pagan daughters of Moab.

- **Numbers 25:4**

"And the LORD said unto Moses, Take all the heads of the people, and hang them up before the LORD against the sun, that the fierce anger of the LORD may be turned away from Israel."

God told Moses to hang the leaders of Israel so that His anger would be turned away from the nation because of this fornication and idolatry.

- **Numbers 25:6-9**

"And, behold, one of the children of Israel came and brought unto his brethren a Midianitish woman in the sight of Moses, and in the sight of all the congregation of the children of Israel, who were weeping before the door of the tabernacle of the congregation. And when Phinehas, the son of Eleazar, the son of Aaron the priest, saw it, he rose up from among the congregation, and took a javelin in his hand; And he went after the man of Israel into the tent, and thrust both of them through, the man of Israel, and the woman through her belly. So the plague was stayed from the children of Israel. And those that died in the plague were twenty and four thousand."

This fornication was judged by the Lord when Phinehas the priest slew the fornicators. The plague was stayed, but God had already slain 23,000 in one day and another 1,000 later, making a total of 24,000 in all.

1 Corinthians 10:9

"Neither let us tempt Christ, as some of them also tempted, and were destroyed of serpents."

As before in the preceding two verses, the prohibition is in the Greek present tense. It means to stop an action already in progress. The true Christians at Corinth were tempting the Lord Jesus Christ. Paul told them to "*Stop it*"!! Some of the Israelites did this and were destroyed by serpents.

- **Numbers 21:5-9**

"And the people spake against God, and against Moses, Wherefore have ye brought us up out of Egypt to die in the wilderness? for there is no bread, neither is there any water; and our soul loatheth this light bread. And the LORD sent fiery serpents among the people, and they bit the people; and much people of Israel died. Therefore the people came to Moses, and said, We have sinned, for we have spoken against the LORD, and against thee; pray unto the LORD, that he take away the serpents from us. And Moses prayed for the people. And the LORD said unto Moses, Make thee a fiery serpent, and set it upon a pole: and it shall come to pass, that every one that is bitten, when he looketh upon it, shall live. And Moses made a serpent of brass, and put it upon a pole, and it came to pass, that if a serpent had bitten any man, when he beheld the serpent of brass, he lived."

Moses followed the instructions that the LORD gave him in the construction of the brass serpent. Then he set it on a pole. Any of the Israelites who were bitten by the poisonous serpents were cured by looking at the brass serpent and lived. Those who did not look on that raised serpent of brass died.

This a picture of the Gospel of the Lord Jesus Christ. It was told to me by my high school janitor. I looked in faith and genuinely believed on the Lord Jesus Christ Who was lifted up on the cross and died for my sins and the sins of the world. I became a genuine Christian in 1944.

The salvation story is that the Lord Jesus Christ was "*lifted up*" on the cross to provide eternal life for those who genuinely trust Him, just as that brass serpent was lifted up on a pole so that everyone who looked upon it might preserve their physical life. The eternal life picture is found in John 3:14-16.

- **John 3:14-16**

"And as Moses lifted up the serpent in the wilderness, even so must the Son of man be lifted up: That whosoever believeth in him should not perish, but have eternal life. For God so loved the world, that he gave his only begotten Son, that whosoever believeth in him should not perish, but have everlasting life."

These are verses that show the hyper-Calvinists' lie who state that the Lord Jesus Christ died ONLY for the "elect" but not for the whole world. These five verses indicate that God so loved humanity so that whosoever genuinely believes in the Saviour can receive God's everlasting life.

1 Corinthians 10:10

"Neither murmur ye, as some of them also murmured, and were destroyed of the destroyer."

As in the three verses above, here is another Greek present tense prohibition which means to stop an action already in progress. Paul is telling the genuine Christians at Corinth that they were to stop murmuring! That's what the Israelites in the Old Testament did and were destroyed of the destroyer.

Verses On Old Testament Murmuring

- **Exodus 15:24**

"And the people murmured against Moses, saying, What shall we drink?"

Thirst caused Israel's murmuring in the wilderness.

- **Exodus 16:2**

"And the whole congregation of the children of Israel murmured against Moses and Aaron in the wilderness:"

All of the Israelites murmured against both Moses and Aaron.

- **Numbers 14:2**

"And all the children of Israel murmured against Moses and against Aaron: and the whole congregation said unto them, Would God that we had died in the land of Egypt! or would God we had died in this wilderness!"

They wished to remain in Egypt and die, or die in the wilderness.

- **Numbers 14:27**

"How long shall I bear with this evil congregation, which murmur against me? I have heard the murmurings of the children of Israel, which they murmur against me."

God heard Israel's murmurings and was angry with them over it.

- **Numbers 16:41**

"But on the morrow all the congregation of the children of Israel murmured against Moses and against Aaron, saying, Ye have killed the people of the LORD."

Israel murmured against these two leaders, blaming them for killing some of the Israelites.

- **Psalms 106:25-27**

"But <u>murmured in their tents, and hearkened not unto the voice of the LORD</u>. Therefore he lifted up his hand against them, to overthrow them in the wilderness: To overthrow their seed also among the nations, and to scatter them in the lands."

Because of their murmuring, God overthrew them in the wilderness.

New Testament Verses On Murmuring

- **Philippians 2:14-15**

"<u>Do all things without murmurings</u> and disputings: That ye may be blameless and harmless, the sons of God, without rebuke, in the midst of a crooked and perverse nation, among whom ye shine as lights in the world;"

Genuine Christians are to do all things without murmuring about anything.

- **Jude 1:16**

"<u>These are murmurers</u>, complainers, walking after their own lusts; and their mouth speaketh great swelling words, having men's persons in admiration because of advantage."

The lost and evil people murmur, but true Christians should not commit this sin, even though many things are difficult. They should praise and honor the Lord Jesus Christ.

1 Corinthians 10:11

"Now all these things happened unto them for ensamples: and they are written for our admonition, upon whom the ends of the world are come."

All the things that happened to the Israelites in the Old Testament happened unto them for examples, either good or bad, for genuine Christians in the New Testament under God's grace. They were written down for admonitions and warnings to the true Christians today.

Verses On Ensamples Or Examples

- **Philippians 3:17**

"Brethren, <u>be followers together of me</u>, and mark them which <u>walk so as ye have us for an ensample</u>."

Paul wanted the genuine Christians at Philippi to follow him as a good example as he followed the Lord Jesus Christ. It's good to have a pattern that can be followed, just as those who sew can follow the pattern that is given in making clothes or other things.
- **1 Thessalonians 1:7**
"So that ye were ensamples to all that believe in Macedonia and Achaia."

The genuine Christians in Thessalonica were good examples to the other true Christians who lived in Macedonia and Achaia.
- **2 Thessalonians 3:9**
"Not because we have not power, but to make ourselves an ensample unto you to follow us."

Paul wanted to make himself a good example for the genuine Christians in Thessalonica to follow.
- **1 Peter 5:3**
"Neither as being lords over God's heritage, but being ensamples to the flock."

Peter is speaking about the pastors/bishops/elders (which is one and the same office with three separate ministries) who should be good examples to the flock to whom they minister.
- **2 Peter 2:6**
"And turning the cities of Sodom and Gomorrha into ashes condemned them with an overthrow, making them an ensample unto those that after should live ungodly;"

God wanted what happened to Sodom and Gomorrha to be an example to all those who would live in an ungodly manner.
- **1 Corinthians 10:6**
"Now these things were our examples, to the intent we should not lust after evil things, as they also lusted."

Paul said about the evil deeds of the Israelites in the wilderness, that they were examples for the genuine Christians at Corinth.
- **1 Timothy 4:12**
"Let no man despise thy youth; but be thou an example of the believers, in word, in conversation, in charity, in spirit, in faith, in purity."

There is no question that young people or older people, no matter what one's age, if you know the Lord Jesus Christ as your Saviour, you should be an example to all true Christians in the following areas: (1) in word, (2) in conversation, (3) in charity, (4) in spirit; (5) in faith, and (6) in purity.
- **Hebrews 4:11**
"Let us labour therefore to enter into that rest, lest any man fall after the same example of unbelief."

Paul is urging these Jews who became genuine Christians, to enter God's perfect rest so as not to follow after the example of the Israelites in their unbelief.
- **James 5:10**
"Take, my brethren, the prophets, who have spoken in the name of the Lord, for an example of suffering affliction, and of patience."

James spoke of the prophets as a good example of suffering and of patience.
- **1 Peter 2:21**
"For even hereunto were ye called: because Christ also suffered for us, leaving us an example, that ye should follow his steps:"

The Lord Jesus Christ urged genuine Christians an example in His suffering, that they should follow in His steps when they are called upon to suffer.

1 Corinthians 10:12
"Wherefore let him that thinketh he standeth take heed lest he fall."

True Christians who think they are standing are to take heed lest the fall. Some of those Israelites who came out of Egypt thought they were all right. They crossed through the Red Sea. They had the cloud to guide them. They had God's protection upon them. They had food to eat. They had water to drink. Everything was fine. They thought they were standing. If genuine Christians think they are standing, they should take heed lest at some point they might fall. That fall can never take them out of their salvation (as some wrongly teach), but they can fall out of sincere fellowship with the Lord Jesus Christ.

The Christian life for the true Christian, as I've said many times before, is like a walk. Remember, a walk is just one step at a time. Every single step could result in a fall, if the other foot doesn't come down properly. Let no genuine Christians think it is impossible to fall. The Greek Word for "*take heed*" is in the Greek present tense. It is a command to continually, moment by moment, take heed, lest a fall takes place.

Verses On Take Heed
- **Deuteronomy 4:9**
"Only take heed to thyself, and keep thy soul diligently, lest thou forget the things which thine eyes have seen, and lest they depart from thy heart all the days of thy life: but teach them thy sons, and thy sons' sons;"

These things that God showed that generation, of His miracles and protection in the wilderness, should be taught to their sons and the following generations also.
- **Deuteronomy 11:16**
"<u>Take heed to yourselves, that your heart be not deceived, and ye turn aside, and serve other gods</u>, and worship them;"

The Israelites were to take heed that their hearts should not be deceived and that they would not serve other gods.
- **Malachi 2:15**
"And did not he make one? Yet had he the residue of the spirit. And wherefore one? That he might seek a godly seed. Therefore <u>take heed to your spirit, and let none deal treacherously against the wife of his youth</u>."

Genuine Christians must take heed in their spirits and be very careful how they treat their wives.
- **Matthew 24:4**
"And Jesus answered and said unto them, <u>Take heed that no man deceive you</u>."

It's very easy for a cleaver deceiver to trick gullible, yet true, Christians. They must continuously take heed.
- **Luke 12:15**
"And he said unto them, <u>Take heed, and beware of covetousness</u>: for a man's life consisteth not in the abundance of the things which he possesseth."

All genuine Christians must take heed of being covetous of wanting more and more money and possessions. This can lead to serious problems.
- **Acts 20:28**
"<u>Take heed therefore unto yourselves</u>, and to all the flock, over the which the Holy Ghost hath made you overseers, <u>to feed the church of God</u>, which he hath purchased with his own blood."

Paul was talking to the pastors/bishops/elders who were pastors of the churches in his day. They must feed the true Christians with the Words of God. Very few pastors in our day really feed and teach the Words of God to their churches in a verse-by-verse manner.
- **1 Corinthians 3:10-12**
"According to the grace of God which is given unto me, as a wise masterbuilder, I have laid the foundation, and another buildeth thereon. <u>But let every man take heed how he buildeth thereupon</u>. For other foundation can no man lay than that is laid, which is Jesus Christ. Now if any man build upon this foundation gold, silver, precious stones, wood, hay, stubble;"

All true Christians are to build on the Lord Jesus Christ as their eternal Foundation, but they must take heed how they build upon this Foundation. May it be with gold, silver, and precious stones instead of wood, hay, and stubble.

- **1 Timothy 4:16**
"Take heed unto thyself, and unto the doctrine; continue in them: for in doing this thou shalt both save thyself, and them that hear thee."

Paul warned Pastor Timothy that he was first of all to take heed to the purity of his own life, and secondly to the sound and Biblical doctrine and teaching of God's Words. He was to continue in both of these areas. This should be the practice of every Bible-believing pastor in the world. It is a sad thing that it is not followed by most of the churches in all the denominations in the world today!

1 Corinthians 10:13

"There hath no temptation taken you but such as is common to man: but God *is* faithful, who will not suffer you to be tempted above that ye are able; but will with the temptation also make a way to escape, that ye may be able to bear *it*."

There are no temptations borne by any of the genuine Christians in the church at Corinth (or of any other true Christians today) but those that are common to mankind. But God is faithful. He will not tempt them above they are able, but will make a way of escape, so they will be continuously (Greek present tense) able to endure it.

Gertrude Grace Sanborn, my wife's mother, wrote a book about my wife's sister, Beverly Grace Sanborn. She was born with brain damage from birth. Mom Sanborn entitled her book, *Able to Bear It*, which was taken right from this verse. God gave her grace to bear up under the care of Beverly who was not able to think, not able to talk, all through her life. But God made her godly mother a way to escape so that she was able to bear it.

1 Corinthians 10:14

"Wherefore, my dearly beloved, flee from idolatry."

Paul discussed what these genuine Christians at Corinth should do about idolatry, which is a terrible thing. What he told them should be applied to every true Christians today.

Idolatry means continually worshipping of false gods and the demons and devils that are in those idols. The Lord God has a remedy for idolatry of all kinds. The remedy is simply to flee from it. Run away from it and don't ever practice any form of the worship of idols, including people who are often worshipped as if they are idols. This was what the Israelites did when wandering in the wilderness for 40 years as well as long after that.

1 Corinthians 10:15

"I speak as to wise men; judge ye what I say."

Paul wanted the genuine Christians at Corinth to know that he considered them wise. As such, he told them to listen to and judge what he was talking about. These experiences of the wayward and sinful actions of the Israelites of old, should not be the actions of those to whom he was speaking. I hope, as did Paul, that present-day true Christians will behold these things and be certain that they will not repeat such things in their lives today.

1 Corinthians 10:16

"The cup of blessing which we bless, is it not the communion of the blood of Christ? The bread which we break, is it not the communion of the body of Christ?"

Now, Paul is getting into a section that he will take up in the next chapter on the Lord's Supper. He mentions the cup of blessing, referring to the grape juice that speaks of the blood of the Lord Jesus Christ Who was sacrificed for the sins of the entire world. He also mentions the unleavened bread of the communion service which speaks of the crucified Body of the Lord Jesus Christ.

1 Corinthians 10:17

"For we *being* many are one bread, *and* one body: for we are all partakers of that one bread."

All of the genuine Christians, wherever they are around the world, are a unity spoken of as *"one bread, and one body."* These true Christians make up what is called in other verses, *"the body of Christ."* They are all joint *"partakers"* of that one bread. They partake of the eternal life which the Lord Jesus Christ has given them by true faith in Him.

1 Corinthians 10:18
"Behold Israel after the flesh: are not they which eat of the sacrifices partakers of the altar?"

Paul is taking the true Christians at Corinth back to the Old Testament as an illustration. They are no longer under the law of Moses, but it is an interesting illustration. He asks a question. He talks about those Priests and Levites to whom were given portions of the clean animals were sacrificed on the brazen altar. The answer to that simple question is this: Because God apportioned to them certain portions of the animals that were sacrificed on that altar, in that sense, they were partakers of the altar.

1 Corinthians 10:19
"What say I then? that the idol is any thing, or that which is offered in sacrifice to idols is any thing?"

Paul asks whether an idol is anything or if that which is offered to an idol is anything. Both are nothing but Satan's counterfeit of God Himself and the one offering for sin forever by the Lord Jesus Christ at Calvary.

An idol is something that is seen. God the Father and God the Holy Spirit are not seen. The Lord Jesus Christ, the Son of God, came to earth in a perfect body as was seen by multitudes, but was never seen from all eternity past when He was with the Father and the Holy Spirit in Heaven.

What are the idols of people generally? Maybe Santa Claus is an idol to some. He's seen everywhere. In fact, he's everywhere you can think, even at food stores and other stores. They have Santa Claus hats. He's almost everywhere. Is that the idol, something seen? Is Rudolph the red-nosed reindeer an idol for some? Is it the Little Drummer Boy? Is it the Grinch that Stole Christmas? Is it Ebenezer Scrooge? Is it Frosty the Snowman? Is it Grandfather Frost? Is it Saint Nicolas?

- **1 Corinthians 5:11**
"But now I have written unto you <u>not to keep company, if any man that is called</u> a brother be a fornicator, or covetous, or <u>an idolater</u>, or a railer, or a drunkard, or an extortioner; with such an one no not to eat."

Genuine Christians should not keep company with those who, though they are true Christians, yet they are also fleshly idolaters.

- **2 Corinthians 6:16**
"And <u>what agreement hath the temple of God with idols</u>? for ye are the temple of the living God; as God hath said, I will dwell in them, and walk in them; and I will be their God, and they shall be my people."

There is no agreement with the temple of God (in this verse, meaning genuine Christians) and idols. They must separate from idols.

- **Galatians 5:19-21**
"Now <u>the works of the flesh are</u> manifest, which are these; Adultery, fornication, uncleanness, lasciviousness, <u>Idolatry</u>, witchcraft, hatred, variance, emulations, wrath, strife, seditions, heresies, Envyings, murders, drunkenness, revellings, and such like: of the which I tell you before, as I have also told you in time past, that they which do such things shall not inherit the kingdom of God."

Idolatry is one of the works of the flesh. It should not be practiced in any form by true Christians.

- **1 Thessalonians 1:9**
"For they themselves shew of us what manner of entering in we had unto you, and how <u>ye turned to God from idols</u> to serve the living and true God;"

These Thessalonian genuine Christians turned from their heathen idols to God. That is the way to go for all former heathen people and all non-Christians today. What is your idol? Is it an athlete? Is it a movie star, a rock star, an Internet or TV star? Is it some preacher?
Is it some friend? Is it some other human being? or is it an image idol? Is it a name of a movie theater? Is it some other Christian?

- **John 4:24**
"God is a Spirit: and they that worship him must worship him in spirit and in truth."

This is the proper way to worship God for genuine Christians. There should be no idolatry whatever.

1 Corinthians 10:20

"But I *say*, that the things which the Gentiles sacrifice, they sacrifice to devils, and not to God: and I would not that ye should have fellowship with devils."

The heathen non-Christian Gentiles sacrifice to devils. No true Christian should have any fellowship with devils or those who sacrifice to them, whether it's the heathen Africans, South Americans, Indians, Eskimos, or whether its idolatry from Buddhists, Shintoists, or any other false and pagan religion.

I was told that missionaries on one of the foreign fields were warned to stay away from a particular bush area which was called the devil bush. One missionary didn't take heed to that warning. He said *"I'll be all right."* Then this missionary went into the devil bush and came out a raving maniac. He swore, he cursed. I don't even know if he was a Christian. He was under the power of the devil. Don't flirt with demonism. Don't flirt with devils. God does not want genuine Christians to have fellowship with devils.

1 Corinthians 10:21

"Ye cannot drink the cup of the Lord, and the cup of devils: ye cannot be partakers of the Lord's table, and of the table of devils."

This is referring to the Lord's Table. Non-Christians should not partake. It should be only genuine Christians. The devil's children (non-Christians) should not be present at the Lord's Table. True Christians should separate from groups that have many lost and compromised people who run them, such as the National and World Councils of Churches, or the New Evangelical groups.

For five years I was on active duty as a Navy Chaplain at the Naval Air Station in Corpus Christi, Texas, I remember that I refused to fellowship with fellow-Chaplains in the communion services. Most (if not all) of them were non-Christian people, so I did not want to take communion with them. One of the reasons was that, like the Roman Catholic Church, they dipped the wafer in the wine (they didn't use grape juice). The senior Chaplain called me into his office and asked why I didn't follow their communion service methods. I reminded him that the motto that was then in practice by the Navy Chaplain Corps was *"Cooperation Without Compromise."* That principle was what I was following.

1 Corinthians 10:22

"Do we provoke the Lord to jealousy? are we stronger than he?"

- 2 Corinthians 11:2

"For <u>I am jealous over you with godly jealousy: for I have espoused you to one husband, that I may present</u> you as a chaste virgin to Christ."

The Lord Jesus Christ is jealous regarding genuine Christians. He does not want them involved with wickedness, and with sin. The Lord Jesus Christ wants them to be faithful to Him. He does not want them to go after idols, false gods, false religions, and any other false things. He wants them for Himself alone. Once the Lord Jesus Christ died for their sins, saved them, and made them new creatures in Christ, He wants to possess them. He wants to keep them and control them. He does not want them to run off into any falsity whatsoever, including false theology of any sort.

Verses On God Being Jealous For His Own
- **Exodus 20:5**

"Thou shalt not bow down thyself to them, nor serve them: for <u>I the LORD thy God am a jealous God</u>, visiting the iniquity of the fathers upon the children unto the third and fourth generation of them that hate me;"

Jealousy might be a sin for human beings, but it is not so with God. He bought true Christians with the sacrifice of His Son and wants them to continue being faithful to Him throughout their lives. He wants us for Himself, just like a bride and groom want each other for themselves alone. They are jealous for their mates. We don't want them to go out after some other mate.

- **2 Corinthians 11:2**

"For <u>I am jealous over you with godly jealousy</u>: for I have espoused you to one husband, that I may present you as a chaste virgin to Christ."

God has espoused all true Christians to the Lord Jesus Christ. God does not want them to be unfaithful to their Saviour, or His cause, once He saves them. None of the genuine Christians are stronger than the Lord Jesus Christ Who saved them. They should look to Him for strength day by day.

1 Corinthians 10:23

"All things are lawful for me, but all things are not expedient: all things are lawful for me, but all things edify not."

Paul said here that though it was lawful for him to do all things that were provided under the law of Moses, yet they would not be expedient for him to do. All these things would not edify either.

Verses On Expedient
- **John 11:50**
"Nor consider that <u>it is expedient for us, that one man should die for the people, and that the whole nation perish not</u>."

It was expedient that the Lord Jesus Christ should die for the sins of all people to give them the opportunity to believe on Him, to receive eternal life, rather than all people and all nations perish and have no opportunity to trust the Lord Jesus Christ as their Saviour.

- **John 16:7**
"Nevertheless I tell you the truth; <u>It is expedient for you that I go away</u>: for if I go not away, the Comforter will not come unto you; but if I depart, I will send him unto you."

The Lord Jesus Christ's departing into Heaven was expedient for His apostles and all genuine Christians. After He went back to Heaven, He would send God the Holy Spirit to all true Christians to indwell them forever.

- **John 18:14**
"Now Caiaphas was he, which gave counsel to the Jews, that <u>it was expedient that one man should die for the people</u>."

It was to the advantage of all the people in the world who ever lived that One Man, the Lord Jesus Christ, should die for them so that they would not have to die and spend eternity in Hell's lake of fire, but have the opportunity to trust in the Saviour and spend eternity with Him in Heaven.

- **1 Corinthians 6:12**
"All things are lawful unto me, but <u>all things are not expedient</u>: all things are lawful for me, but I will not be brought under the power of any."

Though some things might be lawful for Paul, they're not all expedient. For sure, he was not going to be brought under the power of any of them.

1 Corinthians 10:24

"Let no man seek his own, but every man another's wealth."

The words "*let no man seek*," are in the Greek present tense. When you have a negative prohibition in the Greek present tense, it means to stop an action then in progress. The resultant meaning here would be "*stop seeking.*" Apparently some genuine Christians at Corinth were seeking their own things and their own ways. Paul told them to "*Stop it!*" They were probably asking themselves questions like "*What's in it for me*"?

What should be the attitude and action of all these and other true Christians is "How can I seek to help and better another genuine Christian's or even a non-Christian's needs"? One of the most important needs for the non-Christian is to be aware of where they will spend eternity after they die. It will either be Heaven or Hell. If they're not sure which of these two places they will be in after their death, true Christians should be concerned about discussing this with as many as possible.

Think about the Good Samaritan that the Lord Jesus talked about in Luke 10:30-37. Here was a man along the highway who was bleeding and ready to die. A priest came along and a Levite also came along. They both looked the other way and continued on their way. Then came along one who was a Samaritan. He was part Jew and part Gentile. The Jews, in that day, despised such people. That Samaritan did not pass by. He stopped, bound up this man's wounds, set him on his own animal, brought him to an inn, and took care of him. When he departed, he told the inn keeper to take care of him, and if he owed any more money, he would pay him when he came back. This Samaritan truly sought to help someone else rather than himself alone.

1 Corinthians 10:25

"Whatsoever is sold in the shambles, *that* eat, asking no question for conscience sake:"

The word, "*shambles*" is used only here in the New Testament. It refers to various food stores that sell at least some of their meat that had been first offered to idols. Paul told the genuine Christians that they could eat such meat without asking questions for the sake of their conscience.

Verses On Conscience

- **Acts 24:16**

"And herein do I exercise myself, <u>to have always a conscience void of offence toward God, and toward men</u>."

Paul tries very hard to have a clear and undefiled conscience without offence either toward God or toward men.

- **2 Corinthians 4:2c**

". . . <u>commending ourselves to every man's conscience in the sight of God</u>."

Paul wanted to commend himself to every person's conscience in God's sight.

- **1 Timothy 4:2**

"Speaking lies in hypocrisy; <u>having their conscience seared with a hot iron</u>;"

These evil people Paul was speaking about to Pastor Timothy were liars, hypocrites who had consciences *"seared with a hot iron."* Such seared consciences cannot work as consciences should work.

- **Titus 1:15**
"Unto the pure all things are pure: but <u>unto them that are defiled</u> and unbelieving is nothing pure; but <u>even their mind and conscience is defiled</u>."

Non-Christians have defiled minds and consciences. Their consciences cannot work as they were made to work. They have been defiled and broken by their own sins.

1 Corinthians 10:26

"For the earth *is* the Lord's, and the fulness thereof."

God created the earth and its fulness. One of the biggest falsehoods today is the erroneous teaching taught in schools, seminaries, newspapers, radios, and the Internet concerning what they call "evolution." This teaching rules out the need for God and His marvelous creation of the world and all that is in it. Dr. Jack Moorman has an excellent tract against evolution and in favor of creation. The earth is the Lord's. He created it and it belongs to Him, not to the evolutionists! Hymn 144 in our hymn book is entitled: *"This Is My Father's World."* That goes along with this verse.

1 Corinthians 10:27

"If any of them that believe not bid you *to a feast*, and ye be disposed to go; whatsoever is set before you, eat, asking no question for conscience sake."

This describes a non-Christian inviting a genuine Christian to a feast. If they go to that feast, they are not to ask any questions about the food or the meat that is served for conscience sake. They especially are not to ask if the meat had been offered to idols. It was permitted true Christians to eat what was set before them. My mother always told me to eat what was set before me and don't by a picky eater.

1 Corinthians 10:28

"But if any man say unto you, This is offered in sacrifice unto idols, eat not for his sake that shewed it, and for conscience sake: for the earth is the Lord's, and the fulness thereof:"

When this genuine Christian who is attending the feast of the non-Christian who invited him is told by someone who is also at the feast that this meat had been offered in sacrifice to idols, the true Christian is not to eat of that meat for the sake of the person who told him this fact. If he would go ahead and eat it, it would hurt the conscience of the one who told him this fact and was bothered by it. Though the true Christians might eat the vegetables, they should not eat the meat.

1 Corinthians 10:29

"Conscience, I say, not thine own, but of the other: for why is my liberty judged of another *man's* conscience?"

The conscience mentioned here is not the conscience of the genuine Christians, but of the person who told them that the meat had been offered to Satanic idols. The true Christians' liberty should not be judged by some non-Christians' conscience.

1 Corinthians 10:30

"For if I by grace be a partaker, why am I evil spoken of for that for which I give thanks?"

Genuine Christians, who are partakers of God's grace, should not be evil spoken of for the food for which they give thanks. If someone tells the true Christians that the meat was offered to idols, don't eat the meat. If you do eat it, the man who told you about it will speak evil of you for eating it.

1 Corinthians 10:31

"Whether therefore ye eat, or drink, or whatsoever ye do, do all to the glory of God."

Whatever genuine Christians do, whether eating or drinking, or whatever else they might do, they should do all things to and for the glory of God. They should be circumspect and cautious as they're eating and drinking. In the Old Testament, Daniel purposed in his heart that he would not defile himself with the

King's meat or the wine that he drank. He wanted to glorify the Lord; therefore, he abstained from the King's meat and drink.

Verses On Glorifying God

- **Psalms 19:1**

"<u>The heavens declare the glory of God</u>; and the firmament sheweth his handywork."

Even the heavens declare God's glory. How much more should those who are true Christians today.

- **John 11:4**

"When Jesus heard that, he said, <u>This sickness is not unto death, but for the glory of God</u>, that the Son of God might be glorified thereby."

This sickness in this verse was for the glory of God so the Son of God might be glorified by healing it.

- **Acts 7:55**

"But <u>he</u>, being full of the Holy Ghost, looked up stedfastly into heaven, and <u>saw the glory of God</u>, and Jesus standing on the right hand of God,"

Steven, the first Christian martyr, saw the glory of God before the Jews stoned him to death.

- **Romans 3:23**

"For <u>all have sinned, and come short of the glory of God</u>;"

Because all people have sinned, they have come short of the glory of God. This is why they must truly trust the Lord Jesus Christ as their Saviour and be saved.

- **2 Corinthians 4:6**

"For God, who commanded the light to shine out of darkness, hath shined in our hearts, <u>to give the light of the knowledge of the glory of God in the face of Jesus Christ</u>."

That's where the glory of God is. It's in the face of the Lord Jesus Christ.

- **Philippians 2:11**

"And that every tongue should confess that <u>Jesus Christ is Lord, to the glory of God the Father</u>."

God wants all people to confess that Jesus Christ is Lord, to God's glory.

- **Revelation 21:23**

"And the city had no need of the sun, neither of the moon, to shine in it: for <u>the glory of God did lighten it</u>, and the Lamb is the light thereof."

In Heaven, there is no need for the sun or moon because God's glory gives light to it.

1 Corinthians 10:32

"Give none offence, neither to the Jews, nor to the Gentiles, nor to the church of God:"

Since the word "*give*" is in the Greek present tense and it is a negative prohibition, this would indicate, in the Greek, to stop an action already in progress. genuine Christians at Corinth should stop giving offence either to the Jews, the Gentiles, or to the church of God. God doesn't want true Christians to offend people.

Verses On Offence

- **Matthew 16:23**

"But he turned, and said unto Peter, Get thee behind me, Satan: thou art an offence unto me: for thou savourest not the things that be of God, but those that be of men."

When Peter contradicted what the Lord Jesus Christ said to Him, it was an offence to Him. Peter contradicted what the Lord Jesus Christ said was going to happen to Him.

- **Acts 24:16**

"And herein do I exercise myself, to have always a conscience void of offence toward God, and toward men."

Genuine Christians should also strive to have such a conscience, void of offence.

- **2 Corinthians 6:3**

"Giving no offence in any thing, that the ministry be not blamed:"

True Christians should seek to stop giving offence in anything they might say or do.

- **Philippians 1:10**

"That ye may approve things that are excellent; that ye may be sincere and without offence till the day of Christ;"

That's a tough act to follow. Hard to do.

- **1 Peter 2:8**

"And a stone of stumbling, and a rock of offence, even to them which stumble at the word, being disobedient: whereunto also they were appointed."

The Lord Jesus Christ is an offence to those who deny Him and to those who do not want to trust Him as their Saviour.

1 Corinthians 10:33

"**Even as I please all *men* in all *things*, not seeking mine own profit, but the *profit* of many, that they may be saved.**"

Paul says that he did his best to please men (when not in contradiction to God's Words). He didn't want to seek his own profit, but the profit of many that they might become genuine Christians. He did not want to be selfish.

1 Corinthians Chapter Eleven

1 Corinthians 11:1

"Be ye followers of me, even as I also *am* of Christ."

Paul did not want the genuine Christians just to follow him in everything, but he limited the "*following*" only in the ways he followed the Lord Jesus Christ. That's an important distinction.

Verses On Follow

- **Matthew 4:19**

"And he saith unto them, Follow me, and I will make you fishers of men."

Any true Christian should follow the Lord Jesus Christ in the ways specified in the Bible.

- **John 10:27**

"My sheep hear my voice, and I know them, and they follow me:"

The Lord Jesus Christ said that His sheep (genuine, obedient Christians) should follow Him.

- **John 12:26**

"If any man serve me, let him follow me; and where I am, there shall also my servant be: if any man serve me, him will my Father honour."

For the true Christians (then and now) to really serve the Lord Jesus Christ, they must follow the Lord Jesus Christ as specified in the Bible.

- **1 Corinthians 4:16**

"Wherefore I beseech you, be ye followers of me."

Paul urged the genuine Christians at Corinth to follow him as he followed the Lord Jesus Christ.

- **Ephesians 5:1**

"Be ye therefore followers of God, as dear children;"

Paul urged the true Christians in Ephesus to follow God as His dear children.

- **Philippians 3:17**

"Brethren, be followers together of me, and mark them which walk so as ye have us for an ensample."

Paul was a good example for genuine Christians in that day and wanted others to follow him as he followed the Saviour.
- **1 Thessalonians 1:6**
"And ye became followers of us, and of the Lord, having received the word in much affliction, with joy of the Holy Ghost:"

The true Christians followed the Apostles and the Lord Jesus Christ Himself.
- **1 Thessalonians 2:14**
"For ye, brethren, became followers of the churches of God which in Judaea are in Christ Jesus: for ye also have suffered like things of your own countrymen, even as they have of the Jews:"

The genuine Christians at Thessalonica followed other sound churches of God in other areas.
- **2 Thessalonians 3:9**
"Not because we have not power, but to make ourselves an ensample unto you to follow us."

Paul wanted to be a good example for other true Christians to follow.
- **Hebrews 6:12**
"That ye be not slothful, but followers of them who through faith and patience inherit the promises."

Sound Old Testament prophets were to be followed as well.
- **Hebrews 13:7**
"Remember them which have the rule over you, who have spoken unto you the word of God: whose faith follow, considering the end of their conversation."

The faith of the sound and Biblical pastors should be followed.

1 Corinthians 11:2

"Now I praise you, brethren, that ye remember me in all things, and keep the ordinances, as I delivered *them* to you."

The true Christians at Corinth were praised by Paul because they remembered Paul in all things. The second thing Paul praised these Christians for was that they kept the ordinances just as Paul had delivered them unto them.

It is very important to see just what the Biblical ordinances are. The Biblical ordinances are just two: (1) the Lord's Supper; and (2) water baptism. Some churches today practice the ordinance of "foot-washing." Though it was practiced during the apostolic times, it never was commanded to be followed as an ordinance for those of us in the age of Grace.

Certainly the practices of the Roman Catholic Church were never taught in the Bible to be maintained in the form of *"ordinances."* This
includes such things as (1) the last rites; (2) the mass; (3) the various sacraments, and many other things.

There are three things that must be true to qualify as a true Biblical ordinance for our present age of grace:
> (1) First, it must have been taught by the Lord Jesus Christ. (2) Second, it must have been practiced by the apostles.
>
> (3) Third, it must have been written and commanded in one of the epistles.

Verses On Baptism
- **Romans 6:4**

"Therefore <u>we are buried with him by baptism into death</u>: that like as Christ was raised up from the dead by the glory of the Father, even so we also should walk in newness of life."

The picture of water baptism by immersion is a picture of death, burial, and resurrection.
- **Colossians 2:12**

"<u>Buried with him in baptism</u>, wherein also ye are risen with him through the faith of the operation of God, who hath raised him from the dead."

The picture is the same as in Romans 6:4.

1 Corinthians 11:3

"But I would have you know, that the head of every man is Christ; and the head of the woman is the man; and the head of Christ *is* God."

Here are the three Biblical headships mentioned in this verse.
1. Christ is the Head of every man.
2. The man is the head of the woman.
3. God the Father is the Head of Christ.

Verses On Various Headships
- **Acts 4:11**

"This is <u>the stone</u> which was set at nought of you builders, which <u>is become the head of the corner</u>."
s in the world.
- **Ephesians 1:22**

"And hath put all things under his feet, and <u>gave him to be the head over all things to the church</u>,"

The Lord Jesus Christ is the Head of the true Church, the body of Christ.

- **Ephesians 4:15**
  "But speaking the truth in love, may grow up into him in all things, which is the head, even Christ:"

All genuine Christians should recognize that the Lord Jesus Christ is their Head and supreme in every way.

- **Ephesians 5:23**
  "For <u>the husband is the head of the wife</u>, even as Christ is the head of the church: and he is the saviour of the body."

In the New Testament, not only is the Lord Jesus Christ the Head of the man but he's also Head of the true church.

- **Colossians 1:18**
  "And <u>he is the head of the body, the church</u>: who is the beginning, the firstborn from the dead; that in all things he might have the preeminence."

The Lord Jesus Christ is the Head of the true Church which is the body of Christ.

- **Colossians 2:10**
  "And ye are complete in him, which is <u>the head of all principality and power</u>:"

The Lord Jesus Christ is the Head of all principality and power.

- **Colossians 2:19**
  "And <u>not holding the Head</u>, from which all the body by joints and bands having nourishment ministered, and knit together, increaseth with the increase of God."

Genuine Christians should hold up and exalt the Lord Jesus Christ as their Head.

- **1 Peter 2:7**
  "Unto you therefore which believe he is precious: but unto them which be disobedient, <u>the stone which the builders disallowed, the same is made the head of the corner</u>,"

Though the Lord Jesus Christ was rejected by man and crucified, He is made the Head of the corner.

- **Ephesians 5:22-24**
  "Wives, submit yourselves unto your own husbands, as unto the Lord. <u>For the husband is the head of the wife, even as Christ is the head of the church</u>: and he is the saviour of the body. Therefore <u>as the church is subject unto Christ, so let the wives be to their own husbands in every thing</u>."

The husband is the head of the wife. As the genuine Christians are subject to the Lord Jesus Christ, so their wives are to be subject to their own husbands in everything (except anything that is contrary to the Bible, of course.)

Other Verses On Wives To Be Subject To Their Husbands
- **Ephesians 5:33**

"Nevertheless let every one of you in particular so love his wife even as himself; and <u>the wife see that she reverence her husband</u>."

The wife is to have respect to her husband.
- **Colossians 3:18**

"<u>Wives, submit yourselves unto your own husbands</u>, as it is fit in the Lord."

This submission is clear in this verse again.
- **Titus 2:4-5**

"That they may <u>teach the young women to be</u> sober, to love their husbands, to love their children, To be discreet, chaste, keepers at home, good, <u>obedient to their own husbands</u>, that the word of God be not blasphemed."

Older genuine Christian women are to teach the young women to be obedient to their own husbands.
- **1 Peter 3:1**

"Likewise, <u>ye wives, be in subjection to your own husbands</u>; that, if any obey not the word, they also may without the word be won by the conversation of the wives;"

This is another clear verse on the wives' subjection to their husbands.
- **1 Peter 3:5**

"For after this manner <u>in the old time the holy women also</u>, who trusted in God, adorned themselves, <u>being in subjection unto their own husbands</u>:"

Even in the Old Testament times Sarah and others were subject to their own husbands.

The commands for true Christians are plain. The non-Christian world usually pays no heed whatever to these standards. The women's liberation movement disdains these Biblical commands.

Verses On Christ Obeying The Father While On Earth
- **Luke 22:42**

"Saying, Father, if thou be willing, remove this cup from me: nevertheless <u>not my will, but thine, be done</u>."

The Lord Jesus Christ was obedient to God the Father.
- **Mark 14:36**

"And he said, Abba, Father, all things are possible unto thee; take away this cup from me: <u>nevertheless not what I will, but what thou wilt</u>."

The Lord Jesus Christ, while on earth, obeyed the Father's will.
- **1 Corinthians 15:27-28**
"For he hath put all things under his feet. But when he saith all things are put under him, it is manifest that he is excepted, which did put all things under him. And when all things shall be subdued unto him, <u>then shall the Son also himself be subject unto him that put all things under him, that God may be all in all</u>."

It must be made clear that there is no inferiority among either God the Father, God the Son, or God the Holy Spirit. They have co-equality in all of Their attributes. In eternity, the Lord Jesus Christ will again be subject unto God the Father as this verse indicates. This is a matter of organization and order in the Godhead, not a matter of inferiority. There is still an equality among all three Persons in the Trinity, yet They have different tasks and duties.

1 Corinthians 11:4

"Every man praying or prophesying, having *his* head covered, dishonoureth his head."

Before the Bible was completed in 90 or 100 A.D., there was still the temporary gift of prophesying in the church, but not after the Bible was completed. The Charismatics and Pentecostals are in error on this doctrinal area. This is made clear in a proper understanding of 1 Corinthians 13. When a man was either praying or prophesying with his head covered (that is, with long hair, as alluded to in verse 14), it dishonors his Head, even the Lord Jesus Christ.

1 Corinthians 11:5

"But every woman that prayeth or prophesieth with *her* head uncovered dishonoureth her head: for that is even all one as if she were shaven."

From verse 15, it states very, very clearly that the woman's HAIR is given to her by the Lord, for a COVERING. If a genuine Christian woman in Paul's day (before the Bible was completed in 90 to 100 A.D.) prays or prophesies with her head uncovered (without long hair, but only short hair), she dishonors her head, both her husband and the Lord Jesus Christ.

If the woman's hair is short, it is just as if she were shaven with very short hair or almost bald like the prostitutes wore their hair in Paul's day. The Biblical standard for true Christian women is to have their hair long rather than short and for the genuine Christian men to have their hair short. There is no exact length in inches that is specified, but this is relative and contrasting length in both cases.

1 Corinthians 11:6

"For if the woman be not covered, let her also be shorn: but if it be a shame for a woman to be shorn or shaven, let her be covered."

Paul speaks very plainly in this verse. The choice for the genuine Christian woman is threefold: (1) She chooses to have short hair and be "*not covered*," with long hair; (2) She chooses to be shorn; (3) If it's a shame to be shorn or shaven like the prostitutes of the day, the woman should be covered by having long hair which is given to her for a Biblical covering. The women's hair should be of proper length and certainly the world that doesn't believe the Bible has no standards for hair.

1 Corinthians 11:7

"For a man indeed ought not to cover *his* head, forasmuch as he is the image and glory of God: but the woman is the glory of the man."

It is very clear here that genuine Christian men should not cover their heads with long hair. The man was specially created by God. Eve was formed from Adam's rib rather than being created from the dust as Adam was. Woman is the glory of the man because she was taken from the man.

1 Corinthians 11:8

"For the man is not of the woman; but the woman of the man."

Adam was not from the woman. She was taken from Adam's rib. Notice the details of God's making Eve.

- **Genesis 2:22**
  "And the rib, which the LORD God had taken from man, made he a woman, and brought her unto the man."

The man was not of the woman, originally. Today, men today are born from women. Adam, the first man, was created by God.

1 Corinthians 11:9

"Neither was the man created for the woman; but the woman for the man."

Man was not created in behalf of the woman and for the woman. The woman, on the other hand was created for Adam.

God said that it was "*not good that the man should be alone*" (Genesis 2:18). Adam had a need. He was lonely. God met that need and the need for the population of the world by forming Eve from Adam's rib.

1 Corinthians 11:10

"For this cause ought the woman to have power on *her* head because of the angels."

Women ought to have proper covering with long hair because of what the fallen angels did in Genesis 6. It might happen in our days as well if women are not properly attired and obedient to God's Words.

- **Genesis 6:1-6**

"And it came to pass, when men began to multiply on the face of the earth, and daughters were born unto them, That the sons of God saw the daughters of men that they were fair; and they took them wives of all which they chose. And the LORD said, My spirit shall not always strive with man, for that he also is flesh: yet his days shall be an hundred and twenty years. There were giants in the earth in those days; and also after that, when the sons of God came in unto the daughters of men, and they bare children to them, the same became mighty men which were of old, men of renown. And GOD saw that the wickedness of man was great in the earth, and that every imagination of the thoughts of his heart was only evil continually. And it repented the LORD that he had made man on the earth, and it grieved him at his heart."

I believe the sons of God were fallen angels made to look like humans. Here are three verses from Job that identify "*sons of God*" with angels who had access to Heaven:

- **Job 1:6**

Now there was a day when the sons of God came to present themselves before the LORD, and Satan came also among them.

- **Job 2:1**

Again there was a day when the sons of God came to present themselves before the LORD, and Satan came also among them to present himself before the LORD.

- **Job 38:7**

When the morning stars sang together, and all the sons of God shouted for joy?

The wicked union produced a half-breed race that God had to judge by a universal flood of waters, sparing only six people–Noah, Shem, Ham, Japheth and their wives. I believe Jude 1:6 is a reference to these fallen angels.

- **Jude 1:6**
"And <u>the angels which kept not their first estate, but left their own habitation,</u> he hath reserved in everlasting chains under darkness unto the judgment of the great day."

I believe this is a reference to these evil angels of Genesis 6.

- **2 Peter 2:4**
"For <u>if God spared not the angels that sinned</u>, but cast them down to hell, and delivered them into chains of darkness, to be reserved unto judgment;"

This fits in with Genesis 6. There was a judgment of angels. Dr. M. R. DeHaan held this view as well.

So, the woman should have power (long hair) on her head and it should be in line in subjection so that the angels would not be tempted to do this thing again. If the women were in subjection to their husbands on this book of Genesis, the angels probably wouldn't have done this. But when they saw that these women had no subjection to their husbands and families and perhaps their hair was not the proper length, they cohabited with women.

Now, you say, could an angel have a body? The angels at the tomb were seen with bodies. The angels that came to Abraham had bodies. They took the appearance of human beings so they could be seen.

1 Corinthians 11:11

"Nevertheless neither is the man without the woman, neither the woman without the man, in the Lord."

Though the woman, Eve, was made specifically for the man, Adam, neither is the man without the woman, neither the woman without the man, in the Lord. In other words, there is a sharing of each other's needs and a sharing of their lives together, as husband and wife in marriage. The husbands need their wives, and the wives need their husbands. This is the clear position and instruction for genuine Christian husbands and Christian wives. The non-Christians often do not agree with these standards.

1 Corinthians 11:12

"For as the woman *is* of the man, even so *is* the man also by the woman; but all things of God."

In God's original creation of Adam and Eve, Eve was of Adam's rib and in that sense the woman was of or from the man. In natural childbirth, men today are of or from the women. You can't make a man without the woman bearing him. Now, all things of God.

1 Corinthians 11:13

"Judge in yourselves: is it comely that a woman pray unto God uncovered?"

In God's eyes, it is not comely or proper for a woman to pray unto God uncovered, or with short hair. It is not pleasing to God. A woman should have hair that is a proper length; otherwise, she's considered by God as uncovered. We'll see, in verse fifteen of this chapter, that a woman's properly long hair is given to her for a covering.

1 Corinthians 11:14

"Doth not even nature itself teach you, that, if a man have long hair, it is a shame unto him?"

In this verse, God teaches that true Christian men should never have long hair like the women should have. It is a shame unto them if that is the case. Even nature teaches this. I don't believe the Lord Jesus Christ had long hair, even though some pictures today wrongly show this. I believe His hair was the same length as the others in that era. The Roman men, by many pictures of them, had short hair. He was not a Nazarite who let his hair grow long. The Lord Jesus Christ was from Nazareth, so he was a Nazarene, but he was not a Nazarite who was supposed to have long hair, and take certain special vows. There are no provisions for Nazarites in the New Testament under the age of Grace.

1 Corinthians 11:15

"But if a woman have long hair, it is a glory to her: for *her* hair is given her for a covering."

The term, *"long hair,"* is a Biblical term, though the Bible nowhere tells us how many inches *"long hair"* should be. All those verses preceding talked about *"covering."* In this verse *"long hair"* is given unto genuine Christian women who want to follow the Bible as their *"covering."* This *"covering"* is not a hat. It is not a veil. Many commentators and pastors make a false assumption that simply putting a hat or a veil on a true Christian woman going into church is fine, even if they do not qualify for *"long hair."* I believe sincerely that this is a serious violation and a misinterpretation of the clear teachings of the Bible.

1 Corinthians 11:16

"But if any man seem to be contentious, we have no such custom, neither the churches of God."

I believe this verse about being contentious means that the Bible position is clear that genuine Christian women should have "long hair" which is her glory. If any man or women tries to be contentious about God's clear teaching in these verses, Paul is not going to fight about it, nor are the true Biblical churches of God going to fight about it and be contentious. God has spoken and there should be no fighting about this clear Biblical position. This is true also for men who have "*long hair.*" This is forbidden by the Bible. Men should not want to argue about it. The Bible is clear about this.

1 Corinthians 11:17

"Now in this that I declare *unto you* I praise *you* not, that ye come together not for the better, but for the worse."

Paul did not praise the church at Corinth, because, when they met in the church for church meetings, they didn't meet for the better, but for the worse. There was apparently some kind of meanness there. This church was at fault for this conduct. I hope in our local church there will never be meanness during our services. We should come together for the praise and worship of the Lord Jesus Christ.

I think there are many churches like in Corinth. They have their services, but they are divided right up the middle. There might be three or four different divisions in the church. I know, for instance, the church that I was very well acquainted with for a while. I think there are at least three divisions in that church. In fact, in some of the churches, there are even four divisions. They come together, not for the better, but for the worse. Some people don't speak to one another if they're not in the same group.

1 Corinthians 11:18

"For first of all, when ye come together in the church, I hear that there be divisions among you; and I partly believe it."

And so today, in many, if not in most, of our churches, there are divisions. This is a sad situation when this happens. I'm glad that our church does not have major divisions. There is unity here, for which we praise the Lord Jesus Christ. If some of those who attend have different doctrines than our church stands for and that I preach, they stop attending. This brings unity back to our church.

Verses On Divisons
- **John 7:43**

"So there was a division among the people because of him." The Person and Work of the Lord Jesus Christ, when believed Biblically, does cause a division between those who truly believe in Him, His Deity, His miracles, and all that the Bible tells about Him, and those who deny these things.

- **John 9:16**

"Therefore said some of the Pharisees, This man is not of God, because he keepeth not the sabbath day. Others said, How can a man that is a sinner do such miracles? And there was a division among them."

This was another division among the people because some of them denied His miracles.

- **Romans 16:17**

"Now I beseech you, brethren, mark them which cause divisions and offences contrary to the doctrine which ye have learned; and avoid them."

Those people who deny Bible doctrine and cause divisions concerning it should be avoided by genuine Christians.

- **1 Corinthians 1:10**

"Now I beseech you, brethren, by the name of our Lord Jesus Christ, that ye all speak the same thing, and that there be no divisions among you; but that ye be perfectly joined together in the same mind and in the same judgment."

Paul strongly urges the true Christians at Corinth not to be divided but be united in mind and doctrine. I've been in a church that had three or four divided groups. One didn't seem to want to speak to those in the other groups. It's an evidence of carnality and fleshliness.

1 Corinthians 11:19

"For there must be also heresies among you, that they which are approved may be made manifest among you."

There must be heresies among the genuine Christians at Corinth as well. The Greek Word for "heresy" means a holding of certain doctrines or beliefs. Usually, in Scripture, these beliefs are contrary to the Bible doctrines. These heresies must be in existence so that those with true doctrines will be able to find them. Those people who hold such false beliefs must then be put out of the churches so that genuine doctrines can be clearly manifested, and those who hold anti-Biblical doctrines may be put out of true Bible-believing churches.

Verses On Heresies

- **Acts 24:14**
"But this I confess unto thee, that <u>after the way which they call heresy, so worship I the God of my fathers</u>, believing all things which are written in the law and in the prophets:"

> **THE MEANING OF THE GREEK WORD, "HAIRESIS"**
> The Greek Word for *"heresy"* is HAIRESIS. Some of the meanings of this Greek Word are:
> *"1) act of taking, capture: e.g. storming a city; 2) choosing, choice; 3) that which is chosen; 4) a body of men following their own tenets (sect or party); 4a) of the Sadducees; 4b) of the Pharisees; 4c) of the Christians; 5) dissensions arising from diversity of opinions and aims."*

Many people call something "heresy" if it conforms exactly to what the Bible teaches. They hold views contrary to the Bible which, in point of fact, are heretical teachings.

- **Galatians 5:19-20**
"Now <u>the works of the flesh are manifest</u>, which are these; Adultery, fornication, uncleanness, lasciviousness, Idolatry, witchcraft, hatred, variance, emulations, wrath, strife, seditions, <u>heresies</u>,"

One of the works of the flesh are *"heresies"* or doctrines contrary to the Bible.

- **2 Peter 2:1**
"But there were false prophets also among the people, even as <u>there shall be false teachers among you, who privily shall bring in damnable heresies</u>, even denying the Lord that bought them, and bring upon themselves swift destruction."

Peter predicted that during his life and ministry there would be false teachers who will bring in damnable heresies. They would be brought in by false teachers.

Some of the many damnable heresies are teachings of Jehovah Witnesses, Christian Science, all of the other cults, the heresies and apostasies in the Roman Catholic Church, the heresies and apostasies in the liberal churches, the National and World Council of Churches, the compromises of the National Association of New Evangelicals and World Evangelical Fellowship, and even in some of the fundamentalist churches that have left their original doctrinal and Biblical positions.

What To Do When Heresies Come In
- **2 Corinthians 6:14**

"Be ye not unequally yoked together with unbelievers: for what fellowship hath righteousness with unrighteousness? and what communion hath light with darkness?"

Genuine Christians are very clearly commanded here, that if apostasy and unbelievers are present in any of their affiliations, they should not be unequally yoked with such unbelievers who are unrighteous and in darkness.

- **2 Corinthians 6:17**

"Wherefore come out from among them, and be ye separate, saith the Lord, and touch not the unclean thing; and I will receive you,"

True Christians here are told not to even touch any unclean thing or unbelievers, but to come out from among them, and be separate unto the Lord Jesus Christ and the clear doctrines taught in the Bible.

1 Corinthians 11:20

"When ye come together therefore into one place, *this* is not to eat the Lord's supper."

The church at Corinth was having "*love feasts*" as they were called. These were not for the particular purpose for the Lord's Supper. They had their own meals. They were eating in the church with some disorderliness as mentioned in the next verse. Some pastors are opposed to having any meals in their churches, such as my former Pastor in Berea, Ohio, yet other Pastors have no problem with it.

1 Corinthians 11:21

"For in eating every one taketh before *other* his own supper: and one is hungry, and another is drunken."

In the case of the genuine Christians in the church at Corinth, three things were true:
1. Some ate their own supper.
2. Some were hungry.
3. Some were drunken.

This particular service was to commemorate the Lord's Supper which was to remember the death of the Lord Jesus Christ until He returns to this earth to set up His Millennial reign for one thousand years. Instead of that, there was a big feast. This was a matter of disorderliness and eating in the church combined with the Lord's Supper. They should have had only one purpose–the remembering the Saviour in the ordinance of the Lord's Supper.

Instead of one purpose only, they mixed this one purpose with a regular meal. They were out of order mixing these two things.

1 Corinthians 11:22

"What? have ye not houses to eat and to drink in? or despise ye the church of God, and shame them that have not? What shall I say to you? shall I praise you in this? I praise *you* not."

The Apostle Paul scolded these genuine Christians in the church at Corinth for their actions. They have houses to eat and drink in. They should have eaten their meals at home rather than in the church. Some would have sumptuous meals and others would not have any food at all because they were poor. Because of this action, Paul did not praise them, but reproved them for their wrong actions.

1 Corinthians 11:23

"For I have received of the Lord that which also I delivered unto you, That the Lord Jesus the same night in which he was betrayed took bread:"

Paul reminded the true Christians at Corinth that the doctrines he delivered unto them came directly from the Lord Jesus Christ when Paul was taught by Him during his three years in the desert of Arabia. It was a tremendous training by the greatest Teacher that ever lived, the Lord Jesus Christ. One of the teachings that the Saviour taught Paul was the Lord's Supper. This teaching was first taught to the Apostles on the same night that Judas Iscariot betrayed the Lord Jesus Christ.

The Betrayal Of Judas Before The Lord's Supper
- **Matthew 10:4**

"Simon the Canaanite, and <u>Judas Iscariot, who also betrayed him</u>."

Judas Iscariot is named as the Apostle who betrayed his Saviour, the Lord Jesus Christ. May genuine Christians never betray Him!
- **Matthew 17:22**

"And while they abode in Galilee, <u>Jesus said unto them, The Son of man shall be betrayed into the hands of men</u>:"

The Lord Jesus Christ told His apostles before it happened that he

would be betrayed into the hands of men.
- **Matthew 20:18**
"Behold, we go up to Jerusalem; and the Son of man shall be betrayed unto the chief priests and unto the scribes, and they shall condemn him to death,"

The Son of man would be betrayed to the Jewish chief priests and the scribes who would condemn Him to death.
- **Matthew 26:2**
"Ye know that after two days is the feast of the passover, and the Son of man is betrayed to be crucified."

The Lord Jesus Christ named crucifixion as the specific manner in which He would be condemned to death.
- **Matthew 26:16**
"And from that time he sought opportunity to betray him."

Judas sought opportunity to betray the Lord Jesus Christ. May God deliver any genuine Christian anywhere in the world from ever betraying or seeking opportunity to betray the Lord Jesus Christ, the
Lamb of God Who taketh away the sins of the world. Shame on Judas!!
- **Matthew 26:21**
"And as they did eat, he said, Verily I say unto you, that one of you shall betray me."

The Lord Jesus Christ told His twelve apostles, in advance, using His omniscience, that one of them would betray Him.
- **Matthew 26:23-25**
"And he answered and said, He that dippeth his hand with me in the dish, the same shall betray me. The Son of man goeth as it is written of him: but woe unto that man by whom the Son of man is betrayed! it had been good for that man if he had not been born. Then Judas, which betrayed him, answered and said, Master, is it I? He said unto him, Thou hast said."

The Lord Jesus Christ named traitor Judas publicly.
- **Matthew 26:45-46**
"Then cometh he to his disciples, and saith unto them, Sleep on now, and take your rest: behold, the hour is at hand, and the Son of man is betrayed into the hands of sinners. Rise, let us be going: behold, he is at hand that doth betray me."

The Lord Jesus Christ told His apostles that were in the garden with Him that He was about to be betrayed by Judas.

- **Matthew 26:48**

"Now he that betrayed him gave them a sign, saying, Whomsoever I shall kiss, that same is he: hold him fast."
I call that the kiss of betrayal. True kisses seem to be sweet and nice. In Judas' heart, it was the reverse of nice. It was wicked. It was evil. May we not give our Saviour the kiss of betrayal. May not our lips praise Him and yet our heart despise Him, or vice versa. This was indeed a kiss of betrayal.
- **John 6:64**

"But there are some of you that believe not. For Jesus knew from the beginning who they were that believed not, and who should betray him."
Yes, the Lord Jesus Christ knew who should betray Him through His Divine omniscience. Some have asked the question, "*Why did He choose Judas?*" I think He wanted to warn people even in Bible-believing churches that those who seem to be with Bible truth, might be, in reality, just like Judas and be fakes and frauds.
- **John 13:2**

"And supper being ended, the devil having now put into the heart of Judas Iscariot, Simon's son, to betray him;"
It was the Devil himself who was in control of Judas' heart to betray the Lord Jesus Christ. Judas had a heart problem.
- **John 13:11**

"For he knew who should betray him; therefore said he, Ye are not all clean."
Again the Lord Jesus Christ's omniscience is seen in this verse. He knew that all of his Apostles were not clean.
- **John 13:21**

"When Jesus had thus said, he was troubled in spirit, and testified, and said, Verily, verily, I say unto you, that one of you shall betray me."
The Lord Jesus Christ said that one of the Apostles would betray Him. When He said that, everyone but Judas said "*Lord, is it I?*" Judas didn't call Him Lord. He asked, "*Master, is it I?*"

1 Corinthians 11:24

"And when he had given thanks, he brake *it*, and said, Take, eat: this is my body, which is broken for you: this do in remembrance of me."

This is a description of what the Lord Jesus Christ did at what we call the Lord's Supper or the communion service. He first gave thanks to God the Father, (as every genuine Christian should do before taking the Lord's Supper, and at all other times as well), then He broke the bread, and then he told His apostles to take it and eat it.

The most important thing was what He said about the meaning of this ordinance. He said, "*This is my Body.*" This does not mean what the Roman Catholic Church and some other churches falsely teach. It is not His actual perfect Body. This is impossible, because He was right there, in His physical, perfect Body. It would be impossible to have His perfect human Body and having the bread also literally being His Body at the same time. It is obvious, for anyone who is able to think correctly, that this "*is*" is not identity. It is a metaphor, meaning it represents His Body.

Then, the Lord Jesus Christ mentioned that His Body would one day be "*broken for them.*" The Roman Catholic Church Bible doesn't have the word "*broken*" in it, nor do the Gnostic, Critical, and Westcott and Hort texts and all the modern Bibles based upon them (ASV, NASV, NIV, RSV, ESV, etc.) do not have it either.

His Body was crucified on Calvary's cross. He was "broken" in many ways at that time. Before His crucifixion, the Roman soldiers, beat Him, and put a crown with sharp thorns on His head. As He dismissed His spirit, and said, "*It is finished,*" the soldiers pierced His side with a spear, out came some of His Blood. He shed His blood for the sins of the entire world. He indeed had a "*broken*" Body, though none of His bones were broken.

One of the most important things are the words in verse 24, "*for you.*" The death of the Lord Jesus Christ on the cross was for every person who ever lived or will live on the earth. He died as a substitute for everyone. God considers everyone to be a sinner in His sight. On the cross He carried their sins in His own body. Those who genuinely believe they are sinners and that the Lord Jesus Christ took their sins in His own Body on the cross, and trust Him as their Saviour, can receive everlasting and eternal life.

The last clause is also important, "*This do in remembrance of me.*" The entire ordinance of the Lord's Table is an ordinance of remembrance of the Lord Jesus Christ Who bore the sins of entire world in His Body on the cross to make it possible that "whosoever will" might trust Him as their Saviour and possess eternal life.

1 Corinthians 11:25

"**After the same manner also *he took* the cup, when he had supped, saying, This cup is the new testament in my blood: this do ye, as oft as ye drink *it*, in remembrance of me.**"

After taking the bread, the Lord Jesus Christ took the cup filled with the "*fruit of the vine.*" This represented the Blood of the Lord Jesus Christ. The Apostles and other true Christians were to perform this ordinance. As often as they drink it, they are to do it in remembrance of what the Lord Jesus Christ accomplished in His death on the cross of Calvary. This death and provided forgiveness and salvation to whoever realizes they are sinners, that the Saviour carried their sins in His own Body on the cross. If they genuinely believe on Him He will give them forgiveness of their sins and everlasting life with Him in Heaven for all eternity.

1 Corinthians 11:26

"**For as often as ye eat this bread, and drink this cup, ye do shew the Lord's death till he come.**"

There's no limit on remembering the Lord's death until He returns in the Rapture for all genuine Christians. The Lord's Supper is that remembrance until the Lord Jesus Christ returns. Our church remembers the Saviour in this manner once each month. Other churches have other schedules for the Lord's Table. Only true Christians should partake of this ordinance.

Verses On Two Phases Of Christ's Coming
- Matthew 24:3

"And as he sat upon the mount of Olives, the disciples came unto him privately, saying, Tell us, when shall these things be? and <u>what shall be the sign of thy coming, and of the end of the world</u>?"

The Lord Jesus Christ's return is in two phases. (1) The first phase is the Rapture, or the taking away in the air of all genuine Christians, followed by the seven-year Tribulation. (2) The second phase is His coming back to earth after the Tribulation with His true Christians to set up His millennial reign for 1,000 years on earth. There are no signs for the Rapture. It might occur at any moment. There are some signs for His coming back to earth for His millennial reign.
- 1 Corinthians 1:7

"So that ye come behind in no gift; <u>waiting for the coming of our Lord Jesus Christ</u>:"

This is a reference to the Lord Jesus Christ's coming in the clouds to Rapture His genuine Christians and take them to Heaven before

the horrendous Tribulation is ushered in.
- **1 Corinthians 15:23**
"But every man in his own order: Christ the firstfruits; afterward they that are Christ's at his coming."

This verse refers to the Rapture of all true Christians.
- **1 Thessalonians 2:19**
"For what is our hope, or joy, or crown of rejoicing? Are not even ye in the presence of our Lord Jesus Christ at his coming?"

This also refers to the Lord Jesus Christ's coming in the Rapture of all genuine Christians.
- **1 Thessalonians 3:13**
"To the end he may stablish your hearts unblameable in holiness before God, even our Father, at the coming of our Lord Jesus Christ with all his saints."

This verse refers to the 2nd phase of the Lord Jesus Christ's return with all the genuine Christians back to earth to stop the battle of Armageddon and set up His millennial reign for 1,000 years on this earth.
- **1 Thessalonians 4:15**
"For this we say unto you by the word of the Lord, that we which are alive and remain unto the coming of the Lord shall not prevent them which are asleep."

This refers to the 1st phase of the coming of the Lord Jesus Christ at the Rapture to Heaven of all genuine Christians.
- **1 Thessalonians 5:23**
"And the very God of peace sanctify you wholly; and I pray God your whole spirit and soul and body be preserved blameless unto the coming of our Lord Jesus Christ."

This speaks of the Rapture as well as when the Saviour will take all true Christians to Heaven.
- **1 John 2:28**
"And now, little children, abide in him; that, when he shall appear, we may have confidence, and not be ashamed before him at his coming."

Genuine Christians should live daily so as not to be ashamed before the Lord Jesus Christ before He Raptures them Home to Heaven.

1 Corinthians 11:27

"Wherefore whosoever shall eat this bread, and drink this cup of the Lord, unworthily, shall be guilty of the body and blood of the Lord."

This is a warning during the Lord's Supper that affects two classes of people:

(1) Non-Christian people: they should not partake of the Lord's Table because they are "*unworthy.*"

(2) Genuine Christian people who are out of fellowship with the Lord should not partake of the Lord's Supper until they get back into His fellowship by properly following 1 John 1:9 because in this backslidden condition, they are "*unworthy.*"

1 Corinthians 11:28

"But let a man examine himself, and so let him eat of that bread, and drink of that cup."

Only after self-examination should true Christians who are out of fellowship with the Lord get back into fellowship by properly using 1 John 1:9. Only after this is done from the heart should they "*eat of that bread, and drink of that cup.*"

THE MEANING OF THE GREEK WORD, "DOKIMAZO"

The Greek Word for "examine" is DOKIMAZO. Some of the meanings of this Greek Word are:

"1) to test, examine, prove, scrutinise (to see whether a thing is genuine or not), as metals; 2) to recognize as genuine after examination, to approve, deem worthy."

---

1 Corinthians 11:29

"For he that eateth and drinketh unworthily, eateth and drinketh damnation to himself, not discerning the Lord's body."

If non-Christians, or if genuine Christians not in close fellowship with the Lord, partake of the Lord's Table, they are acting "*unworthily.*" If either of these things is true, God promises damnation or judgment on those who eat and drink at the Lord's Table in an unworthy manner because neither group is able to discern the meaning of the Lord Jesus Christ's body and what He accomplished for every one in the world on the cross. In the next verse, we see three kinds of judgments that were given to those in the church at Corinth who took this Lord's Supper in an unworthy manner.

1 Corinthians 11:30

"For this cause many are weak and sickly among you, and many sleep."

In this verse, we see that because of the unworthy partaking at the Lord's Table. This brought three results on the part of either the non-Christians or the genuine Christians who were out of fellowship with the Lord. The results were either:
1. **Weakness,**
2. **Sickness,** or
3. **Sleep** (meaning Death here)

If people in our days partake in the Lord's Table in an unworthy manner, these results might happen to them also. God used this very serious example in the church at Corinth to warn churches even in our days.

Verses Where Sin Brought Immediate Physical Death

- Acts 5:2-5

"And <u>kept back part of the price, his wife also being privy to it, and brought a certain part, and laid it at the apostles' feet</u>. But Peter said, Ananias, why hath Satan filled thine heart to lie to the Holy Ghost, and <u>to keep back part of the price of the land</u>? Whiles it remained, was it not thine own? and after it was sold, was it not in thine own power? why hast thou conceived this thing in thine heart? <u>thou hast not lied unto men, but unto God</u>. And <u>Ananias</u> hearing these words fell down, and <u>gave up the ghost</u>: and great fear came on all them that heard these things."

There is nothing wrong with genuine Christians giving only a portion of their funds to the Lord's ministries, but is a sin to claim or imply that they gave more than they really gave. This is the sin for which both Ananias and Saphira his wife were slain.

- 1 John 5:16-17

"If any man see his brother sin a sin which is not unto death, he shall ask, and he shall give him life for them that sin not unto death. <u>There is a sin unto death</u>: I do not say that he shall pray for it. All unrighteousness is sin: and there is a sin not unto death."

Though the "sin" is not named here, the Apostle John says that there is a sin that true Christians, or, perhaps, non-Christians might commit that lead them to suffer physical death. This is all in the hands of the Lord, but everyone should be made aware of this possibility and stay away from sinning, lest they unknowingly commit a sin that leads to their physical death.

1 Corinthians 11:31

"For if we would judge ourselves, we should not be judged."

God wants all genuine Christians to judge themselves so they will not be judged by others or by the Lord Jesus Christ.

- **1 John 1:9**

"If we confess our sins, he is faithful and just to forgive us our sins, and to cleanse us from all unrighteousness."

This verses is in the Bible so that true Christians can keep in close fellowship with their Saviour, the Lord Jesus Christ. For genuine Christians to properly use this verse to regain God's forgiveness and cleansing from their sins, they must know what it means.

First, they must know what the Word for "confess" means. It is from the Greek Word HOMOLOGEO. HOMO means "the same." LOGEO means "to say." The confession or HOMOLOGEO means that the true Christians, confessing their sins to God, must "say the same thing about their sins that God says about them. They must AGREE with God that the sin or sins that they thought, said, or did were sinful. Only then will God forgive their sin or sins, and only then will He cleanse them from all unrighteousness, thus returning them to the close fellowship they formerly had with Him.

1 Corinthians 11:32

"But when we are judged, we are chastened of the Lord, that we should not be condemned with the world."

When genuine Christians are judged by the Lord, He also chastens them so they will not be condemned with or by the wicked world.

Verses On Chastening

- **Deuteronomy 8:5**

"Thou shalt also consider in thine heart, that, as a man chasteneth his son, so the LORD thy God chasteneth thee."

Fathers should chasten their sons and daughters, but often do not. So the Lord chastens His true Christians who need it.

- **Job 5:17**

"Behold, happy is the man whom God correcteth: therefore despise not thou the chastening of the Almighty:"

Genuine Christians are not to despise God's chastening. He chastens them because He loves them and wants them to be able

to serve Him in a godly fashion.
- **Psalms 94:12**
  "<u>Blessed is the man whom thou chastenest, O LORD</u>, and teachest him out of thy law;"

God always chastens His true Christians for their benefit and their profit. They should be grateful for His loving care.
- **Proverbs 3:11**
  "<u>My son, despise not the chastening of the LORD</u>; neither be weary of his correction:"

God's needed chastening of His genuine Christians should not be despised, but be thanked and respected.
- **Proverbs 13:24**
  "He that spareth his rod hateth his son: but <u>he that loveth him chasteneth him betimes</u>."

Chastening by God of His true Christian sons and daughters is because of His love.
- **Proverbs 19:18**
  "<u>Chasten thy son while there is hope</u>, and let not thy soul spare for his crying."

Often parents don't chasten their children when they need it because of the children's crying. If discipline is needed, administer it, crying or no crying.
- **2 Corinthians 6:9**
  "As unknown, and yet well known; as dying, and, behold, we live; <u>as chastened, and not killed</u>;"

Paul was chastened by the Lord, but was not killed by Him.
- **Hebrews 12:5-11**
  "And ye have forgotten the exhortation which speaketh unto you as unto children, <u>My son, despise not thou the chastening of the Lord, nor faint when thou art rebuked of him: For whom the Lord loveth he chasteneth</u>, and scourgeth every son whom he receiveth. <u>If ye endure chastening, God dealeth with you as with sons; for what son is he whom the father chasteneth not? But if ye be without chastisement, whereof all are partakers, then are ye bastards, and not sons.</u>

Furthermore we have had fathers of our flesh which corrected us, and we gave them reverence: shall we not much rather be in subjection unto the Father of spirits, and live? For <u>they verily for a few days chastened us after their own pleasure; but he for our profit, that we might be partakers of his holiness.</u> Now <u>no chastening for the present seemeth to be joyous, but grievous: nevertheless afterward it yieldeth the peaceable fruit of righteousness unto them which are exercised thereby.</u>"

These are key verses on God's chastening of His genuine Christians. It is because He loves them that He chastens them so they may serve Him faithfully and righteously. And every daughter, too. These verses should be studied and understood about the duty, meaning, and results of proper chastening, whether by parents or by God.

- **Revelation 3:19**

"<u>As many as I love, I rebuke and chasten</u>: be zealous therefore, and repent."

As many of God's true Christians that He rebukes and chastens, He does it because He loves them and wants them to be His obedient and fruitful children.

1 Corinthians 11:33

"Wherefore, my brethren, when ye come together to eat, tarry one for another."

Paul now returns to what the genuine Christians at Corinth should do when they observe the ordinance of the Lord's Table.

They should not partake of the bread or fruit of the vine as soon as they are served it, but should wait until everyone of the genuine Christians are served, and only then should they partake of the elements.

1 Corinthians 11:34

"And if any man hunger, let him eat at home; that ye come not together unto condemnation. And the rest will I set in order when I come."

The Lord's Table ordinance has nothing to do with eating meals as people do daily. It should be a separate ordinance carried out just as the Bible lays out. There was a problem in the church at Corinth because they neglected to follow the Biblical order.

The true Christians who participate in the Lord's Table should eat their meals in their own home so that they would not come

unto condemnation if they attempted to mix their normal meals with participating in the Lord's Table.

Paul intended to set in order other problems that existed in the church at Corinth when he returned to them later. He took up these things in his letter of 2 Corinthians that he sent to them at a later time.

1 Corinthians Chapter Twelve

1 Corinthians 12:1

"Now concerning spiritual *gifts*, brethren, I would not have you ignorant."

This is one of the most crucial passages in 1 Corinthians. It's a very controversial passage. It talks about the nine temporary gifts of the Spirit which the Pentecostals and Charismatics believe are still with us today. I, and many others, believe that these special temporary sign gifts were in the churches until the Bible was completed in 90-100 A.D.

There are five ministries of the Holy Spirit to the genuine Christians:
1. **The baptizing ministry**
2. **The regenerating ministry**
3. **The indwelling ministry**
4. **The sealing ministry**
5. **The filling ministry**

The first four of the Holy Spirit's ministries are accomplished the minute people become true Christians by honestly trusting the Lord Jesus Christ as their Saviour. The fifth of His ministries takes place when genuine Christians are yielded to Him in their lives. It is only then that He manifests His fruits.

On the other hand, there are two more ministries to the non-Christians:
1. **The convicting ministry**
2. **The restraining ministry**

The first five ministries of God the Holy Spirit have been available to genuine Christians from the New Testament days and continuing all during this present age.

The two ministries of God the Holy Spirit towards those who are non-Christians are during this present age.

All seven of these ministries of God the Holy Spirit are like "gifts" of the Holy Spirit, but the temporary sign gifts are something else that Paul does not want these true Christians at Corinth to be ignorant about. He discusses these in the verses below.

There's a lot of ignorance today about the spiritual gifts that were present in the early church, and the temporary spiritual gifts that have ceased after the Bible was completed in about 90 to 100 A.D.

1 Corinthians 12:2

"Ye know that ye were Gentiles, carried away unto these dumb idols, even as ye were led."

The genuine Gentile Christians at Corinth were reminded that their pagan ancestors were heathen idolaters worshipping dumb idols–dumb is in the sense of not being able to talk rather than ignorant. Notice some of the characteristics of these idols worshipped by many even today:

Verses On Idols
- **Psalms 106:35-38**

"But were mingled among the heathen, and learned their works. And they served their idols: which were a snare unto them. Yea, they sacrificed their sons and their daughters unto devils, And shed innocent blood, even the blood of their sons and of their daughters, whom they sacrificed unto the idols of Canaan: and the land was polluted with blood."

When you get into idolatry, you learn the works of the heathen. These heathen practiced human sacrifice because they worshipped devils. The genuine Christians in the church at Corinth were mostly Gentiles. These dumb idols who are worshipped couldn't talk or walk or think. These people did not just worship these idols, but they served them. They were slaves to their idols.

- **Psalms 115:3-9**

"But our God is in the heavens: he hath done whatsoever he hath pleased. Their idols are silver and gold, the work of men's hands. They have mouths, but they speak not: eyes have they, but they see not: They have ears, but they hear not: noses have they, but they smell not: They have hands, but they handle not: feet have they, but they walk not: neither speak they through their throat. They that make them are like unto them; so is every one that trusteth in them. O Israel, trust thou in the LORD: he is their help and their shield."

Formerly, many of these, who were now true Christians, worshipped these idols of silver and gold. The idols were the work of men's hands. How can anybody worship something that they themselves have made, and then say that the idols made those who made them? Seems somewhat inane to me!

Notice the things that these idols have but cannot use: (1) mouths; (2) eyes; (3) ears; (4) noses; (5) hands; (6) feet; (7)

tongues; and a throat. Though idols might have all seven things, none of them can be utilized.

1 Corinthians 12:3

"Wherefore I give you to understand, that no man speaking by the Spirit of God calleth Jesus accursed: and *that* no man can say that Jesus is the Lord, but by the Holy Ghost."

Two things are given in this verse that Paul wanted the genuine Christians at Corinth to understand:

1. No genuine Christian, speaking by the Spirit of God, can call the Lord Jesus Christ accursed.

2. No true Christian can say that the Lord Jesus Christ is the Lord except by the Holy Spirit Who indwells them.

Both of these facts that are mentioned above are absolutely true and can never be denied by anyone. Genuine Christians can neither say the Lord Jesus Christ is in some way accursed by God the Father, nor can they say the Lord Jesus Christ is their Lord except by the Holy Spirit Who lives within them.

1 Corinthians 12:4

"Now there are diversities of gifts, but the same Spirit."

During the early years of the local churches, before the Bible was completed in 90-100 A.D., God the Holy Spirit provided special temporary gifts to inform these churches about what God's will and doctrines. These are sometimes referred to as temporary "sign gifts." I, and many other Bible teachers, pastors, missionaries, and other genuine Christians around the world agree that these temporary "sign gifts" were given and practiced by the true Christians that lived from 90 to 100 A.D., before the Bible was completed. Then these temporary "sign gifts" ceased to be honored and provided by God.

Today, many of these "sign gifts" are thought to be still in existence. They are falsely and unscripturally practiced and performed by such groups as the Pentecostals, Charismatics, and some others. I believe the so-called false "sign gifts" that are practiced today are not of God. They are Satanic and motivated by the Devil himself to lead people astray from following the written Words of God exclusively. They are rather trying to add or take away from His inspired and inerrant Words. To do so is in strict violation of the Bible's clear teachings that we should never add or remove any of those teachings.

Verses on Adding Or Removing God's Words
- **Revelation 22:18**

"For I testify unto every man that heareth the words of the prophecy of this book, If any man shall add unto these things, God shall add unto him the plagues that are written in this book:"
- **Revelation 22:19**

"And if any man shall take away from the words of the book of this prophecy, God shall take away his part out of the book of life, and out of the holy city, and from the things which are written in this book."

1 Corinthians 12:5

"And there are differences of administrations, but the same Lord."

Those who are genuine Christians are not all the same, and do not all have the same abilities or talents to use for the glory of the Lord Jesus Christ. God has differences of administrating and working with all of them around the world and in every country and continent.

The verses below refer to both the temporary "sign gifts" that were given to those genuine New Testament Christians living in the days before the Bible was completed in 90-100 A.D. as well as the permanent gifts which will endure until the return of the Lord Jesus Christ in the Rapture of all genuine Christians.
- **Romans 12:6-8**

"Having then gifts differing according to the grace that is given to us, whether prophecy, let us prophesy according to the proportion of faith; Or ministry, let us wait on our ministering: or he that teacheth, on teaching; Or he that exhorteth, on exhortation: he that giveth, let him do it with simplicity; he that ruleth, with diligence; he that sheweth mercy, with cheerfulness."

Any of the gifts, whether temporary or permanent, were given by God to His true Christians by the working of His grace.
- **Ephesians 4:7-13**

"But unto every one of us is given grace according to the measure of the gift of Christ. Wherefore he saith, When he ascended up on high, he led captivity captive, and gave gifts unto men. (Now that he ascended, what is it but that he also descended first into the lower parts of the earth? He that descended is the same also that ascended up far above all heavens, that he might fill all things.) And he gave some, apostles; and some, prophets; and some, evangelists; and some, pastors and teachers; For the perfecting of the saints, for the work of the ministry, for the edifying of the body of Christ: Till we all come in the unity of the faith, and of the knowledge of the Son of God, unto a perfect man, unto the measure of the stature of the fulness of Christ:"

Though the Mormon Church cult uses apostles, we believe these were only temporary gifts. There are no "apostles" today. They were temporary. Neither are there "prophets." They also were temporary. We believe, however, there are "evangelists," "pastors," and "teachers" that are permanent.

Notice that the gifts of pastors and teachers are *"For the perfecting of the saints, for the work of the ministry, for the edifying of the body of Christ."* This is a needful purpose which many pastors and teachers are not fulfilling. We don't want baby-Christians that know very little about the Words of God. They need to grow in grace and in the Biblical knowledge of God the Father, God the Son, and God the Holy Spirit.

1 Corinthians 12:6

"And there are diversities of operations, but it is the same God which worketh all in all."

It is true that the operations of the gifts that God has provided differ widely, because they were and are necessary for His mighty work to be accomplished in His own way and purpose.

1 Corinthians 12:7

"But the manifestation of the Spirit is given to every man to profit withal."

The main purpose of the gifts of God the Holy Spirit, whether temporary or permanent, is for genuine Christians to whom the gifts were given, and to many other people, might profit thereby. In the verses below, there are a list of nine temporary sign gifts that have passed away, yet many today believe they are still with us.

1 Corinthians 12:8

"For to one is given by the Spirit the word of wisdom; to another the word of knowledge by the same Spirit;"

Here are the first two of the special temporary sign gifts that have expired once the Bible was completed in 90 to 100 A.D.

1. The temporary sign gift of wisdom

This first special sign gift of wisdom was given by God before the entire Bible was completed from Genesis through Revelation. God wanted His genuine Christians to know what they were to do, to believe, and to practice.

2. The temporary sign gift of knowledge

This second special sign gift of knowledge goes right along with the sign gift of wisdom. Knowledge presents certain facts and truths and wisdom makes it possible to understand and use the knowledge. This knowledge God supplied before His completed written revelation in the Bible was completed.

Mrs. Waite and I were reporters on one occasion at a Charismatic meeting in Kansas City, Kansas. The meeting was held in a large stadium which held about 10,000 people. Attending the meeting was a mixture of Charismatics from various denominations including Roman Catholic Charismatics, Baptist Charismatics, Episcopalian Charismatics, Lutheran Charismatics, Baptist Charismatics, Congregational Charismatics, and many others. On the stage were special people who thought that they had various sign gifts, including knowledge and wisdom when they didn't really have them.

1 Corinthians 12:9

"To another faith by the same Spirit; to another the gifts of healing by the same Spirit;"

3. The temporary sign gift of faith

This was not just ordinary faith such as true Christians have exercised in their genuine trust in the Lord Jesus Christ as their Saviour. This was a mighty faith that could move mountains if needed.

Verses On Mighty Faith

- **Matthew 17:20**

"And Jesus said unto them, Because of your unbelief: for verily I say unto you, If ye have faith as a grain of mustard seed, ye shall say unto this mountain, Remove hence to yonder place; and it shall remove; and nothing shall be impossible unto you."

This was the temporary special sign gift of faith.

- **1 Corinthians 13:2**

"And though I have the gift of prophecy, and understand all mysteries, and all knowledge; and though I have all faith, so that I could remove mountains, and have not charity, I am nothing."

He's talking about mountain-moving faith. Now, if any genuine Christians have this in our days, where are they? This sign gift was temporary. Saving faith in the Lord Jesus Christ as the Saviour is still with us and will be with people forever, but not this sign gift of temporary mountain-moving faith.

4. The temporary sign gift of healing

This is another sign gift that was very much present in the New Testament, but was discontinued when the Bible was completed in about 90 to 100 A.D. Those who claim that this temporary sign gift of healing is still with us today have pushed their healing ministries greatly. Many of their fake healings and non-healings, that they pretend to be true, have backfired on them and those who pretended to be healed have later returned to their sickness that they had before. People are very easily deceived about this. I believe that Satan is heavily involved in this false, phony, and fake ministry that has deceived millions of people today!

1 Corinthians 12:10

"To another the working of miracles; to another prophecy; to another discerning of spirits; to another *divers* kinds of tongues; to another the interpretation of tongues:"

In this verse, Paul lists five more of the temporary sign gifts that have passed away with the completion of the Bible in 90 to 100 A.D.

5. The temporary sign gift of miracles

Here we have these remaining temporary gifts, the miracles and the revelation that was there. Now, the Lord Jesus worked miracles, Moses worked miracles, Elijah worked miracles, and the apostles worked miracles. There's no question about that. Mark 16:9-20 has a list of many miracles, all of which were performed in the era of the New Testament days.

6. The temporary sign gift of prophecy

God gave the sign gift of prophecy before the Old and New Testaments were completed so that genuine Christians living then would know about some future events.

7. The temporary sign gift of discerning of spirits

God gave the sign gift of discerning of spirits so the early genuine Christians would be able to tell which spirits were true and which were false.

8. The temporary sign gift of tongues

God gave the early churches the sign gift of tongues or the speaking of foreign languages so they could make known the Gospel of the Lord Jesus Christ to foreigners. This temporary sign gift was used in Acts 2 on the day of Pentecost where the Apostles who were there were able to speak the approximately ten or eleven languages of the people who attended so they could hear the Gospel of God's grace and take it back to their own countries. This temporary sign gift ceased when the Bible was completed in 90 to 100 A.D.

9. The temporary sign gift of interpretation of tongues

The temporary sign gift of interpretation of tongues was practiced in the apostolic time and until the Bible was completed. But when the Bible was completed, and the last book had been written in the New Testament, those temporary signs ceased. We'll see in 1 Corinthians 13 that everyone of these temporary sign gifts were looked at as childish (before the Bible was completed), but now (after the Bible was completed), the genuine Christians became men, and put away these childish things. This is in spite of the false teachings of the Charismatic and Pentecostal movements which are growing and multiplying all around the world. In spite of other sound doctrines these groups might hold, the holding to practicing these nine temporary sign gifts are part of Satan's confusing and divisive strategies. We'll have more details on this when we come to Chapter 13.

1 Corinthians 12:11

"But all these worketh that one and the selfsame Spirit, dividing to every man severally as he will."

In Paul's day, all of these nine temporary sign gifts were present in the churches and were in effect by means of God the Holy Spirit Who divided who divided these gifts to genuine Christians as He willed. The verb, "*worketh*" is a present tense in the Greek and means that these temporary sign gifts were working as Paul wrote to the true Christians at Corinth. If God wanted people to believe that these nine temporary sign gifts were to be permanent, He would have had Paul write in the future Greek tense which would be understood to mean that they will continue to work into the continued future without any let up.

1 Corinthians 12:12

"For as the body is one, and hath many members, and all the members of that one body, being many, are one body: so also *is* Christ."

Many genuine Christians deny this truth that the Body of Christ is one body made up of only those who are true Christians who have accepted the Lord Jesus Christ as their Saviour and Lord. There are many members of that one Body who are scattered around the world in spite of the fact that they might be in many different denominations and churches. If they are attending compromised or doctrinally defective churches, they should leave such churches and find Biblically-sound churches to attend. If they can't find such a church nearby, they could always go to BibleForToday.org and tune into our Sunday a.m. and p.m. and Thursday p.m. services.

Some of my friends have a completely unbiblical position on the Body of Christ with many members. They teach the heresy that their Baptist church, and other Baptist churches who agree with them, are the body of Christ and none other people on this earth. Those who are Genuine Christians, but not part of their specific Baptist church groups are, in their heretical position, not in the "one Body" of Christ, but merely in what they call the "*family of God.*" This heretical group of Baptists also mutilates the King James Bible's accurate translation of this next verse, 1 Corinthians 12:13, in an effort to conform it to their unscriptural position.

1 Corinthians 12:13

"For by one Spirit are we all baptized into one body, whether *we be* Jews or Gentiles, whether *we be* bond or free; and have been all made to drink into one Spirit."

This is a very clear verse on the fact and meaning of baptism by God the Holy Spirit, or Spirit baptism. It states clearly that genuine Christians (the "*we*") when born-again were all baptized into one Body, whether Jews or Gentiles, and were all made to drink into one Spirit.

There is a Baptist group of churches that denies that all true Christians are members of the one Body of Christ. It is presently led by Dr. Thomas Strouse of Connecticut. He teaches that only his own group is the "Body of Christ." All other genuine Christians are only in "the family of God." Though he is Scriptural on many other

Christian doctrines, he has lead his followers to follow two serious, unscriptural, false, and heretical interpretations of this verse.

1. Their misinterpretation of "Spirit"

Though this verse is clearly a reference to God the Holy Spirit, this Baptist group, though they profess to stand for the King James Bible, goes against that Bible that they use and love by changing this word, "*Spirit*" from a reference to God the Holy Spirit, to "spirit" which they misinterpret to be some form of human enthusiasm.

2. Their misinterpretation of "baptized"

The second error made by this group of Baptists is their misinterpretation of the word, "baptized." It is crystal clear that this is a baptism by God the Holy Spirit of all genuine Christians into one body. Their heretical misinterpretation of Spirit baptism is that of water baptism into their local Baptist church.

The baptism of the Holy Spirit does two things, to those of us who are true Christians. Number one, it unites us with the Head of the body, the Lord Jesus Christ. Secondly, it unites us with the other members of the body the Lord Jesus Christ has saved by grace through their genuine faith in Him. The unity to their Head and to the other members of His body--that's what God the Holy Spirit has done in this baptizing work, as soon as people become genuine Christians.

Verses On The Baptism By The Holy Spirit
- **Matthew 3:11**

"<u>I indeed baptize you with water</u> unto repentance: but <u>he that cometh after me</u> is mightier than I, whose shoes I am not worthy to bear: he <u>shall baptize you with the Holy Ghost, and with fire</u>:"

I believe that on the day of Pentecost, the Lord Jesus Christ did fulfil this and baptized them with the Holy Ghost and with fire. That's when the speaking in tongues took place.

- **Mark 1:8**

"I indeed have baptized you with water: but <u>he shall baptize you with the Holy Ghost</u>."

The baptism of the Spirit of God was predicted in Mark 1:8.

- **Luke 3:16**

"John answered, saying unto them all, I indeed baptize you with water; but one mightier than I cometh, the latchet of whose shoes I am not worthy to unloose: <u>he shall baptize you with the Holy Ghost and with fire</u>:"

This prediction was made here and was fulfilled in Acts 2 on the day of Pentecost.

- **Acts 1:5**
"For John truly baptized with water; but ye shall <u>be baptized with the Holy Ghost not many days hence</u>."
That's what happened on the day of Pentecost.
- **Acts 2:4**
"And <u>they were all filled with the Holy Ghost, and began to speak with other tongues, as the Spirit gave them utterance</u>."
This was the result of the apostles being baptized by the Holy Spirit as predicted in Acts 1:5 above. They were able to speak in other languages so that those present from many foreign nations could hear the Gospel of the Lord Jesus Christ.

3. Their misinterpretation of "body"

This group of Baptists have committed a third misinterpretation of 1 Corinthians 12:13. The verse clearly states that they were baptized by God the Holy Sprit *"into one body."* This Baptist group that interprets this verse as "spirited enthusiasm," and "water baptism," limits the "one body" only to a certain group of Baptists that agree with one another. It leaves out many, many who are genuine Christians who are not connected to this group of Baptists. That is not *"one body"* of true Christians, but two bodies–this Baptist group of churches (who may have members attending their services who are lost and bound for Hell) and the true *"one body"* of all genuine Christians from the day of Pentecost to the end of time.

The heresy involved with this group of Baptist churches is that they call their group of Baptist churches "the body of Christ" and they deny the Biblical truth that every genuine Christian who has been born again from the day of Pentecost until the Rapture is a member of the body of Christ–not just a few Baptist churches.

1 Corinthians 12:14

"For the body is not one member, but many."

The "body of Christ" which is the true church, is not merely one member, but many. It consists of every genuine Christian who ever lived or who will live in the future. It certainly is not one group of Baptist churches or any other group of churches.

1 Corinthians 12:15

"If the foot shall say, Because I am not the hand, I am not of the body; is it therefore not of the body?"

In speaking of the literal bodies of human beings, they all have feet, hands, and many other parts of their bodies. This verse is referring to the "Body of Christ" which includes all genuine Christians from the day of Pentecost and beyond.

If the literal feet and hands could talk and the foot would say because it wasn't the hand it was not a part of the body, is it not of the body? Yes, it is a member of the body though not the same as the feet. All the members of our human bodies, though different, are all parts of our bodies. So it is with various true Christians who are all members of the Body of Christ. They are different in many ways with different gifts, abilities, and ministries, but they are all members of that spiritual born-again body.

1 Corinthians 12:16

"And if the ear shall say, Because I am not the eye, I am not of the body; is it therefore not of the body?"

Here we have, sort of an anatomy lesson concerning the Church which is the Body of Christ made up of all genuine Christians around the world. Some are considered as ears and eyes. The ears should not say if they're not the eyes, they are not of the body. Both the ears and the eyes are part of the body, but have different duties to perform.

1 Corinthians 12:17

"If the whole body were an eye, where *were* the hearing? If the whole *were* hearing, where *were* the smelling?"

This is using the human body as an illustration of true Christians who are in the Body of Christ. If the entire body was an eye, there would be noses or other needed members of the body to function properly. To be a properly-functioning human body, or spiritual Body of Christ as genuine Christians, all of the different members need to be present, and working as they are needed to perform their distinctive functions for the betterment of the entire bodies, or Body.

1 Corinthians 12:18

"But now hath God set the members every one of them in the body, as it hath pleased him."

Not only members of our human physical body, our eyes, our ears and so on, but also among the true Christians in the Body of Christ. God has set the members of the Body of Christ in the capacities and places of ministries as it has pleased Him. Each genuine Christian has been given by the Lord differing talents, gifts, purposes, and ideas.

1 Corinthians 12:19

"**And if they were all one member, where *were* the body?**"

Again, we say, if there were only one member of our human bodies, it wouldn't be considered a human body at all. People would be unable to do very many things at all if they had only one member in their body. So if the genuine Christians who are all members of the spiritual Body of Christ were only one type of a member, it would not be a complete, workable, and functional Body of Christ.

1 Corinthians 12:20

"**But now *are they* many members, yet but one body.**"

This is what has been mentioned in the preceding verses. Though there is only one Spiritual Body of the Lord Jesus Christ, yet that one Body is composed of many, many members, composed of all genuinely, born-again, and saved people from the Day of Pentecost until the end of the age of grace.

1 Corinthians 12:21

"**And the eye cannot say unto the hand, I have no need of thee: nor again the head to the feet, I have no need of you.**"

The true Christians who are members of the Body of the Lord Jesus Christ must never scoff at other genuine members of Christ's Body and either say or act like they are worthless people. Whatever their needs might be, they are still members of Christ's Body that He has saved by His grace through their true faith in Him as their Saviour. Courtesy must prevail. Some true Christians are more talented than others. They might be the ones who seem to be "*high and mighty.*" They look down on those that are lesser qualified. That should never take place among the members of the Body of the Lord Jesus Christ.

1 Corinthians 12:22

"**Nay, much more those members of the body, which seem to be more feeble, are necessary:**"

Among the genuine Christians in the Body of the Lord Jesus Christ, there are some who seem to be more feeble than others, but every member is necessary. Just like on a football team, a basketball team, a hockey team, or a baseball team, all players are needed in order to win the games. There is no one person who can do the whole job. So with true Christians in the Body of Christ. All are needed.

- **1 Samuel 30:18-25**

"And David recovered all that the Amalekites had carried away: and David rescued his two wives. And there was nothing lacking to them, neither small nor great, neither sons nor daughters, neither spoil, nor any thing that they had taken to them: David recovered all. And David took all the flocks and the herds, which they drave before those other cattle, and said, This is David's spoil. And <u>David came to the two hundred men, which were so faint that they could not follow David</u>, whom they had made also to abide at the brook Besor: and they went forth to meet David, and to meet the people that were with him: and when David came near to the people, he saluted them. Then answered all the wicked men and men of Belial, of those that went with David, and said, <u>Because they went not with us, we will not give them ought of the spoil that we have recovered</u>, save to every man his wife and his children, that they may lead them away, and depart. <u>Then said David, Ye shall not do so, my brethren, with that which the LORD hath given us</u>, who hath preserved us, and delivered the company that came against us into our hand. For who will hearken unto you in this matter? but <u>as his part is that goeth down to the battle, so shall his part be that tarrieth by the stuff</u>: they shall part alike. And it was so from that day forward, that he made it a statute and an ordinance for Israel unto this day."

There were two hundred of David's men that were too tired to go fight the Amalekites and bring back the wives and children and all the booty and spoil. Some of the men didn't want to give these two hundred tired men any of the spoil, but David shared the spoil with these tired men.

True Christians may not be missionaries or pastors, but can be prayer warriors back home and donors to help those who are on the battlefields for the Lord Jesus Christ. They will be honored by the Lord Jesus Christ at the Judgment Seat of Christ.

1 Corinthians 12:23

"And those *members* of the body, which we think to be less honourable, upon these we bestow more abundant honour; and our uncomely *parts* have more abundant comeliness."

Those genuine Christians are all members of the Body of the Lord Jesus Christ. On those members which are thought to be less honourable, more abundant honour is bestowed on them to make them have more abundant comeliness.

1 Corinthians 12:24

"For our comely *parts* have no need: but God hath tempered the body together, having given more abundant honour to that *part* which lacked:"

In the Body of the Lord Jesus Christ, consisting of all genuine Christians, the comely parts which continue to walk in the Biblical will of God do not need as much care from the Lord as true Christians who do not follow their Lord as they should. In order to take care of these straying members, He gives more honour to those members of the body that lack in some areas.

1 Corinthians 12:25

"That there should be no schism in the body; but *that* the members should have the same care one for another."

God has tempered the true Christian members of the Body of the Lord Jesus Christ so that there should be no schism in that Body. He wants all genuine Christians to have the same care one for another. They should be caring Christians rather than having division and schism.

Verses On Caring

- **Psalms 142:4**

"I looked on my right hand, and beheld, but there was no man that would know me: refuge failed me; no man cared for my soul."

The psalmist needed people who would help him, yet he mentioned that "*no man cared for my soul.*" True Christians need to be caring for one another.

- **Mark 4:38**
  "And he was in the hinder part of the ship, asleep on a pillow: and they awake him, and say unto him, Master, carest thou not that we perish?"

The Lord Jesus Christ cared for his disciples in the stormy Sea of Galilee. He also cares for all of His genuine Christians as well.

- **Luke 10:33-35**
  "But a certain Samaritan, as he journeyed, came where he was: and when he saw him, he had compassion on him. And went to him, and bound up his wounds, pouring in oil and wine, and set him on his own beast, and brought him to an inn, and took care of him. And on the morrow when he departed, he took out two pence, and gave them to the host, and said unto him, Take care of him; and whatsoever thou spendest more, when I come again, I will repay thee."

This half-Jew and half-Gentile Samaritan took good care of this wounded man both on the scene and for many days later as well. True Christians should care for each other as the need arises.

- **John 10:13**
  "The hireling fleeth, because he is an hireling, and careth not for the sheep."

The hireling is not a true shepherd and doesn't really care for the sheep as the shepherd does. There are many hireling Pastors today as well that don't really care for their people.

- **2 Corinthians 8:16**
  "But thanks be to God, which put the same earnest care into the heart of Titus for you."

God put into the heart of Titus to be a caring pastor for those in the Corinthian church as well as for those of his own church on the island of Crete.

- **2 Corinthians 11:28**
  "Beside those things that are without, that which cometh upon me daily, the care of all the churches."

Paul had a care for every one of the churches that he founded at Corinth, Philippi, Colosse, Rome, Galatia, Ephesus, Thessalonica, and elsewhere.

- **Philippians 2:20**
  "For I have no man likeminded, who will naturally care for your state."

Paul was speaking about the excellent care that Timothy gave them.

- **1 Timothy 3:5**
  "(For if a man know not how to rule his own house, how shall he take care of the church of God?)"

If a pastor-bishop-elder doesn't know how to rule his own house, he couldn't take good care of a local church.
- **1 Peter 5:7**
"Casting all your care upon him; for he careth for you."
The Lord Jesus Christ is a caring Saviour. All genuine Christians should cast all of their care and concerns on Him, because He cares for all of them.

1 Corinthians 12:26

"And whether one member suffer, all the members suffer with it; or one member be honoured, all the members rejoice with it."

All genuine Christians and ONLY genuine Christians are members of the Body of the Lord Jesus Christ. If one of these members suffers, all suffer. If a member is honored, all the members rejoice about that.

Other true Christians do not know either the suffering or the rejoicing of other Christians all around the world. But insofar as they know the other Christians' condition, they should suffer with them and also rejoice with them.

1 Corinthians 12:27

"Now ye are the body of Christ, and members in particular."

Paul is sending this letter to the genuine Christians at Corinth. As such, they are members of the Body of the Lord Jesus Christ. He states very clearly that these true Christians are "*the Body of Christ.*"

They are also members of that Body in particular. Though all genuine Christians are the Body of Christ, each member is a distinct, separate, and particular member of that Body.

The Lord Jesus Christ has no other members of His Body except these true Christians who have been regenerated by God the Holy Spirit when they first really and sincerely received and believed on the Lord Jesus Christ as their Saviour.

1 Corinthians 12:28

"**And God hath set some in the church, first apostles, secondarily prophets, thirdly teachers, after that miracles, then gifts of healings, helps, governments, diversities of tongues.**"

In this verse, Paul mentions eight temporary spiritual sign gifts which, though they were present in the church when this book and other New Testament books were written, they have all passed off the scene once the entire Old and New Testaments had been completed in around 90 to 100 A.D. These eight temporary sign gifts include the following:

1. **The temporary sign gift of apostles**
2. **The temporary sign gift of prophets**
3. **The temporary sign gift of teachers**
4. **The temporary sign gift of miracles**
5. **The temporary sign gift of healings**
6. **The temporary sign gift of helps**
7. **The temporary sign gift of governments**
8. **The temporary sign gift of tongues**

Though some of these temporary sign gifts appear to be things that are present today like "*teachers,*" "*helps,*" and "*governments,*" in this verse and as used in this context, they have special and super-human meaning to provide for the true Christians before they had the complete Bible in their hands.

Verses Showing Temporary
Sign Gifts Would Pass Away

- 1 Corinthians 13:8

"Charity never faileth: but <u>whether there be prophecies, they shall fail; whether there be tongues, they shall cease; whether there be knowledge, it shall vanish away</u>."

Those special temporary sign gifts were not permanent (like the Pentecostals, Charismatics, and others wrongly teach in our days) but were only temporary until the entire Bible had been completed. At that point, they all "*failed,*" "*ceased,*" "*vanished away,*" and in verse ten, "*done away.*" Once again, "*knowledge*" in this verse has a special and extended meaning other than the way we used the word today.

- 1 Corinthians 13:10

"But <u>when that which is perfect is come</u>, then that which is in part shall be done away."

As we mentioned last week, the words, *"when that which is perfect is come,"* are impossible to refer to the return of the Lord Jesus Christ, either in the Rapture or in His coming to earth to set up His millennial reign. For that to be the reference, the Greek Word would have to be HO TELEIOS for "*is come.*" Once again, for "*that which is perfect*" to refer to the coming of the Lord Jesus Christ, it would have to read, "*when HE WHO is perfect,*" rather than "when THAT WHICH is perfect. HE WHO is masculine, but THAT WHICH is neuter. The verse uses TO TELEION ("that which is perfect") which is neuter. The neuter Greek noun to which this refers is TO BIBLION which is the Book or the Bible. Think this over carefully before jumping to erroneous conclusions. Ask your Pentecostal and Charismatic friends to think this over carefully as well.

1 Corinthians 12:29

"*Are* all apostles? *are* all prophets? *are* all teachers? *are* all workers of miracles?"

The answer to these four questions is No. But all four of these temporary sign gifts were only temporary and present only until the Bible was completed in 90 to 100 A.D.

But even when these temporary sign gifts were present, these gifts were not available to everyone, but only to certain people to whom God made them available.

1 Corinthians 12:30

"Have all the gifts of healing? do all speak with tongues? do all interpret?"

Even when these temporary sign gifts were available to some of the genuine Christians, every one of them did not have all of the temporary sign gifts. They did not all have the temporary sign gift of healing powers. They did not all have the temporary sign gift of speaking with foreign languages. They did not all have the temporary sign gift of interpretation of foreign languages.

1 Corinthians 12:31

"But covet earnestly the best gifts: and yet shew I unto you a more excellent way."

Even when these sign gifts were temporarily given to some of the genuine Christians before the Bible was completed in 90 to 100 A.D., these Christians were to seek the best sign gifts. But, in the next chapter, Paul will show the true Christians at Corinth that they should desire and seek the more excellent way of charity or love rather than any of the nine temporary sign gifts that were then in the church.

In our days, true Christians have differing natural gifts which are not the temporary miraculous and temporary sign gifts of Paul's day. Some are good speakers. Some are good writers. Some can play music on various instruments. Some can sing well. Yet Paul urges all of these genuine Christians to seek first and foremost charity and love that reaches out to others with genuine concern and care.

1 Corinthians Chapter Thirteen

1 Corinthians 13:1

"Though I speak with the tongues of men and of angels, and have not charity, I am become as sounding brass, or a tinkling cymbal."

In this section of 1 Corinthians, we will find eleven characteristics of charity, which is love in action. Many editors of the new Bible versions (which have many, many mistranslations and are founded on the wrong Hebrew, Aramaic, and Greek Words) remove *"charity"* and use *"love"* in its place. It is true that the Greek Word, AGAPE, means *"love."* But by using the English word, *"charity,"* it adds another dimension to it.

"Charity" is not merely love in the heart and the lips, but it's love in action. It's the kind of love that God had when He sent His Son, the Lord Jesus Christ into the world. He just didn't hope that the world would be all right. He didn't just send an angel, but He sent His only begotten Son, the Lord Jesus Christ. That's the charity of God, giving to all mankind what they did not deserve so that the Lord Jesus Christ could be the Saviour for those who genuinely trust Him by true faith. Paul contrasts "charity" or love with the temporary gift of tongues which was then present in Paul's life until the entire Bible had been completed. He wrote: "*Though I speak with the tongues of men and of angels*" but lack charity, something is lacking in his Christian life. In his day, Paul was given the temporary gift of speaking many foreign languages so people could hear the Gospel. He was also given the temporary gift of the interpretation and translation of languages. He also mentions that sometimes angels spoke.

Verses Where Angels Spoke
- **Matthew 28:5**

"And <u>the angel answered and said unto the women</u>, Fear not ye: for I know that ye seek Jesus, which was crucified."

This angel spoke to the women at the tomb of the Lord Jesus Christ.
- **Luke 1:13**

"But <u>the angel said unto him, Fear not, Zacharias: for thy prayer is heard</u>; and thy wife Elisabeth shall bear thee a son, and thou shalt call his name John."

This angel spoke to Zacharias, the father of John the Baptist.
- **Luke 1:19**

"And <u>the angel answering said unto him, I am Gabriel, that stand in the presence of God; and am sent to</u> speak unto thee, and to shew thee these glad tidings."

This angel who spoke was Gabriel.
- **Luke 1:28**

"And <u>the angel came in unto her, and said, Hail, thou that art highly favoured</u>, the Lord is with thee: blessed art thou among women."

The angel told Mary this concerning the miraculous birth of the Lord Jesus Christ
- **Luke 1:30**

"And <u>the angel said unto her, Fear not, Mary</u>: for thou hast found favour with God."

The angel spoke again to Mary.
- **Luke 4:3**

"And <u>the devil said unto him</u>, If thou be the Son of God, command this stone that it be made bread."

Satan, the fallen angel, spoke again to the Lord Jesus Christ.
- **John 20:12-13**

"And seeth <u>two angels in white sitting</u>, the one at the head, and the other at the feet, where the body of Jesus had lain. And <u>they say unto her, Woman, why weepest thou</u>? She saith unto them, Because they have taken away my Lord, and I know not where they have laid him."

These two angels spoke to this woman at the Lord Jesus Christ's empty tomb.
- **Acts 5:19-20**

"But <u>the angel of the Lord</u> by night opened the prison doors, and brought them forth, and <u>said, Go, stand and speak in the temple to the people all the words of this life</u>."

The angel of the Lord spoke to those released from prison.
- **Acts 8:26**

"And <u>the angel of the Lord spake unto Philip</u>, saying, Arise, and go toward the south unto the way that goeth down from Jerusalem unto Gaza, which is desert."

The angel of the Lord spoke to Philip.
- **Acts 10:7**

"And when <u>the angel which spake unto Cornelius</u> was departed, he called two of his household servants, and a devout soldier of them that waited on him continually;"

This angel spoke to Cornelius.
- **Acts 12:8**

"And <u>the angel said unto him, Gird thyself</u>, and bind on thy sandals. And so he did. And he saith unto him, Cast thy garment about thee, <u>and follow me</u>."

This angel gave instructions to this man to follow him.
- **Acts 27:23-24**

"For there stood by me this night <u>the angel of God</u>, whose I am, and whom I serve, <u>Saying, Fear not, Paul</u>; thou must be brought before Caesar: and, lo, God hath given thee all them that sail with thee."

The angel of God comforted Paul in the storm that would wreck this ship.
- **Galatians 1:8**

"But <u>though we, or an angel from heaven, preach any other Gospel unto</u> you than that which we have preached unto you, let him be accursed."

These angels could possibly preach a false Gospel to people. They were to be accursed.

The word, "charity," is only used twenty-four times in our King James Bible. It only occurs in the New Testament, never in the Old Testament. The word, "love," is used 280 times in the King James Bible. Charity is an outreach. It is love in action. Love or charity spoken of in this chapter, is a love that can only be possessed by genuine Christians who are filled by God the Holy Spirit. This kind of love is listed first in the order of the fruits of the Holy Spirit spoken of in Galatians 5:22-23.

If this temporary sign gift of miraculously speaking in foreign languages is not accompanied by "*charity,*" the person has become like "*sounding brass, or a tinkling cymbal.*" There's nothing wrong with "*sounding brass.*" When you hit it, it makes a sound. There's nothing wrong with a "tinkling cymbal." It also makes a sound when you hit it. But it doesn't have a message of useful and intelligent purpose. It doesn't do any good. It has no effect. Neither of these sounds. There's no action to them.

1 Corinthians 13:2

"And though I have *the gift of* prophecy, and understand all mysteries, and all knowledge; and though I have all faith, so that I could remove mountains, and have not charity, I am nothing."

Here are four more temporary sign gifts that we believe have passed off the scene after the Bible was completed in 90-100 A.D. Here is the list of five sign gifts thus far:

1. **The temporary sign gift of tongues**
2. **The temporary sign gift of prophecy**
3. **The temporary sign gift of mysteries**
4. **The temporary sign gift of knowledge**
5. **The temporary sign gift of faith**

If any of these five temporary sign gifts, properly defined, were possessed when they were still in existence in the church but were not used along with charity or love, they would be incomplete and improperly used.

These sign gifts, and all the others, have been removed because we now have all of God's revelation supernaturally given in the Old Testament and all of God's revelation in the New Testament after 90 to 100 A.D. God does not want us to add to His completed revelation by the false use of any of the nine temporary sign gifts. God has stated in His Word that it is a sin to add to His revealed Words. If any person adds to God's

revealed Words, God will add the plagues written in the book of Revelation.
- **Revelation 22:18**
"For I testify unto every man that heareth the words of the prophecy of this book, <u>If any man shall add unto these things, God shall add unto him the plagues that are written in this book:</u>"

As I have mentioned before, though all the temporary sign gifts mentioned in the New Testament were fine, yet to be effective, all of them must be accompanied with Godly charity and love.

1 Corinthians 13:3

"And though I bestow all my goods to feed *the poor*, and though I give my body to be burned, and have not charity, it profiteth me nothing."

God's standards are not the same as man's standards. He says to us in this verse that even though people might give all their goods to feed the poor, give their bodies to be burned, or suffer other very painful treatment as martyrs yet if they do not have the practical trait of charity, or love in action, it will not profit them. Godly charity is at the top of God's list to accompany all the good deeds done by genuine Christians.

Verses On Helping The Poor And Those In Need
- **Matthew 19:20-22**
"The young man saith unto him, All these things have I kept from my youth up: what lack I yet? Jesus said unto him, If thou wilt be perfect, go and <u>sell that thou hast, and give to the poor, and thou shalt have treasure in heaven: and come and follow me</u>. But when the young man heard that saying, he went away sorrowful: for he had great possessions."

This man went his way. He had no charitable love–no love in action. He wanted to keep his money, and he didn't want to follow the Lord. The Lord knew that. The Lord doesn't require all of our money. He requires our heart. He requires our love for him and trusting him.

- **Luke 14:13-14**
"But <u>when thou makest a feast, call the poor, the maimed, the lame, the blind: And thou shalt be blessed; for they cannot recompense thee</u>: for thou shalt be recompensed at the resurrection of the just."

The Lord will take care of the reward. These people can't pay for anything. They can't recompense you.

- **Luke 19:8-10**

"And <u>Zacchaeus stood, and said unto the Lord; Behold, Lord, the half of my goods I give to the poor</u>; and if I have taken any thing from any man by false accusation, I restore him fourfold. And Jesus said unto him, This day is salvation come to this house, for so much as he also is a son of Abraham. For the Son of man is come to seek and to save that which was lost."

The poor you have with you always. Zacchaeus helped the poor. I hope it was with sound charity.

- **John 12:3-8**

"<u>Then took Mary a pound of ointment of spikenard, very costly, and anointed the feet of Jesus, and wiped his feet with her hair</u>: and the house was filled with the odour of the ointment. Then saith one of his disciples, Judas Iscariot, Simon's son, which should betray him, <u>Why was not this ointment sold for three hundred pence, and given to the poor</u>? This he said, not that he cared for the poor; but because he was a thief, and had the bag, and bare what was put therein. Then said Jesus, Let her alone: against the day of my burying hath she kept this. For <u>the poor always ye have with you; but me ye have not always</u>."

For Mary to do this, her hair had to be long enough, unlike many Christian women today. She had enough hair to do it, by the way. Judas Iscariot had no love or charity for the poor. He just wanted to get his hands on the money this spikenard would bring him when he sold it and kept the money. He had no care for the Lord Jesus Christ Who would soon be crucified.

The last part of 1 Corinthians 13:3 verse mentions "*though I give my body to be burned*" and do not have charity or love in action, it is of no value. This speaks of martyrdom and death as many genuine Christians, in the early years of the Christian faith, suffered.

Material On Torture Methods Used In The Past

There is a book called *Foxes Book of Martyrs*. It tells of many early true Christians who suffered great pain because they refused to recant their faith in the Lord Jesus Christ. In the early days, there were places where genuine Christians were tortured unless they renounced their Saviour. Here's part of an article from the *Wikipedia* on the torture chambers.

> "*A torture chamber is a room where torture is inflicted.[3][4] The medieval torture chamber was windowless and often built underground, was lit by a few candles and*

was specifically designed to induce "horror, dread and despair" to anyone but those possessing a strong mind and "nerves of steel".[5]

Historically, torture chambers were located in royal palaces, in castles of the nobility and even buildings belonging to the church. They featured secret trap-doors which could be activated to throw victims into dark dungeons where they remained and eventually died. The skeletal remains of people who disappeared were strewn on the floor of the hidden dungeons. Other times the dungeons under the trap-doors included pits of water where the victim was thrown to drown after a lengthy torture session in the chamber above.[6]"

I hope none of us have to undergo this as the Christians did in that day, especially in the 1500's as well as in some Communist and terrorist Islamic countries in our days.

"In this "Chamber of Torture," there were instruments for compressing the fingers until the bones should be squeezed to splinters. There were instruments for probing below the fingernails, making an exquisite pain, like a burning fire would run along the nerves. There were instruments for tearing out the tongue, for scooping out the eyes and cutting off the ears. There were bunches of iron cords with a spiked circle at the end of every whip for tearing the flesh from the bone until the sinew lay bare. There were iron cases for the legs which would tighten up the limbs placed in them by means of a screw until flesh and bones were reduced to jelly. There were cradles, set full of sharp spikes in which victims were laid and rolled from side to side, the wretched occupant being pierced at each moment by the machine with innumerable sharp points. There were iron ladles with long handles for holding molten lead for boiling pitch to be poured down the throat of the victim and convert the body into a burning caldron.

What further punishment did the holy officer reserve for those, who even after these torments, failed to recant their faith? The object was to recant faith in the Lord Jesus Christ and in the Scripture."

This is a picture of the *"give my body to be burned,"* not just simple burning--*"and have not charity, it profiteth me nothing."* These are things that our forefathers went through. I don't know whether we are going to escape such persecutions either. The torture, temptations and the privations that the Communists have inflicted upon their people could come into our country as well. If so, the true Christians would be first on the list for suffering and death. There are hit-lists now all over the world, and especially if conquerors come. The ones the leaders want to get rid of first are the Bible-believing, genuine Christians who have standards. They trust in the Lord Jesus Christ and God's Words found in the Bible. They will not recant or change their beliefs. They must be eliminated by the tyrants in authority. They're no good for this One World Government that is coming. This will be a terrible thing!

1 Corinthians 13:4

"Charity suffereth long, *and* is kind; charity envieth not; charity vaunteth not itself, is not puffed up,"

There are 15 characteristics of charity.

The Fifteen Greek Definitions Of Biblical Charity
1. Charity Is Longsuffering.

For each of 15 characteristics of charity, I will give the Greek definitions so the readers can be informed of what Paul meant when he was guided by the Holy Spirit to write these Words.

Here is the Greek definition of the Greek Word for *"longsuffering."*

MEANING OF THE GREEK WORD, "MAKROTHUMEO"

The Greek Word for *"longsuffering"* is, MAKROTHUMEO. Some of the meanings of that Greek Word are: 1) to be of a long spirit, not to lose heart; 1a) to persevere patiently and bravely in enduring misfortunes and troubles; 1b) to be patient in bearing the offenses and injuries of others; 1b1) to be mild and slow in avenging; 1b2) to be longsuffer-ing, slow to anger, slow to punish.

The Lord Jesus Christ was longsuffering, even with those who despised Him. Genuine Christians should be longsuffering as well despite whatever and whoever might confront them.

2. Charity Is Kind.

Here is the Greek definition of the Greek Word for *"kind."*

> **MEANING OF THE GREEK WORD, "CHRESTEUOMAI"**
> The Greek Word for *"kind"* is CHRESTEUOMAI. Some of the meanings of this Greek Word are:
> 1) to show one's self mild, to be kind, use kindness.

The Lord Jesus Christ, the Example for every true Christian, was kind to those who loved Him and kind, as well as sincere, honest, and firm (when needed), to those who hated Him. He was kind to his tormentors. He was kind even to Judas. When the thief on the cross said *"curse God and die,"* the Lord Jesus Christ did not do so. He said, *"Father forgive them, for they know not what they do."* Every genuine Christian should follow the example of their Saviour in this regard, though often very difficult.

3. Charity Envieth Not.

Here is the Greek definition of the Greek Words for the phrase, *"envieth not."*

> **THE MEANING OF THE GREEK WORD, "ZELOO"**
> The Greek Word for *"envieth"* is ZELOO. Some of the meanings of this Greek Word are:
> 1) to burn with zeal; 1a) to be heated or to boil with envy, hatred, anger; 1a1) in a good sense, to be zealous in the pursuit of good; 1b) to desire earnestly, pursue; 1b1) to desire one earnestly, to strive after, busy one's self about him; 1b2) to exert one's self for one (that he may not be torn from me); 1b3) to be the object of the zeal of others, to be zealously sought after; 1c) to envy.

Somebody has a new car, somebody has a new hat, somebody has a new suit, or new shoes, or a new boat, or a new airplane, or a new home. True Biblical charity exercised by genuine Christians will not envy any of these things. We must be content with whatever God has so graciously given us.

4. Charity Vaunteth Not Itself.

Here is the Greek definition of the Greek Words for the expression, *"vaunteth not itself."*

> **MEANING OF THE GREEK WORD, "PERPEREUOMAI"**
>
> The Greek Word for "*vaunteth not itself*" is PERPEREUOMAI. Some of the meanings of this Greek Word are:
>> "1) to boast one's self 2) a self display, employing rhetorical embellishments in extolling one's self excessively."

The Lord Jesus Christ never bragged, yet He was omnipotent and omniscient. He never pushed Himself. Some people brag about the things that they really don't have. They brag about their beauty, and they're ugly. They brag about their strength, and they're weak. They brag about their wealth, and they're impoverished. There's nothing to brag about if they don't have it? But if they do have it, why brag about it. Just go ahead and live.

5. Charity Is Not Puffed Up.

Here is the Greek definition of the Greek Words for the expression, "*puffed up*."

> **THE MEANING OF THE GREEK WORD, "PHUSIOO"**
>
> The Greek Word for "*puffed up*" is PHUSIOO. Some of the meanings of this Greek word are:
>> "1) to make natural, to cause a thing to pass into nature; 2) to inflate, blow up, to cause to swell up; 2a) to puff up, make proud; 2b) to be puffed up, to bear one's self loftily, be proud."

Christian Charity doesn't act in this manner. The Lord Jesus Christ never acted in a proud and arrogant manner. He was perfect God and perfect Man. As such, He was omnipotent, omniscient, and omnipresent. There was never any human being on this earth who had such exalted and Divine abilities, yet He was filled with humility rather than pride. He could have glorified Himself, but He didn't do that. He was in submission to the Father's will as the Son of God. In the Garden of Gethsemane, facing His death on Calvary's cruel cross, He said to God the Father, "*not my will, but Thine be done.*" May every genuine Christian follow their Saviour in such submission.

1 Corinthians 13:5

"Doth not behave itself unseemly, seeketh not her own, is not easily provoked, thinketh no evil;"

In this verse, Paul lists four more characteristics of Christian charity.

6. Charity Does Not Behave Itself Unseemly.

Here is the Greek definition of the Greek Word for *"unseemly."*

THE MEANING OF THE GREEK WORD, "PAROXUNO"

The Greek Word for *"unseemly"* is PAROXUNO. Some of the meanings of this Greek Word are:

"1) to make sharp, sharpen; 1a) to stimulate, spur on, urge; 1b) to irritate, provoke, arouse to anger; 1b1) to scorn, despise; 1b2) provoke, make angry; 1b3) to exasperate, to burn with anger; 1) to make sharp, sharpen; 1a) to stimulate, spur on, urge; 1b) to irritate, provoke, arouse to anger; 1b1) to scorn, despise; 1b2) provoke, make angry; 1b3) to exasperate, to burn with anger."

Christian charity does not irritate and provoke people to anger. On the other hand, it is love in action. This does not mean genuine Christians agree with various people in every detail, but if they are following charity, they will not behave themselves in an angry manner.

7. Charity Does Not Seek Her Own.

"Her own" merely refers to an individual's own self-interest without regard for anyone else.

Here is the Greek definition of the Greek Word for *"seeking."*

THE MEANING OF THE GREEK WORD, "ZETEO"

The Greek Word for *"seeking"* is ZETEO. Some of the meanings of this Greek Word are:

"1) to seek in order to find; 1a) to seek a thing; 1b) to seek [in order to find out] by thinking, meditating, reasoning, to enquire into; 1c) to seek

> after, seek for, aim at, strive after; 2) to seek i.e. require, demand; 2a) to crave, demand something from someone."

The genuine Christians who possess the blessings of Christian charity do not strive after, seek, require, demand, or crave something that belongs to other people. They are content with the things that they have.

8. Charity Is Not Easily Provoked.

Here is the Greek definition of the Greek Word for "*provoked.*"

> **THE MEANING OF THE GREEK WORD, "PAROXUNO"**
>
> The Greek Word for "*provoked*" is PAROXUNO. Some of the meanings this Greek Word are:
>
>> "1) to make sharp, sharpen; 1a) to stimulate, spur on, urge; 1b) to irritate, provoke, arouse to anger; 1b1) to scorn, despise; 1b2) provoke, make angry; 1b3) to exasperate, to burn with anger."

One of the senses of "*provoke*" is to make sharp or sharpen. If someone attacks people with something sharp in their hands, it could result in serious wounds or even death. This word indicates that if genuine Christians possess this trait of not being easily provoked, they will not be sharp, or provoke people, or burn with anger themselves. The Lord will have control of them. This is made possible only if these true Christians are controlled by the Holy Spirit within them and are bearing His fruit.

9. Charity Thinketh No Evil

Here is the Greek definition of the Greek Words for "*think,*" and for "*evil.*" Both words are needed for complete understanding.

> **THE MEANING OF THE GREEK WORD, "LOGIZOMAI"**
>
> The Greek Word for "*think*" is LOGIZOMAI. Some of the meanings of this Greek Word are:
>
>> "1) to reckon, count, compute, calculate, count over; 1a) to take into account, to make an account of; 1a1) metaph. to pass to one's account, to impute; 1a2) a thing is reckoned as or to be something, i.e. as availing for or

1 Corinthians Preaching Verse-By-Verse

> equivalent to something, as having the like force and weight; 1b) to number among, reckon with; 1c) to reckon or account; 2) to reckon inward, count up or weigh the reasons, to deliberate; 3) by reckoning up all the reasons, to gather or infer; 3a) to consider, take into account, weigh, meditate on; 3b) to suppose, deem, judge; 3c) to determine, purpose, decide."

It is very important not only to do no evil, but also to not even think of any evil.

Here is the Greek definition of the Greek Word for "*evil.*"

THE MEANING OF THE GREEK WORD, "KAKOS"

The Greek Word for "evil" is KAKOS. Some of the meanings of this Greek Word are:

> "1) of a bad nature; 1a) not such as it ought to be; 2) of a mode of thinking, feeling, acting; 2a) base, wrong, wicked; 3) troublesome, injurious, pernicious, destructive, baneful."

When genuine Christians are manifesting Christian charity, they do not do any sort of evil, and they do not even think about evil of any kind. This includes any thoughts of murder, suicide, adultery, fornication, smoking pot, or any other evil.

1 Corinthians 13:6

"**Rejoiceth not in iniquity, but rejoiceth in the truth;**"

10. Charity Does Not Rejoice In Iniquity.

In this verse, Paul lists two more characteristics of Christian charity. Here is the Greek definition of the Greek Word for "*iniquity.*"

THE MEANING OF THE GREEK WORD, "ADIKIA"

The Greek Word for "*iniquity*" is ADIKIA. Some of the meanings of this Greek Word are:

> "*1) injustice, of a judge; 2) unrighteous- ness of heart and life; 3) a deed violating law and justice, act of unrighteousness.*"

Christian charity never rejoices in any form of iniquity or

unrighteousness. If genuine Christians rejoice in this, they are not practicing Christian charity.

Verses In Iniquity And Wickedness
- **Psalms 5:5**

"The foolish shall not stand in thy sight: thou hatest all workers of iniquity."

This verse is very clear about God's opinion of iniquity workers.

- **Psalms 26:5**

"I have hated the congregation of evil doers; and will not sit with the wicked."

God will not sit with those who are wicked, nor should genuine Christians.

- **Psalms 45:7**

"Thou lovest righteousness, and hatest wickedness: therefore God, thy God, hath anointed thee with the oil of gladness above thy fellows."

God hates wickedness and all true Christians should hate it also.

- **Psalms 97:10**

"Ye that love the LORD, hate evil: he preserveth the souls of his saints; he delivereth them out of the hand of the wicked."

Genuine Christians should hate evil with a passion.

- **Psalms 119:104**

"Through thy precepts I get understanding: therefore I hate every false way."

This is a good action for all true Christians to hate false ways.

- **Psalms 119:163**

"I hate and abhor lying: but thy law do I love."

Truth should be loved, lying should be hated and abhorred by genuine Christians.

- **Proverbs 8:13**

"The fear of the LORD is to hate evil: pride, and arrogancy, and the evil way, and the froward mouth, do I hate."

God hates all kinds of evil and true Christians should do the same.

- **Amos 5:15**

"Hate the evil, and love the good, and establish judgment in the gate: it may be that the LORD God of hosts will be gracious unto the remnant of Joseph."

Hatred is usually bad, but it is never bad to hate evil.

- **Micah 3:2**

"Who hate the good, and love the evil; who pluck off their skin from off them, and their flesh from off their bones;"

This a sin to love the evil. Evil of all kinds must be hated by all genuine Christians.

- **Zechariah 8:17**

"And <u>let none of you imagine evil in your hearts against his neighbour</u>; and love no false oath: for <u>all these are things that I hate, saith the LORD</u>."

True Christians should hate even the imagination of evil in their hearts.

- **Hebrews 1:9**

"<u>Thou hast</u> loved righteousness, and <u>hated iniquity</u>; therefore God, even thy God, hath anointed thee with the oil of gladness above thy fellows."

This is spoken of about the Lord Jesus Christ. True Christians should follow their Saviour in this hatred of iniquity, but never hatred of truth.

Here is the Greek definition of the Greek Word for the word, "*truth*."

THE MEANING OF THE GREEK WORD, "ALETHEIA."

The Greek Word for "*truth*" is ALETHEIA. Some of the meanings of this Greek Word are:

"1) OBJECTIVELY; 1a) what is true in any matter under consideration; 1a1) truly, in truth, according to truth; 1a2) of a truth, in reality, in fact, certainly; what is true in things appertaining to God and the duties of man, moral and religious truth; 1b1) in the greatest latitude; 1b2) the true notions of God which are open to human reason without his supernatural intervention; the truth as taught in the Christian religion, respecting God and the execution of his purposes through Christ, and respecting the duties of man, opposing alike to the superstitions of the Gentiles and the inventions of the Jews, and the corrupt opinions and precepts of false teachers even among Christians; 2) SUBJECTIVELY; 2a) truth as a personal excellence; 2a1) that candour of mind which is free from affection, pretence, simulation, falsehood, deceit."

Where do genuine Christians go to find truth wherein they may rejoice? Definite truth is not always found in books, newspapers, magazines, schools, or on television, radio, or the Internet.

Reliable and eternal truth is found within the pages of a reliable and accurately translated Bible which has been based on the preserved Masoretic Hebrew, Aramaic, and Greek Words. There are very few such Bibles in the various languages in the world. But in the English language, there is only one Bible which has been based on the properly preserved Hebrew, Aramaic, and Greek Words which have been accurately translated into English. This Bible is the King James Bible.

The other English Bibles have either been based on the erroneous Hebrew, Aramaic, and Greek Words, or have not been accurately translated, or both. For example, in 99% of the modern English Bibles, their New Testaments have been translated from the Gnostic, Critical Greek Words which differ in their New Testament from the King James Bible in over 8,000 places. This has been documented by Dr. Jack Moorman in his book, *8,000 Differences Between The Nestle/Aland Greek And The Traditional Greek New Testaments* **(BFT #3084, 544 pages @ $20.00 + S&H.**) Of these 8,000 differences, there are 356 differences that affect serious differences in Biblical doctrines.

True Christian charity must rejoice in the historical and doctrinal truths that are faithfully represented in the King James Bible or Bibles in other languages that are accurately translated from the same original Words as the King James Bible.

1 Corinthians 13:7

"Beareth all things, believeth all things, hopeth all things, endureth all things."

This chapter of 1 Corinthians will state very clearly that the nine sign gifts of the Holy Spirit will cease. It will also tell us when they ceased.

12. Charity Beareth All Things.

Here is what "*beareth*" means in Greek.

THE MEANING OF THE GREEK WORD, "STEGO"

The Greek Word for "*beareth*" is STEGO. Some of the meanings of this Greek Word are:

"1) deck, thatch, to cover; 1a) to protect or keep by covering, to preserve; 2) to cover over with silence."

Verses On Bearing And Enduring
- **Jeremiah 10:18-19**

"For thus saith the LORD, Behold, I will sling out the inhabitants of the land at this once, and will distress them, that they may find it so. Woe is me for my hurt! <u>my wound is grievous: but I said, Truly this is a grief, and I must bear it</u>."

Jeremiah, when he heard of the distress of his Jewish people, it was a grief, but he realized that he must bear that distress.

- **John 16:12**

"<u>I have yet many things to say unto you, but ye cannot bear them now</u>."

The Lord Jesus Christ said to His disciples, before He went into heaven, that He had many things to say to them, but they were not able to bear them at that time.

- **Acts 15:10**

"Now therefore why tempt ye God, to put <u>a yoke upon the neck</u> of the disciples, <u>which neither our fathers nor we were able to bear</u>?"

The law of Moses was a yoke that no one could bear.

- **1 Corinthians 3:2**

"<u>I have fed you with milk</u>, and <u>not with meat: for hitherto ye were not able to bear it</u>, neither yet now are ye able."

Immature true Christians could not bear the meat of God's Word, but only understand the milk of the Words.

- **1 Corinthians 10:13**

"There hath no temptation taken you but such as is common to man: but <u>God is faithful, who</u> will not suffer you to be tempted above that ye are able; but <u>will with the temptation also make a way to escape, that ye may be able to bear it</u>."

With all the testings and temptations to the genuine Christians, God will make a way to escape so they can bear them.

- **Revelation 2:2**

"I know thy works, and thy labour, and thy patience, and how <u>thou canst not bear them which are evil</u>: and thou hast tried them which say they are apostles, and are not, and hast found them liars:"

True Christians should endure and bear evil people and their evil works. They should oppose them.

13. Charity Believeh All Things.
This is what "*believeth*" means in Greek.

THE MEANING OF THE GREEK WORD, "PISTEUO"

The Greek Word for "believeth" is PISTEUO. Some of the meanings of this Greek Word are:

> "1) to think to be true, to be persuaded of, to credit, place confidence in; 1a) of the thing believed; 1a1) to credit, have confidence; 1b) in a moral or religious reference; 1b1) used in the NT of the conviction and trust to which a man is impelled by a certain inner and higher prerogative and law of soul; 1b2) to trust in Jesus or God as able to aid either in obtaining or in doing something: saving faith; 1bc) mere acknowledgment of some fact or event: intellectual faith; 2) to entrust a thing to one, i.e. his fidelity; 2a) to be entrusted with a thing."

I do not think this characteristic of charity means that genuine Christians are to believe everything that people, radio, televison, the newspapers, the Internet, or any other human source might tell them. There are many, many lies and untruths that are found in this world. I think this refers to "all things" found in God's Words, the Bible (the proper Bible, based on the true Hebrew, Aramaic, and Greek Words and accurately translated, such as the King James Bible.) These Words should be always believed and received by all true Christians. To believe them, they have to read them first.

14. Charity Hopeth All Things.
This is what the Greek Word for "*hopeth*" means.

THE MEANING OF THE GREEK WORD, "ELPIZO"

The Greek Word for "hopeth" is ELPIZO. Some of the meanings of this Greek Word are:

> "1) to hope; 1a) *in a religious sense, to wait for salvation with joy and full confidence;* 2) *hopefully to trust in.*"

The hope that true charity brings is the hope that is found throughout the Bible. Whether in the Old Testament, or the New Testament, what God promises either Israel or the genuine Christians in the New Testament, He always fulfills them. This is why true Christians today can have hope in all of His promises in the New Testament. For example, He has promised that the Lord Jesus Christ will return to take all of His genuine Christians home to Heaven in the Rapture. That is called *"the blessed hope"* in Titus 2:13.

Paul wrote: "*If in this life only we have hope in Christ, we are of all men most miserable*" (1 Corinthians 15:19). Paul was facing death, almost daily. If all he had was this present life, with no hope for eternal life and going home to be with Christ, it would be a terrible life for Paul and for true Christians today.

15. Charity Endureth All Things.

This is what the Greek Word for "*endureth*" means.

THE MEANING OF THE GREEK WORD, "HUPOMENO"

The Greek Word for "endureth" is HUPOMENO. Some of the meanings of this Greek Word are:

"1) to remain; 1a) to tarry behind; 2) to remain i.e. abide, not recede or flee; 2a) to preserve: under misfortunes and trials to hold fast to one's faith in Christ; 2b) to endure, bear bravely and calmly: ill treatments."

True charity "*bears bravely and calmly any ill treatments.*" That is a good definition. It is one thing to go through various difficult circumstances, but it is quite another to endure them and take them in a brave and calm manner. That's what true charity can give the genuine Christians if they walk with the Lord Jesus Christ in a Biblical manner.

1 Corinthians 13:8

"Charity never faileth: but whether *there be* prophecies, they shall fail; whether *there be* tongues, they shall cease; whether *there be* knowledge, it shall vanish away."

Charity, or true love, is contrasted to all these various temporary sign gifts that were then present in the churches until the Bible was completed in 90-100 A.D. True charity will never fail or cease, whether before the Bible was completed or afterwards. It remains forever.

However, the nine temporary sign gifts then in the church in Paul's day will "*fail,*" "*cease,*" and "*vanish away.*" They will not endure forever. This is true of "*prophecies,*" "*tongues,*" special "*knowledge*," and all the other temporary sign gifts. They were to cease.

I, and many other Bible teachers today, differ with those who teach that all nine of these temporary sign gifts are still with us today rather than being false and fake. The time of their departure, we'll take up later in this chapter when we come to verse 10.

1 Corinthians 13:9

"For we know in part, and we prophesy in part."

When Paul was writing this, around 59 AD, the Bible had not yet been fully completed. That took place between 90 and 100 A.D. In 59 A.D. the temporary sign gifts of temporary special knowledge and prophesy were still in effect. However, in verse ten, as we'll see, that when the Scriptures were completed, in 90 AD to 100 AD, all the temporary sign gifts, including special knowledge and prophesy, would cease.

In 59 A.D., the church did not yet have the full written revelation of God in the completed books of the New Testament. Finally, ending with the Book of Revelation, the churches could know the full truth. Before that, they just knew "*in part*" and had the temporary sign gift of "*prophecy*" in part.

1 Corinthians 13:10

"But when that which is perfect is come, then that which is in part shall be done away."

This verse clearly indicates that the two temporary sign gifts mentioned in the previous verse (and, by implication, all the other temporary sign gifts) will be "*done away*" at some future time.

THE MEANING OF THE GREEK WORD, "KATARGEO"

The Greek Word for "*done away*" is KATARGEO. Some of the meanings of that Greek Word are:

> "*1) to render idle, unemployed, inactivate, inoperative; 1a) to cause a person or thing to have no further efficiency; 1b) to deprive of force, influence, power; 2) to cause to cease, put an end to, do away with, annul, abolish; 2a) to cease, to pass away, be done away; 2b) to be severed from, separated from, discharged from, loosed from any one; 2c) to terminate*

| *all intercourse with one."* |

The meanings of this Greek Word could not be any clearer. The specific time when all of these temporary sign gifts would cease and be done away is given in the previous part of this verse. It reads:"**When that which is perfect is come**, *then that which is in part shall be done away.*"

This indicates very clearly that all of these temporary gifts would be completely removed from the church. The question is, **WHEN** will this removal take place. It will be "*when that which is perfect is come.*" There are two interpretations of this phrase: (1) the erroneous interpretation, and (2) the correct interpretation.

1. The Erroneous Interpretation Of "When That Which Is Perfect Is Come." The Pentecostals, the Charismatics, and some others hold to the false interpretation of the phrase: "*when that which is perfect is come.*" They believe that this phrase refers to the coming again of the Perfect Lord Jesus Christ.

2. The Biblical Interpretation of "When That Which Is Perfect Is Come." Those who understand the Greek Bible Words from which our King James Bible was accurately translated, know that this erroneous interpretation could not possibly be true. The truth lies in the gender of the Greek Words, "*that which is perfect is come.*" Even the neuter gender of the English words shows clearly "*that which*" is neuter. It is not "*He who*" which is masculine. It is completely impossible for the neuter phrase, "*that which,*" to refer to the return of the Lord Jesus Christ to meet the genuine Christians in the air as mentioned in 1 Thessalonians 4:16-18.

The Greek Words in which the New Testament was written also bear this out. The Greek Words are: "*HOTAN DE ELTHE TO TELEION TOTE . . .*" The literal order of the Greek Words is: "WHEN BUT COMES THE PERFECT, THEN." This is accurately translated, "*when that which is perfect is come.*"

The Greek Words, "*TO TELEION*" are properly translated in our King James Bible, "*that which is perfect.*" For this to refer to the return of the Lord Jesus Christ, the Greek Word would have to be in the masculine gender (HO TELEIOS) which would be translated when "*He Who is perfect is come.*" It must be "*when IT is perfect.*"

It would be blasphemous to call the Lord Jesus Christ an "IT."

The NEUTER Word in Greek to which "that which is perfect" refers is TO BIBLION ("*the Book*"). I believe it refers to the Bible.

It must rightly be interpreted that when the BIBLION the Book or the Bible which is perfect shall be completed, then all those temporary sign gifts will be "*done away.*" God's BOOK, His complete BIBLE was completed in around 90 to 100 A.D. After that time there was no further need of any of these temporary sign gifts.

Verses On Perfect
- **Deuteronomy 32:4**

"He is the Rock, his work is perfect: for all his ways are judgment: a God of truth and without iniquity, just and right is he."

God's work is absolutely perfect.
- **2 Samuel 22:31**

"As for God, his way is perfect; the word of the LORD is tried: he is a buckler to all them that trust in him."

God's way is also perfect.
- **Job 37:16**

"Dost thou know the balancings of the clouds, the wondrous works of him which is perfect in knowledge?"

The Lord is perfect in knowledge. He's omniscient.
- **Psalms 18:30**

"As for God, his way is perfect: the word of the LORD is tried: he is a buckler to all those that trust in him."

Again, it repeats what we saw in 2 Samuel 22:31.
- **Psalms 19:7**

"The law of the LORD is perfect, converting the soul: the testimony of the LORD is sure, making wise the simple."

God's Words are perfect as well.
- **Matthew 5:48**

"Be ye therefore perfect, even as your Father which is in heaven is perfect."

God is a perfect Heavenly Father to all genuine Christians.
- **Colossians 4:12**

"Epaphras, who is one of you, a servant of Christ, saluteth you, always labouring fervently for you in prayers, that ye may stand perfect and complete in all the will of God."

Epaphras prayed that all the genuine Christians in his days might be perfect and mature in all the will of God.
- **2 Timothy 3:16-17**

"All scripture is given by inspiration of God, and is profitable for doctrine, for reproof, for correction, for instruction in righteousness: That the man of God may be perfect, throughly furnished unto all good works."

The Bible is able to make true Christians mature and full grown.
- **Hebrews 13:20-21**
"Now the God of peace, that brought again from the dead our Lord Jesus, that great shepherd of the sheep, through the blood of the everlasting covenant, <u>Make you perfect in every good work to do his will</u>, working in you that which is wellpleasing in his sight, through Jesus Christ; to whom be glory for ever and ever. Amen."

The Good Shepherd can make genuine Christians to be perfect in every good work to do His will.

The Words of the Lord are perfect. *"That which is perfect"* has come in the completion of our Bible in 90 to 100 A.D. After that date, all nine of these temporary sign gifts passed away. When my wife and I went, as reporters, to a large Stadium, in Kansas City, Kansas, we attended a huge charismatic gathering. The chairman of it was a Roman Catholic young man. We saw and heard their alleged speaking in tongues. It sounded like constant confusion as many spoke in strange sounds that we could not understand at all. It was a grand mess!

1 Corinthians 13:11

"When I was a child, I spake as a child, I understood as a child, I thought as a child: but when I became a man, I put away childish things."

Here is an illustration of the temporary nature of these sign gifts that have passed away since the 90 to 100 A.D. completion of our Old and New Testaments in Hebrew, Aramaic, and Greek. During the time before this completed Bible, when these temporary sign gifts were given by God, this verse describes this past era as being only speaking like, understanding like, and thinking like a little boy *"child."*

But there comes a time when little young boy grows up and becomes a man. When that happens, he puts away and stops playing with baby toys. He puts away and discards his childish things. So with these nine temporary sign gifts, they prevailed in the early childhood of the church. But when the full manhood of the completed Bible arrives, the children's toys of the temporary sign gifts are put away and replaced by the completed Bible. God wants His completed Words to be exalted and never to be interrupted or challenged by any of these temporary sign gifts of the past.

1 Corinthians 13:12

"For now we see through a glass, darkly; but then face to face: now I know in part; but then shall I know even as also I am known."

Paul wrote this book in about 59 A.D. That is his "*now*," before the entire New Testament was completed in about 90 to 100 A.D. His experience is looking at the entire revelation of God's Words at that time, as if he is looking in a glass or mirror. It is "*darkly*." In Paul's day, they didn't use glass mirrors. They used metal mirrors like they used in the Old Testament days. The mirrors were made from the looking glasses of the women in the congregation. They used shiny metal which was by no means as clear as our mirrors today.

Paul is talking about when he is living. It was 40 years or so before the full completion of the entire 66 books of the Bible. We now have 37 books of the Old Testament and 27 books of the New Testament. Paul did not have, at that time, all of the 27 New Testament books. Today, people can see and read all the books of the Bible.

We are now able to translate them into all the languages of the world. We thank God for our English King James Bible which has been accurately translated from the original and preserved Hebrew, Aramaic, and Greek Words. All of the other languages of the world should use these same Hebrew, Aramaic, and Greek Words as their basis, but, sad to say, the current translations have used erroneous original Words and have translated them in many, many places inaccurately.

With accurate translations from the proper Hebrew, Aramaic, and Greek preserved original texts, we can see the truths of the Bible face to face and not through cloudy mirrors. With such accurate Bibles, genuine Christians can know the things of the Lord just as He knows them. I wish all English-speaking true Christian would have a passion daily, and throughout their lives, faithfully to read, study, and obey God's Words that they find in our King James Bible.

Verses On Glass Or Mirror
- **2 Corinthians 3:18**

"But we all, with open face beholding as in a glass the glory of the Lord, are changed into the same image from glory to glory, even as by the Spirit of the Lord."

True Christians can look into the glass or mirror of God's Words and behold His glory.

- **James 1:22-25**

"But be ye doers of the word, and not hearers only, deceiving your own selves. For if any be a hearer of the word, and not a doer, <u>he is like unto a man beholding his natural face in a glass</u>: For he beholdeth himself, and goeth his way, and straightway forgetteth what manner of man he was. But whoso looketh into the perfect law of liberty, and continueth therein, he being not a forgetful hearer, but a doer of the work, this man shall be blessed in his deed."

Here again, we see that "*glass*" is like a mirror.

1 Corinthians 13:13

"And now abideth faith, hope, charity, these three; but the greatest of these is charity."

Though all nine of the temporary sign gifts present in the New Testament until the Bible was completed in 90 to 100 A.D. have passed away, there are three virtues which are permanent and still abide with us even to this day. These three virtues are faith, hope, and charity. The greatest of these three is charity or love in action.

That's a powerful emotion. It will cause a mother to go into a burning building and rescue her baby, even at the risk of her own life. This love in action will cause a father to jump into icy water for his son who is going down and try to rescue him, even at the risk of losing his own life. Genuine love does a lot of good things. The love of God the Father sent God the Son from Heaven to die for the sins of the entire world, making provision to give eternal life to all who truly trust and believe on Him.

Verses On Love

- **John 3:16**

"<u>For God so loved the world, that he gave his only begotten Son</u>, that whosoever believeth in him should not perish, but have everlasting life."

It was God's great love for the whole world that caused Him to send His Son from Heaven to die for all of us sinners.

- **Proverbs 10:12**

"Hatred stirreth up strifes: but <u>love covereth all sins</u>."

Love by genuine Christians puts other's sins in the background and makes it possible to continue their friendship.

- **Proverbs 15:17**

"<u>Better is a dinner of herbs where love is</u>, than a stalled ox and hatred therewith."

Little to eat with love, is better than a great banquet with hatred.

- **John 21:15-17**

"So when they had dined, <u>Jesus saith to Simon Peter, Simon, son of Jonas, lovest thou me more than these</u>? He saith unto him, Yea, Lord; <u>thou knowest that I love thee</u>. He saith unto him, Feed my lambs. He saith to him again the second time, <u>Simon, son of Jonas, lovest thou me</u>? He saith unto him, Yea, Lord; thou knowest that I love thee. He saith unto him, Feed my sheep. He saith unto him the third time, <u>Simon, son of Jonas, lovest thou me</u>? Peter was grieved because he said unto him the third time, Lovest thou me? And he said unto him, Lord, thou knowest all things; <u>thou knowest that I love thee</u>. Jesus saith unto him, Feed my sheep."

The Lord Jesus Christ put His finger on the strong emotion of love that He most wanted from Peter. If genuine love is there for the Saviour, true Christians will not fail or forsake Him no matter what the circumstances are. That kind of love will bring solid obedience to all that the Lord Jesus Christ asks them to do as found within the pages of their Bible.

1 Corinthians
Chapter Fourteen

1 Corinthians 14:1

"Follow after charity, and desire spiritual *gifts*, but rather that ye may prophesy."

Paul wrote 1 Corinthians before the Bible was completed in 90 to 100 A.D. The temporary nine sign gifts were still in the church. This includes tongues, prophecy and all the other 7. Paul wanted them to seek the sign gift of prophecy most of all. Even when these gifts were present, Paul urged them to follow after charity or love in action.

Verses On Follow

- **Matthew 4:19**

"And he saith unto them, Follow me, and I will make you fishers of men."

The Lord Jesus Christ urged these fishermen to follow Him, and fish for men rather than fish.

- **John 12:26**

"If any man serve me, let him follow me; and where I am, there shall also my servant be: if any man serve me, him will my Father honour."

The Saviour urged those who serve Him to follow Him.

- **Romans 14:19**

"Let us therefore follow after the things which make for peace, and things wherewith one may edify another."

Paul urged those at Rome to follow peace and edification of others.

- **1 Thessalonians 5:15**

"See that none render evil for evil unto any man; but ever follow that which is good, both among yourselves, and to all men."

Genuine Christians are to always follow things that are good in the eyes of God.

- **1 Timothy 6:11**

"But thou, O man of God, flee these things; and follow after righteousness, godliness, faith, love, patience, meekness."

Paul listed these six especially to follow.

- **2 Timothy 2:22**

"Flee also youthful lusts: but <u>follow righteousness, faith, charity, peace</u>, with them that call on the Lord out of a pure heart."

Paul told Pastor Timothy to follow especially these four things.

- **Hebrews 12:14**

"<u>Follow peace with all men, and holiness</u>, without which no man shall see the Lord:"

True Christians are to follow peace and holiness.

- **1 Peter 2:21**

"For even hereunto were ye called: because <u>Christ</u> also suffered for us, <u>leaving us an example, that ye should follow his steps</u>:"

Genuine Christians were to follow the steps of the Lord Jesus Christ throughout their lives.

1 Corinthians 14:2

"**For he that speaketh in an *unknown* tongue speaketh not unto men, but unto God: for no man understandeth *him*, howbeit in the spirit he speaketh mysteries.**"

Even before this temporary sign gift disappeared when the Bible was complete in 90 to 100 A.D., Paul is downplaying this special gift of speaking in tongues which spoke to God rather than to men. They would be speaking in a language that nobody knows. If this were the case, there would be no edification or building up the genuine Christians who were assembled, even though "*in the spirit he speaketh mysteries*." We differ strongly in this matter of tongues with our Pentecostal and Charismatic friends who believe the nine temporary sign gifts are still with us, rather than believe they have ceased after that which is perfect (the completed Bible) has come.

1 Corinthians 14:3

"**But he that prophesieth speaketh unto men *to* edification, and exhortation, and comfort.**"

The temporary gift of prophesy (in Paul's day) was like our preaching today. It did three things for those genuine Christians who heard it:

1. **It brought edification.**
2. **It brought exhortation.**
3. **It brought comfort.**

These were beneficial results when this temporary sign gift was with the church before 90 to 100 A.D. when it ceased with the completion of the entire Bible. The completed Bible, if read and followed, also does these three things. (1) it builds up; (2) it exhorts; and (3) comforts the true Christians today.

A Verse On Comfort
- **Romans 15:4**

"For whatsoever things were written aforetime were written for our learning, <u>that we through patience and comfort of the scriptures might have hope</u>."

The Old Testament, though not written TO the genuine Christians today, was written FOR their patience, comfort, and hope.

1 Corinthians 14:4

"He that speaketh in an *unknown* tongue edifieth himself; but he that prophesieth edifieth the church."

When this temporary sign gift was present in the church, it edified only the person who had it. The one who had the temporary sign gift of prophesy, could edify all the genuine Christians who were present. Today, the Bible, when faithfully and correctly preached, can edify and build up the true Christians who receive it, understand it, and follow it.

Some genuine Christians, sad to say, don't want to be edified, built up, and grow in their faith. Apparently, they are content to remain baby, immature Christians. This is what the faithful reading and preaching of God's Words can do today. It can build up, strengthen, and equip true Christians for their daily walk to please God.

1 Corinthians 14:5

"I would that ye all spake with tongues, but rather that ye prophesied: for greater is he that prophesieth than he that speaketh with tongues, except he interpret, that the church may receive edifying."

I don't know how many more times Paul has to say this to this Corinthian church that it's better to have the temporary sign gift of prophesy than to speak in a foreign language unless the language is interpreted so the church may receive edifying. The temporary sign gift of prophesy was to be preferred instead of the temporary sign gift of tongues.

Interpretation is done in places where people from various languages are present so they can understand in their own language, what is being said. This is done in the United Nations meetings as well as in other gatherings where people who speak various languages are in attendance.

1 Corinthians 14:6

"Now, brethren, if I come unto you speaking with tongues, what shall I profit you, except I shall speak to you either by revelation, or by knowledge, or by prophesying, or by doctrine?"

The temporary sign gift of tongues in Paul's day would not profit genuine Christians because they would not understand what was being said. It would be better to come to these true Christians by the temporary sign gifts, then available, of special revelation, special knowledge, special prophesying, or special doctrine.

1 Corinthians 14:7

"And even things without life giving sound, whether pipe or harp, except they give a distinction in the sounds, how shall it be known what is piped or harped?"

The same situation is true with the use of various instruments like a pipe, a harp, a piano, or some other musical instrument. Unless there is a distinction in the notes, no one can tell what music is being played. All of the sounds will sound like a jumble or a cacophony. I want to give a little more time on verse eight, so I'm going rather quickly over these preceding verses.

1 Corinthians 14:8

"For if the trumpet give an uncertain sound, who shall prepare himself to the battle?"

Among other purposes, trumpets, in the Old Testament, were used in calling the nation of Israel to battle. When I was age nine to sixteen, my father and mother sent me to a boys' camp each summer so I could do various things that otherwise I would never experience. I was one of the buglers at this camp. I had to learn various bugle calls. Here are some of the calls we used:

1. **Reveille--the wake-up call**
2. **Taps–the call at bedtime**
3. **Mess Call–the call to eat**
4. **First Call–the call to assemble around the flag**
5. **Assembly–the call when all must be in place**
6. **To The Colors–the call as the flag was raised**

Israel also used their trumpets for many purposes. One purpose was the trumpet call to battle. If that sound was uncertain, who would prepare himself for the battle? It had to be loud enough and clear enough in order to serve its purpose.

Verses On Trumpets In The Old Testament
- **Numbers 10:2**

"Make thee two trumpets of silver; of a whole piece shalt thou make them: that thou mayest use them for the calling of the assembly, and for the journeying of the camps."

Here are two of the uses of Israel's trumpets: the distinctive sounds of the calling of the assembly, and the journeying of the camps.

- **Numbers 10:9**

"And if ye go to war in your land against the enemy that oppresseth you, then ye shall blow an alarm with the trumpets; and ye shall be remembered before the LORD your God, and ye shall be saved from your enemies."

This trumpet sound was an alarm to go to war.

- **Numbers 31:1-6**

"And the LORD spake unto Moses, saying, Avenge the children of Israel of the Midianites: afterward shalt thou be gathered unto thy people. And Moses spake unto the people, saying, Arm some of yourselves unto the war, and let them go against the Midianites, and avenge the LORD of Midian. Of every tribe a thousand, throughout all the tribes of Israel, shall ye send to the war. So there were delivered out of the thousands of Israel, a thousand of every tribe, twelve thousand armed for war. And Moses sent them to the war, a thousand of every tribe, them and Phinehas the son of Eleazar the priest, to the war, with the holy instruments, and the trumpets to blow in his hand."

There were trumpets to be used when Israel went out to a battle.

- **Joshua 6:4**

"And <u>seven priests shall bear before the ark seven trumpets of rams' horns</u>: and the seventh day ye shall compass the city seven times, <u>and the priests shall blow with the trumpets</u>." On this occasion, Israel used seven trumpets to be blown after they had surrounded the city of Jericho seven times.

- **Judges 3:26-29**

"And <u>Ehud</u> escaped while they tarried, and passed beyond the quarries, and escaped unto Seirath. And it came to pass, <u>when he was come, that he blew a trumpet in the mountain of Ephraim</u>, and the children of Israel went down with him from the mount, and he before them. And he said unto them, Follow after me: for <u>the LORD hath delivered your enemies the Moabites into your hand</u>. And they went down after him, and took the fords of Jordan toward Moab, and suffered not a man to pass over. And they slew of Moab at that time about ten thousand men, all lusty, and all men of valour; and there escaped not a man."

- **Jeremiah 4:19**

". . . I am pained at my very heart; my heart maketh a noise in me; <u>I cannot hold my peace, because thou hast heard, O my soul, the sound of the trumpet, the alarm of war</u>." This is one of Dean John William Burgon's favorite verses. He was a mighty defender of the sound and preserved Hebrew, Aramaic, and Greek Words underlying the King James Bible and the King James Bible itself. Forty years ago, I named the Dean Burgon Society after his name because of what he stood for in the battle for the Bible. The Dean Burgon Society has published five of this British scholar's excellent books. Dean Burgon heard "*the sound of the trumpet*" and "*the alarm of* war" in the battle for our Bible.

- **Ezekiel 33:3-3**

"If <u>when he seeth the sword come upon the land, he blow the trumpet, and warn the people</u>; Then whosoever heareth the sound of the trumpet, and taketh not warning; if the sword come, and take him away, his blood shall be upon his own head." Here's the trumpet to warn the people that the battle had come into their land. One of our current hymns is titled "*Sound The Battle Cry.*"

Verses On Fight

- **1 Timothy 6:12**

"<u>Fight the good fight of faith</u>, lay hold on eternal life, whereunto thou art also called, and hast professed a good profession before many witnesses."

In our days, genuine Christians have a battle for our Bibles, our faith, and our doctrines. They must have a certain sound and be prepared for the battle for our King James Bible and its underlying texts.

- **2 Timothy 4:7**

"<u>I have fought a good fight</u>, I have finished my course, I have kept the faith:"

Paul was a fervent fighter for all the doctrines of the Christian faith.

- **1 Timothy 1:18**

"<u>This charge I commit unto thee, son Timothy</u>, according to the prophecies which went before on thee, <u>that thou by them mightest war a good warfare</u>;"

Paul commanded Pastor Timothy to war a good warfare for the Lord Jesus Christ. Genuine Christians today must fight apostasy and false doctrine as well as compromise in doctrines for their Lord and Saviour, Jesus Christ.

1 Corinthians 14:9

"So likewise ye, except ye utter by the tongue words easy to be understood, how shall it be known what is spoken? for ye shall speak into the air."

Paul is insistent that genuine Christians should utter words easy to understand rather than some foreign language so that people would comprehend what was spoken. Otherwise, they would be just speaking into the air for no valid purpose. It is a waste of time both for the speaker and for the listener.

1 Corinthians 14:10

"There are, it may be, so many kinds of voices in the world, and none of them is without signification."

In this world, there are all kinds of languages. Each one of them has meaning for those who understand them. But if people do not understand some of these languages, they are at a loss to find any meaning to them.

1 Corinthians 14:11
"Therefore if I know not the meaning of the voice, I shall be unto him that speaketh a barbarian, and he that speaketh *shall be* a barbarian unto me."

That's just plain, straight logic, isn't it? If people don't know the meaning of the language which is spoken, whether it's Spanish, French, German, or some other foreign language unknown to the listener, both speaker and listener are like barbarians to one another. The Lord used the means of languages to disperse the people around the world. He made many different languages so that those who spoke and understood and spoke the same language went together in their own groups.

1 Corinthians 14:12
"Even so ye, forasmuch as ye are zealous of spiritual gifts, seek that ye may excel to the edifying of the church."

Paul spoke to those in Corinth who wanted some of these temporary sign gifts to seek the gift whereby those in the church might be edified and built up in the things of the Lord, rather than foreign language tongues which to some would just be noisy babble.

I remember when I visited a Pentecostal, Charismatic church. I was a student at the University of Michigan located in Ann Arbor. Some of the genuine Christians went to the Youth for Christ meeting once a month. I thought there was a Youth for Christ meeting, in Detroit, Michigan. I took a bus, I think it was, from Ann Arbor to Detroit, which was about a 40-or 50-minute ride from Ann Arbor. When I arrived in Detroit, I found out they didn't have their Youth for Christ meeting on that date.

It was the wrong Friday night. Since I had taken the bus this far, I thought I should do something in Detroit. There was a church that had a meeting, so I went into the church and I was astounded. I was a young man about twenty or twenty-one at the time. When I went into that church, all I could hear was the noise of everyone in the church speaking strange sounds. They were speaking in tongues. I was scared to death, so I left that church immediately because it sounded like barbaric babble.

1 Corinthians 14:13

"**Wherefore let him that speaketh in an *unknown* tongue pray that he may interpret.**"

In Paul's day, when the temporary sign gift of speaking in foreign languages was present, he told the true Christians at Corinth, that if they had that temporary sign gift, they should pray to be able to interpret what was being said so that others could understand it. I suppose that if he could not interpret, he should not use that temporary sign gift.

When I was in a Bible conference in Liberia, West Africa on one occasion, most of the genuine Christians could not understand English, so I had an interpreter who made clear in the people's language what I was saying in English. The same was true when I ministered in Chinese churches in North New Jersey. I spoke a sentence or two in English, and the Chinese interpreter would translate it into Chinese so that all those who spoke Chinese could understand what I was saying.

1 Corinthians 14:14

"**For if I pray in an *unknown* tongue, my spirit prayeth, but my understanding is unfruitful.**"

If some genuine Christians, in Paul's day (when the temporary sign gifts were present) prayed in an unknown foreign language, their spirits would be praying, but their understanding would be absent. It is important that the understanding of true Christians should be present at all times during their lives. Listening to indiscernible sounds is a waste of time.

1 Corinthians 14:15

"**What is it then? I will pray with the spirit, and I will pray with the understanding also: I will sing with the spirit, and I will sing with the understanding also.**"

Regardless of the temporary sign gifts in Paul's day that were terminated when the Bible was completed in 90 to 100 A.D., he would not only pray with the Spirit, but also understand what he was praying. He would sing with the spirit, but also sing with his understanding.

Genuine Christians should pray knowing the Words of God and the will of God found in those Words. Their songs should be sound Scripturally and written by godly people. It is hard to find a hymn book that has only the traditional hymns in it. Many contemporary songs are also included.

1 Corinthians 14:16

"Else when thou shalt bless with the spirit, how shall he that occupieth the room of the unlearned say Amen at thy giving of thanks, seeing he understandeth not what thou sayest?"

If the temporary sign gift in Paul's day of speaking in foreign languages is used in prayer, how can those who do not know that particular language say Amen since they don't understand any of the words?

Just recently, as this is being written, I was listening to a man who was on the plane with Mrs. Waite and me. He was speaking Spanish and talking to his wife. My wife asked me what he was saying. I told her some of the words. I didn't catch every word because I wasn't close enough to hear every word. He was also talking very fast which made it difficult. Though I speak and understand Spanish, I couldn't agree or disagree with the man because I could not understand everything he was saying. So in the case in this verse. The hearers must understand the speakers.

1 Corinthians 14:17

"For thou verily givest thanks well, but the other is not edified."

It is so true that if genuine Christians, in Paul's day, had the temporary sign gift of speaking in tongues, or foreign languages, and gave thanks in that language, the listeners would not be able to say thanks or be edified because they didn't understood the language. Those listening would not be edified because they did not understand what was spoken.

1 Corinthians 14:18

"I thank my God, I speak with tongues more than ye all:"

Paul testified that he thanked God that he had the temporary sign gift of tongues and spoke in these languages more than anyone else. He was well aware of this sign gift that God gave him, but he never misused this sign gift when it was present before the Bible was complete in 90 to 100 A.D.

Paul was a traveler. He had three missionary journeys, and the journey to Rome as a prisoner. Everywhere he went, God gave him that gift of languages, he could speak to them in their own language. Now, that's what God intended for tongues to be. It was to be an evangelistic and teaching tool so that people who were lost could trust the Lord Jesus Christ as their Saviour and receive His gift of eternal life.

1 Corinthians 14:19

"Yet in the church I had rather speak five words with my understanding, that *by my voice* I might teach others also, than ten thousand words in an *unknown* tongue."

When Paul had the temporary sign gift of the ability to speak in foreign languages, in the church, he would much rather speak only five words with his understanding, rather than 10,000 words in a language that no one could understand. The reason for this is that by his voice, he might teach others also. Paul was a Bible teaching, Bible preaching apostle. This ministry of Paul's teaching God's Words was what he commanded Pastor Timothy to do in this verse.

- 2 Timothy 2:2

"And the things that thou hast heard of me among many witnesses, the same commit thou to faithful men, who shall be able to teach others also."

This chain of teaching God's Words should prevail in the ministries of faithful pastors today as well.

1 Corinthians 14:20

"Brethren, be not children in understanding: howbeit in malice be ye children, but in understanding be men."

Paul did not want the genuine Christians at Corinth to be like children in their understanding. In understanding, they should be like mature men, but they should be like little children in the sin of malice. The man from Africa that Philip was told by God to go out in the desert to meet did not understand Isaiah 53 that he was reading. Philip asked him if he understood what he was reading. The man told Philip he couldn't understand this Scripture unless someone taught him.

> "*He is despised and rejected of men; a man of sorrows, and acquainted with grief: and we hid as it were our faces from him; he was despised, and we esteemed him not. Surely he hath borne our griefs, and carried our*

sorrows: yet we did esteem him stricken, smitten of God, and afflicted. <u>But he was wounded for our transgressions, he was bruised for our iniquities</u>: the chastisement of our peace was upon him; and with his stripes we are healed. <u>All we like sheep have gone astray</u>; we have turned every one to his own way; and <u>the LORD hath laid on him the iniquity of us all</u>." (Isaiah 53:3-6)

When Philip explained these verses and applied them to the Lord Jesus Christ, the eunuch genuinely believed on Him and received Him as his Saviour. Because he was now a true Christian, he asked Philip to baptize him in the river that was there. Philip made sure the eunuch was a genuine Christian and then baptized him.

Verses On Malice
- **1 Corinthians 5:8**

"Therefore let us <u>keep the feast, not</u> with old leaven, neither <u>with the leaven of malice</u> and wickedness; but with the unleavened bread of sincerity and truth."

Malice is hatred. This should not be present in the heart of genuine Christians who are gathered together for any purpose.

- **Ephesians 4:31**

"<u>Let all</u> bitterness, and wrath, and anger, and clamour, and <u>evil speaking, be put away from you, with all malice</u>:"

Be children in malice. It should not be a part of any genuine Christians' lives.

- **Colossians 3:8**

"But now ye also <u>put off</u> all these; anger, wrath, <u>malice</u>, blasphemy, filthy communication out of your mouth."

All genuine Christians should put off and refrain from any malice of heart, of lips, or life.

1 Corinthians 14:21

"In the law it is written, With *men* of other tongues and other lips will I speak unto this people; and yet for all that will they not hear me, saith the Lord."

First of all, notice the words "*it is written.*" In the Greek language, this word is GEGRAPTAI. It is in the Greek perfect tense which means something that was written in the past, preserved down to the present, and preserved on into the future. It has a past, present, and future meaning. This means that God's Words in Hebrew, Aramaic, and Greek have been preserved by the Lord right down to the present day, and on into the future days.

Many of the denominations of churches decades of years ago believed in this Bible preservation of these Hebrew, Aramaic, and Greek Words, but most of them have forsaken this vital doctrine.

The words that are written in this verse are from Isaiah 28:11 from the Old Testament. The verse foreshadows the temporary sign gift of speaking with other languages that occurred in Acts 2. Many Pentecostals, Charismatics, and others are falsely using what they think is this temporary sign gift which expired when the whole Bible was completed in 90-100 A.D. They wrongly believe that this temporary sign gift is permanent.

1 Corinthians 14:22

"Wherefore tongues are for a sign, not to them that believe, but to them that believe not: but prophesying *serveth not* for them that believe not, but for them which believe."

Though it was true that the temporary sign gift of tongues was for those who were genuine Christians, not for those who were non-Christians. This temporary sign gift was given by God to be used by true Christians in communicating the Gospel of the Lord Jesus Christ to the lost world before the Bible was completed in 90 to 100 A.D. This temporary sign gift authenticated God's message and enabled non-Christians who spoke other languages to understand the teachings of God.

The temporary sign gift of prophesying, which passed away around 90 to 100 A.D., was for genuine Christians so they could be instructed in the things that God had for them to learn. It was like Biblical preaching today. The difference is that the temporary sign gift of prophesying was God's special revelation for that day, whereas preaching today, though it should be based on the Bible which has now been completed, it is not from God, but the preaching is not from God, but from pastors who should be using the Words of God to preach and teach God's truths which are written in His Bible.

1 Corinthians 14:23

"If therefore the whole church be come together into one place, and all speak with tongues, and there come in *those that are* unlearned, or unbelievers, will they not say that ye are mad?"

In the New Testament, when the whole church was together in one place, and all were speaking with this temporary sign gift of foreign languages, what if either some unlearned person or unbelievers came into the service? They would say that these people were mad or not in their right mind because of all the not-understood noise and gibberish.

That's the way some Pentecostal and Charismatic churches operate. I went into one years ago (as I mentioned earlier) and just heard a tremendous amount of noise and babble that made me leave immediately. They did sound mad to me.

1 Corinthians 14:24

"But if all prophesy, and there come in one that believeth not, or *one* unlearned, he is convinced of all, he is judged of all:"

When the temporary sign gift of prophesy was present, a non-Christian or one who was unlearned would be able to understand what was being said and would be convinced and judged by all by that which was spoken.

So today, when we have the complete Bible from 90 to 100 A.D., faithful pastors who preach and teach these Words of God will be able to teach those unsaved or unlearned people who enter their churches from the Words of God. When these Words are read and expounded, It is hoped that the people who hear them will accept the truths that are taught.

1 Corinthians 14:25

"And thus are the secrets of his heart made manifest; and so falling down on *his* face he will worship God, and report that God is in you of a truth."

During the temporary use of the sign gift of prophesy, these things mentioned in this verse will take place.

Even in our day, when the Bible has been completed and the sign gifts have passed away, the faithful preaching of God's Words in the Bible will bring a similar reception. If God's Words and the speaker's words are clear and understandable to the listeners, spoken in their own native language, it will then be possible for God's Words to reach the hearts of the listeners. If they are convicted by the Lord and the Holy Spirit, they will accept the Gospel message and genuinely trust the Lord Jesus Christ as their Saviour. They will also recognize that God is leading you to speak His Words to them.

1 Corinthians 14:26

"How is it then, brethren? when ye come together, every one of you hath a psalm, hath a doctrine, hath a tongue, hath a revelation, hath an interpretation. Let all things be done unto edifying."

When the temporary sign gifts were present in Paul's day, he lists five different special sign gifts that might be used in a local church. Whichever of these temporary sign gifts were used, one thing is absolutely certain! All things in the local church must be done, not only in order, but also unto edification to those present so that the hearers might be built up in the teachings of the Bible.

1 Corinthians 14:27

"If any man speak in an *unknown* tongue, *let it be* by two, or at the most by three, and *that* by course; and let one interpret."

Paul was writing in about 59 A.D. when the temporary sign gifts were still in effect. The entire New Testament had not yet been completed as it was in 90 to 100 A.D. If there are people who have this temporary sign gift, this gift should only be used in the church by two, or at the most three people. When they use this temporary gift of speaking in a foreign language, it must by course, or one at a time. There must also be an interpreter so that people in the church can understand what is being said.

1 Corinthians 14:28

"But if there be no interpreter, let him keep silence in the church; and let him speak to himself, and to God."

If this temporary sign gift of foreign languages has no one with their temporary sign gift of interpretation of these tongues, the one who has this temporary sign should keep silence in the church and speak only to himself and to God. This was important then and it is important now when all temporary sign gifts have ceased that people speak clearly in the churches so people can understand what they're saying.

There is much confusion in the Pentecostal and Charismatic churches and others who deny that these nine sign gifts were temporary and God stopped them when the Bible was completed. Even though these gifts are gone, when they use their made-up, demonic, or fake gift of "tongues," there is much confusion and chaos.

1 Corinthians 14:29

"Let the prophets speak two or three, and let the other judge."

When the temporary sign gift of prophesy was in the churches in Paul's day, he made clear that those who had the temporary sign gift of prophesy speak by two or three people in order, and the others in the church evaluate what was said.

1 Corinthians 14:30

"If *any thing* be revealed to another that sitteth by, let the first hold his peace."

If some one who had the temporary sign gift of prophesy was in the church and received a revelation from God, that person should tell what the revelation was and the others should hold their peace and listen to this other person.

In Paul's day, God's complete revelation in the Bible was not complete. Because of this, He used the temporary sign gift of prophesy to reveal His will to the genuine Christians of his day before all 39 books of the Bible had been completed. Since 90 to 100 A.D., however, when the Bible was complete, God has silenced all special revelation which might contradict what is in His completed Words. This is why those who pretend to have these temporary sign gifts today, often contradict the clear teachings of the Bible. In so doing, they are in total disobedience to God.

1 Corinthians 14:31

"For ye may all prophesy one by one, that all may learn, and all may be comforted."

When the temporary sign gift of prophesy was in the church before the Bible was completed, Paul wanted them all of to prophesy one by one so that all in the church might learn what God revealed to them and be comforted. The purpose of the temporary sign gift of prophesy was to give comfort to these genuine Christians.

Verses On Rest And Comfort
- **Matthew 11:29**

"Take my yoke upon you, and <u>learn of me</u>; for I am meek and lowly in heart: and <u>ye shall find rest unto your souls</u>."

There's much to learn from the Lord Jesus Christ. He can also give you His rest and comfort if you genuinely trust and accept Him as your Saviour.

- **Romans 15:4**

"For <u>whatsoever things were written</u> aforetime were written for our learning, <u>that we through</u> patience and <u>comfort of the scriptures might have hope</u>."

This verse is referring to the Old Testament. They were not written to us who are genuine Christians, but they, along with the New Testament, were written to give us comfort and hope.

1 Corinthians 14:32

"And the spirits of the prophets are subject to the prophets."

Paul is speaking to the true Christians at Corinth about the temporary sign gift of prophesy which has now ceased after the completion of the entire Bible. Any genuine Christian at Corinth, or anywhere else, were to keep their human spirits under subjection to themselves. The Greek Word underneath the English word "*subject*" means "*to be under control.*"

Often today, when the temporary gift of prophesy, which has been cancelled, is pretended to be used, those speaking are not under control, but often spew out babble and just noise possibly from Satan.

1 Corinthians 14:33

"For God is not *the author* of confusion, but of peace, as in all churches of the saints."

In Paul's day, those genuine Christians who made use of the temporary gift of tongues or prophesy, but without following the clear rules to go by mentioned in this chapter, brought confusion. God is not the author of confusion, but of peace in all the churches of the true Christians.

If you've ever seen confusion, it's in one of these meetings, with those who believe these temporary sign gifts are for today. There is an abundance of gibbering and jabbering and an abundance of confusion.

I believe the author of confusion is the Devil himself. I believe it started in Heaven when he was a shiny angel who said, in Isaiah 14, five "*I wills*" to God in his rebellion against Him.

From that day, he has caused confusion in the world. He confused Adam and Eve in the Garden of Eden. He is confusing churches today. He has caused confusion in entire church denominations. He has caused confusion in Bible translations. He has caused confusion in countries going to war with one another. He is causing political confusion in this and other countries. He has caused confusion in our educational areas who have wrongly followed the false teachings of John Dewey and others. He has brought doctrinal confusion. He has caused confusion in theological seminaries, Bible institutes, colleges, and universities.

God the Father, the Lord Jesus Christ, and the Holy Spirit are not causing confusion. All the Persons of the Godhead seek to promote and further truth, never confusion.

Verses On Confusion

- **Leviticus 18:23**

"Neither shalt thou lie with any beast to defile thyself therewith: neither shall any woman stand before a beast to lie down thereto: it is confusion."

This wicked sin is called "*bestiality.*" It is being practiced today by both men and women. God calls it confusion!

- **Leviticus 20:12**

"And if a man lie with his daughter-in-law, both of them shall surely be put to death: they have wrought confusion; their blood shall be upon them."

Sexual union with a daughter-in-law either in the Old Testament, or today, is confusion. In the Old Testament, they were both killed.

- **Psalms 71:1**

"In thee, O LORD, do I put my trust: let me never be put to confusion."

The prayer of David was that he would never be brought to confusion in any way. That is a prayer every genuine Christian should make.

- **Isaiah 41:29**

"Behold, they are all vanity; their works are nothing: their molten images are wind and confusion."

Isaiah could see that the idols of the heathen around him were nothing but confusion.

- **Isaiah 45:16**

"They shall be ashamed, and also confounded, all of them: they shall go to confusion together that are makers of idols."

Both the makers of idols and the worshipers of idols will be brought to confusion by the Lord.

- **James 3:16**
"For <u>where envying and strife is, there is confusion</u> and every evil work."
Such things as envying and strife bring massive confusion.

1 Corinthians 14:34

"Let your women keep silence in the churches: for it is not permitted unto them to speak; but *they are commanded* to be under obedience, as also saith the law."

Since this entire chapter is dealing with temporary sign gifts including speaking in tongues, I believe this has to do mainly with the genuine women Christians speaking in the temporary sign gifts of tongues. Those groups like the Pentecostals and Charismatics today who believe these temporary sign gifts have not passed away are violating this rule even as some women violated it in Paul's day.

I believe, by application today for true female Christians, that they should never be preachers. Look at this recent quotation as far as the percentages of females are preachers today:

> "The Faith Communities Today 2010 national survey of a fully representative, multi-faith sample of 11,000 American congregations found that 12% of all congregations in the United States had a female as their senior or sole ordained leader. **For Oldline Protestant congregations this jumps to 24%, and for Evangelical congregations it drops to 9%.**" [From the HARTFORD INSTITUTE FOR RELIGION RESEARCH]

I do not think women should ever be pastors of churches, despite the figures of 9%, 12%, or even 24% given above. It is not Biblical. However, I believe genuine Christian women would be allowed to take part in discussions in Sunday School classes and Bible studies provided they are proper in their remarks and speak in a proper manner when they take part in the discussions.

1 Corinthians 14:35
"And if they will learn any thing, let them ask their husbands at home: for it is a shame for women to speak in the church."

Once again, this was in Paul's day with women using the temporary sign gifts of that day. It was a shame for any true Christian woman to speak in the church in the sense of being an authority on some doctrine or teaching. If they wish to learn more about any thing, they should ask their husbands (if they have them) at home, rather than to interrupt the public services.

I believe the application for today, when all the temporary sign gifts have ceased, is never to interrupt the public church services to ask their pastors questions. They should ask their own husbands or male friends they know outside the church. I believe that informal Sunday School classes or Bible studies are the smaller meetings where they would be allowed to take part in the discussions of Bible teachings, if done in the proper manner and in the proper attitude.

1 Corinthians 14:36
"What? came the word of God out from you? or came it unto you only?"

This refers to the special revelation in the completed Old Testament in Paul's day. Those Words were referred to as "*the Word of God.*" Even in Paul's day, when the temporary sign gifts were in effect, that which God revealed to those who had the temporary sign gifts of prophesy, for example, were but temporary instructions as to what the genuine Christians should do or believe before the Words of God were given by the Lord Jesus Christ to the Holy Spirit to the human writers in the New Testament. None of the things that were given to those who had the temporary sign gifts of that day were considered Scripture. They were just temporary to inform the Genuine Christians of that day certain temporary things that He wanted them to know. ONLY the Words that were written down in either the Old or the New Testaments are the inspired, preserved, inerrant Words of God to be read, followed, and obeyed forever.

1 Corinthians 14:37
"If any man think himself to be a prophet, or spiritual, let him acknowledge that the things that I write unto you are the commandments of the Lord."

Paul makes it very clear in this verse that the words of those who had the temporary sign gifts of prophesy, tongues, or other such sign gifts, were to be temporary. They were not to be considered the "*commandments of the Lord*" for all the ages to come. They were only temporary things for the genuine Christians there at Corinth.

On the contrary, the things that the Apostle Paul said are "*the commandments of the Lord.* Paul was not merely giving suggestions. The Words that God gave him were "*commandments.*" I believe this would apply, as well, to the Words from God found in the other books of the Bible.

I believe Paul wanted to make very clear that all the specific rules to abide by in the exercise of these temporary sign gifts were from God Himself and were to be followed and obeyed as such while exercising their temporary sign gifts.

1 Corinthians 14:38
"But if any man be ignorant, let him be ignorant."

Paul was speaking to those genuine Christians at Corinth. If any of them wanted to be or wanted to remain to be ignorant or not knowing or understanding of these rules and regulations concerning the detailed use of these temporary sign gifts in the church, just let them remain in their ignorance, however sad it may be.

That can be applied to true Christians today. Many of them do know all of the vital and essential Words of God that they should follow because they are reading His Words from Genesis through Revelation. If they insist upon being ignorant of God's Words and following His will for their lives, let them be ignorant of those things. You can try to help them, but you cannot force them to do what is right and proper. The old saying is still true: "*A man convinced against his will is of the same opinion still.*" You can't force people to know God's truth.

I'm sure, some preachers, as they look over the people assembled in their services they preach can see the ones who are not interested in what they're preaching. They can see it in their eyes and in their faces, that they don't care about what is being preached or taught. Some fall asleep during the preaching. Some of them look at their watch several times during the sermon, and probably wonder, "*When is the preaching and teaching going to stop?*"

May God give genuine Christians the desire to hear and obey the milk and the meat of God's Words that they might grow up in the Faith of the Bible as this verse commands:
- **1 Peter 2:2**

"As newborn babes, <u>desire the sincere milk of the word, that ye may grow thereby</u>:"

That's what God has placed in the heart of every born again child of his and sometimes our desire is not right but we are to desire the sincere milk of the Word of God.

1 Corinthians 14:39

"Wherefore, brethren, covet to prophesy, and forbid not to speak with tongues."

Paul is showing what he believes to be true in the importance of these two temporary sign gifts. Of all of the nine sign gifts in the New Testament, Paul rated the temporary sign gift of prophesy the highest. He didn't want any to forbid those who had the temporary sign gift of tongues or foreign languages, but he clearly favoured the temporary sign gift of prophesy. The way the Greek states this not forbidding to speak with tongues is this. The Greek Word for "*forbid*" is in the Greek present tense. It is a negative prohibition. As such, it means to stop an action already in progress. In Paul's day, some were forbidding true Christians to use the temporary sign gift of tongues. Paul told them to stop forbidding it!

1 Corinthians 14:40

"Let all things be done decently and in order."

Paul was very clear here as he wrote to the genuine Christians at Corinth. In everyone of these 9 temporary sign gifts, they were to operate and make use of these sign gifts exactly as Paul stated in this chapter. Nothing was to be overlooked or violated. He ordered that all things should be done decently and in order!

The word, "*decently*" comes from the Greek Word from which we get "*tactics*" in English. In the military, when many troops are marching, they all must act on the same commands so there can be a unity among the 50, or 100, or more. So the rules laid out in this chapter must be followed precisely so there can be order and decency.

As I mentioned before, I went to a boys camp for about six summers. At that camp, we worked for camp letters. One of the classes was tactics. Many of us marched together and the Director of the camp gave us orders such as column right, column left. Company halt. Right dress. Right hand salute. Attention. At ease. And many more commands.

1 Corinthians Chapter Fifteen

1 Corinthians 15:1

"Moreover, brethren, I declare unto you the gospel which I preached unto you, which also ye have received, and wherein ye stand;"

Paul preached the Gospel to these genuine Christians at Corinth when he was visiting them. They not only received it, but they also stood firmly on it. There are many other kinds of false "Gospels" which Paul warned against in his epistle to the Galatians. He repeated his curse on false Gospels twice.

- **Galatians 1:8-9**

"But *though we*, or an angel from heaven, <u>preach any other Gospel unto you</u> than that which we have preached unto you, <u>let him be accursed</u>. As we said before, so say I now again, <u>If any man preach any other Gospel unto you</u> than that ye have received, <u>let him be accursed</u>.

OF THE MANY FALSE GOSPELS

1. The false Gospel of salvation only by good works
2. The false Gospel of salvation only by money gifts
3. The false Gospel of salvation by "penance"
4. The false Gospel of salvation by confession to a priest
5. The false Gospel of salvation by prayer
7. The false Gospel of salvation of thinking everyone is a genuine Christian
8. The false Gospel of salvation by joining a church
9. The false Gospel of salvation by believing you are one of the "elect"
10. The false Gospel of salvation by raising your hand
11. The false Gospel of salvation by only coming forward in a meeting
12. The false Gospel of salvation by only asking Jesus to come into your heart
13. The false Gospel of salvation only by attending a church

14. The false Gospel of salvation only by <u>thinking</u> you are a genuine Christian
15. The false Gospel of salvation only by taking church communion
16. The false Gospel of salvation only by being baptized
17. The many other false Gospels that could be named

There are many, many more false Gospels that are practiced all around the world that make people believe that they need to do or believe something so that they may obtain salvation, eternal life, and the Bible's Heaven. I have used three main things, among others, that are essential for lost non-Christian people to know and truly believe in order to become genuine Christians.

THREE ESSENTIALS TO RECEIVE GOD'S SALVATION
1. There must be an understanding and belief, by all people who want to become genuine Christians, that the Bible is clear, that God considers them all to be lost, and are destined, if they do not wish to become true Bible Christians, to be sent, upon their death, to the everlasting fires of Hell.
2. There must be an understanding and belief, by all people who want to become genuine Christians, that the Bible is clear, that the Lord Jesus Christ died for them as their Substitute and carried all their sins in His own Perfect and Sinless Body in His death upon the cross at Calvary.
3. There must be a true, sincere, heart-belief faith, and trust, in the Lord Jesus Christ as their personal Saviour, on the part of all who wish to receive the forgiveness of all their sins, past, present, and future, and receive everlasting and eternal life from the Lord Jesus Christ, Who then can become their Ever-Living Saviour.

1 Corinthians 15:2

"By which also ye are saved, if ye keep in memory what I preached unto you, unless ye have believed in vain."

By means of the true Gospel of the Lord Jesus Christ, all lost sinners can be saved, unless they believe in vain. It must be a solid and genuine heart belief, not just a belief in the head.

- **John 1:10-12**

"He was in the world, and the world was made by him, and the world knew him not. He came unto his own, and his own received him not. But <u>as many as received him, to them gave he power to become the sons of God, even to them that believe on his name</u>:"

Half-hearted belief is a belief in vain. It's the head belief without the heart belief. The receiving of the Lord Jesus Christ is a heart matter. It's not simply in the head. The devils also "believe" and tremble, it says in the book of James, but they're lost. It's not simply a head belief. It has to be twelve inches down below the head into the heart.

- **Romans 10:10**

"For <u>with the heart man believeth unto righteousness</u>; and with the mouth confession is made unto salvation.

So, it must be a genuine faith and trust in the Lord Jesus Christ Who died for the sins of all the world.

1 Corinthians 15:3

"For I delivered unto you first of all that which I also received, how that Christ died for our sins according to the scriptures;"

The first part of the Gospel of the Lord Jesus Christ is that He died for the sins of all the people in the world. It was according to the Scriptures both of the Old Testament and the New Testament. Psalm 22 is a picture of Calvary and Isaiah 53 is also an Old Testament picture of the Lord Jesus Christ's death on Calvary's cross in the New Testament Scriptures.

That word, *"for"* means *"in place of, for the benefit of and instead of"* He died in the place of, for the benefit of, and made provision for the sins of everyone in the world. But to make it good, they must accept this provision by genuine faith in the Lord Jesus Christ as their Saviour in order to escape the fires of Hell and receive everlasting and eternal life.

1 Corinthians 15:4

"And that he was buried, and that he rose again the third day according to the scriptures:"

Here's the second two parts of the Gospel. (1) He died for our sins, according to the scriptures, (2) He was buried, and (3) He rose again the third day, according to the Scriptures.

Verses On Christ Being Raised From The Dead
- **Matthew 16:21**

"From that time forth began Jesus to shew unto his disciples, how that <u>he must go unto Jerusalem</u>, and suffer many things of the elders and chief priests and scribes, and <u>be killed, and be raised again the third day</u>."

After the betrayal of the Lord Jesus Christ, He predicted His bodily resurrection.

- **Matthew 17:23**

"And they shall kill him, and <u>the third day he shall be raised again</u>. And they were exceeding sorry."

The bodily resurrection of the Lord Jesus Christ is foretold again.

- **Matthew 20:19**

"And shall deliver him to the Gentiles to mock, and to scourge, and to crucify him: and <u>the third day he shall rise again</u>."

Once again, the bodily resurrection of the Lord Jesus Christ was a predicted and firm event. This is part of Paul's Gospel message.

Paul is going to talk about the bodily resurrection of the Lord Jesus Christ throughout the rest of this fifteenth chapter which is the Biblical summary of His bodily resurrection. Other Bible books mention it, but this chapter discusses it in great detail.

1 Corinthians 15:5

"And that he was seen of Cephas, then of the twelve:"

The Apostle Peter saw the resurrected Lord Jesus Christ as well as the other apostles who were still living. As a group, they are referred to as "*the twelve*" even though Judas had committed suicide. Cephas is an Aramaic word for "*stone.*" "*Petros*" is the Greek name for Peter. In the Greek language, it also means "*rock*" or "*stone.*"

- **Mark 16:7**

"But <u>go your way, tell his disciples and Peter</u> that he goeth before you into Galilee: there shall ye see him, as he said unto you."

Mary Magdalene and another Mary were told by the angel at the tomb to tell both His disciples and Peter that the Lord Jesus Christ had been resurrected and had gone into Galilee.

1 Corinthians 15:6

"After that, he was seen of above five hundred brethren at once; of whom the greater part remain unto this present, but some are fallen asleep."

The modernist liberal apostates teach that the bodily resurrection of Christ did not happen. They said it was a hallucination. They said it was a mirage. They said it was some sort of a dream or a vision. How can five hundred brethren, at the same time, take part in a hallucination? That would be a dream of some psychiatrist. It can never happen. This was no hallucination. This was a fact of history and a fact that people saw and believed. Five hundred brethren plus. *"Above five hundred."* Not only five hundred, but above five hundred.

Not only did above five hundred see the bodily resurrected Lord Jesus Christ, but it says, "*of whom the greater part remain unto this present, but some are fallen asleep.*" Some have died. But if need be, Paul implied that people who were still living could be asked about Whom they saw.

Many apostate preachers merely say on Easter Sunday that Christ is "risen," but they deny that the Lord Jesus Christ rose bodily. They mean some sort of a spiritual resurrection.

1 Corinthians 15:7

"After that, he was seen of James; then of all the apostles."

James also and all of the apostles saw the bodily risen Lord Jesus Christ. The apostles saw Him in two successive Sunday evening gatherings. We're not sure which "James" saw Him after he was raised bodily, because there were many named James in the New Testament, but whichever James he was, he was another witness to this miracle. It's amazing why so many apostate ministers and others deny the bodily resurrection of the Lord Jesus Christ even though there were so many witnesses to this event!

1 Corinthians 15:8

"And last of all he was seen of me also, as of one born out of due time."

The Apostle Paul was also an eye-witness of the bodily resurrection of the Lord Jesus Christ. In Acts 9:1-5, Paul was on the road to Damascus, ready to kill and imprison genuine Christians. While on his journey, Paul heard a voice and a voice from heaven, saying: Saul, Saul.

- **Acts 9:4b-5**

"Saul, <u>Saul, why persecutest thou me</u>? And <u>he said, Who art thou, Lord? And the Lord said, I am Jesus whom thou persecutest</u>: it is hard for thee to kick against the pricks."

The Lord Jesus Christ had been raised bodily from the grave, ascended to Heaven, and seated at the right hand of God the Father. The Saviour blinded him and then gave him a call and commission to serve Him as one of His apostles.

The expression he uses, "*as of one born out of due time*," probably refers to the fact that Paul was not one of the original leaders and genuine Christians, but was called into the service of the Lord Jesus Christ as an Apostle after the Saviour had ascended to Heaven.

1 Corinthians 15:9

"For I am the least of the apostles, that am not meet to be called an apostle, because I persecuted the church of God."

Paul showed his humility when writing this verse. He certainly did persecute the church of God. Here are some verses on it.

Verses On Paul's Persecution Of Christians
- **Acts 8:1**

"And <u>Saul was consenting unto his death</u>. And at that time there was a great persecution against the church which was at Jerusalem; and they were all scattered abroad throughout the regions of Judaea and Samaria, except the apostles."

Paul consented unto the stoning and murder of Stephen.

- **Acts 9:4-5**

"And he fell to the earth, and heard a voice saying unto him, Saul, <u>Saul, why persecutest thou me</u>? And he said, Who art thou, Lord? And the Lord said, <u>I am Jesus whom thou persecutest</u>: it is hard for thee to kick against the pricks."

The Lord Jesus Christ asked Paul why he was persecuting Him by persecuting genuine Christians who followed Him.
- **Acts 22:4**
"And I persecuted this way unto the death, binding and delivering into prisons both men and women."

Paul admitted his severe persecution of Christians unto the death as well as imprisoning both men and women.
- **Acts 26:11**
"And I punished them oft in every synagogue, and compelled them to blaspheme; and being exceedingly mad against them, I persecuted them even unto strange cities."

Paul persecuted these true Christians often, even in strange cities.
- **Galatians 1:13b**
". . . how that beyond measure I persecuted the church of God, and wasted it:"

Paul admitted his persecution and wasting of the lives and ministries of many genuine Christians.
- **Galatians 1:23**
"But they had heard only, That he which persecuted us in times past now preacheth the faith which once he destroyed."

Paul no longer persecuted the true Christians. That was all in the past.
- **Philippians 3:6a**
"Concerning zeal, persecuting the church;"

One of the evidences of Paul's zeal as a Jewish Pharisee was his persecution of the genuine Christians.
- **1 Timothy 1:13**
"Who was before a blasphemer, and a persecutor, and injurious: but I obtained mercy, because I did it ignorantly in unbelief."

Before Paul became a true Christian, he admits that he was a persecutor.

1 Corinthians 15:10

"But by the grace of God I am what I am: and his grace which *was bestowed* upon me was not in vain; but I laboured more abundantly than they all: yet not I, but the grace of God which was with me."

Notice the word 'but' at the beginning of verse ten. What a contrast from Paul's former lifestyle! Only by God's matchless grace was he turned around in his life to serve instead of persecute.

This grace that God bestowed upon Paul was not in vain, but because God gave it to him it was not in vain. Because of this gift of God's eternal salvation, Paul was enabled by God's grace to labor for Him more abundantly than all the other genuine Christians around him. God's grace can enable true Christians today as well if they will only use it and not be lazy, true Christians who do not work for their Saviour.

- **Ephesians 2:8**
"For <u>by grace are ye saved through faith; and that not of yourselves: it is the gift of God</u>: Not of works, lest any man should boast."

God's grace is what saves lost sinners, and not by their works. It is by genuine faith in the Lord Jesus Christ as their Saviour and not by any works that they do. The Greek Word for "*labour*" in this verse implies "*to grow weary, tired and exhausted with toil and burdens*." Surely, the Lord Jesus Christ did not save Paul in vain. He was an active worker for Him. I wish all true Christians would labor for their Saviour as hard as Paul labored.

1 Corinthians 15:11

"Therefore whether *it were* I or they, so we preach, and so ye believed."

Paul is saying here that whether genuine Christians who didn't labor as hard as he did, they both preach the Lord Jesus Christ with the result that people believed in Him as their Lord and Saviour. I'm sure both kinds of preachers preached the very Words of God without any compromise whatsoever.

1 Corinthians 15:12

"Now if Christ be preached that he rose from the dead, how say some among you that there is no resurrection of the dead?"

Both kinds of preachers mentioned in the preceding verse faithfully preached God's words of salvation to their hearers. One of the doctrines that they preached faithfully was that the Lord Jesus Christ rose bodily from the dead. Yet some false preachers and teachers at Corinth preached the total lie and falsehood that the Lord Jesus Christ did not rise bodily from among the dead. Sad to say, many, many, pastors and preachers totally deny belief in the bodily resurrection of the Lord Jesus Christ. Sometimes those preachers who deny Christ's bodily resurrection, often hide their denial by just saying "*He arose!*" When this deceptive and unclear wording is used by these unbelieving preachers, they imply "bodily" but do not say it. They only believe in Christ's "spiritual" resurrection, but not "bodily." This is a deceptive heresy!

1 Corinthians 15:13

"But if there be no resurrection of the dead, then is Christ not risen:"

This is a very important theological conclusion that Paul presents. If there is no bodily resurrection at all for genuine Christians, then the Lord Jesus Christ could not rise bodily from the dead either. These two things go together very clearly. This is a serious denial of the third part of Paul's Gospel. *"Christ died for our sins, according to the scriptures, he was buried, and the third day rose again, according to the scriptures."* This is the Gospel that he preached. It's a very important part. *"But if there be no resurrection of the dead, then is Christ not risen:"* This is a very serious matter indeed.

1 Corinthians 15:14

"And if Christ be not risen, then *is* our preaching vain, and your faith *is* also vain."

If Christ is not risen, then Paul's preaching is empty of goal, empty of purpose because he said that he was raised and he wasn't raised if there isn't the resurrection of all the dead. And then your faith is in vain. The people had entrusted the Lord Jesus Christ as being raised and seated at the Father's right hand. Well, if he's not raised from the dead, he's still there. He's not at the Father's right hand, interceding for the believers as the scriptures teach, if the Lord Jesus is not raised. If He was not raised, He could not be the genuine Christian's merciful High Priest to assist them throughout their lives. Nor could He come for His true Christians at the Rapture, nor could He rule and reign one thousand years during the Millennium.

1 Corinthians 15:15

"Yea, and we are found false witnesses of God; because we have testified of God that he raised up Christ: whom he raised not up, if so be that the dead rise not."

If the Lord Jesus Christ was not bodily raised from the dead, Paul would be guilty of being a false witness because he preached that God the Father raised Him up. On the day Paul became a genuine Christian, when he was on the road of Damascus, he asked the Lord Jesus Christ, "*Who art thou?*" The Lord told him, "I *am Jesus whom thou persecutist.*"

1 Corinthians 15:16
For if the dead rise not, then *is* not Christ raised:
Again, he repeats. I don't know how many times Paul has to repeat this to get it through to these Corinthian Christians. If the dead rise not, if there is no such thing as a bodily resurrection of any dead people, then the Lord Jesus Christ was not bodily raised either.

1 Corinthians 15:17
"And if Christ be not raised, your faith *is* vain; ye are yet in your sins."
Another thing would be true if the Lord Jesus Christ were not raised bodily. The faith of true Christians would be in vain. Also, they would yet be in their sins because the Lord Jesus Christ would not be a True and Honest God-Man Who really took their place and died for their sins. They would still be in their sins rather than having been made righteous by their Saviour.

1 Corinthians 15:18
"Then they also which are fallen asleep in Christ are perished."
Another thing would be true if the Lord Jesus Christ did not rise from the dead bodily. Those genuine Christians who had died would be perishing in Hell instead of being in Heaven. This lie against the bodily resurrection of the Lord Jesus Christ would make Him merely a Human Being unable to keep His many promises, including His teachings about Heaven and Hell.

1 Corinthians 15:19
"If in this life only we have hope in Christ, we are of all men most miserable."
If in this life only, true Christians have hope in the Lord Jesus Christ—without any eternal life in Heaven to look forward to, Paul and other genuine Christians would be, of all men, most miserable.

Think of all that the Apostle Paul suffered because he was a faithful and genuine Christian and apostle! To have anyone suffer those things written of Paul's sufferings with no bright and glorious hope of eternal life in the glories of Heaven, that would make anyone miserable.

Paul was persecuted, banished from city to city, stoned, shipwrecked, beaten with rods, whipped and so on. In 2 Corinthians 11:23-28, you can read of 32 different trials, hardships, and punishments that Paul suffered because he was a faithful apostle for the Lord Jesus Christ. If these cruel hardships were all that Paul had for being a faithful servant of the Lord Jesus Christ, with no hope of Heaven and being with His Saviour for all eternity, he would be of all men most miserable.

1 Corinthians 15:20

"But now is Christ risen from the dead, *and* become the firstfruits of them that slept."

The strong truth now comes out. Paul firmly states that now that the Lord Jesus Christ has risen bodily from the dead, He has become the firstfruits of all the genuine Christians that have died as well as all the true Christians who are still living when the Lord Jesus Christ returns in the air to Rapture them to Heaven.

1 Corinthians 15:21

"For since by man *came* death, by man *came* also the resurrection of the dead."

Paul stands for the creation of Adam and Eve. He alludes to Adam's sin of eating from the fruit of the tree that God had forbidden to eat. As such, he brought on physical death to every man, woman, and child through all future history. Though Eve ate of the tree first, God held Adam's eating of it as the cause for this curse of the physical death for all mankind to come.

But, in great contrast, the Lord Jesus Christ, the "*last Adam*" (1 Corinthians 15:45) made provision for the resurrection from the dead to all those who genuinely trust Him as their Saviour Who died in their place on the cross of Calvary.

1 Corinthians 15:22

"For as in Adam all die, even so in Christ shall all be made alive."

Those who are "*in Adam*" includes every man, woman, and child ever born (except for the Lord Jesus Christ). Unless they are genuine Christians and are alive until the Rapture by the Lord Jesus Christ, they will suffer physical death.

By contrast, those "*in Christ*," those who become true Christians by truly trusting the Lord Jesus Christ as their Saviour, will one day, at the Rapture by the Lord Jesus Christ, be transformed and be given new bodies and live forever.

1 Corinthians 15:23

"**But every man in his own order: Christ the firstfruits; afterward they that are Christ's at his coming.**"

The bodily resurrection and entrance into Heaven will follow a set order:

> **THE ORDER FOR THOSE ENTERING HEAVEN**
> 1. The Lord Jesus Christ was the firstfruits of those who will be bodily resurrected and enter Heaven.
> 2. Then, those who were true Christians who have either died, or are still living when the Lord Jesus Christ will come back in the air at the Rapture, will be the next group who will be taken to Heaven either after their bodily resurrection, or after their transformation into new bodies.

After the Rapture of the genuine Christians, there will be the seven-year Tribulation period. It will be followed by the Battle of Armageddon where the Lord Jesus Christ will defeat and conquer Satan and all His enemies. Satan will be bound during the Millennial reign of the Lord Jesus Christ.

At the end of the Millennium, Satan will be loosed from his bondage and will come out of that bottomless pit, where he was bound. Then he will lead all the nations to go up against Jerusalem, against the Lord Jesus Christ, against all genuine Christians alive at that time, and against all of the rest of his enemies. The Lord Jesus Christ will again put down Satan and his followers and win the battle once more.

1 Corinthians 15:24

"**Then *cometh* the end, when he shall have delivered up the kingdom to God, even the Father; when he shall have put down all rule and all authority and power.**"

After the final battle with Satan and his followers, and "*when He shall have put down all rule and all authority and power,*" the conditions spoken of near the end of the book of Revelation will begin.

1 Corinthians 15:25
"For he must reign, till he hath put all enemies under his feet."

This verse explains what happens during the Millennial reign of the Lord Jesus Christ. He will reign until all enemies are put under His feet. As mentioned earlier, Satan will be loosed from being bound, and will try to take over the world once again. The Lord Jesus Christ will defeat him and cast him into the Hell's Lake of Fire for all eternity. The Lord Jesus Christ will put all His other enemies under His feet as well.

1 Corinthians 15:26
"The last enemy *that* shall be destroyed *is* death."

- **Psalms 23:4a**
"Yea, <u>though I walk through the valley of the shadow of death</u>, I will fear no evil:"

It's a valley for the non-Christians, and there's a shadow for the genuine Christians. Physical death is only a shadow for the true Christians, for their spirits and souls will immediately enter the glories of Heaven upon their physical death. The Lord Jesus Christ has snapped the power of the Christians' "*last enemy.*" Death is an enemy. It parts friends, it parts loved ones, it parts spouses, and it parts children from their parents.

- **Romans 5:12**
"Wherefore, as <u>by one man sin entered into the world, and death by sin</u>; and so <u>death passed upon all men</u>, for that all have sinned:"

From the sin of Adam in the Garden of Eden, physical death passed on all human beings. Physical death also was passed upon them.

- **Romans 6:23**
"For <u>the wages of sin is death</u>; but the gift of God is eternal life through Jesus Christ our Lord."

Sin brings wages. One of the wages is physical death of all people.

- **2 Timothy 1:10**
"But is now made manifest by the appearing of <u>our Saviour Jesus Christ, who hath abolished death</u>, and hath brought life and immortality to light through the Gospel:"

The Lord Jesus Christ has abolished physical death for genuine Christians in that He has removed the necessity that they remain dead forever. He takes them immediately to Heaven. Death has no more hold on them. It is abolished in that sense.

- **Hebrews 2:14b-15**
". . that through death he might destroy him that had the power of death, that is, the devil; And deliver them who through fear of death were all their lifetime subject to bondage."

The Lord Jesus Christ will one day destroy Satan who has the power of death.

- **Revelation 1:18**
"I am he that liveth, and was dead; and, behold, I am alive for evermore, Amen; and have the keys of hell and of death."

The Lord Jesus Christ has the keys of physical death. He is in charge of it.

- **Revelation 21:4**
"And God shall wipe away all tears from their eyes; and there shall be no more death, neither sorrow, nor crying, neither shall there be any more pain: for the former things are passed away."

In Heaven, for the genuine Christians who are there, there will be no more physical death, for the former things will all have passed away.

1 Corinthians 15:27

"For he hath put all things under his feet. But when he saith all things are put under *him, it is* manifest that he is excepted, which did put all things under him."

The Lord Jesus Christ, at this point, will have put all things under His feet. He will be completely in control of everything with one exception. God the Father, who put all things under His Son, the Lord Jesus Christ, will not be put under the Lord Jesus Christ. All the members of the Trinity are co-equal. No Member of the Trinity is over any other Member of the Trinity.

1 Corinthians 15:28

"And when all things shall be subdued unto him, then shall the Son also himself be subject unto him that put all things under him, that God may be all in all."

When all things are subdued and put under the control of the Lord Jesus Christ, then the Lord Jesus Christ, the Son of God, Himself will be subject to God the Father Who put all things under Him, including every principality, power, every ruler of this world. Then shall God the Son, be subject unto God the Father so that "*God may be all in all.*" This subjection does not indicate any inferiority among the Persons of the Godhead. It is just God's order.

So in the home. God has placed the father as the head of the home. His wife and children are to be obedient to him. But this certainly does not mean they are inferior to him. They are (or should be) subject to the husband and father, but this does not mean they are inferior to him in any way. This is God's order for the genuine Christian homes. It is very sad that many true Christian homes do not follow God's order in the matter.

1 Corinthians 15:29

"Else what shall they do which are baptized for the dead, if the dead rise not at all? why are they then baptized for the dead?"

This is a verse that some take in a strange and very wrong way. They wrongly take this phrase, "*baptized for the dead,*" to mean something other than what it means. These people, who wear long robes, have many names in a long list of genealogical roles. They select one name and baptize someone for that person. Then they take another and another, and so on.

The proper understanding of this verse is this. When genuine Christians die and their spirits and souls go to Heaven, the churches have lost that true Christian from their church membership. This should make the members of that church give the Biblical Gospel to others and lead them to understand that Gospel and become genuine Christians. When this happens, these true Christians can then be baptized for those who have died and take their place on the rolls of the local church. This the meaning of being "*baptized for* (in the place of those who have died) *the dead.*"

1 Corinthians 15:30

"And why stand we in jeopardy every hour?"

Paul was in jeopardy and danger every day because he believed in the bodily resurrection of the Lord Jesus Christ and other doctrines of the genuine Christian faith. In the verses below, Paul enumerates a total of 19 kinds of difficulties and problems he had to undergo after the Lord Jesus Christ called him as an apostle.

- **2 Corinthians 11:23b-27**

"in labours more abundant, in stripes above measure, in prisons more frequent, in deaths oft. Of the Jews five times received I forty stripes save one. Thrice was I beaten with rods, once was I stoned, thrice I suffered shipwreck, a night and a day I have been in the deep; In journeyings often, in perils of waters, in perils of robbers, in perils by mine own countrymen, in perils by the heathen, in perils in the city, in perils in the wilderness, in perils in the sea, in perils among false brethren; In weariness and painfulness, in watchings often, in hunger and thirst, in fastings often, in cold and nakedness."

Certainly, there were many painful things that Paul had to endure. I don't know if genuine Christian leaders today would be able to endure such jeopardy as Paul had to endure.

1 Corinthians 15:31

"I protest by your rejoicing which I have in Christ Jesus our Lord, I die daily."

He protests by the rejoicing that the true Christians in Corinth had. Perhaps they were rejoicing that Paul was in much trouble. He says that he dies daily in the sense of his pain and persecutions. It seemed as painful as death to him. In fact, he was stoned to death at Lystra and God raised him back to life.

- **Philippians 4:4**

"Rejoice in the Lord alway: and again I say, Rejoice."
Despite Paul's sufferings, he wrote from his Roman imprisonment that these genuine Christians at Philippi rejoice in the Lord always. Though Paul dies daily in many sufferings, he still rejoices in the Lord Jesus Christ his Saviour.

1 Corinthians 15:32

"If after the manner of men I have fought with beasts at Ephesus, what advantageth it me, if the dead rise not? let us eat and drink; for to morrow we die."

If these "*beasts*" were real beasts, rather than the unbelieving "beasts" who fought against him, that is one thought. However, it also might mean that he was one of the genuine Christians who had to fight with wild beasts in one of the amphitheaters of his day like a gladiator. It's not clear. But Paul made it clear that if there was no bodily resurrection from the dead, why would he willingly undergo so many dangers and injuries. If this life is all there is, why not just "*eat and drink; for tomorrow we die.*"

But, it a fact that all true Christians will be raised bodily as their Saviour was raised and have their Home in Heaven with new bodies one day.

1 Corinthians 15:33

"Be not deceived: evil communications corrupt good manners."

The structure of the Greek Words here make it clear that these genuine Christians at Corinth should stop being deceived. This is because it is a Greek present tense prohibition. Apparently these true Christians thought that it was all right to have close associations with evil people. It was not right then, and it is not right in our days. That association always, in some way, corrupts the Biblical standards that genuine Christians should maintain. Paul was a forthright apostle who didn't mind stepping on toes that need stepping on if they are wrong in their actions. Evil communications, associations, friendships, corrupt and continue to corrupt such things as good manners, good ethics, and good morals. So every genuine Christian should watch the company they keep.

Verses On Evil Associations

- **Exodus 23:2**

"<u>Thou shalt not follow a multitude to do evil</u>; neither shalt thou speak in a cause to decline after many to wrest judgment:"

Don't run around with evil people.

- **Numbers 33:55**

"But <u>if ye will not drive out the inhabitants of the land from before you</u>; then it shall come to pass, that those which ye let remain of them shall be pricks in your eyes, and thorns in your sides, and <u>shall vex you in the land wherein ye dwell</u>."

Israel was to drive out the Canaanites.

- **2 Corinthians 6:17**

"Wherefore come out from among them, and <u>be ye separate</u>, saith the Lord, and <u>touch not the unclean thing</u>; and I will receive you,"

Genuine Christians must be careful of their communications and fellowships.

- **Jeremiah 10:2**

"Thus saith the LORD, <u>Learn not the way of the heathen</u>, and be not dismayed at the signs of heaven; for the heathen are dismayed at them."

True Christians have many heathen, foul mouthed, dirty, filthy people that are pigs in morality around them. They must stay away from them. They will corrupt them and their children.

1 Corinthians 15:34

"Awake to righteousness, and sin not; for some have not the knowledge of God: I speak *this* to your shame."

Paul tells the genuine Christians at Corinth to awake to righteousness rather than sinfulness and stop sinning. It is a shame that some people around them don't know the Lord because they haven't been told about Him. Paul was ashamed of them and God is ashamed of genuine Christians today if they are not telling the Gospel of the Lord Jesus Christ, by their lives, by their lips, and in every way possible.

We praise the Lord that we can be on the Internet so that people all over the world can hear our church messages from the Bible. Some months, 1,800 or more people have downloaded the messages from our church.

Verses On The Gospel
- **Mark 16:15**

"And he said unto them, Go ye into all the world, and preach the gospel to every creature."

Th Biblical Gospel must be preached around the world. We can do this now through the Internet.
- **John 1:12**

"But as many as received him, to them gave he power to become the sons of God, even to them that believe on his name:"

People must receive and believe on the Lord Jesus Christ to become sons and daughters of God.

1 Corinthians 15:35

"But some *man* will say, How are the dead raised up? and with what body do they come?"

Now Paul will tell us the method and manner of the bodily resurrection of genuine Christians. There are many people in the resurrection of the dead. How are they raised up and with what body? There are those two questions. The "how" and the "with what" are detailed by Paul in this chapter in later verses.

1 Corinthians 15:36

"*Thou* fool, that which thou sowest is not quickened, except it die:"

God calls those who doubt the bodily resurrection of true Christians *"fools."* That's a harsh name, but God said it, not a man. God used the term again when He said: "*the fool has said in his heart there is no God.*" God calls some people 'fools' that don't believe in him.

The meaning of the Greek Word used here means someone who is:

"*a senseless one, without a mind, mentally disabled, not thinking right, without reflection or intelligence, acting rashly, stupid, foolish, senseless.*"

That's very strong, but straight talk from the Words of God. The seed sown must die or be completely changed. That which grows is different than the seed that was sown. A small kernel of corn when planted, is much different than the large stalk of corn that grows up from that kernel later. So genuine Christians' bodily resurrected bodies will be different than what their natural and mortal bodies were.

1 Corinthians 15:37

"And that which thou sowest, thou sowest not that body that shall be, but bare grain, it may chance of wheat, or of some other *grain*:"

The kernel of corn that a person sows in the ground is not the same thing that grows from that seed, whether the seed is wheat or some other grain. You don't sow the same kind of thing that you're going to get later. For example, you don't sow a whole corn stalk. You'd don't sow a whole field of corn or wheat. You just sow a tiny seed of grain, whether wheat, corn, or some other seed.

1 Corinthians 15:38

"But God giveth it a body as it hath pleased him, and to every seed his own body."

In the area of planting seeds and crops, God causes the resulting body to look and feel as it pleases God Himself. In other words, different seeds have different bodies. This is true whether you plant flowers, vegetables, or any other seed.

1 Corinthians 15:39

"All flesh is not the same flesh: but *there is* one kind of flesh of men, another flesh of beasts, another of fishes, *and* another of birds."

It is obvious that there are various kinds of flesh, whether of men, beasts, fish, birds, or any other kind of flesh. Those who believe in evolution have different views of the origin of human beings. Some believe they came from one kind of animal, whether fish, monkeys or others. If true, which it is not, that would mean they all would be the same flesh. But all flesh mentioned in this verse is not the same. They are all different.

1 Corinthians 15:40

"*There are* also celestial bodies, and bodies terrestrial: but the glory of the celestial *is* one, and the glory of the terrestrial *is* another."

How Many Stars Are There?

"There are about 10 billion galaxies in the observable universe! The number of stars in a galaxy varies, but assuming an average of 100 billion stars per galaxy, it would mean that there are about 1,000,000,000,000, 000,000,000 stars" [from an Internet Site]

These are celestial bodies including all the stars and all the planets. The above quote is amazing, if true! But there are many thousands (or many more) terrestrial bodies living on the earth (and many more living in the rivers, seas, and oceans. They differ in glory, but they are all distinct creations by the Bible's Triune God. Sadly, multitudes deny this truth.

All genuine Christians have terrestrial bodies, but when they are all bodily resurrected, they will have celestial bodies that God Himself will give them. They will be fit for heaven and fit to be in the very presence of God the Father, and to be with the Lord Jesus Christ forever. That's a tremendous thing. Paul says the glory of these two bodies is different. I'm glad we're going to have more glorious new bodies than what we have here.

1 Corinthians 15:41

"*There is* one glory of the sun, and another glory of the moon, and another glory of the stars: for one star differeth from *another* star in glory."

All these heavenly bodies have different glories, whether the sun, the moon, or the stars. They are distinct celestial bodies created separately by the mighty hand of God. He alone knows the glory of each of these heavenly bodies and made them different in glory by His own purpose and will.

1 Corinthians 15:42
"**So also is the resurrection of the dead. It is sown in corruption; it is raised in incorruption:**"

The bodily resurrection of genuine Christians is similar to the various glories of the heavenly bodies of sun, moon, and stars. The earthly bodies of true Christians are sown in death and corruption, but are raised in glory.

1 Corinthians 15:43
"**It is sown in dishonour; it is raised in glory: it is sown in weakness; it is raised in power:**"

In this verse, the bodies of genuine Christians are sown in both dishonor and weakness, but are raised in glory and power.

1 Corinthians 15:44
"**It is sown a natural body; it is raised a spiritual body. There is a natural body, and there is a spiritual body.**"

The bodies of true Christians are sown natural bodies, subjected to the soul, but are raised as spiritual bodies, subjected to the Holy Spirit.

1 Corinthians 15:45
"**And so it is written, The first man Adam was made a living soul; the last Adam *was made* a quickening spirit.**"

When the words, "*it is written*" are used, they are always translated from the Greek perfect tense of GRAPHO which is GEGRAPTAI. The Greek perfect tense always refers to things that occurred in the past, but whose results continue into present and on into the future. This Greek Word therefore means that the written Words of Hebrew, Aramaic, and Greek, though they were written in the past, have been protected by God, and preserved into the future. This is the very essence of Bible preservation.

The only Bible in English that has accurately translated those preserved Hebrew, Aramaic, and Greek Words is the King James Bible. All of the other English Bibles have deviated erroneously in many places, either in a greater or lesser degree with the preserved original language Words that underlie the King James Bible.

The verse below, shows clearly, the first man, Adam, was made a living soul.
- **Genesis 2:7**
"And the LORD God formed man of the dust of the ground, and breathed into his nostrils the breath of life; and <u>man became a living soul</u>."

But the Last Man, the Lord Jesus Christ was made a quickening or life-giving Spirit. He is able to quicken, or give life to lost and wayward sinners.
- **John 3:36**
"<u>He that believeth on the Son hath everlasting life</u>: and he that believeth not the Son shall not see life; but the wrath of God abideth on him."

The Lord Jesus Christ can quicken, or bestow everlasting life to those who genuinely believe on Him as their Saviour.
- **John 3:15**
"That <u>whosoever believeth in him</u> should not perish, but <u>have eternal life</u>."

Eternal life can be given by the Lord Jesus Christ to those who truly believe in Him as their Saviour. He can quicken, or give life to them.

1 Corinthians 15:46

"Howbeit that was not first which is spiritual, but that which is natural; and afterward that which is spiritual."

God's order was first, Adam, who was natural, and then the Lord Jesus Christ, Who was spiritual –The eternal God the Son and the Son of God.

It is true also that genuine Christians were first just natural people. After they received the Lord Jesus Christ as their Saviour, they became spiritual. Their bodies are natural, but when they receive their bodily-resurrected bodies, those bodies will be spiritual.

1 Corinthians 15:47

"The first man *is* of the earth, earthy: the second man *is* the Lord from heaven."

Adam was the first man on the earth. As such, he was earthy. The Lord Jesus Christ is the Lord from Heaven. If you have one of the newer Bible translations which are based on the Gnostic, Critical, or Westcott and Hort texts, you will see that the word, "*Lord,*" is missing. This is because the Gnostics and also Westcott and Hort were Anti-Christian apostates who denied the Deity of the Lord Jesus Christ. The elimination of "*Lord*" is found in such versions as the New International (NIV), the New American Standard (NASV), the Revised Standard (RSV), the English Standard (ESV, and many, more false Bibles.

Verses On Christ Coming Down From Heaven
- **John 6:33**
"For the bread of God is he which cometh down from heaven, and giveth life unto the world."

The Lord Jesus Christ came down from Heaven.
- **John 6:38**
"For I came down from heaven, not to do mine own will, but the will of him that sent me."

The Saviour came from Heaven to do His Father's will.
- **John 6:41**
"The Jews then murmured at him, because he said, I am the bread which came down from heaven."

The unbelieving Jews and Pharisees denied this truth.
- **John 6:51**
"I am the living bread which came down from heaven: if any man eat of this bread, he shall live for ever: and the bread that I will give is my flesh, which I will give for the life of the world."

The Lord Jesus Christ came down from God's Heaven as He mentioned many times, but many people then and now deny this truth.

1 Corinthians 15:48

"As *is* the earthy, such *are* they also that are earthy: and as *is* the heavenly, such *are* they also that are heavenly."

All people born in this world are earthy and have earthy bodies like Adam had. All the genuine Christians also have earthly bodies now, but when they are bodily resurrected, they will have heavenly bodies.

Verses On Christians' New, Resurrected, Bodies
- **Philippians 3:20-21**
"For our conversation is in heaven; from whence also we look for the Saviour, the Lord Jesus Christ: Who shall change our vile body, that it may be fashioned like unto his glorious body, according to the working whereby he is able even to subdue all things unto himself."

The Lord Jesus Christ will change the true Christians' natural bodies into bodies fashioned like that of His own glorious Body.

- **1 John 3:2**
"Beloved, now are we the sons of God, and it doth not yet appear what we shall be: but we know that, <u>when he shall appear, we shall be like him</u>; for we shall see him as he is." At the Rapture of the Lord Jesus Christ, all genuine Christians will be given resurrected bodies like His.

1 Corinthians 15:49

"And as we have borne the image of the earthy, we shall also bear the image of the heavenly."

As true Christians have borne the image of the earthy, Adam, so they will one day be resurrected and will bear the image of the Son.

1 Corinthians 15:50

"Now this I say, brethren, that flesh and blood cannot inherit the kingdom of God; neither doth corruption inherit incorruption."

It is not possible for the flesh and blood bodies, that all genuine Christians possess, to inherit the kingdom of God in Heaven. Corruption which belongs to their earthly bodies cannot inherit incorruption which is required for Heaven. All true Christians will be given incorruptible bodies which can enter Heaven. The Lord Jesus Christ said, of His own resurrected Body, after His bodily resurrection: *"Handle Me and see, for a spirit hath not flesh and bones, as ye see me have"* (Luke 24:39). The Lord Jesus Christ was very careful in what He said. He didn't say *"flesh and blood,"* but He said *"Flesh and bones as ye see me have."* I believe the resurrected body is not dependent upon blood is our present bodies are.

1 Corinthians 15:51

"Behold, I shew you a mystery; We shall not all sleep, but we shall all be changed,"

Paul calls this a mystery. He is writing to the Genuine Christians at Corinth. True Christians shall not all sleep, meaning some will not die before the return of their Saviour at the Rapture. However, all these Christians will be changed, whether if they have died or if they're still living. He means that when the Lord Jesus Christ returns at the Rapture, all these genuine Christians will be changed when they receive their resurrected bodies.

1 Corinthians 15:52

"In a moment, in the twinkling of an eye, at the last trump: for the trumpet shall sound, and the dead shall be raised incorruptible, and we shall be changed."

This miracle of the bodily resurrection of all the genuine Christians will take place, in an instant, as quick as a blink of the eye, when the last trumpet sound occurs. At that point, the dead in Christ will be bodily raised with incorruptible bodies and those true Christians who are still living will also be changed and given incorruptible and resurrected new bodies. This is also explained in the verses below:

- 1 Thessalonians 4:15-17

"For this we say unto you by the word of the Lord, that we which are alive and remain unto the coming of the Lord shall not prevent them which are asleep. For the Lord himself shall descend from heaven with a shout, with the voice of the archangel, and with the trump of God: and the dead in Christ shall rise first: Then we which are alive and remain shall be caught up together with them in the clouds, to meet the Lord in the air: and so shall we ever be with the Lord."

1 Corinthians 15:53

"For this corruptible must put on incorruption, and this mortal *must* put on immortality."

For this event to occur, the bodies of genuine Christians who will take part in this miraculous event, their corruptible bodies must put on incorruptible bodies. Also, these who now have mortal bodies that die, must put on immortality with immortal new bodies.

1 Corinthians 15:54

"So when this corruptible shall have put on incorruption, and this mortal shall have put on immortality, then shall be brought to pass the saying that is written, Death is swallowed up in victory."

When this event has take place, mentioned in the previous verse, then that which is mentioned in this verse and which was prophesied in Isaiah will take place. Physical death for these genuine Christians will be swallowed up in victory. For none of these true Christians will ever die again. They will be forever with the Lord Jesus Christ in Heaven. The "saying that is written" is found in Isaiah 25:8:

- **Isaiah 25:8**
"He will swallow up death in victory; and the Lord GOD will wipe away tears from off all faces; and the rebuke of his people shall he take away from off all the earth: for the LORD hath spoken it."

God promised to swallow up death in victory. Death is a terrible enemy. Cancer is a terrible enemy. Heart trouble is a terrible enemy. All kinds of causes of death are terrible enemies. God says, because the Lord Jesus Christ has been raised, because the world now has been made aware of (though few believe it) the fact the Lord Jesus Christ has been bodily raised from death as payment for the sins of the world, we now have a bodily-resurrected Saviour.

1 Corinthians 15:55

"O death, where *is* thy sting? O grave, where *is* thy victory?"

Paul asks two important questions about death and the grave. The sting of death has been removed for those who have truly received the Lord Jesus Christ as their Lord and Saviour. The grave is no longer victorious over these genuine Christians. No longer will these true Christians have to fear either death or the grave. Their Saviour has given victory over both of these horrendous calamities!

1 Corinthians 15:56

"The sting of death *is* sin; and the strength of sin *is* the law."

Adam's sin in the Garden of Eden brought all mankind the sin of physical death.

The strength of sin is the law, whether the law of Moses, or any other law. When there is a law that forbids any action, and people commit that action, they break that law and receive the punishment and penalty of that sin.

As far as the law of Moses goes, people could never keep it in the past, nor can they keep it now. Salvation can come to people, only by genuine faith in the Lord Jesus Christ as their Saviour Who died for their sins.

1 Corinthians 15:57
"But thanks *be* to God, which giveth us the victory through our Lord Jesus Christ."

Paul was thankful to God Who gives sinners victory because of what the Lord Jesus Christ has done for them. Here is the picture of what alone gives victory to sinful humanity:

      1. When sinful and lost people agree with God that they are sinners and deserve Hell and everlasting punishment in the Lake of Fire;

      2. When these people sincerely believe that the Lord Jesus Christ died as an atonement for all their sins–past, present, and future–on the cross of Calvary, and

      3. When these people truly believe on and trust the Lord Jesus Christ as their Saviour Who died for them and in their place,

      4. These people can rejoice and be thankful to God for providing for them this eternal victory over sin, death, and Hell!

I ask you, who are reading this book, do you understand and sincerely agree with these things in your heart, so you can be thankful to the God of the Bible for His eternal provision for you? I hope and pray that you can.

1 Corinthians 15:58
"Therefore, my beloved brethren, be ye stedfast, unmoveable, always abounding in the work of the Lord, forasmuch as ye know that your labour is not in vain in the Lord."

Verses On Stedfast
- **Hebrews 3:14b**
"if we hold the beginning of our confidence stedfast unto the end;"

God wants genuine Christians to be steadfast until the end of their lives without any wavering.

- **Hebrews 6:19**
"Which hope we have as an anchor of the soul, both sure and stedfast, and which entereth into that within the veil;"

The Lord Jesus Christ is sure and steadfast and so should all true Christians be steadfast in everything they do in behalf of the Lord Jesus Christ.

A Verse On Unmoveable
- Acts 27:41

"And falling into a place where two seas met, <u>they ran the ship aground; and the forepart stuck fast, and remained unmoveable</u>, but the hinder part was broken with the violence of the waves."

When a ship like this one is blown by a tempest into the soft shoreline it remains stuck and unmoveable. May genuine Christians remain unmoveable in their Biblical doctrines of the faith as well.

In our Bible For Today Baptist Church, we must be steadfast and unmoveable in our Bible doctrines without changing them or moving them. Many churches have moved and are moving from the doctrines and teachings of the Bible. They are using perverted and inexact Bible versions based upon the wrong Hebrew, Aramaic, and Greek Words that have been doctored by the Gnostic heretics of Alexandria, Egypt.

We continue to use the accurate King James Bible which has been accurately translated from the proper, preserved Words of the Traditional Hebrew, Aramaic, and Greek originals.

Genuine Christians should always be abounding in the work of the Lord Jesus Christ without ceasing to work for Him in every area found in the Bible. They must be consistent and constant in their seeking to please their Saviour. They must be abounding in their Bible reading, Bible study, and witnessing for their Lord and Saviour Jesus Christ.

1 Corinthians Chapter Sixteen

1 Corinthians 16:1

"Now concerning the collection for the saints, as I have given order to the churches of Galatia, even so do ye."

Paul is talking about the offering for the genuine Christians. This collection was not for Paul and his needs. Paul had given orders to the churches of Galatia about giving gifts to the Lord's work and he is now telling the true Christians in Corinth about their giving. The word, "saints," is not the Roman Catholic saints, but refers to all genuine Christians wherever they might be all around the world.

Verses On Saints

- **Acts 9:13**

"Then Ananias answered, Lord, I have heard by many of this man, how much evil he hath done to <u>thy saints at Jerusalem</u>:"

Before Paul became a true Christian when the Lord Jesus Christ met him on the road to Damascus, he did much evil to the genuine Christians at Jerusalem, and in many other areas as well.

- **Acts 26:10**

"Which thing I also did in Jerusalem: and <u>many of the saints did I shut up in prison</u>, having received authority from the chief priests; and when they were put to death, I gave my voice against them."

Paul sent many genuine Christians to jail before he became a Christian himself.

- **Romans 1:7**

"To all that be in Rome, <u>beloved of God, called to be saints</u>: Grace to you and peace from God our Father, and the Lord Jesus Christ."

These true Christians were beloved of God.

- **Romans 8:27**

"And he that searcheth the hearts knoweth what is the mind of the Spirit, because <u>he maketh intercession for the saints</u> according to the will of God."

God the Holy Spirit makes intercession for every genuine Christian all over the world.
- **Romans 12:13**
"Distributing to the necessity of saints; given to hospitality." This is what Paul was doing. He was making a collection for the saints at Jerusalem and this is what we're doing for believers, saved people.

The true Christians at Corinth were to give to the necessities of the other Christians who had needs.
- **Romans 15:25**
"But now I go unto Jerusalem to minister unto the saints." Paul was going to make a certain contribution for the poor Christians who were at Jerusalem.
- **1 Corinthians 1:2**
"Unto the church of God which is at Corinth, to them that are sanctified in Christ Jesus, called to be saints, with all that in every place call upon the name of Jesus Christ our Lord, both theirs and ours:"

These genuine Christians were called by God.
- **Ephesians 1:1**
"Paul, an apostle of Jesus Christ by the will of God, to the saints which are at Ephesus, and to the faithful in Christ Jesus:"

Paul was writing to the true Christians at Ephesus in this verse.
- **1 Thessalonians 3:13**
"To the end he may stablish your hearts unblameable in holiness before God, even our Father, at the coming of our Lord Jesus Christ with all his saints."

This verse speaks about the 2nd phase of the Lord Jesus Christ's second coming. The Rapture of all genuine Christians, whether dead or alive will take place first. They will receive resurrected bodies and be taken to Heaven. Then the seven-year Great Tribulation will occur.

At the end of the seven-year Great Tribulation, the Lord Jesus Christ will come back to earth and set up His millennial reign for one thousand years on the earth. At this coming, all the true Christians who were Raptured to Heaven will return back to earth with the Lord Jesus Christ. This is the meaning of *"the coming of our Lord Jesus Christ with all His saints."*

1 Corinthians 16:2

"Upon the first *day* of the week let every one of you lay by him in store, *as* God hath prospered him, that there be no gatherings when I come."

Paul gives instructions to the genuine Christians at Corinth about when to bring their offerings to their meetings. It was to be on the *"first day of the week."* They were to put aside their offerings as God has prospered them. It does not name any set amount or percentage. This was so that when Paul would come to visit this church at Corinth, the true Christians there would not have to figure out how much to give in the offerings, because the amount would already be laid aside and could be given when Paul arrived.

Most churches take a collection when they meet on Sundays. Our Bible For Today Baptist Church does not take a collection, but has a box at the door where people may put their offerings if they wish to. Here are some other verses on *"the first day of the week."*

Verses On The First Day Of The Week
- **Matthew 28:1**

"In the end of the sabbath, as it began to dawn toward the first day of the week, came Mary Magdalene and the other Mary to see the sepulchre."

The Lord Jesus Christ rose bodily from the dead on the first day of the week meaning Sunday. This is the day that these two women named Mary visited the tomb where the Lord Jesus Christ had been laid.

- **Mark 16:9**

"Now when Jesus was risen early the first day of the week, he appeared first to Mary Magdalene, out of whom he had cast seven devils."

We worship the Lord Jesus Christ on Sunday, the first day of the week when he rose bodily from the dead.

- **Luke 24:1**

"Now upon the first day of the week, very early in the morning, they came unto the sepulchre, bringing the spices which they had prepared, and certain others with them."

The women came to the tomb early Sunday morning.

- **John 20:1**

"The first day of the week cometh Mary Magdalene early, when it was yet dark, unto the sepulchre, and seeth the stone taken away from the sepulchre."

Mary Magdalene came to the empty tomb Sunday morning.

- **John 20:19**

"Then the same day at evening, being the first day of the week, when the doors were shut where the disciples were assembled for fear of the Jews, came Jesus and stood in the midst, and saith unto them, Peace be unto you."

The apostles worshipped on the first day of the week, which is Sunday. They didn't wait for the Pope of Rome to canonize Sunday as the first day of worship.

- **Acts 20:7**

"And upon the first day of the week, when the disciples came together to break bread, Paul preached unto them, ready to depart on the morrow; and continued his speech until midnight."

The apostles worshipped on the first day of the week as well. So, the Lord's day is a scriptural, New Testament, Biblical day to worship the Lord Jesus Christ.

Verses On Offerings And Giving

- **Exodus 25:2**

"Speak unto the children of Israel, that they bring me an offering: of every man that giveth it willingly with his heart ye shall take my offering."

Genuine Christians should not give their gifts to the Lord grudgingly, but willingly.

- **Deuteronomy 16:17**

"Every man shall give as he is able, according to the blessing of the LORD thy God which he hath given thee."

In both the Old and the New Testaments the offerings were to be as the Lord has prospered them.

- **1 Chronicles 29:9**

"Then the people rejoiced, for that they offered willingly, because with perfect heart they offered willingly to the LORD: and David the king also rejoiced with great joy."

Israel offered to God willingly and with a perfect heart.

- **Joshua 1:8**

"This book of the law shall not depart out of thy mouth; but thou shalt meditate therein day and night, that thou mayest observe to do according to all that is written therein: for then thou shalt make thy way prosperous, and then thou shalt have good success."

Verses On Prospered

- **2 Chronicles 26:5**

"And he sought God in the days of Zechariah, who had understanding in the visions of God: and as long as he sought the LORD, God made him to prosper."

Zechariah was prospered by the Lord as long as he sought the LORD. If true Christians stop seeking the Lord, it is possible even today that they will not prosper.

- **Nehemiah 2:20**

"Then answered I them, and said unto them, The God of heaven, he will prosper us; therefore we his servants will arise and build: but ye have no portion, nor right, nor memorial, in Jerusalem."

God is able to prosper genuine Christians today as well, if they serve Him.

- **Psalms 1:3**

"And he shall be like a tree planted by the rivers of water, that bringeth forth his fruit in his season; his leaf also shall not wither; and whatsoever he doeth shall prosper."

The Lord has promised that the blessed people who serve Him shall prosper in whatsoever they do.

- **Proverbs 28:13**

"He that covereth his sins shall not prosper: but whoso confesseth and forsaketh them shall have mercy."

Those who cover up their sins will not prosper, even today.

- **Isaiah 55:11**

"So shall my word be that goeth forth out of my mouth: it shall not return unto me void, but it shall accomplish that which I

please, and it shall prosper in the thing whereto I sent it."

God's right and true Words will prosper. This is why it so necessary to use the correct Bible, founded upon the traditional and preserved Hebrew, Aramaic, and Greek Words and accurately translated, like the King James Bible is in the English language.

1 Corinthians 16:3

"And when I come, whomsoever ye shall approve by your letters, them will I send to bring your liberality unto Jerusalem."

When Paul came to the church at Corinth, whoever they approved, he would send to bring their offerings unto Jerusalem to help them. It was important to Paul to have trusted and honest men to care for this money rather than to steal any of it.

1 Corinthians 16:4

"And if it be meet that I go also, they shall go with me."

Paul said that he would go with them to Jerusalem if it was fitting for him to go. He didn't push himself to go, but left it up to the faithful men who were handling these gifts for the genuine Christians at Jerusalem.

1 Corinthians 16:5

"Now I will come unto you, when I shall pass through Macedonia: for I do pass through Macedonia."

Paul told the Corinthian church that he would come and visit them when he passed through Macedonia. I'm sure Paul wanted to visit the true Christians in Corinth just as he wanted to visit those in Macedonia.

1 Corinthians 16:6

"And it may be that I will abide, yea, and winter with you, that ye may bring me on my journey whithersoever I go."

Paul told the Corinthian church that he might stay with them through the winter. After that, he hopes that they can give him some food and funds to enable him to continue on his missionary journey.

- **Proverbs 25:17**

"Withdraw thy foot from thy neighbour's house; lest he be weary of thee, and so hate thee."

Don't stay too long when you are visiting somebody lest they get tired of you and begin to hate you.

1 Corinthians 16:7

"For I will not see you now by the way; but I trust to tarry a while with you, if the Lord permit."

Paul told the church at Corinth that he might not see them again for a while, but, if the Lord permits, he will stay a little while with them now.

Verses On If The Lord Wills

- **James 4:13-16**

"Go to now, ye that say, To day or to morrow we will go into such a city, and continue there a year, and buy and sell, and get gain: Whereas ye know not what shall be on the morrow. For what is your life? It is even a vapour, that appeareth for a little time, and then vanisheth away. For that ye ought to say, If the Lord will, we shall live, and do this, or that. But now ye rejoice in your boastings: all such rejoicing is evil."

The lives of genuine Christians should be in the hands of the Lord. They should want to do as He wills in their lives.

- **Proverbs 27:1**
  "Boast not thyself of to morrow; for <u>thou knowest not what a day may bring forth</u>."

True Christians do not know what will take place in the future for them. They should rest in God's will and leading for them because they do not know exactly what each day might bring about for them.

1 Corinthians 16:8

"But I will tarry at Ephesus until Pentecost."

Paul tells the Christians at Corinth that he plans to stay for quite a while, which is the meaning of this Greek Word for "*tarry.*" He gives the reason for this in the next verse.

1 Corinthians 16:9

"For a great door and effectual is opened unto me, and *there are* many adversaries."

Paul explained to these genuine Christians that God had opened a great and effectual door of opportunity for him in the city of Ephesus. Because of this, he planned to stay there until the feast of Pentecost. He also added that, even with this door of opportunity for the Gospel of the Lord Jesus Christ to be preached, there were many adversaries against him and the Gospel message.

Verses On Doors

- **John 10:9**
  "<u>I am the door</u>: by me if any man enter in, he shall be saved, and shall go in and out, and find pasture."

The Lord Jesus Christ Himself is the only door or passageway to salvation and Heaven. People must accept and receive Him as their Saviour in order to be able to enter Heaven.

- **Acts 14:27c**
  ". . . how <u>he had opened the door of faith</u> unto the Gentiles."

Paul mentioned how God had opened the door of faith to the Gentiles as he preached about the Lord Jesus Christ to them. Our Bible For Today Baptist Church has many doors that the Lord has opened for us. At the present time (before they remove the Internet door) our church has a ministry around the world by means of the Internet. The people all around the world are able to hear all three of our weekly preaching and teaching services 24 hours a day and seven days a week through our Website (<u>BibleForToday.org</u>)

In the past month, as I am writing this, the <u>SermonAudio.com</u> has made it possible for people to download

1,934 of our sermons for that month for a total downloads so far. There have been a total of 900,309 downloads to date as well as 24,134 videos. The download from mobile phones to date are 78,233. This covers all 50 states and 53 foreign countries. SermonAudio.Com is broadcasting 4,522 of our sermons 24-hours a day, 7-days a week. We are very grateful to the Lord Jesus Christ for this great open door for our ministry and service to Him!

- **2 Corinthians 2:12**

"Furthermore, when I came to Troas to preach Christ's Gospel, and <u>a door was opened unto me of the Lord</u>,"

The Lord opened a door for Paul at Troas. He is the One Who can open doors for His ministry.

- **Colossians 4:3**

"Withal <u>praying also for us, that God would open unto us a door of utterance, to speak the mystery of Christ</u>, for which I am also in bonds:"

True Christians should pray that the Lord Jesus Christ would open doors for them as well for His glory.

- **Revelation 3:8**

"I know thy works: behold, <u>I have set before thee an open door</u>, and no man can shut it: for thou hast a little strength, and hast kept my word, and hast not denied my name."

It's good to have open doors that God has set before us. We don't want to go through doors that are not opened from Him, though. The devil's got a lot of open doors, too. Don't ever go through his doors!

- **Matthew 7:13-14**

"Enter ye in at the strait gate: for wide is the gate, and broad is the way, that leadeth to destruction, and many there be which go in thereat: Because <u>strait is the gate, and narrow is the way, which leadeth unto life, and few there be that find it</u>."

The Lord Jesus Christ spoke of the strait gate or door that leads to life, but, sad to say, few there be that find it. Genuine Christians must continue to tell people about the Lord Jesus Christ Who is the only Door to salvation and Heaven.

- **Revelation 3:20**

"Behold, <u>I stand at the door, and knock: if any man hear my voice, and open the door, I will come in to him</u>, and will sup with him, and he with me."

The Lord Jesus Christ stands at the door of all the non-Christians' hearts. He wants them to open that door and accept Him as their Saviour.

- **Revelation 4:1**
"After this I looked, and, behold, <u>a door was opened in heaven</u>: and the first voice which I heard was as it were of a trumpet talking with me; which said, Come up hither, and I will shew thee things which must be hereafter."

The Apostle John, as the Lord was leading him to write the Book of Revelation, saw a door opened in Heaven. He heard a voice saying "*Come up hither.*" God showed him the things that must come to pass in the future.

Verses On Adversaries

- **Exodus 23:22b**
". . . then <u>I will be</u> an enemy unto thine enemies, and <u>an adversary unto thine adversaries</u>."

It's good to have the Lord on our side, against our adversaries and enemies.

- **Numbers 22:22**
"And God's anger was kindled because he went: and <u>the angel of the LORD stood in the way for an adversary against him</u>. Now he was riding upon his ass, and his two servants were with him."

Because Balaam was wrong in his actions, the anger of the Lord stood in the way for an adversary against him.

- **1 Samuel 2:10**
"<u>The adversaries of the LORD shall be broken to pieces</u>; out of heaven shall he thunder upon them: the LORD shall judge the ends of the earth; and he shall give strength unto his king, and exalt the horn of his anointed."

God's adversaries will be broken. He is able to do this through His omnipotence.

- **Esther 7:6**
"And Esther said, <u>The adversary and enemy is this wicked Haman</u>. Then Haman was afraid before the king and the queen."

Haman truly was an adversary and enemy of Esther and the Jews in the kingdom.

- **Psalms 38:20**
"<u>They also that render evil for good are mine adversaries</u>; because I follow the thing that good is."

Any who render evil for good are adversaries.

- **Psalms 71:13**
"<u>Let them be confounded and consumed that are adversaries to my soul</u>; let them be covered with reproach and dishonour that seek my hurt."

David said that his adversaries should be confounded and consumed.

- **Psalms 74:10**

"O God, how long shall the adversary reproach? shall the enemy blaspheme thy name for ever?"

David hoped that his adversary would stop his evil working.

- **Psalms 109:29**

"Let mine adversaries be clothed with shame, and let them cover themselves with their own confusion, as with a mantle."

David hoped his adversaries would be clothed with shame.

- **Philippians 1:28**

"And in nothing terrified by your adversaries: which is to them an evident token of perdition, but to you of salvation, and that of God."

Genuine Christians should not be terrified by their adversaries. They should seek the help of the Lord Jesus Christ and His power!

- **1 Timothy 5:14b**

" . . . give none occasion to the adversary to speak reproachfully."

True Christians must guard their lives so as not to give their adversaries occasion to speak against them.

- **Hebrews 10:27**

"But a certain fearful looking for of judgment and fiery indignation, which shall devour the adversaries."

The adversaries of the Lord will be devoured by fiery indignation in Hell's Lake of Fire.

- **1 Peter 5:8**

"Be sober, be vigilant; because your adversary the devil, as a roaring lion, walketh about, seeking whom he may devour:"

The devil is the biggest adversary against genuine Christians. They must be vigilant and aware of his evil powers.

Rome was an adversary to Bible believing Christians, the Roman Catholic system. As a Navy Chaplain on active duty, Roman Catholic chaplains, Episcopalian chaplains, and other apostate chaplains were against my Gospel preaching in the Navy.

New Evangelicalism, compromises against the fundamental, Bible believing Christians, cults, false teachers of all kinds, like John MacArthur's view on the blood of Christ, are all adversaries against the truths of God's Words.

Some otherwise fundamentalists who use and push false Bible versions which are based on false Hebrew, Aramaic, and Greek Words are adversaries against the truth. Schools like Dallas Theological Seminary (my *alma mater*), Bob Jones University, and many other Bible Schools, colleges and seminaries are adversaries in this area and many others, even though they might have some doctrines and teachings that are Biblical.

I have had many experiences too numerous to mention here of those who have been adversaries to me for preaching the truths of the Gospel and the Words of God. In Newton, Massachusetts, when I was Pastor of Faith Baptist Church, someone threw a stone through our downstairs window. Someone else painted our sign advertising our church. Many other adversaries have been against me in my 65 years of my many ministries since my ordination to the Gospel ministry in 1953 to this date in 2018. But the Lord Jesus Christ has been successful in helping me to stay strong and faithful to Him, despite the adversaries during all of these 65 years.

1 Corinthians 16:10

"Now if Timotheus come, see that he may be with you without fear: for he worketh the work of the Lord, as I also do."

Paul praised his friend and co-worker for his work in the Lord. He was a young man, but if he comes to the church at Corinth, they should not be in fear of him because he works for the Lord in the same manner as Paul himself. Paul had an unquestionable approval of Timothy.

Verses On Timothy

- **Acts 16:1b**

". . . a certain disciple was there, named <u>Timotheus, the son of a certain woman, which was a Jewess, and believed</u>; but his father was a Greek:"

Timothy was from a divided home, a genuine Christian (I assume) and a Greek who was a non-Christian.

- **Romans 16:21a**

"<u>Timotheus my workfellow</u>,"

Timothy was Paul's fellow worker and helper for the Lord's work.

- **1 Corinthians 4:17**

"For this cause have I sent unto you <u>Timotheus, who is my beloved son, and faithful in the Lord</u>, who shall bring you into remembrance of my ways which be in Christ, as I teach every where in every church."

Paul led Timothy to the Lord. He was his spiritual "*son*," and faithful in the Lord's work. He knew Paul's ways and teachings.

- **Philippians 2:19**

"But <u>I trust in the Lord Jesus to send Timotheus shortly unto you</u>, that I also may be of good comfort, when I know your state."

Paul told those at Philippi that he was going to send Timothy so he will be comforted when Timothy tells Paul of their condition.

- **Thessalonians 3:2**

"And sent <u>Timotheus, our brother, and minister of God, and our fellowlabourer in the Gospel of Christ</u>, to establish you, and to comfort you concerning your faith:"

Timothy was a minister of God and Paul's fellowlabourer in the Gospel. Paul sent him to Thessalonica to establish them and comfort them in their faith.

- **1 Timothy 1:18**

"This charge I commit unto thee, <u>son Timothy</u>, according to the prophecies which went before on thee, <u>that thou by them mightest war a good warfare</u>;"

Paul wanted Timothy to be able to *"war a good warfare"* for the Lord's cause.

- **1 Timothy 6:20**

"O <u>Timothy, keep that which is committed to thy trust</u>, avoiding profane and vain babblings, and oppositions of science falsely so called:"

The doctrines and teachings that Paul committed to Timothy to his trust were to be kept, guarded, and protected. He was also to avoid babblings and false *"science."*

1 Corinthians 16:11

"Let no man therefore despise him: but conduct him forth in peace, that he may come unto me: for I look for him with the brethren."

When Timothy would come to the genuine Christians at Corinth, no one was to despise him. They were to conduct him forth from them in peace that he might go back to Paul. Paul was looking for him with the other brethren who might come with him.

1 Corinthians 16:12

"As touching *our* brother Apollos, I greatly desired him to come unto you with the brethren: but his will was not at all to come at this time; but he will come when he shall have convenient time."

Paul greatly desired Apollos to go and visit the true Christians at Corinth but he didn't want to come to them at that particular time. Paul told them that Apollos would come to them when the time was convenient.

Verses On Apollos
- **Acts 18:24**
"And <u>a certain Jew named Apollos, born at Alexandria, an eloquent man, and mighty in the scriptures</u>, came to Ephesus."

Apollos, who was mighty in the Scriptures, came to Ephesus as he would some day go to Corinth.

- **1 Corinthians 1:12**
"Now this I say, that every one of you saith, I am of Paul; and I of Apollos; and I of Cephas; and I of Christ."

In the divisions that were in the Church at Corinth, Apollos was one of the leaders that some of the genuine Christians in Corinth followed.

- **1 Corinthians 3:5**
"Who then is Paul, and <u>who is Apollos</u>, but <u>ministers by whom ye believed</u>, even as the Lord gave to every man?"

Apollos led many at Corinth to trust the Lord Jesus Christ as their Saviour.

- **1 Corinthians 3:6**
"I have planted, Apollos watered; but God gave the increase."

Paul told the true Christians at Corinth that he planted the Gospel in Corinth, and Apollos came afterward and watered the Gospel seed, but God alone gave the increase and growth.

- **Titus 3:13**
"<u>Bring Zenas the lawyer and Apollos</u> on their journey diligently, that nothing be wanting unto them."

Paul wanted Zenos and Apollos to come to visit him. He also wanted Pastor Titus and his church at Crete to give him the needed funds for his journey, with nothing wanting.

1 Corinthians 16:13

"Watch ye, stand fast in the faith, quit you like men, be strong."

Paul concluded his letter to the genuine Christians at Corinth with four final commands:
1. **Watch**
2. **Stand fast**
3. **Quit you like men**
4. **Be strong**

Paul's first command for these true Christians was to "*watch.*" It is interesting to note that my name, "Waite," is connected to watching. The origin of that name goes back to those in Scotland and England where the Waites were watchmen on the walls.

Verses On Paul's Command #1: Watch

- **Psalms 127:1b**

". . . except the LORD keep the city, <u>the watchman waketh but in vain</u>."

If the Lord does not keep our cities as He kept those in Israel, the watchmen watch in vain.

- **Isaiah 21:6**

"For thus hath the Lord said unto me, Go, <u>set a watchman, let him declare what he seeth</u>."

Not only must the watchmen watch, but they must declare what they see. They must tell if the enemies are approaching. Pastors today should declare to their people what is going on, both in the churches, and in the world around them.

- **Isaiah 56:10-11**

"<u>His watchmen are blind: they are all ignorant, they are all dumb dogs, they cannot bark; sleeping, lying down, loving to slumber. Yea, they are greedy dogs which can never have enough</u>, and they are shepherds that cannot understand: they all look to their own way, every one for his gain, from his quarter."

Genuine Christians should not have blind, dumb, sleepy, or greedy watchmen in their churches.

- **Isaiah 62:6**

"<u>I have set watchmen upon thy walls, O Jerusalem, which shall never hold their peace day nor night</u>: ye that make mention of the LORD, keep not silence,"

Watchmen should never hold their peace day or night or keep silence.

- **Ezekiel 3:17**

"Son of man, <u>I have made thee a watchman unto the house of Israel</u>: therefore <u>hear the word</u> at my mouth, and <u>give them warning</u> from me."

We need pastors who are watchmen who hear God's warnings and tell them faithfully to their flocks.

- **Ezekiel 33:6**

"But <u>if the watchman see the sword come, and blow not the trumpet, and the people be not warned</u>; if the sword come, and take any person from among them, he is taken away in his iniquity; but <u>his blood will I require at the watchman's hand</u>."

When dangers arise and the watchmen do not warn, God will judge the watchmen for the evils that happen to the people. Pastors today must warn their people of the many religious and secular dangers around them.

1 Corinthians Preaching Verse-By-Verse

- **Matthew 24:42-43**

"<u>Watch therefore</u>: for ye know not what hour your Lord doth come."

Genuine Christians must be looking for the return of the Lord Jesus Christ. They must be watchful.

- **Matthew 25:13**

"<u>Watch therefore</u>, for ye know neither the day nor the hour wherein the Son of man cometh."

The Lord Jesus Christ's return for His true Christians is imminent. It may happen at any time.

- **Matthew 26:41**

"<u>Watch and pray, that ye enter not into temptation</u>: the spirit indeed is willing, but the flesh is weak."

Temptations and testings might come at any moment. Genuine Christians must be watchful for them and avoid them.

- **Ephesians 6:18**

"<u>Praying always</u> with all prayer and supplication in the Spirit, <u>and watching thereunto with all perseverance</u> and supplication for all saints;"

After true Christians pray, they should watch and be alert to God's answers to those prayers and continue with perseverance and continued prayer.

- **Colossians 4:2**

"Continue in prayer, and <u>watch in the same with thanksgiving</u>;"

After prayer, genuine Christians are to watch for the outcome.

- **1 Thessalonians 5:6**

"Therefore <u>let us not sleep</u>, as do others; <u>but let us watch</u> and be sober."

True Christians should not sleep, but keep watching.

- **2 Timothy 4:5**

"But <u>watch thou in all things</u>, endure afflictions, do the work of an evangelist, make full proof of thy ministry."

Genuine Christians should keep watching in all things.

- **1 Peter 4:7**

"But the end of all things is at hand: be ye therefore sober, and <u>watch unto prayer</u>."

Both watching and praying are needful.

Verses On Paul's Command #2: Stand Fast

- **Galatians 5:1**

"<u>Stand fast therefore in the liberty</u> wherewith Christ hath made us free, and be not entangled again with the yoke of bondage."

Genuine Christians are to stand fast in their liberty in Christ.
- **Philippians 1:27c**
"... <u>stand fast in</u> one spirit, with one mind striving together <u>for the faith of the gospel</u>;"

Our church has been standing fast for the doctrines of the faith of the Gospel of Christ.
- **Philippians 4:1**
"Therefore, my brethren dearly beloved and longed for, my joy and crown, so <u>stand fast in the Lord</u>, my dearly beloved."

Genuine Christians should stand fast and fixed in the Lord and His Words, without wavering.
- **1 Thessalonians 3:8**
"For now <u>we live, if ye stand fast in the Lord</u>."

Paul would live rejoicing if the Thessalonians would stand fast in the Lord without compromising.
- **2 Thessalonians 2:15**
"Therefore, brethren, <u>stand fast, and hold the traditions which ye have been taught</u>, whether by word, or our epistle."

Paul exhorts this church to stand fast and keep his teachings by his epistles or by his verbal messages to them. Too many once sound churches have not stood fast for Bible truths, but have drifted away from them.

Verses On Paul's Command #3: Quit You Like Men

That word, "*quit*," is an Old English word for "*equip yourselves.*" Every genuine Christian should do this to prepare for the battles that come upon them.
- **1 Samuel 4:9**
"<u>Be strong, and quit yourselves like men</u>, O ye Philistines, that ye be not servants unto the Hebrews, as they have been to you: quit yourselves like men, and fight."

This expression was used in the Old Testament here when the Philistines were told to equip themselves and not be servants to the Hebrews.

Verses On Paul's Command #4: Be Strong
- **Deuteronomy 11:8**
"Therefore shall ye <u>keep all the commandments which I command you this day, that ye may be strong</u>, and go in and possess the land, whither ye go to possess it;"

Keeping God's commandments, whether in the Old or New Testaments, makes people strong.

- **Deuteronomy 31:6**
"<u>Be strong and of a good courage</u>, fear not, nor be afraid of them: for the LORD thy God, he it is that doth go with thee; he will not fail thee, nor forsake thee."

God does not want His genuine Christians today to be weaklings in their faith in His Words and in the Lord Jesus Christ.

- **Deuteronomy 31:23**
"And he gave Joshua the son of Nun a charge, and said, <u>Be strong and of a good courage</u>: for thou shalt bring the children of Israel into the land which I sware unto them: and I will be with thee."

That was God's command to Joshua for victory against his Old Testament enemies.

- **Joshua 1:9**
"Have not I commanded thee? <u>Be strong and of a good courage; be not afraid, neither be thou dismayed</u>: for the LORD thy God is with thee whithersoever thou goest."

True Christians today must be strong with the strength that God can give them. They should not be weaklings against God's enemies and theirs.

- **Joshua 10:25**
"And Joshua said unto them, Fear not, nor be dismayed, <u>be strong and of good courage</u>: for thus shall the LORD do to all your enemies against whom ye fight."

This is another command by God Himself for Joshua to be strong for Him and against his many enemies.

- **1 Chronicles 28:20**
"And David said to Solomon his son, <u>Be strong and of good courage, and do it</u>: fear not, nor be dismayed: for the LORD God, even my God, will be with thee; he will not fail thee, nor forsake thee, until thou hast finished all the work for the service of the house of the LORD."

God told David to be strong and so that is what He commanded of Him. He was not to be discouraged either.

- **2 Chronicles 32:7**
"<u>Be strong and courageous, be not afraid nor dismayed</u> for the king of Assyria, nor for all the multitude that is with him: for there be more with us than with him:"

Israel was to be strong against the powerful king of Assyria. God would help them.

- **Daniel 11:32**
"And such as do wickedly against the covenant shall he corrupt by flatteries: but <u>the people that do know their God shall be strong, and do exploits</u>."

Even today, the genuine Christians who know and love the Lord

Jesus Christ will be able to be strong in Him and do wonderful things for His glory.
- **Ephesians 6:10**
"Finally, my brethren, <u>be strong in the Lord, and in the power of his might</u>."

The true Christians' power is not in themselves, but in the power of the Lord Jesus Christ, their Saviour.
- **2 Timothy 2:1**
"Thou therefore, my son, be strong in the grace that is in Christ Jesus."

Pastor Timothy was to be strong in the grace that is in the Lord Jesus Christ.

1 Corinthians 16:14
"Let all your things be done with charity."

Charity is love in action. All these four commands that Paul urged upon the genuine Christians at Corinth were to be undertaken with action love of charity. They were to watch with charity; they were to stand fast with charity; they were to quit themselves like men with charity; and they were to be strong with charity. All four of Paul's commands were to be done with charity's love.

1 Corinthians 16:15
"I beseech you, brethren, (ye know the house of Stephanas, that it is the firstfruits of Achaia, and that they have addicted themselves to the ministry of the saints,)"

These "*brethren*" are genuine Christian men and women who have truly trusted the Lord Jesus Christ as their Saviour and Lord. In the parenthesis, Paul reminded them about the house of Stephanas. They were some of the early ones who became true Christians from the area of Achaia. These are those who addicted themselves to the ministry of the true Christians.

The use of the word, "*addicted*," is not used as we have heard it used in our days with those who are addicted to all different kinds of illegal and dangerous drugs. This use of that word deals with those who were strongly and continuously helping those who had needs.

1 Corinthians 16:16

"That ye submit yourselves unto such, and to every one that helpeth with *us*, and laboureth."

Those genuine Christians at Corinth were to submit themselves to those who were ministering to those who had various needs.

Verses On Submission
- **Ephesians 5:22**

"Wives, submit yourselves unto your own husbands, as unto the Lord."

The Greek Word for "*submit*" is a military term. It means to arrange troop divisions in a military fashion, under the command of a leader. In non-military use, it was a voluntary attitude. It is a voluntary attitude of giving in, cooperating, assuming responsibility and caring a burden.

- **Colossians 3:18**

"Wives, submit yourselves unto your own husbands, as it is fit in the Lord."

This verse uses the same words as in Ephesians 5:22. Paul was writing both the book of Ephesians and the book of Colossians from a Roman prison. Sad to say, there are all too many true Christian women who are not obeying the Words of God in this area of submission.

- **Hebrews 13:17**

"Obey them that have the rule over you, and submit yourselves: for they watch for your souls, as they that must give account, that they may do it with joy, and not with grief: for that is unprofitable for you."

This is no doubt referring to genuine Christians obedience to the Words of God that the pastors are preaching and teaching them.

- **James 4:7**

"Submit yourselves therefore to God. Resist the devil, and he will flee from you."

All true Christians should submit themselves to God as clearly spelled out in His Words.

- **1 Peter 2:13**

"Submit yourselves to every ordinance of man for the Lord's sake: whether it be to the king, as supreme;"

There is one qualification on this submission to the ordinances of men. If the ordinance is contrary to God's Words, that ordinance should not be obeyed. As stated in Acts 5:29: "*We ought to obey God rather than men.*" In other words, if it's a lawful ordinance, not contrary to God's Words, submit.

- **1 Peter 5:5**
"Likewise, ye younger, submit yourselves unto the elder. Yea, all of you be subject one to another, and be clothed with humility: for God resisteth the proud, and giveth grace to the humble."

Those who are younger should submit to the elder as long as there is no contradiction to the Words of God.

1 Corinthians 16:17

"I am glad of the coming of Stephanas and Fortunatus and Achaicus: for that which was lacking on your part they have supplied."

These three godly men, who were apparently Bible teachers, had come to the city of Corinth. They helped Paul in things that the church at Corinth was not able to do for Paul.

1 Corinthians 16:18

"For they have refreshed my spirit and yours: therefore acknowledge ye them that are such."

These three Christian leaders, not only helped the Corinthian church, but they also refreshed Paul's spirit and theirs. Paul encouraged the genuine Christians to acknowledge these men as fine helpers of the church.

1 Corinthians 16:19

"The churches of Asia salute you. Aquila and Priscilla salute you much in the Lord, with the church that is in their house."

The churches in Asia Minor sent greetings to the church at Corinth. In addition to those churches, Aquila and Priscilla also greeted them much in the Lord in addition to the church that was in their house. Here was a house church in the days of the New Testament. Today, some people disagree with house churches instead of large buildings that house people. Not only did Aquila and Priscilla have a church in their house, but there were many other house churches in the New Testament. The government might soon shut down church buildings. When this happens, genuine Christians might have to meet in homes or other places like in Communist China today.

Our Bible For Today Baptist Church is in our house. We thank God that through modern techniques, our sermons have been sent to the entire world through our BibleForToday.Org Internet ministry. Last month, as this is being written, here are some of the written statistics given to us by SermonAudio.com that sends out our sermons.

Our Church's Sermon Outreach For The Past Month
1. Downloads of our sermons were 1,934 for the month and a total of 900,309 from the beginning to this date.
2. Downloads of our sermons from mobile phones were 1,050 for the month and a total of 78,233 from the beginning to this date.
3. Our listening audience covered 50 states and 53 countries.
4. SermonAudio.com are currently broadcasting a total of 4,522 sermons for our church 24-hours a day, 7 days a week that carries our sermons, but its ministry goes out by way of the Internet all around the world.

Verses On Churches Meeting In Houses
- Acts 2:46

"And they, continuing daily with one accord in the temple, and breaking bread from house to house, did eat their meat with gladness and singleness of heart,"
Genuine Christians broke the bread of the Lord's Supper and had fellowship house to house.
- Acts 5:42

"And daily in the temple, and in every house, they ceased not to teach and preach Jesus Christ."
These true Christians met in houses and heard the Word of God preached and taught.
- Acts 12:12

"And when he had considered the thing, he came to the house of Mary the mother of John, whose surname was Mark; where many were gathered together praying."
These Christians were assembled in a house and were praying.
- Acts 20:20

"And how I kept back nothing that was profitable unto you, but have shewed you, and have taught you publickly, and from house to house,"
Paul met with genuine Christians and taught them from house to house.
- Romans 16:5

"Likewise greet the church that is in their house. Salute my wellbeloved Epaenetus, who is the firstfruits of Achaia unto Christ."

Here's another reference to a church in a house.
- **1 Corinthians 16:19**
"The churches of Asia salute you. <u>Aquila and Priscilla</u> salute you much in the Lord, <u>with the church that is in their house</u>."
Here is clearly another church meeting in the house of Aquila and Priscilla.
- **Colossians 4:15**
"Salute the brethren which are in Laodicea, and Nymphas, and the church which is in his house."
- **Philemon 1:2**
"And to our beloved Apphia, and Archippus our fellowsoldier, <u>and to the church in thy house</u>:"
Here is another clear reference to the fact that the early churches had churches that met in houses. This is a Biblical location for churches in our days as well.

1 Corinthians 16:20

"All the brethren greet you. Greet ye one another with an holy kiss."

As I said before, "*the brethren*" is a reference to all the genuine men and women who were genuine Christians with Paul. They were to "*Greet one another with an holy kiss*." The Greek Word for "*kiss*" is PHILEMA. It is made up of PHI from PHILOS or love or friendship and the suffix is important. It is -MA which means the result of something. As a result of the friendship of these true Christians, they were to greet them with a greeting of love. Whether it is a friendly smile and handshake, or perhaps a kiss on the cheek as was the custom in Bible times. They were to be kind and charitable to one another.

Verses On The Holy Kiss
- Romans 16:16
"<u>Salute one another with an holy kiss</u>. The churches of Christ salute you."
- **2 Corinthians 13:12**
"<u>Greet one another with an holy kiss</u>."
- **1 Thessalonians 5:26**
"<u>Greet all the brethren with an holy kiss</u>."

You'll notice that in all four of these verses, this greeting must be "*holy*" and not unholy or sexual as some kisses are today.

1 Corinthians 16:21

"The salutation of *me* Paul with mine own hand."

Paul wanted to inform the genuine Christians at Corinth that he wrote this letter with his own hand. He was the author and he did not dictate it for some scribe to write it for him. As God the Holy Spirit led Paul, he wrote down every Word in the Greek language.

1 Corinthians 16:22

"If any man love not the Lord Jesus Christ, let him be Anathema Maranatha."

This is a serious verse. "*If any man love not the Lord Jesus Christ.*" It means that any man or woman who does not love the Lord Jesus Christ is accursed (Anathema) and will spend all eternity in Hell's Lake of Fire. How does a non-Christian genuinely love the Lord Jesus Christ?

There are at least three steps for those who are not genuine Christians to make this come to pass in their lives: (1) They must genuinely believe that they are sinners in the eyes of God. (2) They must genuinely believe that the Lord Jesus Christ took their sins in His own Body on the cross and paid for all their sins; and (3) They must genuinely believe in and genuinely trust the Lord Jesus Christ as their Saviour. If these three conditions are not genuinely met, all of these non-Christians are destined, when they die, to be cast into the Hell's Lake of Fire for all eternity to come.

- **1 Peter 1:8**
"Whom having not seen, ye love; in whom, though now ye see him not, yet believing, ye rejoice with joy unspeakable and full of glory:"

True Christians are able to love the Lord Jesus Christ Who has saved them by His shed blood on the cross even though they have never seen Him. Truly believing in Him and trusting Him for everlasting life brings them rejoicing and unspeakable joy.

1 Corinthians 16:23

"The grace of our Lord Jesus Christ *be* with you."

In the second last verse of this letter, Paul reminds these genuine Christians at Corinth of God's grace–getting something they do not deserve such as salvation, forgiveness of sins, and everlasting life in Heaven. The gifts of God's grace can be received by putting into genuine ACTION the three things mentioned in verse 22 above. Here are two verses where Paul explains to the Ephesians what they and all non-Christians receive by God's grace if they will genuinely trust the Lord Jesus Christ as their Saviour.

- **Ephesians 2:8-9**
"For by grace are ye saved through faith; and that not of yourselves: it is the gift of God: Not of works, lest any man should boast."

1 Corinthians 16:24

"My love *be* with you all in Christ Jesus. Amen."

At the very end of this letter to the true Christians at Corinth, he wants them to know that he wants his love to be in the Lord Jesus Christ.

He ends his long letter with the Word, "*Amen.*" It's originally a Hebrew Word which means "*I believe.*" It's probably the most universal word in every language of the world. It's in English, in French, in German, In Spanish, in Swahili, in Italian, and in most, if not all, of the languages in the entire world. As I said, it means "*I believe what is being spoken.*" May the Words that Paul spoke to these Corinthians be affirmed by all who read them with a solemn and truthful AMEN! Will YOU be one of these individuals? I hope so!

Index Of Words And Phrases

1 Corinthians Chapter One............................ iv
A Verse On Comfort 339
Aaron's Sins While Moses Was On Mount Sinai........... 243
Acknowledgments.................................. ii, iv
ADIKIA.. 323
ADOKIMOS... 234
Adulterers........................ 151, 160, 186, 206, 219
AGORAZO 178
ALETHEIA.. 325
AMERIMNOS 183
ANAKRINO 217
ANEGKLETOS.. 12
ARESKO... 184
ARSENOKOITES 152
Assembly–the call when all must be in place 341
Background Of The Book................................ 1
Be Perfectly Joined Together In The Same Mind And Judgment 5
Be strong 44, 116, 401, 404-406
BFT #4174 i
BLASPHEMEO 109
BROCHOS 186
CHARIS 6
Charity Beareth All Things............................ 326
Charity Believeh All Things 328
Charity Does Not Behave Itself Unseemly................ 321
Charity Does Not Rejoice In Iniquity
 323
Charity Does Not Seek Her Own....................... 321
Charity Endureth All Things 329
Charity Is Kind..................................... 319
Charity Is Longsuffering.............................. 318
Charity Is Not Easily Provoked 322
Charity Is Not Puffed Up 320
Charity Thinketh No Evil 322
Charity Vaunteth Not Itself 192, 195, 318, 319
CHRESTEUOMAI.................................... 319
Come together again................................ 170
Consent... 170
Covetous.................... 141, 152, 197, 200, 250, 253
Date Of 1 Corinthians 1
Dispensations 138

DOULAGOGEO	233
DOULOS	177, 178
Drunkards	152
Effeminate	151
EGKRATEIA	234
EIRENE	6
ERIS	17
EXOUSIAZO	156, 170
Extortioners.	141, 152
First Call–the call to assemble around the flag	341
five ministries of the Holy Spirit.	291
For a time.	170, 214
Foreword	iii, iv
Fornicators	123, 139, 141, 151, 244
GRAPHO	49, 88, 381
growth	66, 67, 72, 74, 191, 401
GUMNETEUO	107
HAGIAZO	4, 102
HAPTOMAI.	168
HEAVEN	3, 8-11, 16, 23, 25, 43, 44, 48, 50-52, 83, 90, 93, 100, 115, 130, 145-148, 151, 155, 158, 162, 165, 196, 197, 202, 203, 213, 227, 240, 253, 257, 258, 261, 272, 283, 284, 313, 315, 327, 329, 332, 335, 353, 361, 362, 366, 370-377, 380, 382-386, 390, 393, 395-397, 411, 446
How Many Stars Are There?	380
HUPOMENO.	329
HUPOPIAZO.	233
Idolaters.	141, 143, 151, 200, 201, 243, 253, 292
Israel Gave 10% To The Lord And His Servants.	225
It brought comfort	338
It brought edification	338
It brought exhortation	338
It must be for a proper purpose	170
It must be only for a short time	170
It must be resumed once again.	170
It must be with consent of both mates	170
It must prevent Satan's temptations for being apart	170
KAKIA	134
KALOS	167
KATARGEO.	35, 330
KERUGMA	29
KOLLAO	161
KOPIAO.	108
KOSMOS	54

LOGIZOMAI 322
MALAKOS 151
Material On Torture Methods Used In The Past........... 316
MEANING OF THE GREEK WORD, "ARSENOKOITES" .. 151
MEANING OF THE GREEK WORD, "BLASPHEMEO" 109
MEANING OF THE GREEK WORD, "CHRESTEUOMAI".. 319
MEANING OF THE GREEK WORD, "DOULAGOGEO".... 233
MEANING OF THE GREEK WORD, "MAKROTHUMEO" . 318
MEANING OF THE GREEK WORD, "PERIKATHAMA" ... 109
MEANING OF THE GREEK WORD, "PERPEREUOMAI".. 320
MERIMNAO 183, 185
Mess Call–the call to eat 341
New Testament Verses On Temples 163
OIKODOMEO 191
OIKONOMOS 95
Old Testament Verses On Temples 162
Other Verses On Wives To Be 269
Our Church's Sermon Outreach For The Past Month 409
PARISTEMI....................................... 207
PAROXUNO 321, 322
Pastor D. A. Waite, Th.D., Ph.D .... i, iii, 446
Patricia Canter...................................... iii
Paul Was Born Free 229
Paul's conversion to Christ 3
PERIKATHAMA 109
PERPEREUOMAI.................................. 320
PHUSIOO............................. 102, 115, 191, 320
PISTEUO 328
PORNEIA........................... 121, 122, 139, 140, 168
PROSKOMA....................................... 210
PSUCHIKOS 58
PUROO... 172
Quit You Like Men 401, 404
Rapture....... 8-13, 16, 36, 59, 75, 84, 139, 158, 159, 213, 232, 283, 284, 294, 301, 309, 329, 369, 371, 372, 384, 390
Revilers.. 152
SARKIKOS... 66
SCHEMA 182
sign gift.................... 296-298, 308, 309, 314, 330, 337-340, 345-347, 349-353, 358
SKANDALON 30
Some Background Verses From Acts 18.................... 2
Speak The Same Things Without Divisions................ 14
Stand fast 401, 403, 404, 406
Subject To Their Husbands 269

Table of Contents iv
Taps–the call at bedtime 341
temporary .. 8, 195, 270, 291-298, 308-311, 314, 315, 329-333, 335, 337-340, 344-347, 349-353, 355-358
That Satan tempt you not 170
That Which Is Perfect 308, 309, 330, 331, 338
That Which Is Perfect Is Come 308, 309, 330, 331
That ye may give yourselves 170
The Betrayal Of Judas Before The Lord's Supper 279
The dispensation of conscience 139
The dispensation of grace 139, 176
The dispensation of human government 139
The dispensation of innocence 138
The dispensation of law 139
The dispensation of promise 139
The dispensation of the millennial kingdom of Christ 139
The first phase of His coming 8
The Help Of The Lord Jesus Christ 35, 398
THE MEANING OF THE GREEK WORD, ... 4, 6, 12, 17, 29, 30, 35, 42, 49, 54, 58, 66, 84, 94, 95, 102, 105, 107, 108, 110, 115, 121, 134, 140, 151, 156, 160, 161, 167, 168, 170, 172, 178, 179, 182-184, 186, 191, 207, 210, 217, 233, 234, 277, 285, 319-323, 325, 326, 328-330
THE MEANING OF THE GREEK WORD, CHARIS 6
THE MEANING OF THE GREEK WORD, EIRENE 6
THE MEANING OF THE GREEK WORD, "ADIKIA" 323
THE MEANING OF THE GREEK WORD, "ADOKIMOS" .. 234
THE MEANING OF THE GREEK WORD, "AGORAZO" ... 178
THE MEANING OF THE GREEK WORD, "AMERIMNOS" 183
THE MEANING OF THE GREEK WORD, "ANAKRINO" .. 217
THE MEANING OF THE GREEK WORD, "ARESKO" 184
THE MEANING OF THE GREEK WORD, "BROCHOS" ... 186
THE MEANING OF THE GREEK WORD, "DOULOS" 178
THE MEANING OF THE GREEK WORD, "EGKRATEIA" . 234
THE MEANING OF THE GREEK WORD, "EXOUSIAZO" . 156, 170
THE MEANING OF THE GREEK WORD, "GRAPHO" 49
THE MEANING OF THE GREEK WORD, "GUMNETEUO" 107
THE MEANING OF THE GREEK WORD, "HAIRESIS" 277
THE MEANING OF THE GREEK WORD, "HAPTOMAI" .. 168
THE MEANING OF THE GREEK WORD, "HUPERETES" .. 94
THE MEANING OF THE GREEK WORD, "HUPOPIAZO" . 233
THE MEANING OF THE GREEK WORD, "KAKIA" 134
THE MEANING OF THE GREEK WORD, "KAKOS" 323
THE MEANING OF THE GREEK WORD, "KALOS" 167

THE MEANING OF THE GREEK WORD, "KATARGEO" . . 330
THE MEANING OF THE GREEK WORD, "KOLLAO" 160
THE MEANING OF THE GREEK WORD, "KOPIAO". 108
THE MEANING OF THE GREEK WORD, "KOSMOS". 54
THE MEANING OF THE GREEK WORD, "LOGIZOMAI". . 322
THE MEANING OF THE GREEK WORD, "MALAKOS". . . . 151
THE MEANING OF THE GREEK WORD, "MERIMNAO". . 183
THE MEANING OF THE GREEK WORD, "OIKODOMEO". 191
THE MEANING OF THE GREEK WORD, "OIKONOMOS". . 95
THE MEANING OF THE GREEK WORD, "PAROXUNO". 321, 322
THE MEANING OF THE GREEK WORD, "PERIPSEMA". . 110
THE MEANING OF THE GREEK WORD, "PHTHEIRO". . . . 84
THE MEANING OF THE GREEK WORD, "PHUSIOO" 102, 115, 191, 320
THE MEANING OF THE GREEK WORD, "PORNEIA" 121, 140, 168
THE MEANING OF THE GREEK WORD, "PROSKOMA". . 210
THE MEANING OF THE GREEK WORD, "PSUCHIKOS". . . 58
THE MEANING OF THE GREEK WORD, "PUROO" 172
THE MEANING OF THE GREEK WORD, "SARKIKOS" 66
THE MEANING OF THE GREEK WORD, "SCHEMA". 182
THE MEANING OF THE GREEK WORD, "THEATRON" . . 105
THE MEANING OF THE GREEK WORD, "TIME" 179
THE MEANING OF THE GREEK WORD, "ZELOO". 319
THE MEANING OF THE GREEK WORD, "ZETEO". 321
The Meaning Of Works Tested By Fire 81
THE ORDER FOR THOSE ENTERING HEAVEN. 372
the planting 72
The second phase of His Coming 8
The Seven Dispensations In The Bible 138
The Sinful And Pagan Practices At Corinth. 1
The temporary sign gift of apostles. 308
The temporary sign gift of discerning of spirits 297
The temporary sign gift of faith. 296, 314
The temporary sign gift of governments 308
The temporary sign gift of healing 297, 309
The temporary sign gift of healings 308
The temporary sign gift of helps 308
The temporary sign gift of interpretation of tongues 298
The temporary sign gift of knowledge 296, 314
The temporary sign gift of miracles 297, 308
The temporary sign gift of prophecy 297, 314
The temporary sign gift of prophets 308
The temporary sign gift of teachers 308

The temporary sign gift of tongues 298, 308, 314, 339, 340, 346, 349, 358
The temporary sign gift of wisdom 296
The Three Most Wicked Ancient Cities 1
The Two Phases Of Christ's Second Coming. 8
the watering. 72, 74
The Wrong Choice of Matthias As An Apostle 216
THEATRON 105
Their misinterpretation of "baptized" 300
Their Misinterpretation of "body" 301
Their misinterpretation of "Spirit" 300
They have divisions 68
They have envying 68
They have strife...................................... 68
They walk as men, as natural, unsaved people............ 68
Thieves.. 152, 230
Three Cases Of Christians' Incest Without Penalty 124
THREE ESSENTIALS TO RECEIVE GOD'S SALVATION .. 362
TIME 1, 3, 8, 9, 12, 18, 19, 27, 36-38, 41, 47, 54, 56, 66, 67, 69, 71, 80, 91, 101, 104, 105, 107, 112, 118, 120, 123-125, 138, 139, 149, 159, 163, 170, 176, 179-181, 184, 188, 193, 201, 210, 214, 216, 217, 219, 221, 224, 249, 254, 269, 280, 282, 290, 298, 301, 327, 330-334, 336, 340, 342-345, 351, 364-366, 372, 394, 395, 400, 403
To Jews, Paul Was As A Jew......................... 229
To The Colors–the call as the flag was raised 341
To Those Who Are Weak, Paul Was As Weak. 230
To Those Without Law, Paul Was As Without Law 230
TROMOS 42
Verse On The Need For Spiritual Growth 67
Verse On Unmoveable 388
Verses About Paul: 229
Verses Calling Paul An Apostle....................... 215
Verses In Iniquity And Wickedness 324
Verses In The New Testament On Marriage Until Death ... 188
Verses on Adding Or Removing God's Words 294
Verses On Adversaries 397
Verses On Angels 147
Verses On Apollos................................. 18, 401
Verses On Babes 66
Verses On Baptism 267
Verses On Bearing And Enduring...................... 327
Verses On Begotten 112
Verses On Being Bought Or Redeemed By Christ 163

1 Corinthians Preaching Verse-By-Verse 419

Verses On Blameless.................................. 12
Verses On Boasting................................... 196
Verses On Body...................................... 157
Verses On Calling 33
Verses On Caring..................................... 305
Verses On Carnal Or Fleshly 65
Verses On Charity or Love 195
Verses On Chastening................................. 287
Verses On Christ Being Raised From The Dead 364
Verses On Christ Knowing His Genuine Christians 198
Verses On Christ Obeying The Father While On Earth 269
Verses On Christian Spiritual Babies 67
Verses On Churches Meeting In Houses 409
Verses On Commending.............................. 208
Verses On Confusion................................. 354
Verses On Conscience........................... 205, 258
Verses On Contention................................. 17
Verses On Crucifixion................................. 41
Verses On Defilement................................. 85
Verses On Discerning 59
Verses On Divisions 70
Verses On Divisons 276
Verses On Doors 395
Verses On Ensamples Or Examples 247
Verses On Envy 68
Verses On Evil 125, 377
Verses On Evil Associations........................... 377
Verses On Excellency 39
Verses On Expedient............................ 155, 257
Verses On Faithfulness........................... 13, 95
Verses On Fight...................................... 343
Verses On Follow........................... 113, 265, 337
Verses On Foolishness 59
Verses On Fornication 121, 140, 156
Verses On Genuine Christians Owned By God 90
Verses On Glass Or Mirror............................ 334
Verses On Glorify 164
Verses On Glorifying God............................. 261
Verses On Glory............................ 36, 48, 89, 103
Verses on Glory And Glorying.......................... 89
Verses On God Being Jealous For His Own............... 256
Verses On God's Creation............................. 202
Verses On God's Leading Cloud 237
Verses On Helping The Poor And Those In Need.......... 315
Verses On High And Low Estimation 149

Verses On Idols	198, 292
Verses On If The Lord Wills	394
Verses On Israel's Fornication Practices	244
Verses On Judging	60, 146
Verses On Judgment	99
Verses On Justification	154
Verses On Knowledge	192
Verses On Labor	108
Verses On Leaven	129
Verses On Liberty	209
Verses On Love	335
Verses On Lust	124
Verses On Malice	134, 348
Verses On Many Of Israel Who Were Disobedient	242
Verses On Marriage	219
Verses On Married Love	160
Verses On Mighty Faith	296
Verses On Ministers	71
Verses On Natural	58
Verses On Offence	262
Verses On Offences	212
Verses On Old Testament Murmuring	246
Verses On Opening The Red Sea	238
Verses On Passover	131
Verses On Paul Seeing The Lord Jesus Christ	216
Verses On Paul's Command #2: Stand Fast	403
Verses On Paul's Command #3:	404
Verses On Paul's Command #4: Be Strong	404
Verses On Paul's Persecution Of Christians	366
Verses On Perfect	332
Verses On Power	25, 43, 115
Verses On Preaching	27, 225
Verses On Prepared Things	50
Verses On Puff Up	192
Verses On Puffed Up	102
Verses On Putting Way	143
Verses On Remembrance	114
Verses On Rest And Comfort	353
Verses On Revealed	52
Verses On Rewards	75
Verses On Saints	389
Verses On Sanctification	4, 153
Verses On Satan	128
Verses On Signs	29
Verses On Sincerity	135

1 Corinthians Preaching Verse-By-Verse 421

Verses On Sowing And Reaping 72
Verses On Speech 40
Verses On Spirit...................................... 54
Verses On Spiritual................................... 60
Verses On Stedfast 387
Verses On Stewards 93
Verses On Stumblingblock............................ 209
Verses On Submission 407
Verses On Take Heed 249
Verses On The Apostles Working 220
Verses On The Baptism By The Holy Spirit.............. 300
Verses On The Church Gathered Together 127
Verses On The Cross of Christ.......................... 22
Verses On The Death Of Christ 210
Verses On The First Day Of The Week 391
Verses On The Five Crowns......................... 75, 82
Verses On The Five Crowns Of Rewards 82
Verses On The Gospel................................ 378
Verses On The Heart.................................. 51
Verses On The Holy Kiss 410
Verses On The Mind 61
Verses On The Rod 117
Verses On The Second Coming Of Christ 9
Verses On The Water Out Of The Rock 240
Verses On The Work Of The Holy Spirit 65
Verses On Things Being Manifested 80
Verses On Thoughts 88
Verses On Timothy 399
Verses On True Christians Being Soldiers For Christ....... 221
Verses On Trumpets In The Old Testament 341
Verses On Truth 136
Verses On Two Other Crowns 232
Verses On Two Phases Of Christ's Coming 283
Verses On Unjust.................................... 145
Verses On Various Headships 267
Verses On Warning.................................. 110
Verses On Wash..................................... 153
Verses On Watering By Preaching God's Words............ 72
Verses On Wickedness 135
Verses On Wisdom 23, 32, 45
Verses On Wise And Wisdom 86
Verses On Words.................................... 56
Verses On "For You" Or "For Us" 132
Verses Where Angels Spoke........................... 312
Verses Where Sin Brought Immediate Physical Death 286

Watch 111, 220, 358, 377, 401-403, 406, 407
Website: www.BibleForToday.org i
What Fire Does To Gold, Silver, And Precious Stones 81
What Fire Does To Wood, Hay, And Stubble 81
What Gold, Silver, And Precious Stones Mean. 81
What To Do When Heresies Come In 278
What Wood, Hay, And Stubble Mean 81
Why Paul Wrote This Letter 2
ZELOO 319
ZETEO 181, 321

About The Author

The author of this book, Dr. D. A. Waite, received a B.A. (Bachelor of Arts) in classical Greek and Latin from the University of Michigan in 1948, a Th.M. (Master of Theology), with high honors, in New Testament Greek Literature and Exegesis from Dallas Theological Seminary in 1952, an M.A. (Master of Arts) in Speech from Southern Methodist University in 1953, a Th.D. (Doctor of Theology), with honors, in Bible Exposition from Dallas Theological Seminary in 1955, and a Ph.D. in Speech from Purdue University in 1961. He held both New Jersey and Pennsylvania teacher certificates in Greek and Language Arts.

He has been a teacher in the areas of Greek, Hebrew, Bible, Speech, and English for over thirty-five years in ten schools, including one junior high, one senior high, four Bible institutes, two colleges, two universities, and one seminary. He served his country as a Navy Chaplain for five years on active duty; pastored three churches; was Chairman and Director of the Radio and Audio-Film Commission of the American Council of Christian Churches; since 1969, has been Founder, President, and Director of THE BIBLE FOR TODAY; since 1978, has been Founder and President of the DEAN BURGON SOCIETY; has produced over 700 other studies, books, cassettes, VHS's, CD's, or VCR's on various topics; and is heard IN DEFENSE OF TRADITIONAL BIBLE TEXTS and verse-by-verse preaching, by streaming on the Internet at BibleForToday.org, 24/7/365 on the BROWN BOX.

Dr. and Mrs. Waite have been married since 1948; they have four sons, one daughter, and, at present, eight grandchildren, and seventeen great-grandchildren. Since October 4, 1998, he has been the Pastor of the Bible For Today Baptist Church in Collingswood, New Jersey. His sermons are heard, all over the world on the Internet 24 hours a day and 365 days a year over www.BibleForToday.org on the BROWN BOX.

Order Blank (p. 1)

Name:_____
Address:_____
City & State:_____Zip:_____
*Credit Card #:*_____*Expires:*_____

Verse by Verse Preaching Books By Dr. D. A. Waite

[ ] Send 1 Corinthians–Preaching Verse By Verse By Dr. D. A. Waite (447 pages ($25.00 + $10.00 S&H) fully indexed.

[ ] Send Titus–Preaching Verse By Verse By Pastor D. A. Waite, (142 pages ($15.00 + $7.00 S&H) fully indexed

[ ] Send James–Preaching Verse By Verse By Pastor D. A. Waite, (218 pages (16.00 + $7.00 S&H) fully indexed.

[ ] Send *1,2, & 3 John–Preaching Verse By Verse* By Pastor D. A. Waite, 202 pages ($14.00 + $7.00 S&H) fully indexed.

[ ] Send *2 Peter & Jude–Preaching Verse By Verse* By Pastor D. A. Waite, 237 pages ($16.00 +$7.00 S&H) fully indexed.

[ ] Send *1 & 2 Thessalonians–Preaching Verse By Verse* By Pastor D. A. Waite, 360 pages ($20.00 + $8.00 S&H) fully indexed.

[ ] Send *Hebrews–Preaching Verse by Verse*, By Pastor D. A. Waite, 616 pages ($34.00 +$10.00 S&H) fully indexed.

[ ] Send *Revelation–Preaching Verse by Verse*, By Pastor D. A. Waite, 1032 pages ($55.00 + $10.00 S&H) fully indexed.

[ ] Send *1 Timothy--Preaching Verse by Verse*, by Pastor D. A. Waite, 288 pages, hardback ($18+$7 S&H) fully indexed.

[ ] Send *2 Timothy--Preaching Verse by Verse*, by Pastor D. A. Waite, 250 pages, hardback ($16+$7 S&H) fully indexed.

Send or Call Orders to:
THE BIBLE FOR TODAY
900 Park Ave., Collingswood, NJ 08108
Phone: 856-854-4452; FAX:--2464; Orders: 1-800 JOHN 10:9
E-Mail Orders: BFT@BibleForToday.org; Credit Cards OK

Order Blank (p. 2)

Name:_____
Address:_____
City & State:_____Zip:_____
Credit Card #:_____Expires:_____

Other Books By Dr. D. A. Waite

[ ] Send *Romans--Preaching Verse by Verse* by Pastor D. A. Waite 736 pp. Hardback ($35+$8 S&H) fully indexed
[ ] Send *Colossians & Philemon--Preaching Verse by Verse* by Pastor D. A. Waite ($16+$7 S&H) hardback, 240 pages.
[ ] Send *Philippians--Preaching Verse by Verse* by Pastor D A. Waite ($14+$7 S&H) hardback, 176 pages. fully indexed.
[ ] Send *Fundamentalist Deception on Bible Preservation* by Dr. D. A. Waite, ($8+$4 S&H), paperback, fully indexed
[ ] Send *Fundamentalist MIS-INFORMATION on Bible Versions* by Dr. Waite ($7+$4 S&H) perfect bound, 136 pages
[ ] Send *Fundamentalist Distortions on Bible Versions* by Dr. Waite ($6+$3 S&H) A perfect bound book, 80 pages
[ ] Send *Fuzzy Facts From Fundamentalists* by Dr. D. A. Waite ($8.00 + $4.00) printed booklet
[ ] Send *Foes of the King James Bible Refuted* by DAW ($10 +$4 S&H) A perfect bound book, 164 pages in length.
[ ] Send *Central Seminary Refuted on Bible Versions* by Dr. Waite ($10+$4 S&H) A perfect bound book, 184 pages
[ ] Send *The Case for the King James Bible* by DAW ($7 +$3 S&H) A perfect bound book, 112 pages in length.
[ ] Send *Theological Heresies of Westcott and Hort* by Dr. D. A. Waite, ($7+$3 S&H) A printed booklet.
[ ] Send *Westcott's Denial of Resurrection*, Dr. Waite ($4+$3)
[ ] Send *Four Reasons for Defending KJB* by DAW ($3+$3)

Send or Call Orders to:
THE BIBLE FOR TODAY
900 Park Ave., Collingswood, NJ 08108
Phone: 856-854-4452; FAX:--2464; Orders: 1-800 JOHN 10:9
E-Mail Orders: BFT@BibleForToday.org; Credit Cards OK

Order Blank (p. 3)

Name:_____
Address:_____
City & State:_____ Zip:_____
Credit Card #:_____ Expires:_____

[ ] Send *Galatians--Preaching Verse By Verse* by Pastor D. A. Waite ($15+$7 S&H) hardback, 216 pages. fully indexed.
[ ] Send *1 Peter–Preaching Verse By Verse* by Pastor D. A. Waite ($15.00 + $7.00 S&H) hardback, 176 pages. fully indexed.
[ ] Send *Ephesians--Preaching Verse by Verse* by Pastor D. A. Waite ($15+$7 S&H) hardback, 224 pages. fully indexed.
[ ] Send *BJU's Errors on Bible Preservation* by Dr. D. A. Waite, 110 pages, paperback ($8+$4 S&H) fully indexed
[ ] Send *A Critical Answer to God's Word Preserved* by Pastor D. A. Waite, 192 pp. perfect bound ($11.00+$4.00 S&H)
[ ] Send *Defending the King James Bible* by DAW ($12+$5 S&H) A hardback book, indexed with study questions.
[ ] Send *Holes in the Holman Christian Standard Bible* by Dr. Waite ($3+$2 S&H) A printed booklet, 40 pages
[ ] Send *Contemporary Eng. Version Exposed*, DAW ($3+$2)
[ ] Send *NIV Inclusive Language Exposed* by DAW ($5+$3)
[ ] Send *26 Hours of KJB Seminar* (4 videos*)* by DAW($50.00*)*
[ ] Send *Making Marriage Melodious* by Pastor D. A. Waite ($7+$4 S&H), perfect bound, 112 pages.
[ ] Send *Burgon's Warnings on Revision* by DAW ($7+$4 S&H) A perfect bound book, 120 pages in length.
[ ] Send *The Superior Foundation of the KJB* By Dr. D. A. Waite ($10.00 + $7.00 S&H)
[ ] Send *Biblical Separation–1,896 Bible Verses About It* by Dr. D. A. Waite ($14.00 + $7.00 S&H)

Send or Call Orders to:
THE BIBLE FOR TODAY
900 Park Ave., Collingswood, NJ 08108
Phone: 856-854-4452; FAX:--2464; Orders: 1-800 JOHN 10:9
E-Mail Orders: BFT@BibleForToday.org; Credit Cards OK

Order Blank (p. 4)

Name:_____
Address:_____
City & State:_____ Zip:_____
Credit Card #:_____ Expires:_____

Books By Dean John William Burgon

[ ] Send *The Last 12 verses of Mark* by Dean Burgon ($15+$5 S&H) A hardback book 400 pages.
[ ] Send *The Traditional Text* hardback by Burgon ($16+$5
[ ] Send *The Revision Revised* by Dean Burgon ($25 + $5 S&H) A hardback book, 640 pages in length.
[ ] Send *Dean Burgon's Confidence in KJB* by DAW ($3+$3)
[ ] Send *Vindicating Mark 16:9-20* by Dr. Waite ($3+$3S&H)
[ ] Send *Summary of Traditional Text* by Dr. Waite ($3 +$3)
[ ] Send *Summary of Causes of Corruption*, DAW ($3+$3)
[ ] Send *Summary of Inspiration* by Dr. Waite ($3+$3 S&H)

Books By Dr. Jack Moorman

[ ] Send *The Doctrinal Heart of the Bible--Removed from Modern Versions* by Dr. Jack Moorman, VCR, $15 +$4 S&H
[ ] Send *Modern Bibles--The Dark Secret* by Dr. Jack Moorman, $5+$3 S&H
[ ] Send *The Manuscript Digest of the N.T.* (721 pp.) By Dr. Jack Moorman, copy-machine bound ($50+$7 S&H)
[ ] *Early Manuscripts, Church Fathers, & the Authorized Version* by Dr. Jack Moorman, $18+$5 S&H. Hardback
[ ] Send *Forever Settled--Bible Do*cuments *& History Survey* by Dr. Jack Moorman, $20+$5 S&H. Hardback book.
[ ] Send *When the KJB Departs from the So-Called "Majority Text"* by Dr. Jack Moorman, $16+$5 S&H
[ ] Send *Missing in Modern Bibles--Nestle-Aland/NIV Errors* by Dr. Jack Moorman, $8+$4 S&H

Send or Call Orders to:
THE BIBLE FOR TODAY
900 Park Ave., Collingswood, NJ 08108
Phone: 856-854-4452; FAX:--2464; Orders: 1-800 JOHN 10:9
E-Mail Orders: BFT@BibleForToday.org; Credit Cards OK

Order Blank (p. 5)

Name:_____

Address:_____

City & State:_____Zip:_____

Credit Card #:_____Expires:_____

[ ] Send *Westcott & Hort's Greek Text & Theory Refuted by Burgon's Revision Revised--Summarized* by Dr. D. A. Waite ($7.00+$4 S&H), 120 pages, perfect bound.

[ ] Send *Soulwinning's Versions-Perversions* By Dr. D. A. Waite ($6.00 + $5.00 S&H)

[ ] Send *Causes of Corruption* by Burgon ($15+$5 S&H) A hardback book, 360 pages in length.

[ ] Send *Inspiration and Interpretation*, Dean Burgon ($25+$5 S&H) A hardback book, 610 pages in length.

Books By Miscellaneous Authors

[ ] Send *Guide to Textual Criticism* by Edward Miller ($7+$4) Hardback book

[ ] Send *Scrivener's Greek New Testament Underlying the King James Bible*, hardback, ($14+$5 S&H)

[ ] Send *Samuel P. Tregelles--The Man Who Made the Critical Text Acceptable to Bible Believers* by Dr. Moorman ($2+$1)

[ ] Send *8,000 Differences Between TR & CT* by Dr. Jack Moorman [$65 + $7.50 S&H] Over 500-large-pages of data

[ ] Send *356 Doctrinal Errors in the NIV & Other Modern Versions*, 100-large-pages, $10.00+$6 S&H.

[ ] Send *Scrivener's <u>Annotated</u> Greek New Testament*, by Dr. Frederick Scrivener: Hardback--($35+$5 S&H); Genuine Leather--($45+$5 S&H)

[ ] Send *Why Not the King James Bible?--An Answer to James White's KJVO Book* by Dr. K. D. DiVietro, $10+$5 S&H

[ ] Send Brochure #1: "*1000 Titles Defending the KJB/TR*" No Charge

Send or Call Orders to:
THE BIBLE FOR TODAY
900 Park Ave., Collingswood, NJ 08108
Phone: 856-854-4452; FAX:--2464; Orders: 1-800 JOHN 10:9
E-Mail Orders: BFT@BibleForToday.org; Credit Cards OK

Order Blank (p. 6)

Name:_____
Address:_____
City & State:_____ Zip:_____
Credit Card #:_____ Expires:_____

More Books By Miscellaneous Authors

[ ] Send *The LIE That Changed the Modern World* by Dr. H. D. Williams ($16+$5 S&H) Hardback book
[ ] Send *With Tears in My Heart* by Gertrude G. Sanborn. Hardback 414 pp. ($25+$5 S&H) 400 Christian Poems
[ ] Send *Able To Bear It* By Gertrude Sanborn ($14.00 + $7.00 S&H
[ ] Send *Visitation In Action* By Mr. R. O. Sanborn ($10.00 + $7.00 S&H)
[ ] Send *Daily Bible Blessings From Daily Bible Readings* By Yvonne Sanborn Waite ($30.00 + $10.00 S&H)
[ ] Send *Husband-Loving Lessons* By Yvonne Sanborn Waite ($25.00 + $8.00 S&H)
[ ] Send *Gnosticism–The Doctrinal Foundation of New Bibles* by J. Moser ($20.00 + $8.00 S&H)
[ ] Send *Dean Burgon's Defense of the Authorised Version* By Dr. David Bennett ($14.0 + 8.00 S&H)
[ ] Send *Drift in Baptist Missions, Churches & Schools* by Dr. David Bennett ($12.00 + $8.00 S&H)
[ ] Send *God's Marvelous Book* By Dr. David Bennett ($15.00 + $8.00 S&H)
[ ] Send *CCM Not The Problem–Only A Symptom* By Dr. David Bennett ($12.00 + $7.00 S&H)
[ ] Send *English Standard Bible (ESV) Deficiencies* By several authors ($7.00 + $4.00 S&H)
[ ] Send *Strong's Micro-Print Concordance* By the Sherbornes ($21.00 + $8.00 S&H)

Send or Call Orders to:
THE BIBLE FOR TODAY
900 Park Ave., Collingswood, NJ 08108
Phone: 856-854-4452; FAX:--2464; Orders: 1-800 JOHN 10:9
E-Mail Orders: BFT@BibleForToday.org; Credit Cards OK

Order Blank (p. 7)

Name:_____
Address:_____
City & State:_____Zip:_____
Credit Card #:_____Expires:_____

Books by D. A. Waite, Jr.

[ ] Send *The Doctored New Testament* by D. A. Waite, Jr. ($25+$5 S&H) Greek MSS differences shown, hardback
[ ] Send *Readability of A.V. (KJB)* by D. A. Waite, Jr. ($6+$3)
[ ] Send *4,114 Definitions from the Defined King James Bible* by D. A. Waite, Jr. ($7.00+$4.00 S&H)

Question And Answer Books By Dr. D. A. Waite

[ ] Send *The First 200 Questions Answered* By Dr. D. A. Waite ($15.00 + $7.00 S&H)
[ ] Send *The Second 200 Questions Answered* By Dr. D. A. Waite ($15.00 + $7.00 S&H)
[ ] Send *The Third 200 Questions Answered* By Dr. D. A. Waite ($15.00 + $7.00 S&H)
[ ] Send *The Fourth 200 Questions Answered* By Dr. D. A. Waite ($15.00 + $7.00 S&H)
[ ] Send *The Fifth 200 Questions Answered* By Dr. D. A. Waite ($15.00 + $7.00 S&H)
[ ] Send *The Sixth 200 Questions Answered* By Dr. D. A. Waite ($15.00 + $7.00 S&H)

Send or Call Orders to:
THE BIBLE FOR TODAY
900 Park Ave., Collingswood, NJ 08108
Phone: 856-854-4452; FAX:--2464; Orders: 1-800 JOHN 10:9
E-Mail Orders: BFT@BibleForToday.org; Credit Cards OK

The Defined King James Bible

UNCOMMON WORDS DEFINED ACCURATELY

I. Deluxe Genuine Leather

✦Large Print--Black or Brgundy✦

1 for $44.00+$12.00 S&H

✦Case of 12 for✦

$34.00 each+$50.00 S&H

✦Medium Print--Black or Burgundy

1 for $39.00+$8.00 S&H

✦Case of 12 for✦

$29.00 each+$40.00 S&H

II. Deluxe Hardback Editions

1 for $22.00+12.00 S&H (Large Print)

✦Case of 12 for✦

$17.00 each+$40.00 S&H (Large Print)

1 for $19.50+$8.00 S&H (Medium Print)   ✦Case of 12 for✦

1 For $19.50 +$12.00 S&H (Large Print)

Order Phone: 1-800-JOHN 10:9

CREDIT CARDS WELCOMED

Pastor D. A. Waite, Th.D., Ph.D.

Christ's Bodily Resurrection

The Bodily Resurrection of the Lord Jesus Christ Is Doubted By Many Today. Though doubted by many so-called Pastors in many churches of the U.S.A. and around the world, it is clearly taught in 1 Corinthians 15 and elsewhere in the New Testament.

The Angel Of The Lord Was A Witness. When the two Mary's came to Christ's tomb early on the first day of the week, the angel of the Lord told them *"He is not here: for He is risen . . . come, see the place where the Lord lay"* (Matthew 28:6).

More Than "*500 Brethren at once*" Were Also Witnesses. (1 Corinthians 15:6). Many of those brethren were still alive when Paul wrote the book of 1 Corinthians. What greater witness is needed to establish Christ's bodily resurrection?

Eleven Apostles Were Witnesses. At the second Sunday evening service, the Lord Jesus Christ appeared before them in the upper room. Even Thomas was there on that occasion though absent the week before.

The Apostle Paul Was A Witness. The Lord Jesus Christ appeared to Paul from Heaven when he was on his way to imprison Christians at Emmaus. Paul asked *"Who art thou, Lord?"* The Lord Jesus Christ replied, "I am Jesus Whom thou persecutest." (Acts 9:5).

www.BibleForToday.org

BFT 4174   ISBN #978-1-56848-117-3

www.ingramcontent.com/pod-product-compliance
Lightning Source LLC
Chambersburg PA
CBHW070612230426
43670CB00010B/1504